CHAUCER
Sources and Backgrounds

CHAUCER
Sources and Backgrounds

Edited by
Robert P. Miller
Queens College of the City University of New York

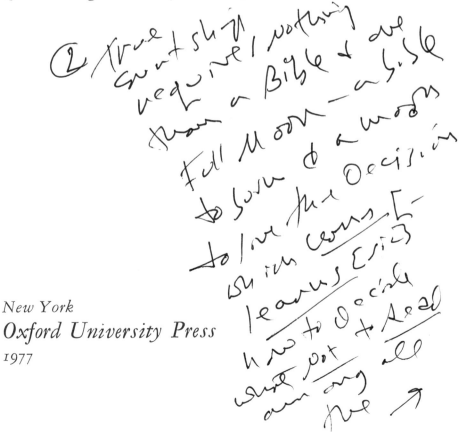

New York
Oxford University Press
1977

20 19 18 17 16 15

Printed in the United States of America
on acid-free paper

For Daphne
Non extinguetur in nocte lucerna eius.

Preface

This anthology is intended to provide for the study of Chaucer's works the kind of textual supplement that I have found helpful over many years in the classroom. The selections are drawn from works Chaucer is known to have used, as well as from works representing significant medieval attitudes toward matters with which he, like many other authors of his day, concerned himself. As for the former, I have always felt that much more was to be gained from a direct comparison of, say, a section of Boccaccio's *Filostrato* with its counterpart in *Troilus and Criseyde*, than from a reading of any number of essays on "What Chaucer Did with the *Filostrato*." Such comparison also has the advantage of providing documentary evidence to test the conclusions of critics. As for the latter, I have found it helpful to have at hand such texts as the Marriage Ceremony, or portions of a chivalric manual, to illustrate at first hand what were at least the formally received notions concerning these central topics. Again, statements about the nature of literature by respected medieval authors can provide a basis for discussion of Chaucer's actual practice—or, indeed, that of any author of the late Middle Ages.

An effort has been made here to include texts of sufficient length to provide the context within which particular points may appear. The topical organization of these texts has been a matter of convenience, not always satisfactory since materials in one section are often closely related to those in another. Numerous cross-references have been provided to help link related matters, and to lead the reader into the intricate fabric of medieval thought. If the notes sometimes seem elementary, they reflect my reaction to the annotations in many modern texts, which leave the average student stranded. The many notes to allusions to earlier authors, with which medieval writers loved to embellish their work, would ideally have included the actual texts referred to. A few have escaped the constraints upon space imposed on a volume such as this. As a body, however, the notes are meant to direct the reader back into the literary tradition that these writings shared, to indicate the continuity of that tradition, and to illustrate the richness of literary reference which characterizes much important medieval expression.

During the compilation of this anthology I have spoken with many fellow medievalists, whose suggestions have significantly contributed to its present design. I am grateful to them, and grateful as well to the generation of students who have made me aware of the kind of information a modern student finds most helpful. I wish particularly to thank Dean Nathaniel Siegel of Queens College for financial assistance; Jane Licht for her scholarly editorial assistance; Howard Schless for his most helpful suggestions; and my colleagues Charles Dahlberg, Daniel Donno, Diane Bornstein, and Douglas Butturff for having read portions of the manuscript. To E. Talbot Donaldson I apologize for being unable to incorporate fully some sterling suggestions about the Ovidian influence upon the formalities of courtly loving. Finally, my debt to D. W. Robertson, Jr., whose perception of the critical utility of sources and backgrounds has renovated medieval studies, cannot be expressed.

NOTE:

All scriptural texts and citations follow the Douay Rheims Version of the Bible. Where individual translators use the wording of other versions, their texts have been left unaltered.

Contents

List of Figures

Figure 1. Fortune's Wheel. Oxford, Bodleian Library MS Douce 332, fol. 58 (*Roman de la rose*). The four figures on the Wheel represent the attitudes each person takes toward Fortune's "gifts," which are limited to worldly pleasures. The individual may plead, exult, lament, or suffer (as is shown clockwise from the left). (See figure 18.) Fortune is represented as a queen, because she controls material goods; she is represented as "blinded" because she apportions her gifts without regard to merit. This illumination illustrates the speech of Reason in the *Romance of the Rose*.

INTRODUCTION

In Chaucer's Nun's Priest's Tale, Chauntecleer defends his concern over a prophetic dream by citing "auctorite" respecting such visions, in the manner of a medieval clerk (2870 ff.). He urges his wife to "rede" the "auctours" who have written on the subject: Cicero, the *Golden Legend*, Macrobius, the Old Testament, Ovid, Boethius, and Homer, among others. His idea that truth is preserved in the writings of authors who, taken collectively, make up a kind of authority useful to human life is not simply a debating tactic; it closely reflects the Latin etymology of his terms. Latin *auctor*, which gives us *auctoritas*, derives from the verb *augere* ("to increase"). "Authors" were, for medieval clerks as well as cocks, increasers of knowledge who set down their findings in memorable form for the benefit of future generations. In his bookish appeal to the library, Chauntecleer subjects his own present experience to certain established criteria, and in doing so he reflects a typical medieval habit of thought.

The literature of the Middle Ages provides rich and varied testimony of the force of authority in medieval thought. This fact is no less true of Chaucer than it is of the more pedestrian John Gower; it is equally evident in compilations such as the vast *Speculum* (or "Mirror") of Vincent of Beauvais, who sought to collect and arrange all knowledge, often in the very words of his authors, and in the encyclopedic *Romance of the Rose*, which amassed clerkly clichés on a wide range of topics in prolonged speeches by a series of allegorical figures. That the same set of clichés concerning marriage should reappear more than a century later in Eustache Deschamps' *Mirror of Marriage* and in Chaucer's Canterbury Tales does not mean that either writer was lacking in inventiveness. Both Chaucer and Deschamps expected their audience to recognize these commonplaces and even, in some cases, to recall the sources from which they were drawn. What it does mean is that both authors saw themselves and their work as part of a tradition of "authority" reaching back through their immediate literary predecessors to the great "clerks" of classical antiquity, and, indeed, to the six days of Creation.

Medieval regard for this particular kind of literary authority was intimately related to a complex but highly unified and coherent view of reality. According to this view, the only true reality was God, the Creator of all things. All else was a phenomenal sign of God's infinite and eternal Will as it was manifested in space and time. A favorite medieval metaphor describing the relationship between man the creature and his Creator pictured God as an Author whose Word had been published in two great Books. The first of these Books was called the "Book of Nature"—that is, the created universe, in which the divine Will is crystallized, so to speak, in time and space. The second was the Bible, in which God speaks to man, communicating His Word by way of the written words of inspired authors and the revealed Word of Christ, the Incarnate God. Since all existence was an expression of God's Will, these two Books obviously contained all the Truth that God had seen fit to reveal to mankind. God the Author was thus the source of all succeeding authority regarding the true nature of things.

Christian doctrine taught that man could achieve salvation only by conforming to God's Will. In the schools the liberal arts were those studies designed to free the student, or "artist," from the bondage in sin which was fostered by ignorance of that Will. What he studied were, in effect, the works of individual authorities who explained the art and the meanings to be found in the two Books of the Author of all. The somewhat mystical concept of a divine Word, in which all truths were simultaneously contained, diffusing itself into the discrete and fragmentary knowledge of man, and of man's difficulties in reaching through words and signs to the ineffable purity of Truth itself, is dramatically explored in the *Confessions* of Saint Augustine. Here the reader will find that Augustine's "education" leads him finally to contemplation of the account of Creation in the Book of Genesis—the statement of one of God's Books concerning the other.

In the Book of Nature, first of His revelations in point of time, God could be discovered through close observation and informed analysis. The idea that Truth was immanent in all details of Creation is similar to the modern idea that the genetic code of any living creature is entirely contained in each of its cells—an equally mystical notion. Pagans such as Pliny and Aristotle were highly respected as observers, and became authorities for what man unaided by revelation could sense concerning God's works and their rationale. But revelation in the Bible added a dimension of understanding which offered meaning within observed phenomena, for the original Author had there used aspects of His Creation in figurative contexts. At the end of the fourth century Saint Augustine, in his *On Christian Doctrine*, had called for the compilation of dictionaries to aid in the interpretation of the Holy Scriptures:

> . . . I think it might be possible, if any capable person could be persuaded to undertake the task for the sake of his brethren, to collect in order and write down singly explanations of whatever unfamiliar geographical locations, animals, herbs and trees, stones, and metals are mentioned in the Scripture. The same thing could be done with numbers. . . . (II, xxxix)

During the Middle Ages just such collections were made, growing in the course of time to encyclopedic proportions. Appearing as bestiaries (describing animate creatures), herbals (trees and flowers), lapidaries (stones), numerologies, and so forth, they could be called "chapters" in the Book of Nature. In this way, standard definitions of the natures and significance of things entered the library of medieval authority.

The importance of the second Book for medieval thought and expression cannot be overestimated. Holy Scripture, properly interpreted, was the ultimate authority in all matters. In the Old Testament God had revealed His Law directly to mankind through inspired, but as yet unredeemed, prophets. The New Testament recorded the divine Incarnation, the ministry, and the sacrifice of Christ in the Gospels; and the Epistles announced the apostolic mission to teach the Word to all people. The New Testament was said to teach the "New Law," a fulfillment and completion of the "Old Law" revealed before the Incarnation. The Old Law was God's authority literally perceived; uninformed by the new light brought into the world by Christ, it was limited to a prudential version of virtue based on the fear of the Lord. Christ's new perception of the Law (which is put most succinctly in the Sermon on the Mount: Matthew v–vii) views it spiritually as a way of life to be spontaneously followed out of the love of God. The New Law thus "frees" the Christian, since he does not feel constrained to behave virtuously; in effect, its spiritual meaning abrogates the "letter" of the Old Law. This revelation was supposed to be symbolized by the rending of the veil of the temple at the moment of Christ's death (see Matthew xxvii, 50–51), and the image of showing forth a truth previously present though secret reappears in different guises in all areas of thought throughout the Middle Ages, as in the discovery of hidden meanings in the natures of created things.

Interpretation of different Scriptural texts took the form of "commentaries" or "glosses." These scholarly expositions sought to explain the divine Truth veiled behind the limitations of purely human language, and to reveal the "inner meaning" of texts which, if taken literally, would not completely reflect the New Law. By way of such commentaries Truth was "increased" and, since the major authors in this endeavor were the Church "Fathers," it has been called "patristic exegesis." Those explications considered most instructive were organized into an authoritative gloss inscribed around the margins of manuscript Bibles (later in printed copies), known as the *Ordinary Gloss*. These authors, augmenting the understanding of the words of the divine Author, were, of course, included in the library of medieval authority.

Since the literal meaning of Old Testament texts could not overtly express the divine intent that, as Chaucer's Parson puts it, we should all come "to the knoweleche of hym, and to the blisful lif that is perdurable" (Parson's Tale, 75), the Christian exegete followed the example of Christ and His apostles in explicating the true Word as it had been later revealed by the Incarnation. This process was, in essence, a "converting" of the Old Testament, for it was now viewed as a veiled expression of God's Will. The Old Testament thus became a storehouse of "types" in which the revealed Truth of the New Testament had been implied. God had, it was held, tested unredeemed mankind by speaking in a language which could be interpreted either literally or spiritually, so that both Nature and the Old Testament contained His true meaning but in an allegorical form unavailable to the unregenerate.

Allegorical interpretation established standard higher meanings for figures and events in Scripture, often on more than one "level" of signification. For example, the Samaritan woman (John iv) who, like the Wife of Bath, has had five husbands was interpreted on one level as a type of *Synagoga*, the Church before its conversion to Christ, the five "husbands" representing the five books of the Old Law. On another level she was seen as a type of man's carnal nature not yet regenerate, the "husbands" standing for the five senses. Such meanings were conveniently gathered in dictionaries like Rabanus Maurus' *Allegories in Sacred Scripture*, which also became part of the medieval library of authority.

The pagan authors of antiquity, finally, had their own place in this library. Although deprived by history of the benefits of revelation, they were yet thought to have perceived Truth in a limited way. Classical poets provided useful examples which could, as Augustine said, be converted to Christian purposes, just as the Israelites made use of the golden vessels of the Egyptians, and, of course, they offered models of rhetoric for later writers. In a most important sense the medieval author of a poetic fiction thought himself to be a part of a continuous literary tradition reaching back to the masters of Rome and Greece. So Chaucer, dedicating his Troilus and Criseyde, requires his "litel bok" to

> . . . kis the steppes, where as thow seest pace
> Virgile, Ovide, Omer, Lucan, and Stace. (V, 1791–92)

Not only are Virgil, Ovid, Homer, Lucan, and Statius all admired classical authors; the lines themselves paraphrase lines at the end of Statius' *Thebaid* (XII, 816 ff.), thus illustrating, at least for those who had the Latin of Statius' epic in mind, the reverence they recommended.

Minds trained to read Nature and the Bible allegorically had little difficulty uncovering inner meanings beneath the "veil" of pagan fictions. Moralizations of Virgil's *Aeneid* and Statius' *Thebaid* were published under the name of Fulgentius at an early date. In *On the The-*

baid the author prefaces his work with the observation that poets "usefully provide moral instructions beneath the seductive . . . covering of poetic fictions." Christian scholars who explicated pagan fictions, and who were known as "mythographers," sought to extract a kernel of truth from the shell of such fictions. The favorite text of the mythographers was Ovid's *Metamorphoses*, an unparalleled storehouse of classical myth. The classical gods and goddesses quickly acquired standardized moral and philosophical "meanings" which brought them into conformity with Christian thought, and which turned them, as a consequence, into "figures" available to medieval poets. Mythographic analysis, amounting to the "conversion" of the pagan classics, culminated in an enormous French poem, the *Moralized Ovid* ("Ovide moralisée," c. 1316–28), in which even Christological meanings flourish. Boccaccio compiled a more scholarly mythological manual, *The Genealogy of the Pagan Gods* (c. 1345–75), and such manuals remained an important literary resource throughout the Renaissance.

In all these areas of inquiry medieval authors were concerned with augmenting God's Truth. It can be seen that the process of interpretation, whether it applied to the text of Nature, of Holy Scripture, or of a pagan poet, always involved the notion that human experience (man's "natural" or sensible perceptions), because of its attachment to appearances, had to be intellectually surmounted if the true reality were to become accessible. The function of the authorities was to make possible the penetration of "seductive coverings" which would otherwise distract the unaided mind of Adam's progeny. In the light of such an attitude, of course, the Wife of Bath's proposal, in lines 1–2 of her Prologue, to displace "auctoritee" with "experience" is more than a little revealing of the kind of wisdom she can be expected to provide.

To help illuminate some aspect of reality, a medieval author habitually turned to the authorities at his disposal, as the notes to the texts in this anthology abundantly illustrate. His arrangement of these materials was sometimes called a *conjunctura* (or "fitting-together"). Into the texture of his fiction he could weave the work of previous "clerks" who made up the literary tradition in which he wrote, and in this way he assembled his own delightful "covering"—what Dante called the "outside" which contained an "inside" of value. Truth could not be altered, but the means of expressing it in the "language of men" could be usefully varied.

One result of this deliberate use of authorities, whether pagan, Hebrew, or Christian, is that authors like Chaucer turn out to be surprisingly bookish. For illustration, the reader might compare the work of the "clerks" Jerome and Theophrastus, printed below, pp. 411–14 and

415–36, with the famous Prologue of the Wife of Bath, the great opponent of "auctoritee." Readers should be constantly alert for the possibility of ironies arising from misinterpretation or eccentric use of earlier texts. Thus, the description of the Prioress's table-manners, in the General Prologue portrait, 127–36, is drawn from the *Romance of the Rose*, where the Old Woman instructs the Rose on methods of attracting men; and this counsel is itself developed from a passage in Ovid's *Art of Love* (see below, p. 284). If we are to understand the kind of "gentility" Chaucer attributes to his Prioress, not only the source of these graces, but the context in which they originally occurred and their literary ancestry as well, are helpful.

The present anthology seeks to present an introduction to the tradition of literary authority within which Chaucer wrote. The selections are drawn from works which he knew and used or which illustrate the kind of thing he would have known, and the notes are intended to indicate their place in this ongoing tradition. The individual texts are meant to be, in general, of sufficient length to provide larger units of thought and narrative, rather than isolated fragments, because the larger context is often of considerable, even crucial, interest. Unfortunately, this collection could never claim to be anything approaching a complete "Chaucer library" or a "library of the medieval mind." Such endeavors are the province of others. It is hoped, however, that these selections will serve to introduce a wide and representative number of "clerks," both scholars and poets, to whom the Middle Ages turned, like Chauntecleer, for authority.

one

CREATION & FALL

Important for any true understanding of an author's art is his concept of humanity—its origins, nature, and destiny. Medieval authorities could be very intricate and subtle in their analysis of these matters, but the salient features of the accepted view, which Chaucer shared with his audience, are quite straightforward. For an understanding of human nature one turned not, in the first instance, to self-analysis, but rather to the truths expressed in God's own revelations. Divine authority took precedence over experience because the perceptions of fallen human nature were necessarily fallible. God's Will concerning man was thought to be implied in all Creation as well as all parts of Holy Scripture, if they were properly interpreted; but the divine design appeared most directly in two texts—the account of the creation and fall of Adam in Genesis, and the story of the life of Christ in the Gospels. The first could be analyzed to discover the primal nature God conferred on man before he fell into sin; in the second, God Himself took on flesh to provide a living model for human nature.

In the texts printed below we can see how contemplation of the rather simple account of the Creation and Fall in Genesis could lead to an extended series of coherently related concepts, most of which appear in Chaucer's work. Among these are the ideas of obedience and rebellion, freedom and servitude of the will, the three stages of sin, the three temptations, order and disorder, good and evil, innocence and experience, the different categories of knowledge, the oppositions between the fallen self and God, and between Adam and Christ—and, in fact, a model of marriage (see below, pp. 371–72). Such topics make up the fabric of medieval humanistic thought, and were so well known by the audience Chaucer wrote to that he could depend on his public to recognize, for instance, the "upside-down" character of the Wife of Bath's version of "obedience" or of the Franklin's view of "freedom."

According to the great Providential pattern which organized these different concepts, a good Creator created a good world in six days. Man, the last and highest of His earthly creatures, was distinguished by his possession of reason—a faculty which was useless without free will. Through misuse of his reason and will Adam disobeyed the just Law of his Creator, lost all the advantages of the state of innocence which had been intended as his proper condition, and, by preferring his own will to his Lord's, created in himself the lack of good which is called "evil" or "vice." The just consequence of this first sin was Original Sin (a sinful condition stemming from man's origin), which has been inherited through the flesh by all the descendants of Adam. Man is still required by God's Law to live the life designed for him at the Creation, but his vitiated nature now prevents such obedience. Yet in each failure to abide by the original law of his nature he suffers pain.

This picture of mankind's destiny is, of course, tragic. It is the philo-

sophical basis for Chaucer's idea of "tragedye" in Troilus and Criseyde
(V, 1786). However, the Providential pattern also provided for a release
from such a fatality. Christ's Incarnation and Passion, and the New
Testament of His apostles, revealed to erring mortals the "way" of re-
claiming their lost innocence, through a reformation of the reason—the
end to which medieval schools were officially dedicated. Such an end
(that is, salvation) provides for the medieval concept of comedy, which
Dante explains in his description of his own Commedia *(see below,*
p. 81). After he has described his Troilus and Criseyde as a "tragedye,"
Chaucer goes on to pray that

> . . . God thi makere yet, er that he dye,
> So sende mygth to make in som comedye! (V, 1787–88)

The "comedye" is, most critics believe, the Canterbury Tales. The
General Prologue begins with echoes of the order of Creation. Corrup-
tion of the perfection of the created world by Adam's sin was the be-
ginning of "the period of error," according to Jacobus de Voragine
(see below, p. 14). This period of erring was succeeded, as the Christian
viewed history, by "the period of pilgrimage" which "is that of our
present life," in which man looks forward to the reconciliation which
God has made possible. That the Canterbury pilgrimage symbolically
reflects this stage of human history is certainly possible, and it is con-
sistent with this Providential scheme that Chaucer, like Dante and
many other authors before him, should end his work with a vision of
blessedness (see below, pp. 491–96).

Jacobus de Voragine:
from *The Golden Legend*

The Legenda aurea *is a collection of saints' lives, accounts from the lives of Christ and the Virgin Mary, and discussions of holy days and seasons, which are arranged as readings* (legenda) *for the different days of the liturgical year. Its enormous popularity in the Middle Ages is reflected by the fact that the large number of surviving manuscripts include translations into all the languages of western Europe. Since it was gradually enlarged in the fourteenth century, it now exists in several versions. One of the first books printed in English was Caxton's translation of it* (1483).

Jacobus de Voragine (c. *1228–98) was a Dominican preacher, theologian, and chronicler, provincial of Lombardy, and archbishop of Genoa* (1292–98).

Chaucer's translation of the life of Saint Cecilia (see below, pp. 112–20) for his Second Nun shows his knowledge of the Legenda aurea. *The Legend of Good Women, referred to in the Introduction to the Man of Law's Tale, 61, as "the Seintes Legende of Cupide," is a secular parody of Jacobus' work. The significance attached to the different parts of the liturgical year warns us to consider carefully the dates and seasons in medieval writings. For example, as references such as General Prologue, 8, and the Man of Law's Prologue, 5–6, indicate that Chaucer's pilgrims set out about April 17, the date would place the Canterbury Tales in the first period "of erring, or wandering from the way," looking forward to the "period of reconciliation," to begin at Easter, as Winter looks forward to Spring.*

This text begins the Prologue *to* The Golden Legend.

Trans. Granger Ryan and Helmut Ripperger, The Golden Legend of Jacobus de Voragine (New York: Longmans, Green and Co., 1941), pp. 1–2. Reprinted by permission of Granger Ryan.

"The Divisions of the Year"

HERE BEGINS THE BOOK OF THE LEGENDS OF THE SAINTS COLLECTED BY BROTHER JACOBUS OF GENOA, OF THE ORDER OF PREACHERS.

The whole of this fugitive life is divided into four periods: the period of erring, or wandering from the way;[1] the period of renewal, or returning to the right way; the period of reconciliation; and the period of pilgrimage. The period of erring began with Adam and lasted until Moses, for it was Adam who first turned from God's way. And this first period is represented, in the Church, by the part of the year which runs from Septuagesima[2] to Easter. During this part of the year the Book of Genesis is recited, this being the Book which contains the account of the sin of our first parents. The period of renewal began with Moses and lasted until the birth of Christ, for this is the period during which man was renewed and called back to the faith through the mouth of the Prophets. It is represented, in the Church, by the part of the year which runs from Advent[3] until Christmas. Isaias is then recited, because he revealed this divine renewal most clearly. The period of reconciliation is that in which Christ, through the merits of His life and death, reconciled us with God the Father. It is represented, in the Church, by the part of the year from Easter to Pentecost.[4] The Apocalypse is read, for the mystery of this reconciliation is revealed therein in symbols and visions. Finally, the period of pilgrimage is that of our present life, in which we wander as pilgrims amidst a thousand obstacles. It is represented, in the Church, by the part of the year between the Octave of Pentecost[5] and Advent; and the Books of Kings and Maccabees are recited, wherein are set forth many wars, to symbolize the spiritual struggle which we must undertake. As for the part of the year between Christmas and Septuagesima, it is divided into two parts. The first is within the period of reconciliation and is a time of rejoicing, which lasts from Christmas to the Octave of the Epiphany;[6] the other is within the period of pilgrimage and is a time of sadness, which lasts from the Octave of the Epiphany to Septuagesima.

These four divisions of the spiritual life are comparable to the four parts of the natural year, so that the first is the Winter, the second the Spring, the third the Summer, and the fourth the Autumn, and the meaning of this comparison is apparent. Another comparison may be made with the times of the day, so that the first spiritual period is like the Night, the next like the Morning, the third like Noon, and the fourth like Evening.

But although the time of erring preceded the time of renewal, the Church prefers to begin its year with Advent, and not with Septuagesima, and this for two reasons: because, due to the fact that this is the time of renewal, the Church then turns back to the beginning of her offices; and because, by beginning with the time of the transgression, she would seem to begin with error. Therefore she does not hold strictly to the order of time, just as the Evangelists frequently do not follow it in their accounts of the life of the Lord. Then too, with the advent of the Lord everything is renewed, and that is why this period is called the time of renewal.

NOTES

1. See General Prologue, 467. The reference corresponds well with what we later learn of the Wife of Bath's knowledge.
2. Two Sundays before the beginning of Lent.
3. Sunday nearest November 30 (see below, pp. 479–80).
4. The fiftieth day after Easter.
5. A week after Pentecost.
6. Epiphany is January 6; its Octave is a week later.

Saint Augustine:
from *The City of God*

Saint Augustine shaped the thought of the Catholic Middle Ages more pro-
foundly than any other man. He was born in 354, in the North African
Roman province of Numidia, and, despite a wayward youth recorded in his
Confessions, was a brilliant student in the Roman schools. By 373 he had
sufficiently mastered the curriculum in rhetoric to turn to teaching—first at
Tagaste, his home town, then at Carthage and at Rome. In 384 he was ap-
pointed municipal professor of rhetoric by the city of Milan. Here the
preaching of Ambrose, bishop of Milan, was instrumental in bringing
about his famous conversion (386), at the symbolic age of thirty-three. He
was baptized by Saint Ambrose himself in 387.

Augustine's new life as a convert was immensely productive, though
complicated by official duties. In 391 he was ordained as priest at Hippo
Regius in North Africa, and in 396 succeeded as bishop of Hippo, a post
he filled with distinction until his death in 430. Besides theological treatises
which were destined to become standard "authorities" in the Middle Ages,
he produced numerous polemical works against Manichaeans, Donatists,
and Pelagians, in which he articulated the theological views which were to
prevail thereafter. Counting his sermons, letters, and Biblical commentaries
(notably on Genesis and Psalms), his bibliography contains about a thou-
sand works. Among them many remain classics of their kinds: the auto-
biographical Confessions *(c. 400);* On the Trinity *(400–416); On Christian*
Doctrine *(397–426), an educational treatise (see below, pp. 53–57); and*
The City of God *(413–26). Augustine was cited as an authority by virtually*
every succeeding medieval author, most notably for medieval thought by
Peter Lombard in his Sentences, *a summa accepted as authoritative by the*
fourth Lateran Council (1215).

The City of God (De civitate Dei) was written at a time immediately

Trans. Gerald G. Walsh and Grace Monahan (Washington, D.C.: The Catholic
University of America Press, 1952), Vol. II, pp. 190, 191, 240–42, 288–90, 330–
32, 316–18, 375–80, 384–91. Reprinted by permission of the publisher.

following the sack of Rome by Alaric the Goth (410). In it Augustine distinguishes between the destinies of purely human institutions, typified by the Roman State—the "City of Man"—and the spiritual community of the Christian faithful, ranging in time from the Creation to the future Day of Judgment (see below, pp. 490–95). This work has been said to elaborate "the first Christian philosophy of history"; its encyclopedic scope made it an essential reference book.

The chapters excerpted here contain Augustine's view of Creation and of the Fall of man, the first representing his speculation concerning God's Will, the second analyzing the failure of man's will. Medieval "psychology" always relates fundamentally to the intended original design of the Author of "human nature" and to the causes and consequences of its corruption. Chaucer's many references to Adam and Eve illustrate his awareness of the principles discussed here.

[The Creation and Fall of Man]

XI, 4 [handwritten annotation]

Of all visible things, the universe is the greatest; of all invisible realities, the greatest is God. That the world exists we can see; we believe in the existence of God. But there is no one we can more safely trust than God Himself in regard to the fact that it was He who made the world. Where has He told us so? Nowhere more distinctly than in the Holy Scriptures where His Prophet said: "In the beginning God created the heavens and the earth."[1] Well, but was the Prophet present when God made heaven and earth? No; but the Wisdom of God by whom all things were made was there.[2] And this Wisdom, entering into holy souls, makes of them the friends and prophets of God[3] and reveals to them, silently and interiorly, what God has done.

They are taught, also, by the angels of God who "always behold the face of the Father"[4] and are commissioned to announce His will to others. Among these Prophets was the one who announced in writing: "In the beginning God created the heavens and the earth." And it was so fitting that faith in God should come through such a witness that he was inspired by the same Spirit of God, who had revealed these truths to him, to predict, far in advance, our own future faith.[5]

XI, 33

The Apostle Peter clearly teaches that certain angels, having sinned, were hurled down to the lowest depths of the universe, as to a prison dungeon, there to remain until their final damnation on the day of judgment. His words are: "God did not spare the angels when they sinned, but thrust them into the dark prisons of hell and delivered them to be tortured and kept in custody for judgment."[6] No one, then, can doubt that God, either in foreknowledge or in fact, separated the sinful angels from the others. And, as for these others, no reader will dispute that they are rightly called "light." For, even we, who are still living by faith in this world, still hoping to be "as the angels," though we are not yet like them, are called "light" by the Apostle: "For you were once darkness, but now you are light in the Lord."[7] And, as for the deserter-angels, those who hold, whether by reason or by Revelation, that they are worse than human traitors, remark how suitably they are called "darkness," even though quite a different kind of light and darkness is signified in the following passages of Genesis: "God said, 'Let there be light,' and there was light," and "God separated the light from the darkness."[8]

At any rate, for us there are two societies of angels, one in the enjoyment of God, the other swelling with pride. The Psalmist refers to one in the verse: "Praise ye him, all his angels,"[9] and the Gospel records the speech of the prince of the other: "All these things will I give thee, if thou wilt fall down and worship me."[10] One is aflame with the holy love of God; the other is reeking with the impure desire for its own exaltation. Since, as Scripture warns us, "God resists the proud, but gives grace to the humble,"[11] one group dwells in the highest courts of heaven; the other, hurled down, rages in the lowest regions of the air. One is tranquil with radiant holiness; the other is troubled with dark desires. One, by the will of God, aids us with kindness and avenges us with justice; the other, in arrogance, seethes with the desire of dominating and doing us damage. One group, as ministers of God's goodness, are free to do all the good they desire; the others are bridled by the power of God to keep them from doing all the harm they would. The good angels laugh at the others when these unwillingly do more good than harm by their persecutions; the latter envy the former when they bring their pilgrims home.

For us, then, these two angelic societies are dissimilar and opposed one to the other. One is good by nature and upright in will; the other is also good by nature, but perverse by choice. The difference between the two societies is much more explicitly expressed in other Scriptural texts, but even in the Book of Genesis these angels, I think are intimated by the terms light and darkness, even though the author may have had something else in mind when he wrote these words.

My only hope is that our discussion of this obscure passage has not been a waste of time. At any rate, even though we have failed to discover the intention of the author of Genesis, we have not abandoned the rule of faith which, from other Scriptural passages of equal authority, is sufficiently well known to the faithful.

Even though this text of Genesis does indicate the material works of God, these, certainly, suggest certain spiritual analogies, as is clear from what the Apostle had in mind when he wrote: "For you are all children of the light and children of the day. We are not of night, nor of darkness."[12] And if the author of Genesis himself had this in mind, then we have reached a very satisfactory conclusion to our discussion, namely, that this man of God, who was so eminent in divine wisdom, or, rather, the Spirit of God, who inspired him, so recorded the works of creation completed on the sixth day that he by no means failed to mention the angels. We may believe that he included them in the words, "in the beginning," in the sense that God made them first, or, as seems more likely, in the sense that God created them in the only-begotten Word.

Scripture says: "In the beginning God created the heavens and the earth." By these two words, heaven and earth, all of creation is signified. They may mean spiritual and material creation, as seems very probable, or they may refer to the two major elements of the world which contain all that has been created. In this case, the writer spoke first on creation as a whole and then described it part by part according to the mystical number of days.

XII, 22

Now that I have explained, as well as I could, this difficult question of the eternal God creating new things without any change in His will, it is simple enough to see how much better it was for God to multiply the human race from one man whom He created rather than to develop it from many.

In regard to other animals, we see that He created some to be solitary, lone rangers, so to speak, like eagles, hawks, lions, wolves, and so on; and others to be gregarious, animals that prefer to live together in flocks, such as doves, starlings, stags, and others of the kind. However, He propagated neither of these classes from a single pair, but ordered the creation of several at the same time.

On the other hand, He created man with a nature midway between angels and beasts, so that man, provided he should remain subject to his true Lord and Creator and dutifully obey His commandments, might pass into the company of the angels, without the intervention of death, thus to attain a blessed and eternal immortality. But, should he offend his Lord and God by a proud and disobedient use of his free will, then, subject to death and a slave to his appetites, he would have to live like a beast and be destined to eternal punishment after death. Therefore, God created one sole individual, not that he was meant to remain alone deprived of human companionship, but in order that the unity of society and the bond of harmony might mean more to man, since men were to be united not only by the likeness of nature but also by the affection of kinship. God did not even wish to create the woman who was to be mated with man in the same way that He created man but, rather, out of him, in order that the whole human race might be derived entirely from one single individual.

XII, 23

God was not unaware that man would sin and, being subjected to death, would propagate mortals destined to die; and that these mortals would go so far in the monstrousness of sin that even the beasts without power of rational choice, that had been created in numbers from the waters and the earth, would live more securely and peacefully among their own kind than men—even though the human race had been given a single progenitor for the very purpose of promoting harmony. And, in fact, neither lions nor dragons have ever waged such wars with their own kind as men have fought with one another.

However, God also foresaw that a community of saints would be called to supernatural adoption, would have their sins forgiven, be sanctified by the Holy Spirit, and finally be united with the holy angels in eternal peace, so that, at last, the enemy death will be destroyed. And God knew how good it would be for this community often to recall that the human race had its roots in one man, precisely to show how pleasing it is to God that men, though many, should be one.

XII, 24

When God made man according to His own image, He gave him a soul so endowed with reason and intelligence that it ranks man higher than all the other creatures of the earth, the sea, the air, because they lack intelligence. God, then, formed man out of the dust of the earth and, by His breath, gave man a soul such as I have described. It is not certain whether God's breathing imparted to man a soul previously created or whether God created the soul by the act of breathing, as though He wanted the soul of man to be the very breath of God. (Notice that to breathe is the same as to *make* a breathing.)

Next, He took a bone from the man's side and made of it a mate to collaborate in procreation. Of course, all this was done in a divine way. We must not imagine the process in a material way, as though God worked, as ordinary artists do, with hands, shaping, as best they can, some earthly material into a form dictated by the rules of art. The "hand" of God means the power of God which works in an invisible way to produce even visible results. If some people take these true facts for mere fables it is because they use familiar, everyday craftsmanship to measure that power and wisdom of God which not merely can but does produce even seeds without seeds. And as for those things which God first created, they refuse to believe them on the ground that they have no way to know them. Yet, they know facts about human conception and birth which would seem far more incredible if they were told to others who did not know them and, what is more, they often think such things can be attributed to natural, physical causes rather than to the efficacy of any divine action.

XIII, 21

. . . There are some who have allegorized the entire Garden of Eden where, according to Holy Scripture, the first parents of the human race actually lived. The trees and fruit-bearing shrubs are turned into symbols of virtues and ways of living, as though they had no visible and material reality and as if Scripture had no purpose but to express meanings for our minds. The assumption here is that the possibility of a spiritual meaning rules out the reality of a physical Paradise. That is like saying that Agar and Sara, the mothers of the two sons of Abraham, "the one by a slave-girl and the other by a free woman," had no historical existence simply because the Apostle has said that "by way of allegory . . . these are the two covenants,"[13] or that Moses struck no rock nor did water actually flow simply because the story can also be read as an allegory of Christ, as the same Apostle does read it: "but the rock was Christ."[14]

There is no reason, then, for anyone forbidding us to see in the Garden, symbolically, the life of the blessed; in its four rivers, the four virtues of prudence, fortitude, temperance, and justice; in its trees, all useful knowledge; in the fruits of the trees, the holy lives of the faithful; in the tree of life, that wisdom which is the mother of all good; and in the tree of the knowledge of good and evil, the experience that results from disobedience to a command of God. The punishment which God imposed on the sinners was just and, therefore, good in itself, but not for man who experienced the taste of it.

This account can be even better read as an allegory of the Church, prophetical of what was to happen in the future. Thus, the Garden is the Church itself, as we can see from the Canticle of Canticles;[15] the four rivers are the four Gospels; the fruit-bearing trees are the saints, as the fruits are their works; and the tree of life is, of course, the Saint of saints, Christ; and the tree of the knowledge of good and evil is the free choice of our own will.[16] For, if a man disdains the divine will, he can only use his own to his own destruction, and, thus, he comes to the knowledge of the difference between obedience to the good common to all and indulgence in a good proper to oneself. For, anyone who loves himself is left to himself until, filled with fears and tears, he cries out, if he has any sensitivity to his own sufferings, like the psalmist: "My soul is troubled within myself,"[17] so that, when he has learned his lesson, he may cry: "I will keep my strength to thee."[18]

No one should object to such reflections and others even more appropriate that might be made concerning the allegorical interpretation of the Garden of Eden, so long as we believe in the historical truth manifest in the faithful narrative of these events.

XIII, 13

As soon as our first parents had disobeyed God's commandment, they were immediately deprived of divine grace, and were ashamed of their nakedness. They covered themselves with fig leaves, which, perhaps, were the first thing noticed by the troubled pair. The parts covered remained unchanged except that, previously, they occasioned no shame. They felt[19] for the first time a movement of disobedience in their flesh, as though the punishment were meant to fit the crime of their own disobedience to God.

The fact is that the soul, which had taken perverse delight in its own liberty and disdained the service of God, was now deprived of its original mastery over the body; because it had deliberately deserted the Lord who was over it, it no longer bent to its will the servant below it, being unable to hold the flesh completely in subjection as would always have been the case, if only the soul had remained subject to God. From this moment, then, the flesh began to lust against the spirit.[20] With this rebellion we are born, just as we are doomed to die and, because of the first sin, to bear, in our members and vitiated nature, either the battle with or defeat by the flesh.

XIII, 14

God, the Author of all natures but not of their defects, created man good; but man, corrupt by choice and condemned by justice, has pro-

Figure 2. Adam and Eve at labor, outside Paradise. British Library MS Add. 47682, fol. 4 (Picture Bible). The distaff symbolizes the "labor" of Eve, and the spade that of Adam, according to God's curse (Genesis iii, 17–19). The goats in this fallen world are explained by Matthew xxv, 32–34. An angel guards the gates of Eden, the "garden of pleasure."

duced a progeny that is both corrupt and condemned. For, we all existed in that one man, since, taken together, we were the one man who fell into sin through the woman who was made out of him before sin existed. Although the specific form by which each of us was to live was not yet created and assigned, our nature was already present in the seed from which we were to spring. And because this nature has been soiled by sin and doomed to death and justly condemned, no man was to be born of man in any other condition.

Thus, from a bad use of free choice, a sequence of misfortunes conducts the whole human race, excepting those redeemed by the grace of God, from the original canker in its root to the devastation of a second and endless death.

XIII, 15

Since there is no mention of more than one death in the Scriptural passage: "Thou shalt die the death,"[21] we should interpret it to mean that particular death which occurs when the life of the soul (which is God) abandons it. (The soul was not first deserted by God and so deserted Him, but it first deserted God, with the result that it was deserted by Him. For, as regards man's evil, it is his will that comes first, but where his good is in question, it is the Creator's will that is responsible, both for creating him out of nothing and for restoring him to life after he had fallen, and was dead.)[22] However, although we may take it that God intimated only this one death in the words: "In what day soever thou shalt eat of it, thou shalt die the death," by which He meant: "In whatever day you will leave me through disobedience I shall leave you without grace," nevertheless, the mention of this one death includes all the other deaths which were certainly to follow.

In so far as a rebellion of the flesh against the rebellious soul prompted our parents to cover their shame, they experienced one kind of death—God's desertion of the soul. It was this death which was intimated when God asked Adam, beside himself with fear and in hiding: "Where art thou?"[23] not, of course, because God did not know the answer, but to scold Adam by reminding him that there really was nowhere that he could be, once God was not in him.

Then when the soul departed from Adam's body, wasted and worn out with old age, he experienced a second kind of death, one which God specified when He pronounced this sentence upon man: "Dust thou art, and into dust thou shalt return."[24] Now, what I call the first death—that of the entire man—embraces these two deaths. Ultimately, it will be followed by a second one, unless, by God's grace, man is delivered from it.

The body of man would never return to the earth out of which it was formed unless it did so by its own death, which occurs when the soul, the life of the body, abandons it. Consequently, all Christians who really hold to the Catholic faith believe that it is not by a law of nature that man is subject to bodily death—since God created for man an immortal nature—but as a just punishment for sin. For, it was in retribution for sin that God said to the man, in whose existence we all shared: "Dust thou art, and into dust thou shalt return."

XIV, 11

Since God foresaw all things and, hence, that man would sin, our conception of the supernatural City of God must be based on what God foreknew and forewilled, and not on human fancies that could never come true, because it was not in God's plan that they should. Not even by his sin could man change the counsels of God, in the sense of compelling Him to alter what He had once decided. The truth is that, by His omniscience, God could foresee two future realities: how bad man whom God had created good was to become, and how much good God was to make out of this very evil.

Though we sometimes hear the expression, "God changed His mind," or even read in the figurative language of Scripture that "God repented,"[25] we interpret these sayings not in reference to the decisions determined on by Almighty God but in reference to the expectations of man or to the order of natural causes. So, we believe, as Scripture tells us that God created man right[26] and, therefore, endowed with a good will, for without a good will he would not have been "right."

The good will, then, is a work of God, since man was created by God with a good will. On the contrary, the first bad will, which was present in man before any of his bad deeds, was rather a falling away from the work of God into man's own works than a positive work itself; in fact, a fall into bad works, since they were "according to man" and not "according to God."[27] Thus, this bad will or, what is the same, man in so far as his will is bad is like a bad tree which brings forth these bad works like bad fruit.

A bad will, however, contrary as it is to nature and not according to nature, since it is a defect in nature, still belongs to the nature of which it is a defect, since it has no existence apart from this nature. This nature, of course, is one that God has created out of nothing, and not out of Himself, as was the case when He begot the Word through whom all things have been made. Though God has fashioned man from the dust of the earth, that same dust, like all earthly matter, has been made out of nothing. And it was a soul made out of nothing which God united to the body when man was created.

In the long run, however, the good triumphs over the evil. It is true, of course, that the Creator permits evil, to prove to what good purpose His providence and justice can use even evil. Nevertheless, while good can exist without any defect, as in the true and supreme God Himself, and even in the whole of that visible and invisible creation, high in the heavens above this gloomy atmosphere, evil cannot exist without good, since the natures to which the defects belong, in as much as they are natures, are good. Moreover, we cannot remove evil by the destruction of the nature or any part of it, to which the damage has been done. We can only cure a disease or repair the damage by restoring the nature to health or wholeness.

Take the case of the will. Its choice is truly free only when it is not a slave to sin and vice. God created man with such a free will, but, once that kind of freedom was lost by man's fall from freedom, it could be given back only by Him who had the power to give it. Thus, Truth tells us: "If therefore the Son makes you free, you will be free indeed."[28] He might equally have said: "If, therefore, the Son saves you, you will be saved indeed." For the same reason that God's Son is our Saviour He is also our Liberator.

XIV, 12

Some one may be puzzled by the fact that other sins do not change human nature in the way that the transgression of our first parents not merely damaged theirs but had the consequence that human nature, ever since, has been subject to death, to the great corruption which we can see and experience, and to so many and such opposing passions which disturb and disorder it, which was not the case in Eden before there was sin, even though the human body was animal then as now. However, no one has a right to be puzzled, on the assumption that our first parents' sin must have been a small, venial sin, since it involved merely a matter of food—a thing good and harmless in itself apart from being forbidden, as everything else was good which God had created and planted in that place of perfect happiness.

However, what is really involved in God's prohibition is obedience, the virtue which is, so to speak, the mother and guardian of all the virtues of a rational creature. The fact is that a rational creature is so constituted that submission is good for it while yielding to its own rather than its Creator's will is, on the contrary, disastrous. Now, this command to refrain from a single kind of food when they were surrounded by an abundance of every other kind of food was so easy to obey and so simple to remember for anyone still free from passion resisting the will (as would be the case later on, in punishment for sin) that the sinfulness involved in breaking this precept was so very great precisely because the difficulty of submission was so very slight.

XIV, 14

There is a worse and more execrable kind of pride whereby one seeks the subterfuge of an excuse even when one's sin is manifest. There was an example of this in the case of our first parents when the woman said: "The serpent deceived me and I did eat," and when Adam said: "The woman, whom thou gavest me to be my companion, gave me of the tree and I did eat."[29] There is not a hint here of any prayer for pardon, not a word of entreaty for any medicine to heal their wound. They do not, it is true, deny like Cain that they had sinned. Still, their pride seeks to put the blame for the sin on someone else. The pride of the woman blames the serpent; the man's pride blames the woman. But where there is a case, as here, of an open transgression of a divine command, they did more to increase their guilt than to lessen it. For, where there is a question of believing or obeying, no one can be preferred to God, and, therefore the blame was in no way lessened merely because the woman believed the suggestion of the serpent and the man obeyed the woman who gave him the fruit.

XIV, 15

For many reasons, then, the punishment meted out for disobeying God's order was just. It was God who had created man. He had made man to His own image, set man above all other animals, placed him in Paradise, and given him an abundance of goods and of well-being. God had not burdened man with many precepts that were heavy and hard, but had propped him up with a single precept that was momentary and utterly easy and that was meant merely as a medicine to make man's obedience strong, and as a reminder that it was good for man who is a creature to give his service freely to God who is his Master.

This just punishment involves many consequences. Man who was destined to become spiritual even in his flesh, if only he had kept the commandment, became, instead, fleshly even in his soul.

Man who, by human pride, had had his own way was abandoned, by divine justice, to his own resources—not, that is, to his power but to his

Figure 3. Man the master and man the mastered. British Library MS Add. 42130, fol. 60 (Luttrell Psalter). At the top, man "controls the fish and fowl of the earth," as if God's gift in Genesis i, 29–30 were still valid. Below, woman uses her distaff (compare figure 2) to subdue man, contrary to the original terms of marriage in Genesis ii. The source of the wife's "power" after the Fall is indicated by the sexual symbolism of the husband's pocket.

weakness. The very self that had been obeyed when he sinned now became a tyrant to torment and, in place of the liberty he longed for, he had to live in the misery of servitude. He had chosen freely the death of his soul; he was now condemned, unwillingly, to the death of his body. He had been a deserter from eternal life; he was now doomed to eternal death—from which nothing could save him but grace.

This punishment was neither excessive nor unjust. Anyone who thinks otherwise merely proves his inability to measure the magnitude of this sinfulness in a case where sin was so easy to avoid. For, just as the obedience of Abraham is rightly regarded as magnificent precisely because the killing of his son was a command so difficult to obey,[30] so in Paradise the lack of obedience was so lamentable because the prohibition imposed was so easy to respect. And just as the obedience of the Second Man is so marvelous because He made Himself obedient unto death,[31] so is the disobedience of the first man so malignant because he made himself disobedient unto death. It was the Creator Himself who commanded; the thing commanded was perfectly easy; the penalty attached was known to be great. Surely, then, the malice is incalculable when the creature defies, in a matter so simple and in the face of so fearful a penalty, the supreme authority of Omnipotence.

Actually, in the punishment for that sin the only penalty for disobedience was, to put it in a single word, more disobedience. There is nothing else that now makes a man more miserable than his own disobedience to himself. Because he would not do what he could, he can no longer do what he would. It is true that even in the Garden, before man sinned, he could not do everything; but he could still do all he desired to do, since he had no desire to do what he could not do. It is different now. As Scripture says: "Man is like to a breath of air."[32] That is what we see in Adam's progeny. In too many ways to mention, man cannot do what he desires to do, for the simple reason that he refuses to obey himself; that is to say, neither his spirit nor even his body obeys his will. For, in spite of his will, his spirit is frequently troubled and his body feels pain, grows old, and dies. Now, if only our nature, wholly and in all its parts, would obey our will, we would not have to suffer these and all our other ills so unwillingly.

XIV, 16

There are, then, many kinds of lusts for this or that, but when the word is used by itself without specification it suggests to most people the lust for sexual excitement. Such lust does not merely invade the whole body and outward members; it takes such complete and passionate possession of the whole man, both physically and emotionally, that what results is the keenest of all pleasures on the level of sensation; and, at the crisis of excitement, it practically paralyzes all power of deliberate thought.

This is so true that it creates a problem for every lover of wisdom and holy joys who is both committed to a married life and also conscious of the apostolic ideal, that every one should "learn how to possess his vessel in holiness and honor, not in the passion of lust like the Gentiles who do not know God."[33] Any such person would prefer, if this were possible, to beget his children without suffering this passion. He could wish that, just as all his other members obey his reason in the performance of their appointed tasks, so the organs of parenthood, too, might function in obedience to the orders of will and not be excited by the ardors of lust.

Curiously enough, not even those who love this pleasure most— whether legitimately or illegitimately indulged—can control their own indulgences. Sometimes, their lust is most importunate when they least desire it; at other times, the feelings fail them when they crave them most, their bodies remaining frigid when lust is blazing in their souls. Thus, lust itself, lascivious and legitimate, refuses to obey, and the very passion that so often joins forces to resist the soul is sometimes so divided against itself that, after it has roused the soul to passion, it refuses to awaken the feelings of the flesh.

XIV, 17

It is no wonder that everyone feels very much ashamed of this kind of lust; hence, those organs, which lust in its own right, if I may so speak, sways or allays in defiance of the will's decision, are properly called *pudenda*. Things were different before man sinned as we can see from the text: They "were naked, but they felt no shame."[34] They were aware, of course, of their nakedness, but they felt no shame, because no desire stirred their organs in defiance of their deliberate decision, for the time had not yet come when the rebellion of the flesh was a witness and reproach to the rebellion of man against his Maker.

Of course, it is merely a popular misunderstanding to imagine that, "because their eyes were opened," they had been created blind.[35] Actually, Adam saw the animals he named and Eve "saw that the tree was good to eat, and fair to the eyes, and delightful to behold."[36] Their eyes, then, could see, but they were not open enough in the sense that they themselves had not been observant enough to realize in what a raiment of grace they must have been robed to have been unaware so long of any war between their members and their will. But, once the raiment of grace was removed, they were taught the lesson that disobedience to God is punishable by disobedience to oneself.[37] A strange and irrepressible commotion sprang up in their bodies that made nakedness indecent. They realized the rebellion and it made them ashamed.

That explains what is said after they violated the commandment of God by their open transgression: "And the eyes of both of them were opened: and when they perceived themselves to be naked, they sewed together fig leaves, and made themselves aprons."[38] It was not, then, in order to see outward things that their "eyes were opened," because they could see such things already; it was in order that they might see the difference between the good they had lost and the evil into which they had fallen. That is why the tree is called the tree of the knowledge of good and evil. They had been forbidden to touch it because, if they did, it would bring on the experience of this distinction. It takes the experience of the pains of sickness to open our eyes to the pleasantness of health.

"They perceived themselves to be naked" because they had been stripped of that grace which—so long as there had been no law in their members, warring, because of sin, against the law of their minds[39]—had taken away all shame from nakedness. All that they had really learned was what sinful experience was bound to teach them, namely, how harmful it is not to believe and not to obey. Had they not sinned, had they believed and obeyed God, they would have been happier in their ignorance. And, so, it was because they were ashamed of the rebellion in their flesh, which was at once a proof and a penalty of their rebellion against God, that they "sewed together fig leaves and made themselves aprons," to cover their loins as athletes do.

NOTES

1. Genesis i, 1.
2. Proverbs viii, 27.
3. Wisdom vii, 14.
4. Matthew xviii, 10.
5. Result of Augustine's belief that the Old Testament contains types or prefigurations of the New Testament. See below, pp. 54–57.
6. 2 Peter ii, 4.
7. Ephesians v, 8.
8. Genesis i, 3–4.

9. Psalm cxlviii, 2.
10. Matthew iv, 9.
11. James iv, 6; 1 Peter v, 5.
12. 1 Thessalonians v, 5.
13. Galatians iv, 22–24.
14. 1 Corinthians x, 4; compare Exodus xvii, 6, and Numbers, xx, 11.
15. Canticles iv, 12–13.
16. These two allegorizations would have been understood to be, respectively, "tropological" and "allegorical" (see below, pp. 56–57).
17. Psalm xli, 6.
18. Psalm lviii, 10.
19. I.e., "experienced." This moment, a most crucial one for human nature, Augustine defines with the concept of "experience." Adam and Eve knew Truth according to the authority of the Word; their new knowledge arose from their own sensations. Thus they erected a new "knowledge of good and evil" which related to self rather than to God, but which was consequently "disobedient" and began the "period of erring" (see above, p. 14). This kind of "experience," the basis of a wisdom informed by fallen human nature, is thus a source of mortal error. Chaucer often uses *experience, expert,* and similar terms in this sense, most notably in the Wife of Bath's Prologue, 1. For further discussion of the two kinds of knowledge, see especially XIV, 17 (below, pp. 31–32).
20. Galatians v, 17.
21. Genesis ii, 17.
22. This is a basis for Augustine's famous distinction between the two loves, "charity" and "cupidity" (see below, p. 53).
23. Genesis iii, 9.
24. Genesis iii, 19. See 1 Corinthians xv, 47, and the Pardoner's Tale, 729–31.
25. Genesis vi, 6; 1 Kings xv, 11.
26. Ecclesiastes vii, 30.
27. This important principle, developed in many texts by Augustine, was also stressed in Boethius' *De consolatione Philosophiae.* Since a good God could create only a good reality, evil had to be a negation, or privation, or "falling off" from the created good nature. God was infinitely good; hence an absolute denial of His Will was, as Boethius said, nothing, or "naught." Disobedient children are thus called "naughty."
28. John viii, 36.
29. Genesis iii, 12, 13.
30. Genesis xxii; the event was regarded as a prefiguration of the sacrifice of Christ.
31. Philippians ii, 8.
32. Psalm cxliii, 4.
33. 1 Thessalonians iv, 4. Despite the difficulty, readers of medieval stories of passionate love should remember that sexual pleasure was widely regarded as a penalty for Original Sin. The point is implicit in much of the discussion on love, below pp. 271 ff.
35. I.e., by a literal reading of Genesis iii, 7: "And the eyes of them both were opened." Compare the analogy in the Merchant's Tale, 2354–75.
36. Genesis iii, 6.
37. In developing the image of clothing Augustine had in mind the Pauline figure of "putting off" the old man and "putting on" the new man, as in Ephesians iv, 22–24.
38. Genesis iii, 7.
39. Romans vii, 23.

Geoffrey Chaucer:
from *The Parson's Tale*

In the Prologue to the Parson's Tale, as evening approaches and the pil-
grims are about to enter a village, seemingly near the end of their pilgrim-
age, the Host calls on the Parson to "knytte up wel a greet mateere" (28).
The Parson responds with a final tale that is, in effect, a penitential manual
to which has been added an account of the Seven Deadly Sins and their
"remedies." For the portion on penance Chaucer drew his text principally
from the Summa on Penitence of Raymund de Pennaforte (c. 1240); ma-
terials concerning the sins are based mainly on Gulielmus Peraldus' Summa
on the Vices (c. 1260). Such manuals were extremely popular in the Mid-
dle Ages, and we may assume that this combination of these standard sub-
jects was Chaucer's means of "summing up" the concerns which have been
so variously treated in the Canterbury Tales. In the Parson's Tale Chaucer
provides us with an ordered exposition of the "authority" which has ap-
peared shattered, distorted, disguised, rejected, as well as promoted, in the
course of the journey to Canterbury. Other passages from this rather un-
usual "tale" appear in connection with different issues, below, pp. 360–62,
366–69, 496–97.

When a medieval author refers to Adam and Eve, as Chaucer frequently
does, it is likely that the reference is intended to bring to mind such ex-
tended meanings as those discussed in the following excerpts. Both the
Nun's Priest's Tale and the Merchant's Tale, for instance, contain actions
reminiscent of the Fall in Genesis, and these actions invite us to bring to
the tales the allegorical significance thought to reside in the Fall story.
Similarly, courtly lovers who "serve" their ladies, and even the Wife of
Bath, who exacts "obedience" from her husbands, create an order of au-
thority which, according to the Parson's standards, is "upside-down," and
thus an expression of fallen human nature.

A modernization of lines 259–71 and 322–36.

[Original Sin and the Fall of Adam]

'You should understand that in man's sin every order or ordinance is turned upside-down. For it is true that God, and reason, and sensuality, and the body of man have been ordained so that each of these four should have lordship over the one below it. Thus: God should have lordship over the reason, and reason over sensuality, and sensuality over the body of man. But when a man sins, all this order or ordinance is turned upside-down. And therefore, inasmuch as man's reason will not be subject or obedient to God, who is rightfully his Lord, it loses the lordship which it should have over sensuality and also over the body. Why? Because sensuality then rebels against the reason, and in that way the reason loses its dominion over sensuality and the flesh. For just as reason is rebel to God, just so both sensuality and the flesh rebel against reason. And, in fact, our Lord Jesus Christ paid very dearly with His precious body for this disorder and rebellion; and hear in what way. When the reason rebels against God, man deserves to suffer sorrow and to die. Our Lord Jesus Christ suffered these things for men, after He had been betrayed by His disciple, and been seized and bound so that the blood burst out at every nail of His hands, as says Saint Augustine.[1] And furthermore, when the reason will not subdue sensuality when it may, man is worthy of shame; and this our Lord Jesus Christ suffered when they spit in His face. And furthermore, when the wretched body of man rebels against both reason and sensuality, it is worthy of death. And this our Lord Jesus Christ suffered for man upon the cross, where there was no part of His body free from great pain and bitter passion.

Of the beginning of sin Saint Paul says this: "As by one man sin first entered into this world, and by that sin death, so death passed upon all men, in whom all have sinned."[2] And this man was Adam, by whom sin entered into this world when he broke the commandments of God. And therefore he who at first was so mighty that he would never have died became such a one that must needs die, whether he like it or not, and also all his progeny in this world, since they have sinned in that man. Behold, in the state of innocence, when Adam and Eve were naked in Paradise yet had no shame of their nakedness,[3] how the serpent, which was the wiliest of all the beasts that God had made, said to the woman: "Why hath God commanded you, that you should not eat of every tree of Paradise?" The woman answered: "Of the fruit," she said, "of the trees that are in Paradise we do eat: but of the fruit of the tree which is in the midst of Paradise, God hath commanded us that we should not eat; and that we should not touch it, lest perhaps we die." The serpent said to the woman: "Nay, nay, you shall not die the death. For God doth know that in what day soever you shall eat thereof, your eyes shall be opened: and you shall be as gods, knowing good and evil." The woman then saw that the tree was good to eat, and fair to the eyes, and delightful to behold. She took of the fruit of the tree, and ate it, and gave to her husband, and he ate, and the eyes of them both were immediately opened. And when they knew themselves to be naked, they sewed out of fig leaves a kind of breeches to hide their members.[4] There may you see that in deadly sin there is, first, the suggestion of the Fiend, as is here shown by the adder; and after that the delight of the flesh, as is shown here by Eve; and after that the consent of the reason, as is shown here by Adam.[5] For trust well that, if the Fiend had tempted Eve, that is to say, the flesh, and the flesh had delight in the beauty of forbidden fruit, it is certain that until the reason, that is to say, Adam, consented to the eating of the fruit, he remained in the state of innocence. From that same Adam we inherited original sin, for we are all descended from him in the flesh, engendered of vile and corrupt matter. And when the soul is put in our body, original sin is immediately contracted;[6] and what was at first only the penalty of concupiscence becomes afterwards both penalty and sin. And therefore we are all born sons of wrath and of eternal damnation, were it not for the baptism that we receive, which takes away our guilt. But the penalty continues to dwell in us, in the form of temptation, which penalty is called concupiscence. And this concupiscence, when it is wrongfully disposed or ordered in man, makes him desire fleshly sin by concupiscence of the flesh, earthly things by concupiscence of his eyes, and high place by the pride of the heart.[7]

NOTES

1. Reference not traced.
2. Romans v, 12.
3. See Merchant's Tale, 1326.
4. Genesis iii, 1–7.
5. This allegory of the Fall was the most common medieval interpretation. One of its consequences was that the figure of "woman" in medieval literature could carry an allegorical signification of "flesh," in the broad sense of the term employed here (as carnal knowledge or desire). It is doubtful that the Wife of Bath would have disputed this view. See Wife of Bath's Prologue, 440–42.
6. Original Sin is frequently referred to as a "disease" of the soul for which

Christ is the "only Physician." His apostles were supposed to carry on His practice.

7. See 1 John ii, 16. The pattern of these three temptations was found in many places in Scripture, such as in Eve's temptation (Genesis iii, 6) and in Christ's temptations in the wilderness (Matthew iv). For a literary application of the pattern, see below, pp. 129–34.

two

MEDIEVAL LITERARY THEORY

In the medieval schools poetic theory was primarily a branch of rhetoric. In the works of the masters of rhetoric and in the comments of poets on their craft, we can discern two major interests. The first, which could be called technical, dealt with the disposition of the various parts of a discourse or fiction, treating such matters as the order of presentation, methods of amplifying or abbreviating a particular passage, levels of style, and the variety of figures of speech (conventionally termed "flowers" or "colors") available to an author. The principal sources for these topics were classical: Horace's Art of Poetry, Cicero's On Invention, and the Rhetoric for Herennius attributed to Cicero in the Middle Ages. This category of medieval study was thus inherited directly from the Roman schools, and represent the kind of thing Saint Augustine taught when he "sold the ability to lie" at Carthage and Milan before his conversion.

Codifications of these topics for the medieval schools are abundant and often elaborate, the main innovation being the view, held by such authorities as Augustine, Jerome, and Bede, that Holy Scripture provided better examples of rhetorical figures and devices than did the pagan authors. The most famous such work in the later Middle Ages was the Poetria nova ("The New Poetry") by Geoffrey of Vinsauf (see below, pp. 66–68). Some idea of how these subjects were managed in the schools may be gained from the Parisiana poetria of John of Garland, excerpted below. Such technical rules were oriented toward the composition of epistles, sermons, or poetry, and were used to analyze what medieval critics called the "letter" of a text.

In the other category of major interest the emphasis lay in interpretation, and enquiry concerned the workings of allegory. Allegorical interpretation was not unknown in pagan antiquity, but in the Christian schools it flourished in new ways which profoundly affected the concept of literature, both Christian and pagan, and consequently the author's view of his own creations. Undoubtedly the study of the Bible, and the necessity of harmonizing the Old Testament with the revelation of the New, gave special impetus to the process by which an "inner" or "higher" meaning was sought beneath the "veil" of a literal meaning. But the technique was soon applied to classical poets such as Virgil, Ovid, and Statius. Dante (below, pp. 79–81) gives easy examples of both methods, in the course of elucidating his own literary practice. It is not difficult to see how Christian authors, trained to read God's own writ allegorically and striving to compose in the tradition of classical models whose "fabulous narrations" were read allegorically, should feel it appropriate to make use of the same techniques in their own constructions.

The exact nature of medieval allegory, and the manner in which it was employed, are currently the subject of serious debate. The texts *below must speak for themselves; but the following observations may aid the nonspecialist.*

"Allegory" had a much broader meaning in the Middle Ages than it has today. In his De schematibus et tropis ("Concerning Figures and Tropes," c. 700), Bede states that "Allegory is a trope in which a meaning other than the literal is indicated," and cites irony, sarcasm, and enigma among its varieties. The idea of "other-meaning" lies behind the conventional comparison of poetry to a nut which has a cortex and a nucleus, or a "shell" and a "kernel" (see below, p. 55), and Dante's view (below, p. 80) that literature has an "inside" and an "outside." The medieval habit of schematizing created distinctions among the kinds of meanings other than the literal to be found beneath the letter. These could be threefold, as Hugh of St. Victor represents them (below, p. 63), or more commonly, fourfold, as in Dante's scheme (below, p. 79).

Hugh of St. Victor's Didascalicon (below, p.59–62) asks the reader to consider in order the letter, sense, and sentence of a text. Letter here means such matters as grammar, style, and the management of rhetorical colors. Sense is the open and obvious meaning conveyed by the letter. Together these two aspects of a text form what discussions of allegory refer to as the "literal" level of meaning, and they would exhaust the significance of the technical mechanics mentioned earlier. Sentence refers to ulterior meanings contained in the literal sense.

In the more common system, these ulterior meanings could refer to any (or all) of three aspects of Christian truth. Hence arises the idea of "fourfold allegory." The literal meaning is often called "historical," and may express the entire content of a text, as in the works of historians. Ulterior aspects of meaning were labeled allegorical, tropological (or moral), and anagogical. Allegorical meanings—not to be confused with allegory as a controlling trope—referred to the mission of the Church on earth; tropological meanings referred to the moral duties and struggles of human nature; while anagogical meanings concerned mysteries of faith, such as the afterlife or the operation of Grace, known only through revelation. Dante analyzes a single text which contains all four meanings (below, p. 81). Such multileveled significance in a single text was, however, considered to be rare.

Chaucer signaled his concern for sentence in the General Prologue to the Canterbury Tales when the Host promises a prize to the pilgrim who tells tales "of best sentence and moost solaas" (798); and some pilgrims, such as the Clerk and the Nun's Priest, explicitly warn against an exclusively literal reading. The student will find, however, a great *deal of critical debate concerning the nature and extent of allegory in Chaucer's works; what is presented here is a selection from those medieval writers who addressed themselves to the problem of allegory itself, as well as those who treated rhetorical techniques.*

Macrobius:
from the *Commentary on the Dream of Scipio*

Chaucer's interest in Macrobius' Commentary on the Dream of Scipio is attested by his references to this authority. In the Book of the Duchess (lines 280–89) he couples him as an expounder of dreams with Joseph, who interpreted Pharaoh's dream in Genesis xli. Neither Joseph nor "Macrobeus"

(He that wrot al th'avysyoun
That he mette, kyng Scipioun,
The noble man, the Affrikan,—
Suche marvayles fortuned than) (285–88)

could properly interpret his dream. In The House of Fame, 514, the narrator again compares his "avisyon" to that of "Scipion," and in fact begins the poem (lines 1–65) with a discussion of the different kinds of dreams. In The Parliament of Fowls, 29–84, he provides a résumé of "Tullyus of the Drem of Scipioun" which he reads before his own dream begins, and of which Africanus says "Macrobye roughte nat a lyte" (111). Though he jokingly suggests in the Parliament, 99–108, that his dream may be only a meaningless "nightmare" (insomnium) of the sort described by Macrobius, his practice of citing the "interpreter of dreams" suggests that he wished his dream-visions to be regarded as "fabulous narrations" making use of types of significant dreams. In the Nun's Priest's Tale, 3122–26, Chantecleer similarly claims his "avisioun" to be prophetic, on the authority of "Macrobeus."

Macrobius' (fl. 400 A.D.) defense of the "fabulous narration" in certain areas of philosophical discourse is an answer to critics of Plato's "Vision of Er" in The Republic—critics whom he indentifies as "the whole sect of Epicureans" (I, ii, 3), "men who concealed their fundamental ignorance by a display of apparent wisdom" (I, ii, 1). In Cicero's case, the narration

Trans. William Harris Stahl, Macrobius: Commentary on the Dream of Scipio (New York: Columbia University Press, 1952), pp. 84–91. Reprinted by permission of Columbia University Press.

is presented in the form of a dream. Chaucer's dream-visions take this form. In The House of Fame *and* The Parliament of Fowls, *speaking animals introduce elements of the "fable" into his narration. His form of dream-vision falls primarily under the category of a personal* somnium, *or "enigmatic dream," for which his term seems to have been "avisioun." Chantecleer's dream is clearly a* visio, *or true prophecy, as are the dreams in the cock's clerkly examples.*

Chaucer's literary practice was probably influenced by the greatest of all medieval dream-visions, the Romance of the Rose. *The opening lines of that poem (1–20) justify the literary form on the authority of Macrobius: "Many men say that there is nothing in dreams but fables and lies, but one may have dreams which are not deceitful, whose import becomes quite clear afterward. We may take as witness an author named Macrobius, who did not take dreams as trifles, for he wrote of the vision which came to King Scipio. Whoever thinks or says that to believe in a dream's coming true is folly and stupidity may, if he wishes, think me a fool; but, for my part, I am convinced that a dream signifies the good and evil that comes to men, for most men at night dream many things in a hidden way which may afterward be seen openly."*

The Dream of Scipio *itself, which Chaucer adapted in* The Parliament of Fowls, *may be found below, pp. 96–105.*

[On the Fabulous Narration]

[6] Philosophy does not discountenance all stories nor does it accept all, and in order to distinguish between what it rejects as unfit to enter its sacred precincts and what it frequently and gladly admits, the points of division must needs be clarified. [7] Fables—the very word acknowledges their falsity[1]—serve two purposes: either merely to gratify the ear or to encourage the reader to good works. [8] They delight the ear as do the comedies of Menander and his imitators, or the narratives replete with imaginary doings of lovers in which Petronius Arbiter so freely indulged and with which Apuleius, astonishingly, sometimes amused himself.[2] This whole category of fables that promise only to gratify the ear a philosophical treatise avoids and relegates to children's nurseries. [9] The other group, those that draw the reader's attention to certain kinds of virtue, are divided into two types. In the first both the setting and plot are fictitious, as in the fables of Aesop, famous for his exquisite imagination. The second rests on a solid foundation of truth, which is treated in a fictitious style. This is called the fabulous narrative (*narratio fabulosa*) to distinguish it from the ordinary fable; examples of it are the performances of sacred rites, the stories of Hesiod and Orpheus that treat the ancestry and deeds of the gods, and the mystic conceptions of the Pythagoreans. [10] Of the second main group, which we have just mentioned, the first type, with both setting and plot fictitious, is also inappropriate to philosophical treatises. The second type is subdivided, for there is more than one way of telling the truth when the argument is real but is presented in the form of a fable. [11] Either the presentation of the plot involves matters that are base and unworthy of divinities and are monstrosities of some sort (as, for example, gods caught in adultery, Saturn cutting off the privy parts of his father Caelus and himself thrown into chains by his son and successor), a type which philosophers prefer to disregard altogether; or else a decent and dignified conception of holy truths, with respectable events and characters, is presented beneath a modest veil of allegory. This is the type of fiction approved by the philosopher who is prudent in handling sacred matters.

[12] Therefore, since the treatises of Plato and Cicero suffer no harm from Er's testimony or Scipio's dream, and the treatment of sacred subjects is accomplished without loss of dignity by using their names,

let our critic at last hold his peace, taught to differentiate between the fable and the fabulous narrative.

[13] We should not assume, however, that philosophers approve the use of fabulous narratives, even those of the proper sort, in all disputations. It is their custom to employ them when speaking about the Soul, or about spirits having dominion in the lower and upper air, or about gods in general. [14] But when the discussion aspires to treat of the Highest and Supreme of all gods, called by the Greeks the Good (*tagathon*) and the First Cause (*proton aition*), or to treat of Mind or Intellect, which the Greeks call *nous*, born from and originating in the Supreme God and embracing the original concepts of things, which are called Ideas (*ideai*), when, I repeat, philosophers speak about these, the Supreme God and Mind, they shun the use of fabulous narratives. When they wish to assign attributes to these divinities that not only pass the bounds of speech but those of human comprehension as well, they resort to similes and analogies. [15] That is why Plato, when he was moved to speak about the Good, did not dare to tell what it was, knowing only this about it, that it was impossible for the human mind to grasp what it was. In truth, of visible objects he found the sun most like it, and by using this as an illustration opened a way for his discourse to approach what was otherwise incomprehensible. [16] On this account men of old fashioned no likeness of the Good when they were carving statues of other deities, for the Supreme God and Mind sprung from it are above the Soul and therefore beyond nature. It is a sacrilege for fables to approach this sphere.

[17] But in treating of the other gods and the Soul, as I have said, philosophers make use of fabulous narratives; not without a purpose, however, nor merely to entertain, but because they realise that a frank, open exposition of herself is distasteful to Nature, who, just as she has withheld an understanding of herself from the uncouth senses of men by enveloping herself in variegated garments, has also desired to have her secrets handled by more prudent individuals through fabulous narratives. [18] Accordingly, her sacred rites are veiled in mysterious representations so that she may not have to show herself even to initiates. Only eminent men of superior intelligence gain a revelation of her truths; the others must satisfy their desire for worship with a ritual drama which prevents her secrets from becoming common. [19] Indeed, Numenius, a philosopher with a curiosity for occult things, had revealed to him in a dream the outrage he had committed against the gods by proclaiming his interpretation of the Eleusinian mysteries. The Eleusinian goddesses themselves, dressed in the garments of courtesans, appeared to him standing before an open brothel, and when in

his astonishment he asked the reason for this shocking conduct, they angrily replied that he had driven them from their sanctuary of modesty and had prostituted them to every passer-by. [20] In truth, divinities have always preferred to be known and worshipped in the fashion assigned to them by ancient popular tradition, which made images of beings that had no physical form, represented them as of different ages, though they were subject neither to growth nor decay, and gave them clothes and ornaments, though they had no bodies. [21] In this way Pythagoras himself, and Empedocles, Parmenides, and Heraclitus spoke of the gods, and Timaeus, their disciple, continued the tradition that had come down to him.

NOTES

1. *Fabula* is derived from Latin *fari*, "to tell," "to sing (as a poet)." See Varro, *De lingua Latina*, VI, 55; Isidore, *Etymologiae*, I, xl, 1–2.
2. Menander (342–291 B.C.) wrote over one hundred comedies, none of which survives intact. Both Plautus (c. 254–184 B.C.) and Terence (c. 190–159 B.C.) wrote close imitations of his work in Latin. Petronius Arbiter (d. 66 A.D.), reputed author of the *Satyricon*, was identified with a public official under the Emperor Nero, noted for his voluptuary excesses. Apuleius (fl. 2nd century A.D.), on the other hand, was a leading philosopher of the Platonic school. Macrobius is here thinking of *The Golden Ass*, a work which he feels is unbefitting the author of the *De deo Socratis*.

[On Dreams]

CHAPTER iii

[1] After these prefatory remarks, there remains another matter to be considered. . . . We must first describe the many varieties of dreams recorded by the ancients, who have classified and defined the various types that have appeared to men in their sleep, wherever they might be. Then we shall be able to decide to which type the dream we are discussing belongs.

[2] All dreams may be classified under five main types: there is the enigmatic dream, in Green *oneiros*, in Latin *somnium*; second, there is the prophetic vision, in Green *horama*, in Latin *visio*; third, there is the oracular dream, in Greek *chrematismos*, in Latin *oraculum*; fourth, there is the nightmare, in Greek *enypnion*, in Latin *insomnium*; and last, the apparition, in Greek *phantasma*, which Cicero, when he has occasion to use the word, calls *visum*.[1]

[3] The last two, the nightmare and the apparition are not worth interpreting since they have no prophetic significance. [4] Nightmares may be caused by mental or physical distress, or anxiety about the future: the patient experiences in dreams vexations similar to those that disturb him during the day. As examples of the mental variety, we might mention the lover who dreams of possessing his sweetheart or of losing her, or the man who fears the plots or might of an enemy and is confronted with him in his dream or seems to be fleeing him.[2] The physical variety might be illustrated by one who has overindulged in eating or drinking[3] and dreams that he is either choking with food or unburdening himself, or by one who has been suffering from hunger or thirst and dreams that he is craving and searching for food or drink or has found it. Anxiety about the future would cause a man to dream that he is gaining a prominent position or office as he hoped or that he is being deprived of it as he feared.[4]

[5] Since these dreams and others like them arise from some condition or circumstance that irritates a man during the day and consequently disturbs him when he falls asleep, they flee when he awakes and vanish into thin air. Thus the name *insomnium* was given, not because such dreams occur "in sleep" [i.e., *in somnio*]—in this respect nightmares are like other types—but because they are noteworthy only during their course and afterwards have no importance or meaning.

[6] Virgil, too, considers nightmares deceitful: "False are the dreams

49

(*insomnia*) sent by departed spirits to their sky."⁵ He used the word "sky" with reference to our mortal realm because the earth bears the same relation to the regions of the dead as the heavens bear to the earth. Again, in describing the passion of love, whose concerns are always accompanied by nightmares, he says: "Oft to her heart rushes back the chief's valor, oft his glorious stock; his looks and words cling fast within her bosom, and the pang withholds calm rest from her limbs."⁶ And a moment later: "Anna, my sister, what dreams (*insomnia*) thrill me with fears?"⁷

[7] The apparition (*phantasma* or *visum*) comes upon one in the moment between wakefulness and slumber, in the so-called "first cloud of sleep." In this drowsy condition he thinks he is still fully awake and imagines he sees specters rushing at him or wandering vaguely about, differing from natural creatures in size and shape, and hosts of diverse things, either delightful or disturbing. To this class belongs the incubus, which, according to popular belief, rushes upon people in sleep and presses them with a weight which they can feel.⁸ [8] The two types just described are of no assistance in foretelling the future; but by means of the other three we are gifted with the powers of divination.

We call a dream oracular (*oraculum*) in which a parent, or a pious or revered man, or a priest, or even a god clearly reveals what will or will not transpire, and what action to take or to avoid. [9] We call a dream a prophetic vision (*visio*) if it actually comes true. For example, a man dreams of the return of a friend who has been staying in a foreign land, thoughts of whom never enter his mind. He goes out and presently meets his friend and embraces him. Or in his dream he agrees to accept a deposit, and early the next day a man runs anxiously to him, charging him with the safekeeping of his money and committing secrets to his trust. [10] By an enigmatic dream (*somnium*) we mean one that conceals with strange shapes and veils with ambiguity the true meaning of the information being offered, and requires an interpretation for its understanding.⁹ We need not explain further the nature of this dream since everyone knows from experience what it is. There are five varieties of it: personal, alien, social, public, and universal. [11] It is personal when one dreams that he himself is doing or experiencing something; alien, when he dreams this about someone else; social, when his dream involves others and himself; public, when he dreams that some misfortune or benefit has befallen the city, forum, theater, public walls, or other public enterprise; universal, when he dreams that some change has taken place in the sun, moon, planets, sky, or regions of the earth.¹⁰

[12] The dream which Scipio reports that he saw embraces the three

reliable types mentioned above, and also has to do with all five varieties of the enigmatic dream. It is oracular since the two men who appeared before him and revealed his future, Aemilius Paulus and Scipio the Elder, were both his father, both were pious and revered men, and both were affiliated with the priesthood. It is a prophetic vision since Scipio saw the regions of his abode after death and his future condition. It is an enigmatic dream because the truths revealed to him were couched in words that hid their profound meaning and could not be comprehended without skillful interpretation.

It also embraces the five varieties of the last type. [13] It is personal since Scipio himself was conducted to the regions above and learned of his future. It is alien since he observed the estates to which the souls of others were destined. It is social since he learned that for men with merits similar to his the same places were being prepared as for himself. It is public since he foresaw the victory of Rome and the destruction of Carthage, his triumph on the Capitoline, and the coming civil strife. And it is universal since by gazing up and down he was initiated into the wonders of the heavens, the great celestial circles, and the harmony of the revolving spheres, things strange and unknown to mortals before this; in addition he witnessed the movements of the stars and planets and was able to survey the whole earth.

NOTES

1. Macrobius' classification of dreams derives in most part from the *Oneirocriton* of Artemidorus (fl. 2nd century A.D.), a work which has been called "a main source of the leading dream books of the Middle Ages." Macrobius' *Commentary*, however, was the chief means of its transmission to European Latinists. See, for example, John of Salisbury, *Policraticus*, II, xv; Vincent of Beauvais, *Speculum naturale*, XXVI, 32 ff.; Bartholomaeus Anglicus, *De proprietatibus rerum*, VI, 24–27 (*De somno*); Robert Holkot, *Liber Sapientiae*, Lectio ccii.
2. See Troïlus and Criseyde, V, 246–52, for example, and Pandarus' analysis of dreams in V, 358–85. Chaucer playfully suggests that his dream in the Parliament of Fowls is an *insomnium* (99–105). The actual dream, however, obviously shares characteristics with "significant" dreams. Compare *Roman de la rose*, 18,366–410; *Romeo and Juliet*, I, iv, 70–88. If it is read as sheer autobiography, equating the authors with the Lover, the *Roman de la rose* would also amount to no more than an *insomnium*; the poets' invitation to read the poem in this way is clearly a French joke.
3. See Cicero, *De divinatione*, I, 60. Chantecleer calls him "Oon of the gretteste auctour that men rede" (Nun's Priest's Tale, 2984), and draws his stories of prophetic dreams from *De diviantione*, I, 27. The nature of the *insomnium* may explain why lovers sleep "namoore than dooth a nyghtyngale" (General Prologue, 98). Pertelote seeks to interpret Chantecleer's *visio* as an *insomnium* (Nun's Priest's Tale, 2921 ff.).
4. See John of Salisbury, *Policraticus*, II, xv.

5. *Aeneid,* VI, 896.
6. *Aeneid,* IV, 3–5.
7. *Aeneid,* IV, 9; this and the previous reference describe the fated passion of Dido for Aeneas.
8. See John of Salisbury, *Policraticus,* II, xv; Wife of Bath's Prologue, 880.
9. As Troilus' dream in Troilus and Criseyde, V, 1233–43, and Cassandra's interpretation in V, 1513–19.
10. See John of Salisbury, *Policraticus,* II, xv.

Saint Augustine:
from *On Christian Doctrine*

St. Augustine's De doctrina Christiana was completed in 427. Basically intended to explain the principles of interpreting the Bible, it nevertheless incorporated, as a reflection of the extraordinary unity of Augustine's mind, the fundamental principles of his view of Christian thought. For example, the treatise provides his famous distinction between charity and cupidity (III, x [16]):

I call "charity" the motion of the soul toward the enjoyment of God for His own sake, and the enjoyment of one's self and of one's neighbor for the sake of God; but "cupidity" is a motion of the soul toward the enjoyment of one's self, one's neighbor, or any corporal thing for the sake of something other than God.

And this concept of charity becomes an important critical premise for the understanding of Scripture, which, according to Augustine, "teaches nothing but charity, nor condemns anything except cupidity, and in this way shapes the minds of men" (III, x [15]).

The following selections can only isolate a few of the literary principles treated in this influential treatise. The passage on "Egyptian gold," itself an example of an allegorical interpretation of Scripture, became a standard argument for the Christian use of pagan authors. Augustine's comments on figurative language reflect his insistence upon the necessity of piercing the letter to arrive at an "inner meaning" consistent with God's Word, a technique fundamental to medieval allegory.

Trans. D. W. Robertson, Jr., On Christian Doctrine (New York: The Liberal Arts Press, 1958), pp. 75, 83–84, 90, 99–101. Copyright © 1958 by The Liberal Arts Press, Inc. Reprinted by permission of The Bobbs-Merrill Co., Inc.

53

[Gold out of Egypt]

If those who are called philosophers, especially the Platonists, have said things which are indeed true and are well accommodated to our faith, they should not be feared; rather, what they have said should be taken from them as from unjust possessors and converted to our use. Just as the Egyptians had not only idols and grave burdens which the people of Israel detested and avoided, so also they had vases and ornaments of gold and silver and clothing which the Israelites took with them secretly when they fled, as if to put them to a better use. They did not do this on their own authority but at God's commandment, while the Egyptians unwittingly supplied them with things which they themselves did not use well.[1] In the same way all the teachings of the pagans contain not only simulated and superstitious imaginings and grave burdens of unnecessary labor, which each one of us leaving the society of pagans under the leadership of Christ ought to abominate and avoid, but also liberal disciplines more suited to the uses of truth, and some most useful precepts concerning morals. Even some truths concerning the worship of one God are discovered among them. These are, as it were, their gold and silver, which they did not institute themselves but dug up from certain mines of divine Providence, which is everywhere infused, and perversely and injuriously abused in the worship of demons. When the Christian separates himself in spirit from their miserable society, he should take this treasure with him for the just use of teaching the gospel. And their clothing, which is made up of those human institutions which are accommodated to human society and necessary to the conduct of life, should be seized and held to be converted to Christian uses.

NOTE

1. Exodus iii, 22; xi, 2; xii, 35.

[Figurative Language]

III, 5

But the ambiguities of figurative words, which are now to be treated, require no little care and industry. For at the outset you must be very careful lest you take figurative expressions literally. What the Apostle says pertains to this problem: "For the letter killeth, but the spirit quickeneth."[1] That is, when that which is said figuratively is taken as though it were literal, it is understood carnally. Nor can anything more appropriately be called the death of the soul[2] than that condition in which the thing which distinguishes us from beasts, which is the understanding, is subjected to the flesh in the pursuit of the letter. He who follows the letter takes figurative expressions as though they were literal and does not refer the things signified to anything else. For example, if he hears of the Sabbath, he thinks only of one day out of the seven that are repeated in a continuous cycle; and if he hears of Sacrifice, his thoughts do not go beyond the customary victims of the flocks and fruits of the earth. There is a miserable servitude of the spirit in this habit of taking signs for things, so that one is not able to raise the eye of the mind above things that are corporal and created, to drink in eternal light.

III, 12

Those things which seem almost shameful to the inexperienced, whether simply spoken or actually performed either by the person of God or by men whose sanctity is commended to us, are all figurative, and their secrets are to be removed as kernels from the husk, as nourishment for charity.[3] Whoever uses transitory things in a more restricted way than is customary among those with whom he lives is either superstitious or temperate. But whoever so uses them that he exceeds the measure established by the custom of the good men among his neighbors either signifies something or is vicious. In all instances of this kind it is not the use of the things but the desire of the user which is culpable. Thus no reasonable person would believe under any circumstances that the feet of the Lord were anointed with precious ointment by the woman[4] in the manner of lechcrous and dissolute men whose banquets we despise. For the good odor is good fame which

55

anyone in the works of a good life will have when he follows in the footsteps of Christ, as if anointing His feet with a most precious odor. In this way what is frequently shameful in other persons is in a divine or prophetic person the sign of some great truth. Certainly union with a prostitute is one thing when morals are corrupted and quite another thing in the prophecy of the prophet Osee.[5] If, moreover, it is shameful to strip the body of clothing at the banquet of the drunken and lascivious, it is not on this account shameful to be naked in the baths.

III, 25

Since things are similar to other things in a great many ways, we must not think it to be prescribed that what a thing signifies by similitude in one place must always be signified by that thing. For the Lord used "leaven" in vituperation when He said, "Beware of the leaven of the Pharisees,"[6] and in praise when He said, "The kingdom of God . . . is like to leaven, which a woman took and hid in three measures of meal, till the whole was leavened."[7]

This variation takes two forms. Thus one thing signifies another thing and still another either in such a way that the second thing signified is contrary to the first or in such a way that the second thing is entirely different from the first. The things signified are contrary, that is, when one thing is used as a similitude in a good sense and in another place in an evil sense, like "leaven" in the above example. This is the situation where the lion is used to signify Christ, when it is said, "The lion of the tribe of Juda . . . has prevailed,"[8] but also signifies the Devil, when it is written, "Your adversary the devil, as a roaring lion, goeth about seeking whom he may devour."[9] Thus the serpent appears in a good sense in "wise as serpents,"[10] but in a bad sense in "the serpent seduced Eve by his subtilty."[11] Bread is used in a good sense in "I am the living bread which came down from heaven,"[12] but in a bad sense in "hidden bread is more pleasant."[13] Many other things are used in the same way. Those examples which I have mentioned create little doubt as to their meaning, for things ought not to be used as examples unless they are clear. There are, however, instances in which it is uncertain whether the signification is to be taken in a good sense or in an evil sense, like "in the hand of the Lord there is a cup of strong wine full of mixture."[14] It is uncertain whether this may signify the wrath of God but not to the ultimate penalty, or, that is, "the dregs," or whether it may signify rather the grace of the Scriptures passing from the Jews to the Gentiles, because "he hath poured it out from this to that," certain practices remaining among the Jews which they understand carnally because "the dregs thereof are not emptied."[15] To show that one thing may have significations which are not contrary but diverse, we may use as an example the fact that water is used in the Apocalypse to signify people,[16] but it also signifies the Holy Spirit, as in "out of his belly shall flow rivers of living water."[17] And thus water may be seen to signify one thing and another in accordance with the passages in which it is used.

NOTES

1. 2 Corinthians iii, 6.
2. Romans viii, 6.
3. The image of the kernel and husk became a commonplace. The moralized account of Statius' *Thebaid*, written in the sixth century and attributed to Fulgentius, states: "Not uncommonly poetic songs are seen to be comparable with nuts. For as in a nut there are two parts, the shell and the kernel, so also there are two parts in poetic songs: the literal and the mystical senses. The kernel lies hidden beneath the shell; beneath the literal sense lies the mystic understanding. If you wish to have the kernel, you must break the shell; if the figures are to be made plain, the letter must be shattered. The shell is tasteless; the kernel is flavorful to the taster. Similarly, the palate of the understanding relishes not the letter but the figure. A boy likes a nut whole to play with: but a wise adult breaks it to taste it. Similarly, if you are a boy, you have the plain literal sense entire without any subtle exposition in which you may delight. If you are an adult, the letter is to be broken and the kernel extracted from the literal meanings so that you may be refreshed by the taste of it." See Richard de Bury's use of the image, below, p. 75, and compare Nun's Priest's Tale, 3438–43.
4. Luke vii, 37–38; John xii, 3.
5. Osee i, 2.
6. Matthew xvi, 11.
7. Luke xiii, 20–21; Matthew xiii, 33. In dictionaries of Scriptural signs, figures are often given in both a good sense and a bad sense (*in bono* or *in malo*).
8. Apocalypse v, 5.
9. 1 Peter v, 8.
10. Matthew x, 16.
11. 2 Corinthians xi, 3.
12. John vi, 51.
13. Proverbs ix, 17.
14. Psalm lxxiv, 9.
15. Psalm lxxiv, 9.
16. Apocalypse xvii, 15; xix, 6.
17. John vii, 38.

Hugh of St. Victor:
from the *Didascalicon*

*Hugh of St. Victor is often regarded as the leading theologian at the com-
mencement of Europe's twelfth-century renaissance. Born in Saxony in
1096, he became a canon regular of St. Augustine at an early age. From
1115 until his death in 1141 he lived and taught at the Augustinian Abbey
of St. Victor in Paris. Besides the* Didascalicon *("On the Study of Read-
ing"), he wrote commentaries and a number of mystical works. His greatest
work, the* De sacramentis Christianae fidei *("The Sacraments of the Chris-
tian Faith," 1134), has been called "the first complete theological treatise
of the medieval schools."*

*So steeped was Hugh in the thought of Saint Augustine, he is sometimes
referred to as the "Second Augustine." The* Didascalicon, *composed late
in the 1120s, is an educational treatise in the tradition of Augustine's* De
doctrina Christiana. *It is a detailed survey of the arts, originally written for
his students at St. Victor, but copied extensively for schools throughout
Europe in succeeding centuries. His "allegorical" approach to reading Scrip-
ture was, presumably, part of the curriculum for many generations of schol-
ars and future authors.*

Trans. Jerome Taylor, The Didascalicon of Hugh of St. Victor *(New York: Colum-
bia University Press, 1961), pp. 120–22, 147–50. Reprinted by permission of Co-
lumbia University Press.*

[On the Order of Exposition]

VI, 8. *CONCERNING THE ORDER OF EXPOSITION*

Exposition includes three things: the letter, the sense, and the deeper meaning (*sententia*).[1] The letter is found in every discourse, for the very sounds are letters; but sense and a deeper meaning are not found together in every discourse. Some discourses contain only letter and sense, some only the letter and a deeper meaning, some all these three together. But every discourse ought to contain at least two. That discourse in which something is so clearly signified by the mere telling that nothing else is left to be supplied for its understanding contains only letter and sense. But that discourse in which the hearer can conceive nothing from the mere telling unless an exposition is added thereto contains only the letter and a deeper meaning in which, on the one hand, something is plainly signified and, on the other, something is left which must be supplied for its understanding and which is made clear by exposition.[2]

VI, 9. *CONCERNING THE LETTER*

Sometimes the letter is perfect, when, in order to signify what is said, nothing more than what has been set down needs to be added or taken away—as, "All wisdom is from the Lord God";[3] sometimes it is compressed, when something is left which must be supplied—as, "The Ancient to the lady Elect";[4] sometimes it is in excess, when, either in order to inculcate an idea or because of a long parenthetical remark, the same thought is repeated or another and unnecessary one is added, as Paul, at the end of the Epistle to the Romans, says: "Now to him . . ." and then, after many parenthetical remarks, concludes, "to whom is honor and glory."[5] The other part of the passage seems to be in excess. I say "in excess," that is, not necessary for making the particular statement. Sometimes the literal text is such that unless it is stated in another form it seems to mean nothing or not to fit, as in the following: "The Lord, in heaven the throne to him,"[6] that is, "the throne of the Lord in heaven"; "the sons of men, the teeth of those are weapons and arrows,"[7] that is, "the teeth of the sons of men"; and "man, like grass the days of him,"[8] that is, "man's days": in these examples the nominative case of the noun and the genitive case of the pronoun are put for a singular genitive of the noun; and there are many other things which are similar. To the letter belong construction and continuity.

VI, 10. CONCERNING THE SENSE

Some sense is fitting, other unfitting. Of unfitting sense, some is incredible, some impossible, some absurd, some false. You may find many things of this kind in the Scriptures, like the following: "They have devoured Jacob."[9] And the following: "Under whom they stoop that bear up the world."[10] And the following: "My soul hath chosen hanging."[11] And there are many others.

There are certain places in Divine Scripture in which, although there is a clear meaning to the words, there nevertheless seems to be no sense, either because of an unaccustomed manner of expression or because of some circumstance which impedes the understanding of the reader, as in the case, for example, in that passage in which Isaias says: "In that day seven women shall take hold of one man, saying: We will eat our own bread, and wear our own apparel: only let us be called by thy name. Take away our reproach."[12] The words are plain and open. You understand well enough, "Seven women shall take hold of one man." You understand, "We will eat our own bread." You understand, "We will wear our own apparel." You understand, "Only let us be called by thy name." You understand, "Take away our reproach." But possibly you cannot understand what the sense of the whole thing together is. You do not know what the Prophet wanted to say, whether he promised good or threatened evil. For this reason it comes about that you think the passage, whose literal sense you do not see, has to be understood spiritually only. Therefore you say that the seven women are the seven gifts of the Holy Spirit, and that these take hold of one man, that is, Christ, in whom it pleased all fulness of grace to dwell because he alone received these gifts without measure; and that he alone takes away their reproach so that they may find someone with whom to rest, because no one else alive asked for the gifts of the Holy Spirit.[13]

See now, you have given a spiritual interpretation, and what the passage may mean to say literally you do not understand. But the Prophet could also mean something literal by these words. For, since he had spoken above about the slaughter of the transgressing people, he now adds that so great would be the destruction of that same people and to such an extent were their men to be wiped out that seven women will hardly find one husband, for one woman usually has one man; and, while now women are usually sought after by men, then, in contrary fashion, women will seek after men; and, so that one man may not hesitate to marry seven women at the same time, since he might not have the wherewithal to feed and clothe them, they say to him: "We will eat our own bread, and wear our own apparel." It will not be necessary for you to be concerned about our well-being, "only let us be called by thy name," so that you may be called our husband and *be* our husband so that we may not be heralded as rejected women, and die sterile, without children—which at that time was a great disgrace. And that is why they say, "Take away our reproach."

You find many things of this sort in the Scriptures, and especially in the Old Testament—things said according to the idiom of that language and which, although they are clear in that tongue, seem to mean nothing in our own.

VI, 11. CONCERNING THE DEEPER MEANING

The divine deeper meaning can never be absurd, never false. Although in the sense, as has been said, many things are found to disagree, the deeper meaning admits no contradiction, is always harmonious, always true. Sometimes there is a single deeper meaning for a single expression; sometimes there are several deeper meanings for a single expression; sometimes there is a single deeper meaning for several expressions; sometimes there are several deeper meanings for several expressions. "When, therefore, we read the Divine Books, in such a great multitude of true concepts elicited from a few words and fortified by the sound rule of the catholic faith, let us prefer above all what it seems certain that the man we are reading thought. But if this is not evident, let us certainly prefer what the circumstances of the writing do not disallow and what is consonant with sound faith. But if even the circumstances of the writing cannot be explored and examined, let us at least prefer only what sound faith prescribes. For it is one thing not to see what the writer himself thought, another to stray from the rule of piety. If both these things are avoided, the harvest of the reader is a perfect one. But if both cannot be avoided, then, even though the will of the writer may be doubtful, it is not useless to have elicited a deeper meaning consonant with sound faith."[14] "So too, if, regarding matters which are obscure and farthest removed from our comprehension, we read some of the Divine Writings and find them susceptible, in sound faith, to many different meanings, let us not plunge ourselves into headlong assertion of any one of these meanings, so that if the truth is perhaps more carefully opened up and destroys that meaning, we are overthrown; for so we should be battling not for the thought of the Divine Scriptures but for our own thought, and this in such a way that we wished the thought of the Scriptures to be identical with our own, whereas we ought rather to wish our thought identical with that of the Scriptures."[15]

NOTES

1. As in Chaucer's word *sentence*: for example, General Prologue, 798; Nun's Priest's Tale, 3165.
2. Such expressions were commonly called *enigmas*.
3. Ecclesiasticus i, 1.
4. 2 John i, 1.
5. Romans xvi, 25–27.
6. Psalm x, 15.
7. Psalm lvi, 5.
8. Psalm cii, 15.
9. Psalm lxxviii, 7.
10. Job ix, 13.
11. Job vii, 15.
12. Isaias iv, 1.
13. The exclusively allegorical interpretation is Origen's, as translated by Saint Jerome. Jerome himself, in his commentary on Isaias, gives both a literal and an allegorical interpretation.
14. Quoted from Augustine, *De Genesi ad litteram* ("On Genesis According to the Letter"), I, 21.
15. *Ibid.*, I, 18.

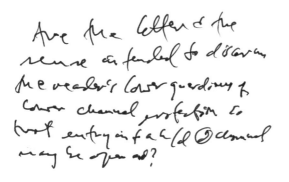

[On the Threefold Understanding]

V, 2. *CONCERNING THE THREEFOLD UNDERSTANDING*

First of all, it ought to be known that Sacred Scripture has three ways of conveying meaning—namely, history, allegory, and tropology. To be sure, all things in the divine utterance must not be wrenched to an interpretation such that each of them is held to contain history, allegory, and tropology all at once. Even if a triple meaning can appropriately be assigned in many passages, nevertheless it is either difficult or impossible to see it everywhere.[1] "On the zither and musical instruments of this type not all the parts which are handled ring out with musical sounds; only the strings do this. All the other things on the whole body of the zither are made as a frame to which may be attached, and across which may be stretched, those parts which the artist plays to produce sweetness of song."[2] Similarly, in the divine utterances are placed certain things which are intended to be understood spiritually only, certain things that emphasize the importance of moral conduct, and certain things said according to the simple sense of history. And yet, there are some things which can suitably be expounded not only historically but allegorically and tropologically as well. Thus it is that, in a wonderful manner, all of Sacred Scripture is so suitably adjusted and arranged in all its parts through the Wisdom of God that whatever is contained in it either resounds with the sweetness of spiritual understanding in the manner of strings; or, containing utterances of mysteries set here and there in the course of a historical narrative or in the substance of a literal context, and, as it were, connecting these up into one object, it binds them together all at once as the wood does which curves under the taut strings; and, receiving their sound into itself, it reflects it more sweetly to our ears—a sound which the string alone has not yielded, but which the wood too has formed by the shape of its body. Thus also is honey more pleasing because enclosed in the comb, and whatever is sought with greater effort is also found with greater desire.[3] It is necessary, therefore, so to handle the Sacred Scripture that we do not try to find history everywhere, nor allegory everywhere, nor tropology everywhere but rather that we assign individual things fittingly in their own places, as reason demands. Often, however, in one and the same literal context, all may be found together, as when a truth of history both hints at some mystical meaning by way of allegory, and equally shows by way of tropology how we ought to behave.

V, 3. THAT THINGS, TOO, HAVE A MEANING IN SACRED SCRIPTURE

It ought also to be known that in the divine utterance not only words but even things have a meaning[4]—a way of communicating not usually found to such an extent in other writings. The philosopher knows only the significance of words, but the significance of things is far more excellent than that of words, because the latter was established by usage, but Nature dictated the former.[5] The latter is the voice of men, the former the voice of God speaking to men. The latter, once uttered, perishes; the former, once created, subsists. The unsubstantial word is the sign of man's perceptions; the thing is a resemblance of the divine Idea. What, therefore, the sound of the mouth, which all in the same moment begins to subsist and fades away, is to the idea in the mind, that the whole extent of time is to eternity.[6] The idea in the mind is the internal word, which is shown forth by the sound of the voice, that is, by the external word. And the divine Wisdom, which the Father has uttered out of his heart, invisible in Itself, is recognized through creatures and in them. From this is most surely gathered how profound is the understanding to be sought in the Sacred Writings, in which we come through the word to a concept, through the concept to a thing, through the thing to its idea, and through its idea arrive at Truth. Because certain less well instructed persons do not take account of this, they suppose that there is nothing subtle in these matters on which to exercise their mental abilities, and they turn their attention to the writings of philosophers precisely because, not knowing the power of Truth, they do not understand that in Scripture there is anything beyond the bare surface of the letter.

That the sacred utterances imply the meaning of things, moreover, we shall demonstrate by a particular short and clear example. The Scripture says: "Watch, because your adversary the Devil goeth about as a roaring lion."[7] Here, if we should say that the lion stands for the Devil, we should mean by "lion" not the word but the thing. For if the two words "devil" and "lion" mean one and the same thing, the likeness of that same thing to itself is not adequate. It remains, therefore, that the word "lion" signifies the animal, but that the animal in turn designates the Devil. And all other things are to be taken after this fashion, as when we say that worm, calf, stone, serpent, and other things of this sort signify Christ.[8]

NOTES

1. In assigning a threefold "deeper meaning" to Scripture, Hugh was following the principles expounded by Saints Jerome and Gregory the Great. A fourfold interpretation, more common in the following centuries, is found in the commentaries of Augustine, Bede, and Rabanus Maurus. Compare Dante's account of these levels of meaning, below, p. 79.
2. The image appears in Augustine's *Contra Faustum Manichaeum* ("Against Faustus The Manichaean"), XXII, xciv, but the text quoted is from Isidore of Seville, *Quaestiones in Vetus Testamentum* ("Problems in the Old Testament"), Praefatio, iv.
3. A favorite idea of Augustine's concerning the utility of allegory, as in *De doctrina*, II, vi, 8: allegory exercises the minds of the worthy and excludes the unworthy.
4. See Augustine's *De doctrina*, I, ii; II, i; III, v ff. (above, p. 55).
5. Hugh equates Nature with divine Wisdom, which is also Christ. The concept is that of God's Word in the "Book of Nature."
6. The relationship between the human "word," limited to time and space, and the eternal Word of God (Truth) is explored in great detail as a major concern in Augustine's *Confessions*.
7. 1 Peter v, 8.
8. *Worm*—Psalm xii, 7; *calf*—Psalm xxviii, 6; *stone*—Psalm cxvii, 22; Isaias xxviii, 16, Matthew xxi, 42, Romans ix, 33, and 1 Peter ii, 7; *serpent*—John iii, 14.

Geoffrey of Vinsauf: from *The New Poetry*

When the Nun's Priest seeks a rhetoric sufficient to lament the downfall of his rooster Chauntecleer, he turns somewhat mockingly to apostrophe:

> O Gaufred, deere maister soverayn,
> That whan thy worthy kyng Richard was slayn
> With shot, compleynedest his deeth so soore,
> Why ne hadde I now thy sentence and thy loore,
> The Friday for to chide, as diden ye? (3347–51)

The authority is Geoffrey of Vinsauf, who provided in his New Poetry, *as an example of apostrophe designed to express great grief, a formal "chiding" of Friday—the day on which Richard I was slain.*

Although his rhetorical treatise the Poetria nova *is, on the evidence of surviving manuscripts, the most widely known medieval "art of poetry," virtually nothing is known of Geoffrey himself. Probably an Englishman, he seems to have studied in Paris and returned to England as a teacher. The* New Poetry *has been dated c. 1200–1215.*

The major sources for the treatise are Horace's Ars poetica *and the* Rhetorica ad Herennium *attributed to Cicero. Geoffrey speaks of the ordering of literary materials, devices for amplification and abbreviation, and the figures of speech (called "colors" or "flowers," as in Franklin's Prologue, 723–26). The present selection deals with* descriptio, *a device for amplifying a work. The particular "description" chosen is at the same time an example of* effictio, *a rhetorical convention for literary portraiture, particularly of women. Examples of Chaucer's use of the* effictio *occur in the Miller's Tale, 3233–70 (perhaps 3312–38 as well) and the Book of the Duchess, 817–1014. Elements of the* effictio *appropriately stress the feminine charm of the Prioress (General Prologue, 118–62).*

Trans. Margaret F. Nims, Poetria Nova of Geoffrey of Vinsauf *(Toronto: Pontifical Institute, 1967), pp. 36–38. Reprinted by permission of the Pontifical Institute of Mediaeval Studies.*

[Examples of *Effictio*]

Description, pregnant with words, follows as a seventh means of amplifying the work. But although the path of description is wide, let it also be wise, let it be both lengthy and lovely. See that the words with due ceremony are wedded to the subject. If description is to be the food and ample refreshment of the mind, avoid too curt a brevity as well as trite conventionality. Examples of description, accompanied by novel figures, will be varied, that eye and ear may roam amid a variety of subjects.

If you wish to describe, in amplified form, a woman's beauty:

Let the compass of Nature first fashion a sphere for her head; let the colour of gold give a glow to her hair, and lilies bloom high on her brow. Let her eyebrows resemble in dark beauty the blackberry, and a lovely and milk-white path separate their twin arches. Let her nose be straight, of moderate length, not too long nor too short for perfection. Let her eyes, those watch-fires of her brow, be radiant with emerald light, or with the brightness of stars. Let her countenance emulate dawn: not red, nor yet white—but at once neither of those colours and both. Let her mouth be bright, small in shape—as it were, a half-circle. Let her lips be rounded and full, but moderately so; let them glow, aflame, but with gentle fire. Let her teeth be snowy, regular, all of one size, and her breath like the fragrance of incense. Smoother than polished marble let Nature fashion her chin—Nature, so potent a sculptor. Let her neck be a precious column of milk-white beauty, holding high the perfection of her countenance. From her crystal throat let radiance gleam, to enchant the eye of the viewer and ensnare his heart. Let her shoulders, conforming to beauty's law, not slope in unlovely descent, nor jut out with an awkward rise; rather, let them be gracefully straight. Let her arms be a joy to behold, charming in their grace and their length. Let soft and slim loveliness, a form shapely and white, a line long and straight, flow into her slender fingers. Let her beautiful hands take pride in those fingers. Let her breast, the image of snow, show side by side its twin virginal gems. Let her waist be close girt, and so slim that a hand may encircle it. For the other parts I am silent—here the mind's speech is more apt than the tongue's. Let her leg be of graceful length and her wonderfully tiny foot dance with joy at its smallness.

So let the radiant description descend from the top of her head to her toe, and the whole be polished to perfection.

If you wish to add to the loveliness thus pictured an account of attire:

Let her hair, braided and bound at her back, bind in its gold; let a circlet of gold gleam on her ivory brow. Let her face be free of adornment, lovely in its natural hue. Have a starry chain encircle her milk-white neck. Let the border of her robe gleam with fine linen; with gold let her mantle blaze. Let a zone, richly set with bright gems, bind her waist, and bracelets enrich her arms. Have gold encircle her slender fingers, and a jewel more splendid than gold shed its brilliant rays. Let artistry vie with materials in her fair attire; let no skill of hand or invention of mind be able to add aught to that apparel. But her beauty will be of more worth than richness of vesture. Who, in this torch, is unaware of the fires? Who does not find the flame?

John of Garland:
from the *Parisiana Poetria*

The English poet and grammarian John of Garland (c. 1195–c. 1272) was a lifelong academic. After attending Oxford (1210–13), he moved to Paris, where he studied under Alanus de Insulis and taught grammar and literature at the University, except for a period between 1229–31 when he accepted an invitation to serve as Master of Grammar at the newly established University of Toulouse. John wrote five major Latin poems, among them the Integumenta Ovidii, an important mythographic gloss to the Metamorphoses. He compiled dictionaries, and wrote at least five grammatical or rhetorical works, of which the Parisiana poetria is an example.

The Parisiana poetrica (c. 1233) seems to have been written as a textbook for his students at Paris, to be consulted in connection with his lectures. It is a conservative work, depending primarily on Horace's Ars poetica, the pseudo-Ciceronian Rhetorica ad Herennium, and treatises by Geoffrey of Vinsauf (see above, pp. 67–68). The "vices" of poetry in this selection, stemming from those listed in Horace's Ars 1–37, are generously illustrated in the Squire's Tale, Chaucer's deliberate exercise in literary "vices."

Trans. Traugott Lawler, The Parisiana Poetria of John Garland (New Haven: Yale University Press, 1974), pp. 85–91. Reprinted by permission of the publisher.

[On the Six Vices Peculiar to Verse]

FROM CHAPTER V

There are six vices to avoid in a poem. The first is incongruous arrangement of parts; the second, incongruous digression from the subject; the third, obscure brevity; the fourth, incongruous variation of styles; the fifth, incongruous variation of subject matter; the sixth, an awkward ending.

The First Vice to Avoid in Verse. The ideal is a consistent arrangement of parts, from which a writer deviates when he appropriates bits and pieces from another subject, as when someone writing a comedy, all of whose elements should be suited to light entertainment, shifts to elements of tragedy, which are made up of serious characters and sentiments suited to them. Avoid this by holding strictly to similar elements; Horace says of this vice in his *Art of Poetry*:

Serpents are paired with birds, lambs with tigers.[1]

Serpents mean lowly men, birds lofty men; tigers fierce men, lambs gentle men, between whom there will never be any fitness.

The Second Vice. An incongruous digression from the subject deviates from the ideal. For ideally there are only two excuses to digress from the subject, namely, to explain a difficulty, and to move the minds of one's audience and to instruct them in hard matters. But it becomes an incongruous digression when a description or comparison or similitude is put forward, for the sake of moving, when it should not be done, of which vice Horace says:

A purple patch or two is sewn on, and sticks out all over.[2]

This vice is avoided whenever, for either of two reasons—the reasons given above—a digression is made either to what is itself part of the subject matter, as when a place or a castle or the like is described, or to what is not part of the subject matter, but is aptly fitted to it, such as a comparison.

The Third Vice to Avoid. Here the ideal is to speak as briefly as circumstances permit; but this sometimes declines into a vice, when brevity leads to obscurity. To do away with that vice, choose words that make the matter plain. For example: Jupiter is a guest in the home of Lycaon, who has killed a hostage in order that he might place human flesh on Jove's table; when Jupiter found out, he changed Lycaon into a wolf and set fire to his house. Choose words of this sort: "Jupiter," "guest," "hostage," "the Arcadian," "wolf," "is changed," "is burnt." When the list is complete, turn it into poetry, thus:

> Jupiter is as a guest; as food for him, a hostage falls; the Arcadian is changed; he is a wolf, and his house is burnt.[3]

The Fourth Vice, and the Three Styles. There are, again, three styles, corresponding to the three estates of men. The low style suits the pastoral life; the middle style, farmers; the high style, eminent personages, who are set over shepherds and farmers. Shepherds find riches in animals; farmers accumulate them by cultivating the earth; but princes possess them by giving them away to inferiors. Virgil composed three works to correspond to these three types, the *Eclogues*, the *Georgics*, and the *Aeneid*. High matter can be lowered, in imitation of Virgil, who calls Caesar—or himself—Tityrus and Rome a beech;[4] and low matter can be exalted, as when in a treatment of a high subject women's distaffs are called "the spears of peace." Here is an example of the high style:

> Charles, the shield of the Church and the column of peace, tames arms with arms and the fierce with ferocity.

In this style, nouns should be chosen which signify things placed in the top row; in the middle style, things placed in the middle row; in the low style, things placed in the bottom row.

On Avoiding the Vices Associated with the Several Styles. The high style has two vices associated with it, bombast and inflation: bombast is a function of words, inflation of ideas. Here is an example:

> That most supernal peak of wars, the warrioress Rolandina, was the hand and club of peace.

The middle style has two vices associated with it, fluctuation and looseness: fluctuation is a function of words or diction, looseness of ideas. For since the middle style is a compromise between extremes, that is, between the high and the low, sometimes a poet fluctuates in diction and is loose in ideas. Here is an ideal example of the middle style:

> Charles was the guardian of the Church, the protection of the people, a cultivator of justice, a lover of peace.

The following lines exemplify the vices to which this style is liable:

The king is the staff of the army and a smooth lover to his wife; he bids his men be brave.

The following lines are an ideal example of the low style:

The shepherd carries his club over his shoulder; he uses it to beat the priest his wife has been playing with.

The two vices associated with this style are aridity and bloodlessness: aridity refers to ideas that are not juicy and tasty; bloodlessness refers to works whose surface is not purpled, as here:

The peasant draws the club from his shoulder, and in three strokes removes that shorn sheep's testicles; he has a happy supper.

Notice, by the way, that "style" is used metaphorically. For a style is the middle section of a column, on which rests the epistyle, and whose lower section is called the base.[5] "Style," then, in this sense is "the poetic quality," or an "uprightness" preserved throughout the body of the matter. Sometimes style means the poem itself. Style means the office of a poet, as in the *Anticlaudianus*:

I beg the style of an author and the trappings of a poet.[6]

Finally, style means the pen we write with.

The Fifth Vice. The fifth vice of a poem, as I said above, is called incongruous variation of the subject matter. The ideal here is to vary the subject matter in order to forestall revulsion and avoid monotony; for monotony is the mother of satiety, which in turn produces boredom in the audience. To forestall that, vary the subject matter. In an amusing piece, bring in amusing things, as Horace did in one of his satires by introducing a city mouse and a country mouse for a comparison of city life and country life.[7] In a grave subject, bring in grave things, as Lucan did by telling the story of the wrestling match between the giant Antaeus and Hercules.[8] But a poet falls into vice if he tries to describe a grave subject by means of amusing and comic details, or an amusing subject by means of grave details, of which Horace says:

The man who has an urge to vary one thing a thousand ways paints dolphins in the woods, bears on the waves.[9]

That is to say, "he attributes the properties of the sea to woods, and the properties of the woods to the sea." And note that a digression is made in order to amplify the subject matter in order to avoid monotony.

The Sixth Vice, and the Various Kinds of Endings. The sixth vice is an awkward ending, which means a conclusion inappropriate to its work; to avoid it, the ending or conclusion should be derived sometimes from the body of the matter, by way of recapitulation of what has gone before, which is appropriate for orators and preachers; sometimes purely from the poet's pleasure, as Virgil does in the *Eclogues*:

> Go home fully fed, Hesperus comes, go home, she-goats.[10]

And Statius:

> O Thebaid, the subject of my waking hours for twice six years, etc.[11]

Sometimes it takes place by means of an example which contains a similitude, as in the end of the *Art of Poetry*:

> But anyone he has got hold of, he clings to and reads to death—a leech who won't let go of the skin till he has had his fill of blood.[12]

Sometimes it is taken from a proverb, as in the epistles of Horace:

> You have played enough, eaten and drunk enough; it is time for you to pass on, lest playful youth—whose behavior would be more becoming than yours—mock you and beat you for having drunk more than you should.[13]

NOTES

1. *Ars poetica*, 13. Compare Squire's Tale, 543–46.
2. *Ars poetica*, 15–16.
3. John's Latin lines, which are metrical and contain rhyme, are here literally translated.
4. See *Eclogue*, I, 1.
5. In this metaphor, the *basis* is the subject matter, the *epistilium* the work itself: the *style* rests on the subject matter, but is the means of raising the work higher than the subject matter alone could do.
6. Alanus de Insulis, *Anticlaudianus*, Prologue, 1.
7. *Satires*, II, vi, 79–117.
8. *Pharsalia*, IV, 609–55.
9. *Ars poetica*, 29–30.
10. *Eclogue*, X, 77.
11. *Thebaid*, XII, 811–12.
12. *Ars poetica*, 475–76.
13. *Epistles*, II, ii, 214–16.

Richard de Bury:
from the *Philobiblon*

Richard de Bury (1287–1345), bishop of Durham, was not only a bibliophile, but also a respected scholar and statesman. He was High Chancellor of England (1334–35) and Treasurer (1336–39) under Edward III, whose tutor he had been. He was twice ambassador to Pope John XXII at Avignon. During the first of these visits, in 1330, he met Petrarch, who wrote of their acquaintance in his Familiar Epistles, III, 1. *At home the bishop cultivated the friendship of scholars, among them Thomas Bradwardine and Richard FitzRalph. Bradwardine, to whose* De causa Dei *Chaucer's Nun's Priest refers (Nun's Priest's Tale, 3242), later became Archbishop of Canterbury; FitzRalph, later Archbishop of Armagh, was a leader among antifraternal clerks (see below, pp. 255–58). The* Philobiblon *("The Love of Books") is dated 1345.*

Trans. E. C. Thomas, The Philobiblon of Richard de Bury (London: Kegan Paul, 1888; rept. New York: Cooper Square Publishers, 1966), pp. 83–87.

[The Fables of Poets]

CHAPTER XIII

All the varieties of attack directed against the poets by the lovers of naked truth may be repelled by a two-fold defence: either that even in an unseemly subject-matter we may learn a charming fashion of speech, or that where a fictitious but becoming subject is handled, natural or historical truth is pursued under the guise of allegorical fiction.

Although it is true that all men naturally desire knowledge, yet they do not all take the same pleasure in learning. On the contrary, when they have experienced the labor of study and find their senses wearied, most men inconsiderately fling away the nut, before they have broken the shell and reached the kernel.[1] For man is naturally fond of two things, namely, freedom from control and some pleasure in his activity; for which reason no one without reason submits himself to the control of others, or willingly engages in any tedious task. For pleasure crowns activity, as beauty is a crown to youth, as Aristotle truly asserts in the tenth book of the *Ethics*.[2] Accordingly the wisdom of the ancients devised a remedy by which to entice the wanton minds of men by a kind of pious fraud, the delicate Minerva secretly lurking beneath the mask of pleasure.[3] We are wont to allure children by rewards, that they may cheerfully learn what we force them to study even though they are unwilling. For our fallen nature does not tend to virtue with the same enthusiasm with which it rushes into vice. Horace has expressed this for us in a brief verse of the *Ars Poetica*, where he says:

All poets sing to profit or delight.[4]

And he has plainly intimated the same thing in another verse of the same book, where he says:

He hits the mark, who mingles joy with use.[5]

. . . So much we have alleged in defence of the poets; and now we proceed to show that those who study them with proper intent are not to be condemned in regard to them. For our ignorance of one single word prevents the understanding of a whole long sentence. . . . As now the sayings of the saints frequently allude to the inventions of the poets, it must needs happen that through our not knowing the poem referred to, the whole meaning of the author is completely obscured, and assuredly, as Cassiodorus says in his book *Of the Institutes of Sacred Literature:* "Those things are not to be considered trifles without which great things cannot come to pass."[6] It follows therefore that through ignorance of poetry we do not understand Jerome, Augustine, Boethius, Lactantius, Sidonius, and very many others, a catalogue of whom would more than fill a long chapter. . . .

Taking this salutary instruction to heart, let the detractors of those who study the poets henceforth hold their peace, and let not those who are ignorant of these things require that others should be as ignorant as themselves, for this is the consolation of the wretched. And therefore let every man see that his own intentions are upright, and he may thus make of any subject, observing the limitations of virtue, a study acceptable to God. And if he have found profit in poetry, as the great Virgil relates that he had done in Ennius, he will not have done amiss.[7]

NOTES

1. The image of the nut is a critical commonplace. See Augustine, *De doctrina*, III, 12 (above, p. 55); Alanus de Insulis, *De planctu Naturae*, Prose iv. Gregory the Great provides a similar image in the Proemium to his Commentary on the Canticle of Canticles: *"The letter killeth* as it is written, *but the Spirit quickeneth* [2 Corinthians iii, 6]: thus the letter covers the spirit as the chaff covers the grain; but to eat the chaff is to be a beast of burden; to eat the grain is to be human. He who uses human reason, therefore, will cast aside the chaff fit for beasts and hasten to eat the grain of the spirit. For this reason it is useful that the mystery be covered in the wrapping of the letter." Compare Nun's Priest's Tale, 3438–43.
2. X, 1174 b.
3. Minerva stands for wisdom.
4. *Ars poetica*, 333.
5. *Ars poetica*, 343.
6. From Jerome, Épistle vii.
7. From Donatus' life of Virgil, xviii.

Dante Alighieri:
from the *Convivio*
and the *Letter to Can Grande*

The stature and influence of Dante are so great that his understanding of the nature of poetry, particularly with reference to his own practice, must be most seriously weighed. Born in Florence in 1265, he was a pupil of the Florentine encyclopedist and statesman Brunetto Latini, whom his Commedia later confined in the seventh circle of Hell for his sins against nature. Dante's involvement in the politics of his city brought about his banishment in 1302, and he spent the rest of his life in exile, serving, however, on frequent ambassadorial missions. About 1316 he joined the court of Can Grande della Scala, who had been appointed imperial vicar of Verona. Dante dedicated his Paradise *to this patron in Letter X, in which he undertook to explain the structure and technique of the* Commedia. *After 1318 he moved to Ravenna, where he died in 1321.*

Dante's works include the Vita nuova *("The New Life," c. 1293), a memorial of his youthful love for Beatrice, whom he later makes his guide in* Paradise. *The* Convivio *("Banquet," c. 1304–7) is an unfinished commentary on lyric poetry with philosophical meanings. Between c. 1304 and 1309 he composed* De vulgari eloquentia *("On the Eloquence of the Vernacular"), a study of the relative merits of various vernacular languages and dialects as literary media. This incomplete tract is written in Latin. In the* De monarchia, *written before 1313, Dante argued in favor of the restoration of the Empire under a powerful but divinely ordained Emperor.*

The Divine Comedy *(c. 1307–21) is the artistic pinnacle and summation of medieval Christian culture. Three great books trace the journey of the pilgrim Dante from the abyss of the* Inferno, *through Purgatory, to a final vision of blessedness in Paradise—the movement, on one level of allegory, reflecting the disentanglement of the Christian soul from the bonds of sin to achieve salvation and experience of divine glory. This movement is, as*

Selections trans. Robert S. Haller, Literary Criticism of Dante Alighieri *(Lincoln: University of Nebraska Press, 1973), pp. 99, 112–13. Reprinted by permission of The University of Nebraska Press.*

Dante himself pointed out, comedic, as it "introduces a situation of adversity, but ends its matter in prosperity" (Letter to Can Grande).

Dante was especially revered by Petrarch and by Boccaccio, whose own poems abound with echoes of the master and who devoted himself to writing a commentary on the Commedia. *Chaucer's frequent reflections of Dante's works show that he knew them well.*

[On Levels of Interpretation]

[2] I say . . . that the interpretation should be both literal and allegorical. For the understanding of this, it should be realized that texts can be understood and should be explicated primarily on four levels. [3] The first of these is called the literal level, the level which does not extend beyond the letter of the fictive discourse, which is what the fables of the poets are. The second is called allegorical, and is hidden under the cloak of these fables, a truth disguised under a beautiful lie; as for example when Ovid says that Orpheus with his lyre made the wild beasts tame, and caused the trees and the stones to move,[1] this means that the wise man with the instrument of his voice makes cruel hearts tame and humble, and causes the wills of those who do not have a life of learning and art to be moved (for those who do not possess the life of reason are like stones). [4] . . . Of course, the theologians understand this sense in another way than do the poets.[2] But because my purpose is to follow the mode of the poets, I understand the allegorical sense as it is used by poets.

[5] The third sense is called the moral,[3] and it is this one which teachers should seek out with most diligence when going through texts, because of its usefulness to them and to their pupils. One may discover, for example, from the Gospel, that when Christ went up to the mountain to be transfigured, he took only three of the twelve disciples with him:[4] this may be interpreted morally to mean that in the most secret affairs we should have few companions.

[6] The fourth sense is called the anagogical, or the "sense beyond." This sense occurs when a spiritual interpretation is to be given a text which, even though it is true on the literal level, represents the supreme things belonging to eternal glory by means of the things it represents. It may be perceived in that song of the Prophet which says that, in the departure of the people of Israel from Egypt, Judea was made holy and free.[5] [7] For even though the literal truth of this passage is clear, what it means spiritually is no less true, that in the departure of the soul from sin, it is made holy and free in its power. [8] In bringing out this meaning, the literal sense should always come first, it being the meaning in which the others are contained and without which it would be impossible and irrational to come to an understanding of the others, particularly the allegorical. [9] It would be impossible because, in the

case of anything which has an outside and an inside, it is impossible to come to the inside without first coming to the outside. Thus, since in a text the literal meaning is always the outside, it is impossible to come to the others, particularly the allegorical, without first coming to the literal.

NOTES

1. *Metamorphoses*, X, 86–105, 143–47; XI, 1–2.
2. In theology "allegory" normally refers to Christ and the Church on earth. In poetry "allegory" provides practical examples of conduct. But such a distinction becomes blurred when a poet uses allegorical figures drawn from the Bible or Nature, rather than pagan "fictions" or "beautiful lies." See below, p. 83.
3. The "moral" corresponds to what is elsewhere called the "tropological" meaning.
4. Matthew xvii, 1–8; Mark ix, 1–7; Luke ix, 28–36.
5. Psalm cxiii, 1–2. See the *Letter to Can Grande*, below.

[On His *Commedia*]

FROM *THE* LETTER TO CAN GRANDE

For the clarification of what I am going to say, then, it should be understood that there is not just a single sense in this work: it might rather be called *polysemous*, that is, having several senses. For the first sense is that which is contained in the letter, while there is another which is contained in what is signified by the letter. The first is called literal, while the second is called allegorical, or moral or anagogical. And in order to make this manner of treatment clear, it can be applied to the following verses: "When Israel went out of Egypt, the house of Jacob from a barbarous people, Judea was made his sanctuary, Israel his dominion."[1] Now if we look at the letter alone, what is signified to us is the departure of the sons of Israel from Egypt during the time of Moses; if at the allegory, what is signified to us is our redemption through Christ; if at the moral sense, what is signified to us is the conversion of the soul from the sorrow and misery of sin to the state of grace; if at the anagogical, what is signified to us is the departure of the sanctified soul from bondage to the corruption of this world into the freedom of eternal glory. And although these mystical senses are called by various names, they may all be called allegorical, since they are all different from the literal or historical. For allegory is derived from the Greek *alleon*, which means in Latin *alienus* ("belonging to another") or *diversus* ("different").[2]

NOTES

1. Psalm xciii, 1–2. All of the meanings Dante goes on to mention appear in Saint Augustine's commentary on the psalm. The inner meanings aptly illustrate Dante's plan for the inner meaning of the *Commedia*.
2. Isidore of Seville translated *allegoria* as *alieniloquium* ("other-speaking"): *Etymologiae*, I, xxxvii, 22.

Francis Petrarch:
from *Familiar Epistles, X, 4,*
"To His Brother Gherardo"

Francis Petrarch (1304–74) was the most distinguished literary authority of his day. Crowned poet laureate in 1341, he is referred to as "the lauriat poet" by Chaucer's Clerk (Clerk's Tale, 31). Boccaccio, who considered him his "revered teacher, father, and master," wrote:

Not many years ago at Rome, by vote of the senate and approval of the famous King Robert of Sicily and Jerusalem, he received the decoration of the laurel crown from the very hands of the senators. He really deserves to be counted not among the moderns, but among the illustrious ancients. His great eminence as a poet has been recognized by—I will not say merely all Italians, for their glory is singular and perennial—but by all France, and Germany, and even that most remote little corner of the world, England; and, I must add, many of the Greeks. Surely his great fame has reached Cyprus. . . . Many memorable works from his hand in prose and verse yield patent proof to all the world of his heaven-sent genius. First is his divine poem *Africa*, written in heroics to extoll the deeds of the first Africanus. . . . Second, is his *Bucolics*, famous the world over. Third, the book of metrical epistles to his friends. Fourth, are two great volumes of letters in prose, so replete with thought and fact, so resplendent with artistic embellishment, that no fair-minded reader would judge them in any respect inferior to Cicero's. Fifth, are his *Invectives against the Physician*. Sixth, his book *On the Solitary Life*. Last is . . . his book *On the Remedies of Fortune*. . . . Who then will repudiate his testimony? Who will refuse to trust him?

(*Genealogy of the* Gods XV, 6)

The present selection, "On the Nature of Poetry," is drawn from the Epistolae de rebus familiaribus. In its complete form it includes his personal allegorization of one of his own Bucolics. The letter is written to his brother Gherardo, a Carthusian monk.

Trans. J. H. Robinson and H. W. Rolfe, Petrarch *(New York: Putnam's, 1896), pp. 261–65.*

[On the Nature of Poetry]

LETTER X, 4, TO HIS BROTHER GHERARDO

I judge, from what I know of your religious fervor, that you will feel a sort of repugnance toward the poem which I enclose in this letter,[1] deeming it quite out of harmony with all your professions, and in direct opposition to your whole mode of thinking and living. But you must not be too hasty in your conclusions. What can be more foolish than to pronounce an opinion upon a subject that you have not investigated? The fact is, poetry is very far from being opposed to theology. Does that surprise you? One may almost say that theology actually is poetry, poetry concerning God. To call Christ now a lion, now a lamb, now a worm, what pray is that if not poetical?[2] And you will find thousands of such things in the Scriptures, so very many that I cannot attempt to enumerate them. What indeed are the parables of our Savior, in the Gospels, but words whose sound is foreign to their sense, or allegories, to use the technical term?[3] But allegory is the very warp and woof of all poetry. Of course, though, the subject matter in the two cases is very different. That everyone will admit. In the one case it is God and things pertaining to Him that are treated, in the other mere gods and mortal men.

Now we can see how Aristotle came to say that the first theologians and the first poets were one and the same. The very name of poet is proof that he was right. Inquiries have been made into the origin of that word; and, although the theories have varied somewhat, the most reasonable view on the whole is this: that in early days, when men were rude and unformed, but full of a burning desire—which is part of our very nature—to know the truth, and especially to learn about God, they began to feel sure that there really is some higher power that controls our destinies, and to deem it fitting that homage should be paid to this power, with all manner of reverence beyond that which is ever shown to men, and also with an august ceremonial. Therefore, just as they planned for grand abodes, which they called temples, and for consecrated servants, to whom they gave the name of priests, and for magnificent statues, and vessels of gold, and marble tables, and purple vestments, they also determined, in order that this feeling of homage might not remain unexpressed, to strive to win the favor of the deity by lofty words, subjecting the powers above to the softening influences of songs of praise, sacred hymns remote from all the forms of speech that pertain to common usage and to the affairs of state, and embellished moreover by numbers, which add a charm and drive tedium away. It behoved of course that this be done not in every-day fashion, but in a manner artful and carefully elaborated and a little strange. Now speech which was thus heightened was called in Greek *poetices*; so, very naturally, those who used it came to be called *poets*.[4]

Who, you will ask, is my authority for this? But can you not dispense with bondsmen, my brother, and have a little faith in me? That you should trust my unsupported word, when I tell you things that are true and bear upon their face the stamp of truth, is nothing more, it seems to me, than I have a right to ask of you. Still, if you find yourself disposed to proceed more cautiously, I will give you bondsmen who are perfectly good, witnesses whom you may trust with perfect safety. The first of these is Marcus Varro, the greatest scholar that Rome ever produced,[5] and the next is Tranquillus, an investigator whose work is characterised always by the utmost caution. Then I can add a third name, which will probably be better known to you, Isidore. He too mentions these matters, in the eighth book of his *Etymologies*, although briefly and merely on the authority of Tranquillus.

But you will object, and say, "I certainly can believe the saint, if not the other learned men; and yet the fact remains that the sweetness of your poetry is inconsistent with the severity of my life." Ah! but you are mistaken, my brother. Why, even the Old Testament fathers made use of poetry, both heroic song and other kinds. Moses, for example, and Job, and David, and Solomon, and Jeremiah. Even the psalms, which you are always singing, day and night, are in meter, in the Hebrew; so that I should be guilty of no inaccuracy or impropriety if I ventured to style their author the Christian's poet. Indeed the plain facts of the case inevitably suggest some such designation. . . . Of course these sacred poems, these psalms, which sing of the blessed man, Christ,—of His birth, His death, His descent into hell, His resurrection, His ascent into heaven, His return to judge the earth,—never have been, and never could have been, translated into another language without some sacrifice of either the meter or the sense. So, as the choice had to be made, it has been the sense that has been considered. And yet some vestige of metrical law still survives, and the separate fragments we still call verses, very properly, for verses they are.[6]

NOTES

1. This is the first of his Latin *Bucolics* (or *Eclogues*: 1346–48, rev. 1364). See n. 6, below.

2. See pp. 65n, 88 for a list including the sources of these figures.
3. See below, p. 91 for Boccaccio's statement.
4. As indicated in the next paragraph, the idea is developed primarily from Isidore of Seville, *Etymologiae*, VIII, vii, 1–2. The same passage appears as well in Servius' commentary on the *Aeneid* III, 443; in Rabanus Maurus' *De universo*, XV, 2; and in the *Speculum Doctrinale*, IV, 110, of Vincent of Beauvais.
5. Compare Boccaccio's *Genealogy of the Gods* XV, 8: "There are certain pietists who, in reading my words, may be moved by holy zeal to charge me with injury to the most sacrosanct Christian religion; for I allege that the pagan poets are theologians—a distinction which Christians grant only to those instructed in sacred literature. . . . But the carelessness of their remarks shows clearly the narrow limitations of their reading. If they had read widely, they would not have overlooked that very well-known work on the *City of God;* they might have seen how, in the Sixth Book, Augustine cites the opinion of the learned Varro, who held that theology is threefold in its divisions—mythical, physical, and civil." The reference is to *De civitate Dei* VI, 5. Caius Suctonius Tranquillus' *De poetis*, 2, is quoted by Isidore of Seville.
6. Petrarch goes on with a detailed allegorical analysis of the first of his *Bucolics*, which concerns the pursuit of poetry and the scholarly life.

Giovanni Boccaccio:
from *The Genealogy of the Pagan Gods*

*For some reason Chaucer never mentioned Giovanni Boccaccio (1313–75)
by name. Yet by making him one of his chief sources he at least tacitly rec-
ognized Boccaccio as one of the great Italian triumvirate of scholar-poets,
along with Petrarch and Dante.*

*Traditional reconstructions of Boccaccio's life have depended upon pur-
portedly autobiographical references in his fictional works. Unfortunately,
a great deal of what he presented as reflections of his personal life now
appears to be equally fictional. Son of a Florentine businessman, he was
sent, about 1328, to Naples to study business and law, materialistic careers
which interested him less, he later recalled, than the pursuit of "poetry."
His youthful love affair with Maria d'Aquino, whom he called "Fiam-
metta," is supposed to have occurred at this time. Evidence for this affair,
however, derives only from his fictional allusions.*

*The most significant of these earlier works are long romances: the
Filocolo (c. 1336; see below, pp. 121–35), the Filostrato (c. 1338; see be-
low, pp. 314–21), and the epical Teseide (1340–41; see below, pp. 323–
43)—each of which was adapted by Chaucer. During the 1340s and 1350s
Boccaccio also wrote many shorter poems and lyrics, in which "Fiammetta"
is sometimes celebrated. After 1340, when he returned from Naples to
Florence, he was, as well, occupied by frequent ambassadorial missions for
the Florentine court.*

*In 1350 Boccaccio welcomed at the gates of Florence Francis Petrarch,
the scholar and laureate poet who was thereafter to be his revered master
and friend. About 1353 he published the Decameron, upon which his repu-
tation now rests almost exclusively. His contemporaries, however, and
Renaissance authors were impressed primarily with his romances, and the*

Trans. Charles G. Osgood, Boccaccio on Poetry (Princeton: Princeton University
Press, 1930), pp. 39–42. Copyright © 1930 by Princeton University Press, 1956 by
The Liberal Arts Press, Inc. Reprinted by permission of The Liberal Arts Press Divi-
sion of The Bobbs-Merrill Company, Inc.

scholarly works which, the result of his preparation for his own profession of poetry, became handbooks for poets who would follow him.

The most important of these is the De genealogia deorum gentilium. *Written and revised between 1350 and 1374, it is an encyclopedic compilation of materials available to him concerning pagan mythology. This mythographic treatise is the fruit of the same scholarly activity that produced his other Latin handbooks.* De montibus, silvis, fontibus, lacubus, fluminibus *("Mountains, Forests, Fountains, Lakes, and Rivers," 1355–74) is an encyclopedia of classical geography.* De casibus virorum illustrium *("Falls of Famous Men," 1355–74) provides a series of examples of "falls from high estate" in a Boethian convention which Lady Reason had earlier used in the* Roman de la rose. *It was probably one of the models for Chaucer's "Monkes Tale De Casibus Virorum Illustrium" and was translated by John Lydgate as* The Falls of Princes *(1430–38).* De claris mulieribus *("Famous Women," 1360–74), a companion-piece for Petrarch's* De viris illustribus *("Famous Men"), provided Chaucer's Monk with the example of Zenobia (Monk's Tale, 2247–73) and served as a model for* The Legend of Good Women.

The first thirteen Books of the Genealogy *describe the ancient myths, often providing allegorical interpretations of their significance. "Perhaps as you read," he says, "you will wonder to see the meaning that was lately hidden under a rough shell brought forth now into the light—as if one were to see fresh water gushing from a globe of fire" (XIV, 1). In Book XV he justifies his own methods and style. Book XIV is his Defense of Poetry against those who take the poets for "mere story-tellers," rather than "men of great learning, endowed with a sort of divine intelligence and skill" (XIV, 1).*

Boccaccio's Defense depends upon the idea that fiction is allegorical: "Fiction [fabula] is a form of discourse which, under guise of invention, illustrates or proves an idea; and, as its superficial aspect is removed, the meaning of the author is clear. If, then, sense is revealed from under the veil of fiction, the composition of fiction is not idle nonsense" (XIV, 9). "Such then is the power of fiction that it pleases the unlearned by its external appearance, and exercises the minds of the learned with its hidden truth; and thus both are edified and delighted with one and the same perusal" (XIV, 9).

Boccaccio justifies poetry again and again by referring to the similarity between its technique and that of Holy Writ. To condemn poetry "is the same as condemning the form which our Savior Jesus Christ, the Son of God, often used when He was in the flesh, though Holy Writ does not call it 'poetry,' but rather 'parable'; some call it 'exemplum,' because it is used as such" (XIV, 9). This similarity undermines the position of his pious opponents (XIV, 14):

They would cease to wonder that the poets call Jove, now god of heaven, now lightning, now an eagle, or a man, or whatever, if they had only reminded themselves that Holy Writ itself from time to time represents the one true God as sun, fire, lion, serpent, lamb, worm, or even a stone. Likewise our most venerable mother the Church is prefigured in the sacred books, sometimes as a woman clothed with the sun, or arrayed in varied garb, sometimes as a chariot, or a ship, or an ark, a house, a temple, and the like. No less is this true of the Virgin Mother, or of the Great Enemy of mankind, as I remember to have read, time and again. I can say the same also of the multiplicity of sacred epithets; these applied to God alone are indeed innumerable at present, as are those of the Virgin Mary and the Church. Such forms and epithets are not devoid of mystic meaning; no more are those employed by poets.

For these figures Boccaccio had in mind: God as sun—*Wisdom v, 6;* fire—*Luke xii, 49;* lion—*Amos iii, 8, and Apocalypse v, 5;* serpent—*Numbers xxi, 8–9, and John iii, 14;* lamb—*Apocalypse xiv;* worm—*Psalm xxi, 7;* stone—*Ephesians ii, 20. Church as* ship—*Matthew viii, 24, and Luke v, 3;* ark—*Psalm cxxxi, 8, and the story of Noah* [*Genesis vi–ix*]; house—*Psalm xcii, 5;* temple—*Psalm xxviii, 9; a* woman clothed with the sun—*Apocalypse xii, 1;* chariot—*Habacuc iii, 8. Figures of this sort are conveniently collected in works such as Rabanus Maurus'* Allegoriae in Sacram Scripturam.

[The Definition of Poetry]

This poetry, which ignorant triflers cast aside, is a sort of fervid and exquisite invention, with fervid expression, in speech or writing, of that which the mind has invented.[1] It proceeds from the bosom of God, and few, I find, are the souls in whom this gift is born; indeed so wonderful a gift it is that true poets have always been the rarest of men. This fervor of poesy is sublime in its effects: it impels the soul to a longing for utterance; it brings forth strange and unheard-of creations of the mind; it arranges these meditations in a fixed order, adorns the whole composition with unusual interweaving of words and thoughts; and thus it veils truth in a fair and fitting garment of fiction. Further, if in any case the invention so requires, it can arm kings, marshall them for war, launch whole fleets from their docks, nay, counterfeit sky, land, sea, adorn young maidens with flowery garlands, portray human character in its various phases, awake the idle, stimulate the dull, restrain the rash, subdue the criminal, and distinguish excellent men with their proper meed of praise: these, and many other such, are the effects of poetry. Yet if any man who has received the gift of poetic fervor shall imperfectly fulfil its function here described, he is not, in my opinion, a laudable poet. For, however deeply the poetic impulse stirs the mind to which it is granted, it very rarely accomplishes anything commendable if the instruments by which its concepts are to be wrought out are wanting—I mean, for example, the precepts of grammar and rhetoric, an abundant knowledge of which is opportune. I grant that many a man already writes his mother tongue admirably, and indeed has performed each of the various duties of poetry as such; yet over and above this, it is necessary to know at least the principles of the other Liberal Arts, both moral and natural, to possess a strong and abundant vocabulary, to behold the monuments and relics of the Ancients, to have in one's memory the histories of the nations, and to be familiar with the geography of various lands, of seas, rivers and mountains.[2]

Futhermore, places of retirement, the lovely handiwork of Nature herself, are favorable to poetry, as well as peace of mind and desire for worldly glory; the ardent period of life also has very often been of great advantage.[3] If these conditions fail, the power of creative genius frequently grows dull and sluggish.

Now since nothing proceeds from this poetic fervor, which sharpens and illumines the powers of the mind, except what is wrought out by art, poetry is generally called an art. Indeed the word poetry has not the origin that many carelessly suppose, namely *poio, pois*, which is but Latin *fingo, fingis*; rather it is derived from a very ancient Greek word *poetes*, which means in Latin exquisite discourse (*exquisita locutio*).[4] For the first men who, thus inspired, began to employ an exquisite style of speech, such, for example, as song in an age hitherto unpolished, to render this unheard-of discourse sonorous to their hearers, let it fall in measured periods; and lest by its brevity it fail to please, or on the other hand, become prolix and tedious, they applied to it the standard of fixed rules, and restrained it within a definite number of feet and syllables. Now the product of this studied method of speech they no longer called by the more general term poesy, but poem. Thus as I said above, the name of the art, as well as its artificial product, is derived from its effect.

Now though I allege that this science of poetry has ever streamed forth from the bosom of God upon souls while even yet in their tenderest years, these enlightened cavillers will perhaps say that they cannot trust my words. To any fair-minded man the fact is valid enough from its constant recurrence. But for these dullards I must cite witnesses to it. If, then, they will read what Cicero, a philosopher rather than a poet, says in his oration delivered before the senate in behalf of Aulus Licinius Archias, perhaps they will come more easily to believe me. He says: "And yet we have it on the highest and most learned authority, that while other arts are matters of science and formula and technique, poetry depends solely upon an inborn faculty, is evoked by a purely mental activity, and is infused with a strange supernal inspiration."[5]

But not to protract this argument, it is now sufficiently clear to reverent men, that poetry is a practical art, springing from God's bosom and deriving its name from its effect, and that it has to do with many high and noble matters that constantly occupy even those who deny its existence. If my opponents ask when and in what circumstances, the answer is plain: the poets would declare with their own lips under whose help and guidance they compose their inventions when, for example, they raise flights of symbolic steps to heaven, or make thick-branching trees spring aloft to the very stars, or go winding about mountains to their summits. Haply, to disparage this art of poetry now unrecognized by them, these men will say that it is rhetoric which the poets employ. Indeed, I will not deny it in part, for rhetoric has its own inventions. Yet, in truth, among the disguises of fiction rhetoric has no part, for whatever is composed as under a veil, and thus exquisitely wrought, is poetry and poetry alone.[6]

NOTES

1. "Invention" is one of the five "divisions" of classical rhetoric: "The discovery of things that are true, or sufficiently similar to the true to be probable" (see Cicero, *De inventione*, I, 7; *Rhetorica ad Herennium*, I, 2).
2. Thus Boccaccio's own contribution for poets: *De montibus, silvis, fontibus, lacubus, fluminibus*.
3. He may be thinking of his own youthful poetry in the vernacular.
4. An etymology which reflects that of Isidore of Seville, *Etymologiae* VIII, vii, 2. Boccaccio cited the passage earlier in the *Genealogy* (XI, 2). Latin *fingo* means "to fashion," "to invent."
5. Cicero, *Pro Archia*, 18.
6. Boccaccio describes his method of "unveiling" thus: "The first meaning is the superficial, which is called literal. The others are deeper, and are called allegorical. To make the matter easier, I will give an example. According to the poetic fiction, Perseus, son of Jupiter, killed the Gorgon, and flew away victorious into the air. Now, this may be understood superficially in its literal or historical sense. In the moral sense it shows a wise man's triumph over vice and his attainment of virtue. Allegorically it figures the pious man who scorns worldly delight and lifts his mind to heavenly things. It admits also an anagogical sense, since it symbolizes Christ's victory over the Prince of this World, and his Ascension. But all these secondary meanings, by whatever name, are essentially allegorical. For 'allegory' is from *allo*, Latin *alienum*, and is so called being alien from the literal or historical sense" (I, 3).

three

SELECTED NARRATIVE SOURCES

The literary texts to which Chaucer had access seem to have been remarkably varied. His familiarity with the available literature of antiquity, with the authorities in matters of scholarship, and with the vernacular works of his own contemporaries is everywhere apparent. This "bookishness"—this conscious reference to images, phrases, examples, theories, and texts of previous writers within a literary tradition—is characteristic of much medieval expression, as the annotations in this volume should show. The result is a composition of allusion and reference, often quite complex, in which the colors of the past are an intimate part of the new design. As Chaucer put in the Parliament of Fowls, 22–25, with reference to his own compulsive reading,

> . . . out of olde feldes, as men seyth,
> Cometh al this newe corn from yer to yere,
> And out of olde bokes, in good feyth,
> Cometh al this newe science that men lere.

The texts translated here represent works which Chaucer either used as narrative sources or paraphrased extensively. Just as an allusion to a figure of speech from Boethius can recall the philosophical context in which it appeared, so the source Chaucer selects can involve its own literary implications. His account of Cicero's Dream of Scipio suggests a way of reading the Parliament of Fowls as a "dream-vision" and directs our attention to the theme of "commune profyt." The narrator's alterations of Ovid's "Ceyx and Alcyone" are symptomatic of his particular lack of insight. In the Canterbury Tales, Chaucer assigns to his Clerk a clerk's translation of another clerk's story; his Second Nun obediently Englishes without frills a Saint's Life from the most respected authority; and his Franklin revises part of an aristocratic romance with rhetorical embroideries which turn it into a show-piece unfortunately marred by his failure to read the analysis following the narration he adapts.

Cicero:
The Dream of Scipio

Chaucer's résumé of Cicero's Somnium Scipionis at the beginning of his
Parliament of Fowls (29–84) testifies to his familiarity with this work.
There he calls it "Tullyus of the Drem of Scipioun" (31); comparison will
show that his résumé is complete, if succinct.

Cicero's fable, originally the concluding section to a longer work, De re
publica, was thought to be an imitation of the fabulous "Vision of Er"
with which Plato had concluded his own Republic. The body of Cicero's
treatise was not known in the Middle Ages, but the present part was im-
mensely popular as the text for a lengthy commentary by Macrobius (fl.
400 A.D.). Macrobius used Cicero as a springboard to elaborate Neoplatonic
theories concerning Arithmetic, Geometry, Astronomy, and Music—the
four subjects of the quadrivium—and his work became an important school-
text. His discussion of the nature of dreams, for which he earned the title
somniorum interpres ("interpreter of dreams"), really expounds an aspect
of Rhetoric (see above, pp. 44–52); and his treatment of the cardinal vir-
tues impinges on Ethics.

The real subject of Cicero's Somnium Scipionis is the justification of
political Virtue and a love of Justice, without which no practicable republic
can be predicated. Here such virtue is said to be an expression of man's
immortal soul, consonant with cosmic design; to be independent of the re-
wards of temporal fame; and to guarantee its own reward—eternal life in
the country of stars from which all souls originally descend. Macrobius him-
self says that Cicero was as judicious and clever as Plato in recommending
the pursuit of justice: "After giving the palm to justice in all matters con-
cerning the welfare of the state, he [Cicero] revealed, at the very end of his
work, the sacred abode of immortal souls and the secrets of the heavens and
pointed out the place to which the souls of those who had served the repub-
lic prudently, justly, courageously, and temperately must proceed, or rather,
must return" (Comm. I, 8).

Trans. William Harris Stahl, Macrobius: Commentary on the Dream of Scipio
(New York: Columbia University Press, 1952), pp. 69–77. Reprinted by permission
of Columbia University Press.

The Dream of Scipio

CHAPTER I

[1] When I arrived in Africa in the consulship of Manius Manilius (I was military tribune in the fourth legion, as you know), the intention that was uppermost in my mind was to meet King Masinissa, who for very good reasons was most friendly to my family.[1] [2] When I came before him, the old man embraced me with tears in his eyes and, after a pause, gazing heavenward, said: "To you, O Sun on high, and to you other celestial beings, my thanks are due for the privilege, before I pass from this life, of seeing in my kingdom and beneath this very roof Publius Cornelius Scipio, at the mere mention of whose name I am refreshed; for the memory of that excellent and invincible leader never leaves my mind."

Then we questioned each other, I about his kingdom and he about our commonwealth, and in the ensuing conversation we spent the whole day. [3] Moreover, enjoying the regal splendor of our surroundings, we prolonged our conversation far into the night; the aged king could talk of nothing but Scipio Africanus, recollecting all his words as well as his deeds.

After we parted for the night, I fell into a deep slumber, sounder than usual because of my long journey and the late hour of retirement. [4] I dreamt that Africanus was standing before me—I believe our discussion was responsible for this, for it frequently happens that our thoughts and conversations react upon us in dreams somewhat in the manner of Ennius' reported experiences about Homer,[2] of whom he used to think and speak very often in his waking hours. My grandfather's appearance was better known to me from his portrait-mask than from my memories of him. Upon recognizing him I shuddered, but he reproved my fears and bade me pay close attention to his words.[3]

CHAPTER II

[1] "Do you see that city which I compelled to be obedient to the Roman people but which is now renewing earlier strife and is unable to remain at peace?" (From our lofty perch, dazzling and glorious, set among the radiant stars, he pointed out Carthage.) "To storm it you

have now come, ranking not much higher than a private soldier. Two years hence as consul you will conquer it, thus winning for yourself the cognomen which until now you have had as an inheritance from me. After destroying Carthage and celebrating your triumph, you will hold the office of censor; you will go as legate to Egypt, Syria, Asia, and Greece; you will be chosen consul a second time in your absence, and you will bring to a close a great war, destroying Numantia. [2] Arriving at the Capitol in a chariot, you will find the commonwealth gravely disturbed because of the policies of my grandson.⁴ Then, Scipio, it will behoove you to display to your people the brilliance of your intellect, talents, and experience.

"But at that point I see the course of your life wavering between two destinies, as it were. When your age has completed seven times eight recurring circuits of the sun, and the product of these two numbers, each of which is considered full for a different reason, has rounded out your destiny, the whole state will take refuge in you and your name; the Senate, all good citizens, the Allies, and the Latins will look to you; upon you alone will the safety of the state depend; and, to be brief, as dictator you must needs set the state in order, if only you escape death at the hands of your wicked kinsmen."

[3] Hereupon Laelius⁵ let out a cry, and the others groaned deeply; but Scipio said with a smiling expression: Hush! please; don't awaken me from my sleep; hear the rest of the dream.

CHAPTER III

[1] "But that you may be more zealous in safeguarding the commonwealth, Scipio, be persuaded of this: all those who have saved, aided, or enlarged the commonwealth have a definite place marked off in the heavens where they may enjoy a blessed existence forever. Nothing that occurs on earth, indeed, is more gratifying to that supreme God who rules the whole universe than the establishment of associations and federations of men bound together by principles of justice, which are called commonwealths. The governors and protectors of these proceed from here and return hither after death."

[2] At this point, though I was greatly dismayed, not at the fear of dying but rather at the thought of being betrayed by relatives, I nevertheless asked whether he and my father Aemilius Paulus⁶ and the others whom we think of as dead were really still living.

"Of course these men are alive," he said, "who have flown from the bonds of their bodies as from a prison; indeed, that life of yours, as it is called, is really death. Just look up and see your father Paulus approaching you."

[3] When I saw him, I wept profusely, but he embraced and kissed me and forbade me to weep. As soon as I could check my tears and speak out, I said: "I pray you, most revered and best of fathers, since this is truly life, as I hear Africanus tell, why do I linger on earth? Why do I not hasten hither to you?"

[4] "You are mistaken," he replied, "for until that God who rules all the region of the sky at which you are now looking has freed you from the fetters of your body, you cannot gain admission here. Men were created with the understanding that they were to look after that sphere called Earth, which you see in the middle of the temple. Minds have been given to them out of the eternal fires you call fixed stars and planets, those spherical solids which, quickened with divine minds, journey through their circuits and orbits with amazing speed.[7] [5] Wherefore, Scipio, you and all other dutiful men must keep your souls in the custody of your bodies and must not leave this life of men except at the command of that One who gave it to you, that you may not appear to have deserted the office assigned you. But, Scipio, cherish justice and your obligations to duty, as your grandfather here, and I, your father, have done; this is important where parents and relatives are concerned, but is of utmost importance in matters concerning the commonwealth. [6] This sort of life is your passport into the sky, to a union with those who have finished their lives on earth and who, upon being released from their bodies, inhabit that place at which you are now looking" (it was a circle of surpassing brilliance gleaming out amidst the blazing stars), "which takes its name, the Milky Way, from the Greek word [*galaxias*]."

[7] As I looked out from this spot, everything appeared splendid and wonderful. Some stars were visible which we never see from this region, and all were of a magnitude far greater than we had imagined. Of these the smallest was the one farthest from the sky and nearest the earth, which shone forth with borrowed light. And, indeed, the starry spheres easily surpassed the earth in size. From here the earth appeared so small that I was ashamed of our empire which is, so to speak, but a point on its surface.

CHAPTER IV

[1] As I gazed rather intently at the earth, my grandfather said: "How long will your thoughts continue to dwell upon the earth? Do

you not behold the regions to which you have come? The whole universe is comprised of nine circles, or rather spheres.[8] The outermost of these is the celestial sphere, embracing all the rest, itself the supreme god, confining and containing all the other spheres. In it are fixed the eternally revolving movements of the stars. [2] Beneath it are the seven underlying spheres, which revolve in an opposite direction to that of the celestial sphere. One of these spheres belongs to that planet which on earth is called Saturn. Below it is that orb, propitious and helpful to the human race, called Jupiter. Next comes the ruddy one, which you call Mars, dreaded on earth. Next, and occupying almost the middle region, comes the sun, leader, chief, and regulator of the other lights, mind and moderator of the universe, of such magnitude that it fills all with its radiance. The sun's companions, so to speak, each in its own sphere, follow—the one Venus, the other Mercury—and in the lowest sphere the moon, kindled by the rays of the sun, revolves. [3] Below the moon all is mortal and transitory, with the exception of the souls bestowed upon the human race by the benevolence of the gods. Above the moon all things are eternal.[9] Now in the center, the ninth of the spheres, is the earth, never moving and at the bottom. Towards it all bodies gravitate by their own inclination."

CHAPTER V

[1] I stood dumbfounded at these sights, and when I recovered my senses I inquired: "What is this great and pleasing sound that fills my ears?"[10]

"That," replied my grandfather, is a concord of tones separated by unequal but nevertheless carefully proportioned intervals, caused by the rapid motion of the spheres themselves. The high and low tones blended together produce different harmonies. Of course such swift motions could not be accomplished in silence and, as nature requires, the spheres at one extreme produce the low tones and at the other extreme the high tones. [2] Consequently the outermost sphere, the star-bearer, with its swifter motion gives forth a higher-pitched tone, whereas the lunar sphere, the lowest, has the deepest tone. Of course the earth, the ninth and stationary sphere, always clings to the same position in the middle of the universe. The other eight spheres, two of which move at the same speed, produce seven different tones, this number being, one might almost say, the key to the universe. Gifted men, imitating this harmony on stringed instruments and in singing, have gained for themselves a return to this region, as have those who have devoted their exceptional abilities to a search for divine truths. [3] The ears of mortals are filled with this sound, but they are unable to hear it. Indeed, hearing is the dullest of the senses: consider the people who dwell in the region about the Great Cataract, where the Nile comes rushing down from lofty mountains; they have lost their sense of hearing because of the loud roar. But the sound coming from the heavenly spheres revolving at very swift speeds is of course so great that human ears cannot catch it; you might as well try to stare directly at the sun, whose rays are much too strong for your eyes.

I was amazed at these wonders, but nevertheless I kept turning my eyes back to earth.

CHAPTER VI

[1] My grandfather then continued: "Again I see you gazing at the region and abode of mortals. If it seems as small to you as it really is, why not fix your attention upon the heavens and contemn what is mortal?[11] Can you expect any fame from these men, or glory that is worth seeking? You see, Scipio, that the inhabited portions on earth are widely separated and narrow, and that vast wastes lie between these inhabited spots, as we might call them; the earth's inhabitants are so cut off that there can be no communication among different groups; moreover, some nations stand obliquely, some transversely to you, and some even stand directly opposite you; from these, of course, you can expect no fame. [2] You can also discern certain belts that appear to encircle the earth; you observe that the two which are farthest apart and lie under the poles of the heavens are stiff with cold, whereas the belt in the middle, the greatest one, is scorched with the heat of the sun. [3] The two remaining belts are habitable; one, the southern, is inhabited by men who plant their feet in the opposite direction to yours and have nothing to do with your people; the other, the northern, is inhabited by the Romans. But look closely, see how small is the portion allotted to you! The whole of the portion that you inhabit is narrow at the top and broad at the sides and is in truth a small island encircled by that sea which you call the Atlantic, the Great Sea, or Ocean. But you can see how small it is despite its name! [4] Has your name or that of any Roman been able to pass beyond the Caucasus, which you see over here, or to cross the Ganges over yonder? And these are civilized lands in the known quarter of the globe. But who will ever hear of your

name in the remaining portions of the globe? With these excluded, you surely see what narrow confines bound your ambitions. And how long will those who praise us now continue to do so?"[12]

CHAPTER VII

[1] "Not even if the children of future generations should wish to hand down to their posterity the exploits of each one of us as they heard them from their fathers, would it be possible for us to achieve fame for a long time, not to mention permanent fame, owing to the floods and conflagrations that inevitably overwhelm the earth at definite intervals. [2] What difference does it make whether you will be remembered by those who came after you when there was no mention made of you by men before your time? They were just as numerous and were certainly better men. Indeed, among those who can possibly hear of the name of Rome, there is not one who is able to gain a reputation that will endure a single year. [3] Men commonly reckon a year solely by the return of the sun, which is just one star; but in truth when all the stars have returned to the same places from which they started out and have restored the same configurations over the great distances of the whole sky, then alone can the returning cycle truly be called a year; how many generations of men are contained in a great year I scarcely dare say. [4] As, long ago, the sun seemed to be failing and going out when Romulus' soul reached these very regions, so at the time when it will be eclipsed again in the very same quarter, and at the same season, and when all constellations and planets have been returned to their former positions, then you may consider the year complete; indeed, you may be sure that not a twentieth part of that year has yet elapsed.

[5] "Therefore, if you despair of ever returning to this region in which great and eminent men have their complete reward, how insignificant will be that human glory which can scarcely endure for a fraction of a year? But if you will look upwards and contemplate this eternal goal and abode, you will no longer give heed to the gossip of the common herd, nor look for your reward in human things. Let Virtue, as is fitting, draw you with her own attractions to the true glory; and let others say what they please about you, for they will talk in any event. All their gossip is confined to the narrow bounds of the small area at which you are gazing, and is never enduring; it is overwhelmed with the passing of men and is lost in the oblivion of posterity."

CHAPTER VIII

[1] After he said these words, I interrupted: "If, as you say, Africanus, a man who has served his country steadfastly finds a passage to the sky, so to speak, then, though I have walked in your steps and those of my father from boyhood and have never forsaken your brilliant example, I shall now strive much more zealously, with the promise of such a reward before me."

[2] "Do you then make that effort," he said, "and regard not yourself but only this body as mortal; the outward form does not reveal the man but rather the mind of each individual is his true self, not the figure that one designates by pointing a finger. Know, therefore, that you are a god if, indeed, a god is that which quickens, feels, remembers, foresees, and in the same manner rules, restrains, and impels the body of which it has charge as the supreme God rules the universe; and as the eternal God moves a universe that is mortal in part, so an everlasting mind moves your frail body.

[3] "For that which is always self-moved is eternal, but when that which conveys motion to another body and which is itself moved from the outside no longer continues in motion, it must of course cease to be alive. Therefore, only that which is self-moved never ceases to be moved, since it never abandons itself; rather, it is the source and beginning of motion for all other things that move. [4] Now a beginning has no origin: all things originate in a beginning, but a beginning itself cannot be born from something else, since it would not be a beginning if it originated elsewhere. But if it has no beginning, then indeed, it has no ending: for if a beginning were destroyed it could not be reborn from anything else; nor could it create anything else from itself if, indeed, everything has to come from a beginning. [5] Thus it happens that the beginning of motion, that which is self-moved, originates in itself; moreover, it cannot experience birth or death; otherwise the whole heavens and all nature would have to collapse and come to a standstill and would find no force to stir them to motion again."

CHAPTER IX

[1] "Therefore, since it is clear that that which is self-moved is eternal, is there anyone who would deny that this is the essence possessed by souls? Everything that is set in motion by an outside force is inani-

mate, but that which has soul is moved by its own inward motion, for this is the peculiar function and property of soul. If the soul is unique in being self-moved, surely it is without birth and without death.

[2] "Exercise it in the best achievements. The noblest efforts are in behalf of your native country; a soul thus stimulated and engaged will speed hither to its destination and abode without delay; and this flight will be even swifter if the soul, while it is still shut up in the body, will rise above it, and in contemplation of what is beyond, detach itself as much as possible from the body. [3] Indeed, the souls of those who have surrendered themselves to bodily pleasures, becoming their slaves, and who in response to sensual passions have flouted the laws of gods and of men, slip out of their bodies at death and hover close to the earth, and return to this region only after long ages of torment."

He departed, and I awoke from sleep.

NOTES

1. King of Numidia, who had helped the elder Scipio Africanus defeat Hannibal in 202 B.C. Cicero (106–43 B.C.) made his narrator the younger Scipio, whose father, Aemelius Paulus, was a Roman hero. The younger Scipio was adopted by the son of Scipio Africanus. The consulship of Manilius dates the dream in 149 B.C.
2. See Lucretius, *De rerum natura*, I, 124–26; Cicero, *Academica*, II, 51; Persius, *Satire* VI, 10–11.
3. According to Macrobius' *Commentary*, I, iii, 12, Scipio's dream embraces the three types of meaningful dreams—*oraculum*, *visio*, and *somnium*. See above, pp. 49–51.
4. Tiberius Gracchus.
5. A friend of the younger Scipio.
6. Scipio's father, who defeated Perseus, King of Macedonia, in 168 B.C.
7. Macrobius explains (I, xiv) that God creates Mind (*nous*) from himself. As long as this Mind "fixes its gaze upon the Father" it "retains a complete likeness of its Creator, but when it looks away at things below [it] creates from itself Soul. Soul, in turn, as long as it contemplates the Father, assumes his part, but by diverting its attention more and more, though itself incorporeal, degenerates into the fabric of bodies."
8. The following account, along with Macrobius' commentary, of the Ptolemaic universe had a great influence on medieval cosmology.
9. A common idea which strengthens the association of the moon with matters of Fortune, who operates in its sphere. Mortal and transitory things are consequently the concerns of "sublunary lovers." See Macrobius, *Commentary*, I, xi.
10. The following passage introduces the subject of Music in the medieval curriculum, and provides a philosophical context for related imagery in literature, such as images of harmony and discord. The "music of the spheres" is identified with Justice, an expression of cosmic Law. Terrestrial noise deafens the human ear to this perfect Music; instrumental music distracts the ear in sensual pleasures.

11. The following passage introduces the subject of geography, a significant part of Geometry in the medieval *quadrivium*.
12. Compare Boethius' discussion of the vanity of earthly fame, *De consolatione Philosophiae*, III, pros. iv–met. vi.

Ovid:
from the *Metamorphoses*

Publius Ovidius Naso (43 B.C.–18 A.D.) was twelve years old when Augustus Caesar defeated Antony at the battle of Actium (31 B.C.) and unified the Roman Empire. Sent to Rome at an early age to study rhetoric, as preparation for the practice of law or public administration, he grew up in the Augustan age when, through military expansion, patronage of the arts, and policies of moral reform, the Emperor deliberately cultivated a sense of Roman grandeur. Ovid was of the equestrian class, which made him roughly the social equivalent of the medieval knight, but after serving in a few minor administrative positions he devoted his life to poetry. He was part of a literary circle which included Tibullus (d. 19 B.C.) and Propertius (d. 15 B.C.?), both love poets, and he wrote in a Rome where Virgil (d. 19 B.C.) and Horace (d. 8 B.C.) still walked. His third marriage, to a patrician lady for whom he apparently maintained a constant affection, lasted until he died.

Ovid's amatory and mythological works have achieved enduring popularity. The Amores *("The Loves"),* Heroides *("Letters of Heroines"),* Ars amatoria *("Art of Love"), and* Remedia amoris *("Remedies of Love") deal with love that is frankly sensual or passionate, with unceasing wit and irony. The* Metamorphoses *("Transformations") and the* Fasti *("Festival Days," a kind of calendar) present an incredible profusion of classical myth and fable. In 8 A.D. Ovid was exiled by Augustus Caesar to Tomi, a barren outpost on the Black Sea. Ovid reports that his* Ars amatoria *contributed to the Emperor's decision: not only does the* Ars *seem to recommend adulterous love (specifically outlawed in Augustus' program of moral reform), but a strain of social satire on the "Golden Age" envisioned by the Emperor runs through the work. In exile Ovid wrote the* Tristia *("The Sorrows") and the* Epistolae ex Ponto *("Letters from the Black Sea"), letters*

Trans. Frank Justus Miller, Ovid: Metamorphoses (Cambridge, Mass.: Harvard University Press, 1916: Loeb Classical Library), pp. 161–73. Reprinted by permission of the publishers and The Loeb Classical Library.

*of autobiography and lament to friends in Rome, seeking reversal of his
sentence.*

Ovid's works were preserved in manuscripts copied for monastic libraries
of the eleventh and twelfth centuries. He very quickly became a "school
author," read in the schools as a model of rhetoric (and often morality). So
great did his popularity become, the twelfth and thirteenth centuries have
often been called the aetas Ovidiana ("the age of Ovid").

The Metamorphoses *seems to have been nearly complete c. 8* A.D., *the
year of his exile to Tomi. It is a vast collection (nearly 12,000 lines arranged
in 15 books) of about 250 tales drawn from Greek and Roman mythology,
related in roughly chronological order, from a description of primal chaos
to the apotheosis of Julius Caesar into a star (whose brightness, the poet
predicts, will be dimmed when Augustus Caesar is deified). If there is any
philosophical theme in the* Metamorphoses, *it may be indicated by the dis-
cussion in Book XV of Pythagorean philosophy, which recognized growth
and change as a universal law. Despite Ovid's fulsome praise of Augustus at
the end of the book, such a principle could hardly have endeared the author
to the Emperor whose social programs stressed stability.*

For the Christian Middle Ages the Metamorphoses *was a primary source-
book for a knowledge of pagan mythology. In the hands of mythographers
the tales were allegorized to provide physical, moral, and even theological
meanings consonant with Christianity. This mythographic tradition cul-
minated in the huge fourteenth-century Old French* Ovide moralisée, *al-
though such allegorical interpretation continued to flourish through the
seventeenth century.*

The story of Ceyx and Alcyone was adapted by Chaucer for his Book of
the Duchess. *The reader may wish to speculate on the significance of the
many changes from the original, which appear in his retelling. In Book XI
Ovid describes how King Ceyx of Trachis makes a sea-voyage to Claros to
consult an "oracle that helps mankind in trouble." His ship is destroyed in
a storm, and he is drowned. The present excerpt picks up the narrative as
Queen Alcyone, daughter of Aeolus, awaits the return of her husband.*

[Ceyx and Alcyone]

Meanwhile the daughter of Aeolus,[1] in ignorance of this great disaster, counts off the nights; now hastens on to weave the robes which he is to put on, and now those which she herself will wear when he comes back, and pictures to herself the home-coming which can never be. She dutifully burns incense to all the gods; but most of all she worships at Juno's[2] shrine, and approaches the altars on behalf of the man who is no more, that her husband may be kept safe from harm, that he may return once more, loving no other woman more than her. And only this prayer of all her prayers could be granted her.

But the goddess could no longer endure these entreaties for the dead. And that she might free her altar from the touch of the hands of mourning, she said: "Iris, most faithful messenger of mine, go quickly to the drowsy house of Sleep, and bid him send to Alcyone a vision in dead Ceyx' form to tell her the truth about his fate." She spoke; and Iris put on her cloak of a thousand hues and, trailing across the sky in a rainbow curve, she sought the cloud-concealed palace of the king of sleep.

Near the land of the Cimmerians[3] there is a deep recess within a hollow mountain, the home and chamber of sluggish Sleep. Phoebus can never enter there with his rising, noontide, or setting rays. Clouds of vapour breathe forth from the earth, and dusky twilight shadows. There no wakeful, crested cock with his loud crowing summons the dawn; no careful watch-dog breaks the deep silence with his voice, or goose, still shrewder than the dog. There is no sound of wild beast or of cattle, of branches rustling in the breeze, no clamorous tongues of men. There mute silence dwells. But from the bottom of the cave there flows the stream of Lethe, whose waves, gently murmuring over the gravelly bed, invite to slumber. Before the cavern's entrance abundant poppies bloom, and countless herbs, from whose juices dewy night distils sleep and spreads its influence over the darkened lands. There is no door in all the house, lest some turning hinge should creak; no guardian on the threshold. But in the cavern's central space there is a high couch of ebony, downy-soft, black-hued, spread with a dusky coverlet. There lies the god himself, his limbs relaxed in languorous repose. Around him on all sides lie empty dream-shapes, mimicking many forms, many as ears of grain in harvest-time, as leaves upon the trees, as sands cast on the shore.

When the maiden entered there and with her hands brushed aside the dream-shapes that blocked her way, the awesome house was lit up with the gleaming of her garments. Then the god, scarce lifting his eyelids heavy with the weight of sleep, sinking back repeatedly and knocking his breast with his nodding chin, at last shook himself free of himself and, resting on an elbow, asked her (for he recognized her) why she came. And she replied: "O Sleep, thou rest of all things, Sleep, mildest of the gods, balm of the soul, who puttest care to flight, soothest our bodies worn with hard ministries, and preparest them for toil again! Fashion a shape that shall seem true form, and bid it go in semblance of the king to Alcyone in Trachis, famed for Hercules. There let it show her the picture of the wreck. This Juno bids." When she had done her task Iris departed, for she could not longer endure the power of sleep, and when she felt the drowsiness stealing upon her frame she fled away and retraced her course along the arch over which she had lately passed.

But the father rouses Morpheus from the throng of his thousand sons, a cunning imitator of the human form. No other is more skilled than he in representing the gait, the features, and the speech of men; the clothing also and the accustomed words of each he represents. His office is with men alone: another takes the form of beast or bird or the long-bodied serpent. Him the gods call Icelos, but mortals name him Phobetor. A third is Phantasos, versed in different arts. He puts on deceptive shapes of earth, rocks, water, trees, all lifeless things. These shapes show themselves by night to kings and chieftains, the rest haunt the throng of common folk. These the old sleep-god passes by, and chooses out of all the brethren Morpheus alone to do the bidding of Iris, Thaumas' daughter. This done, once more in soft drowsiness he droops his head and settles it down upon his high couch.

But Morpheus flits away through the darkness on noiseless wings and quickly comes to the Haemonian city. There, putting off his wings, he takes the face and form of Ceyx, wan like the dead, and stands naked before the couch of the hapless wife. His beard is wet, and water drips heavily from his sodden hair. Then with streaming eyes he bends over her couch and says: "Do you recognize your Ceyx, O most wretched wife? or is my face changed in death? Look on me! You will know me then and find in place of husband your husband's shade. No help, Alcyone, have your prayers brought to me: I am dead. Cherish no longer your vain hope of me. For stormy Auster[4] caught my ship on the Aegean sea and, tossing her in his fierce blasts, wrecked her there. My lips, calling vainly upon your name, drank in the waves. And this tale no uncertain messenger brings to you, nor do you hear it in the words of vague report; but I myself, wrecked as you see me, tell you of my fate. Get you up, then, and weep for me; put on your mourning garments and let me not go unlamented to the cheerless land of shades." These words spoke Morpheus, and that, too, in a voice she might well believe her husband's; he seemed also to weep real tears, and had the very gesture of her Ceyx' hands. Alcyone groaned, shed tears, and in sleep seeking his arms and to clasp his body, held only air in her embrace. She cried aloud: "Wait for me! Whither do you hasten? I will go with you." Aroused by her own voice and by the image of her husband, she started wide awake. And first she looked around to see if he was there whom but now she had seen. For her attendants, startled by her cries, had brought a lamp into her chamber. When she did not find him anywhere, she smote her cheeks, tore off her garment from her breast and beat her breasts themselves. She stayed not to loose her hair, but rent it, and to her nurse, who asked what was her cause of grief, she cried: "Alcyone is no more, no more; she has died together with her Ceyx. Away with consoling words! He's shipwrecked, dead! I saw him and I knew him, and I stretched out my hands to him as he vanished, eager to hold him back. It was but a shade, and yet it was my husband's true shade, clearly seen. He had not, to be sure, his wonted features, nor did his face light as it used to do. But wan and naked, with hair still dripping, oh, woe is me, I saw him. See there, on that very spot, he himself stood, piteous"—and she strove to see if any footprints still remained. "This, this it was which with foreboding mind I feared, and I begged you not to leave me and sail away. But surely I should have wished, since you were going to your death, that you had taken me as well. How well had it been for me to go with you; for in that case neither should I have spent any of my life apart from you, nor should we have been separated in our death. But now far from myself I have perished; far from myself also I am tossed about upon the waves, and without me the sea holds me. My heart would be more cruel to me than the sea itself if I should strive still to live on and struggle to survive my sorrow. But I shall neither struggle nor shall I leave you, my poor husband. Now at least I shall come to be your companion; and if not the entombed urn, at least the lettered stone shall join us; if not your bones with mine, still shall I touch you, name with name." Grief checked further speech, wailing took place of words, and groans drawn from her stricken heart.

Morning had come. She went forth from her house to the seashore and sadly sought that spot again from which she had watched him sail. And while she lingered there and while she was saying: "Here he loosed his cable, on this beach he kissed me as he was departing"; while she was thus recalling the incidents and the place and gazing seaward, away out upon the streaming waters she saw something like a corpse. At first she was not sure what it was; but after the waves had washed it a little nearer, although it was still some distance off, yet it clearly was a corpse. She did not know whose it was; yet, because it was a shipwrecked man, she was moved by the omen and, as if she would weep for the unknown dead, she cried: "Alas for you, poor man, whoever you are, and alas for your wife, if wife you have!" Meanwhile the body had been driven nearer by the waves, and the more she regarded it the less and still less could she contain herself. Ah! and now it had come close to land, now she could see clearly what it was. It was her husband! " 'Tis he!" she shrieked and, tearing her cheeks, her hair, her garments all at once, she stretched out her trembling hands to Ceyx, crying: "Thus, O dearest husband, is it thus, poor soul, you come back to me?" Near by the water was a mole built which broke the first onslaught of the waters, and took the force of the rushing waves. Thither she ran and leaped into the sea; 'twas a wonder that she could; she flew and, fluttering through the yielding air on sudden wings, she skimmed the surface of the water, a wretched bird. And as she flew, her croaking mouth, with long slender beak, uttered sounds like one in grief and full of complaint. But when she reached the silent, lifeless body, she embraced the dear limbs with her new-found wings and strove vainly to kiss the cold lips with her rough bill. Whether Ceyx felt this, or whether he but seemed to lift his face by the motion of the waves, men were in doubt. But he did feel it. And at last, through the pity of the gods, both changed to birds. Though thus they suffered the same fate, still even thus their love remained, nor were their conjugal bonds loosened because of their feathered shape. Still do they mate and rear their young; and for seven peaceful days in the winter season Alcyone broods upon her nest floating upon the surface of the waters. At such a time the waves of the sea are still; for Aeolus guards his winds and forbids them to go abroad and for his grandsons' sake gives peace upon the sea.[5]

NOTES

1. God of the winds.
2. Juno's attribute as goddess of wedlock is probably referred to.
3. The Cimmerii were said by Homer to have dwelt farthest west on the ocean, in a land enveloped in constant darkness.
4. The southwest wind.
5. These are the so-called "halcyon days," around the shortest day of the year. The couple were metamorphosed into kingfishers, which nest at this time.

Jacobus de Voragine:
from *The Golden Legend*

The Second Nun's Tale is an example of that most popular medieval literary genre, the saint's life or "legende." As the narrator claims, Chaucer's versification of the Life of Saint Cecilia is a very close rendering of "the wordes and sentence/ Of hym that at the seintes reverence/ The storie wroot" (81–83). That author was Jacobus de Voragine, who is discussed above, p. 13.

Saint Cecilia is memorialized on November 22, and has by tradition been regarded as the patron saint of church music and of the blind.

A new translation.

[The Life of Saint Cecilia]

Cecilia is as much as to say the "lily of heaven,"[1] or "a way for blind men."[2] Or she is named for *caelum* and *lya;*[3] or else Cecilia, as "lacking blindness."[4] Or she is named for *caelum*, that is "heaven," and *leos,* that is "people."[5] She was a heavenly lily by shamefastness of virginity. Or she is said to be a "lily" because she had the whiteness of purity, strength of conscience, and the odor of good fame. She was a "way to blind men" by her example, "heaven" by her devout contemplation, "lya" by her busy labor. Or she is named for "heaven" because, according to Isidore, the philosophers say that heaven is movable, round, and burning.[6] Just so she was moving in her busy works, round in her perseverence, and burning in fiery charity. She was "lacking blindness" through the illumination of wisdom. And she was "heaven of the people," for the people beheld in her, as if following the spiritual heaven, the sun, the moon, and the stars: that is to say, shining of wisdom, magnanimity of faith, and diversity of virtues.

Saint Cecilia, the holy virgin, came from the noble lineage of the Romans, and from the time that she lay in her cradle she was fostered and nourished in the faith of Christ. She always bore the gospel hidden in her breast, and never ceased day or night from holy prayers and divine discourse, but always commended her virginity to God. And when this blessed virgin was to be espoused to a young man named Valerian, and the day of the wedding had come, she was clad in royal clothes of gold, but under them she wore a hair shirt. And hearing the organs making melody, she sang in her heart only to God, saying, "O Lord, I beseech thee that my heart and body may be undefiled, so that I be not confounded." And every second and third day she fasted praying, commending herself unto our Lord, whom she feared.

The night came in which she was to share the secret silences of the bridal chamber alone with her husband, and she said to him: "O most beloved and sweet youth, I have a secret to tell you, if you will keep it secret and swear that you will reveal it to no man." When Valerian swore that under no circumstances would he reveal it, nor for any reason, she said to him: "I have an angel as my lover, which keeps watch over my body with extreme jealousy, and if he finds that you touch me even lightly in polluted love, he will slay you at once, and you will lose the flower of your most gracious youth.[7] But if he knows that you love me with pure love, he will love you as he loves me, and will show you his glory." Then Valerian, fearing the will of God, said to her: "If you

De sca cecilia uirgi
Ecilia uirgo clari
er nobili romano.
gue exorta rab ip
amabilis i fitei n
tea absconditu sp e
gelium e gerebat
fectore in diebz no
noctibz a colloqui
diuinis. rozone diuina cessabat suan
uirginitate cfuati a domino exorab

wish me to believe what you say to me, show me that angel, and if I find that he is truly an angel of God, I will do as you say; but if it happens that you love another man than me, I will slay both him and you with my sword." Cecilia answered him: "If you will believe in the true God and promise to be baptised, you shall have the power to see him. Go then forth to the Via Appia, to the third milestone from the city, and say to the poor folk whom you will find there, 'Cecilia has sent me to you, so that you can lead me to the holy old man, Urban,[8] because I bear a secret message for him.' When you see him, tell him the words that I have said; and after you have been purified by him, then when you return you shall see the angel."

Valerian went forth and, following the signs he had received, found this holy bishop Urban hiding among the sepulchres of the martyrs, to whom he reported all the words that Cecilia had said. And Saint Urban, raising his hands to heaven, wept and said: "O Lord Jesus Christ, sower of chaste counsel and keeper of us all, receive the fruit of the seed that thou hast sown in Cecilia. O Lord Jesus Christ, good Shepherd, your servant Cecilia, like a busy bee, serveth Thee. For the spouse whom she hath taken, who was like a wild lion, she hath sent hither to Thee like a most gentle lamb." And with that word there suddenly appeared an old man clad in clothes as white as snow, holding a book written with letters of gold. When Valerian saw him, he for fear fell down to the ground as if he were dead. The old man raised him up, and read in this manner: "One God, one faith, one baptism, one God and Father of all, above all, and in us all, everywhere."[9] And when the old man had read this, he said: "Do you believe this, or do you still doubt it?" Then Valerian cried out, saying: "Nothing under heaven can be believed more truly." The old man vanished on the spot. Then Valerian received baptism from Saint Urban, and returning home he found Cecilia within their chamber speaking with an angel.

And this angel had two crowns of roses and lilies which he held in his hands, of which he gave one to Cecilia and the other to Valerian, saying: "Keep these crowns with an undefiled heart and clean body, for I have brought them to you from God's Paradise, and they shall never wither, nor lose their fragrance, nor may they be seen by any but those to whom chastity is pleasing.[10] And thou, Valerian, because thou hast used profitable counsel, demand whatever thou wilt." Valerian said: "There is nothing in this life more dear to me than the love of my only brother. Therefore I pray that he might know this truth with

---

Figure 4. Torture and martyrdom of Saint Cecilia. Huntington Library MS H.M. 3027, fol. 161 (Jacobus de Voragine, *Legenda Aurea*).

me." The angel said: "Thy petition pleaseth our Lord, and ye both shall come to Him with the palm of martyrdom."

At that moment Tyburtius, his brother, entered the chamber, and as he smelled the sweet odor of roses, he said: "I wonder where this odor of roses and lilies can come from, this time of the year, for if I were holding those roses and lilies in my own hands, perfumes of such sweetness could not so penetrate my senses. I confess, I am so refreshed that I think I have been suddenly transformed." Then Valerian said: "We have crowns that bloom with rose red and snow white flowers which your eyes have no power to see, and as by my prayers you have smelled their odor, so, if you will believe, shall you be able to see them." Tyburtius replied: "Do I hear this in my dreams or do you speak to me in very truth, Valerian?" Valerian said: "We have been in dreams up to now, but now we reside in the truth indeed." Tyburtius inquired: "Where have you learned this?" Valerian said: "An angel of God has taught me, whom you will be able to see if you will be purified and renounce all idols."

To this miracle of the crowns of roses Ambrose testifies in his *Preface*,[11] saying: Saint Cecilia was so filled with the heavenly gift that she took up the martyr's palm. She renounced the world itself along with her marriage chamber. Witness is the confession of Valerian her husband and of Tyburtius, whom, O Lord, you crowned by an angelic hand with perfumed flowers; a virgin led these men to glory; the world acknowledges how great is the power of devout chastity. Thus Ambrose.

Then Cecilia showed him plainly that all idols were mute and without senses, so that Tyburtius responded, saying: "Whoever does not believe this is a beast." Then Cecilia, kissing his breast, said: "Today I acknowledge you as my relative. For just as the love of God made your brother my husband, so your contempt of idols will make you one of our family. Now go with your brother to receive baptism, and you will be able to see the faces of the angels." And Tyburtius asked his brother: "I beseech you, brother, to tell me to whom you are taking me." Valerian replied: "To the bishop Urban." Tyburtius inquired: "Do you mean that Urban who has so often been condemned to death and who still lurks in secret hiding places? If he is found he will be burned, and we will be wrapped in the same flames. And while we seek out the divinity hidden in heaven, we will incur the fury of fire on earth."

Cecilia answered him: "If this life were the only one, we might justly fear to lose it. There is, however, another better life, which can never be lost, which the Son of God has told us of. All things created have been made by the Son born of the Father, and the whole, which was created, was animated by the Spirit proceeding from the Father. This very Son of God, coming into the world with words and miracles, showed us that there is another life." Tyburtius asked: "You have said that there is one God; how can you now speak of three?" Cecilia replied: "Just as in the single wisdom (*sapientia*) of a man there are three things: reason (*ingenium*), memory (*memoria*), and understanding (*intellectus*), so can there be three persons in the one essence of divinity." Then she began to preach to him of the coming of the Son of God and of His passion, and to show the many pertinent applications of his martyrdom. "For," she said, "the Son of God was slain so that human nature bound by sin should be freed; blessed, he was reviled, so that the reviled man should receive blessing; he permitted himself to be mocked, so that man should be freed from the mocking of demons; he received on his head a crown of thorns, in order to remove from us the sentence of death ('capital sentence'); he drank the bitter gall, in order to restore a sweet taste to man; he was stripped, in order to cover the nakedness of our first parents; he was hanged on a tree, to lift the burden of the lie of the first tree." Then Tyburtius said to his brother: "Have pity on me, and take me to the man of God so that I may be baptised." He was taken and baptised, and thereafter he often saw angels of God, and he obtained all that he ever required of God.

After this, Valerian and Tyburtius devoted themselves to giving alms to the poor, and they gave burial to the bodies of the saints whom the prefect Almachius had put to death. Almachius called them before him, and inquired why they were burying those condemned for their crimes. Tyburtius replied: "Would that we were the servants of those whom you call criminals! They rejected what appeared to be but was not true, and they discovered that what did not seem to be was true." The prefect asked: "Now, what could that be?" Tyburtius replied: "That which seems to be but is not, is all that is in this world, which leads men to nothingness. And that which does not seem to be but is, is the life of the just and the punishment of the evil." The prefect said: "I do not think you speak reasonably." Then he ordered Valerian to stand forth, saying: "Since your brother is not of sound mind, you, at all events, can answer for him. Most people hold that you are wrong—you who contemn worldly pleasure and welcome all sorts of suffering as pleasures." Then Valerian said that he had seen idle men joking and deriding workers in the field in cold weather, but in summer time, when the blessed came into the fruits of their labor, to the joy of those who were thought to be foolish, then those who were thought so witty were reduced to weeping. "Thus is it with us who even now undergo ignominy and labor. In the future, however, we will receive our glory and our eternal reward.[12] But you who now enjoy temporal pleasures will, in the future, find eternal ruin." Then the prefect said: "Therefore we who are invincible princes will suffer eternal sorrow, and you who are most worthless will possess eternal joy?" Valerian answered: "You are but little men, not princes, born in our own time, destined soon to die and to render account to God more than other men." But the prefect said: "Why should I put up with your twisted words? Offer sacrifice to the gods and depart without harm." The holy men answered: "We offer sacrifice to the true God every day." The prefect demanded: "What is his name?" Valerian responded: "You could not discover His name even if you could fly with wings." The prefect asked: "Therefore Jupiter is not the name of god?" Valerian said: "That is the name of a murderer and a ravisher of women." Almachius asked him: "Therefore the whole world is in error, and only you and your brother know who is the true god?" Valerian answered: "We are not alone: a great multitude of people has accepted this doctrine."

The holy men were turned over to the custody of Maximus. He said to them: "O bright flower of youth, O mutual brotherly devotion, how is it that you hasten to death as if to a feast?" Valerian answered that if he would promise to believe their faith, he would see the glory which their souls would receive after death. Maximus said: "May I be blasted by thunderbolts if I do not confess Him whom you worship to be the only God, if He can bring about what you say." Then this Maximus, with all his household and all the executioners, were turned to the faith and received baptism from the holy Urban, who came there secretly. And afterwards, when the morning came, Saint Cecilia said to them: "Hail, you knights of Christ; cast off the works of darkness and clothe yourselves with the arms of light." And then they were led four miles out of the town to the statue of Jupiter, and when they refused to sacrifice they were beheaded together. Then Maximus, who saw this thing, swore that in the hour of their passion he saw clear shining angels, and their souls leave like virgins from their chamber, borne up by the angels to heaven. Many believed him, and, converted from the error of idolatry, returned to faith in their Creator.

When Almachius heard that Maximus had been made a Christian, he ordered him beaten with whips of lead until he gave up his spirit and died. Saint Cecilia buried his body by Valerian and Tyburtius. Then Almachius began to inquire into the relationships of the two men, and he brought Cecilia before him inasmuch as she was the wife of Valerian, and ordered that she sacrifice unto the idols or accept the sentence of death. When the officers came to press her on this matter, they wept bitterly that so fair and so noble a maid should be put to death. Then she said to them: "O good young men, this is not to lose my youth, but to change it: that is, to give clay and receive gold, to give up a vile habitation and receive a precious one, to give up a little corner and receive a bright open space. For each offering God repays a hundredfold. Do you believe what I say?" And they said: "We believe Christ to be very God, who has such a servant." Bishop Urban was called, and four hundred and more were baptised.

Then Almachius, calling Saint Cecilia before him, said to her: "Of what condition are you?" And she said: "I am native born, and a noble." Almachius asked her: "I demand to know of you your religion." Then Cecilia said: "You began your interrogation foolishly, since you would have two answers to one question." Almachius answered: "What is the cause of your rude answer?" And she said: "A good conscience and a faith not feigned." Almachius said: "Do you not know my power?" And she said: "Your power is like a bladder full of wind; its rigor can be deflated by a needle's prick, and whatever seems straight in it will be twisted." Almachius replied: "You began with injurious words, and you continue with injurious words." Cecilia answered: "Only if I have put my case with deceiving words can what I have said be called injurious; therefore, either show that I have spoken falsely, or condemn yourself for making false accusations. But we who know the holy name of God are entirely unable to deny it. It is better to die with joy, than to live in misery." Almachius asked her: "How is it that you speak with such pride?" And she said: "It is not pride, but constancy." Almachius said: "Wretch, don't you know that I have been given the power over life and death?" And she said: "Now shall I prove you a liar against accepted truth. You may indeed take life from those who live, but to those who are dead you can give no life. Therefore you are a minister not of life, but of death." Almachius returned: "Now put aside your madness, and sacrifice unto the gods." Cecilia answered: "I do not know where you lost your eyes; for those whom you call gods, we all can see are only stones. Put your hands on them, and by touching learn what your eyes are unable to see."[13]

Then Almachius became angry, and commanded that she be led to her house, and commanded that she be burned there day and night in a boiling bath. In this she remained, as if she were in a cold place, and she did not feel even a drop of sweat. When Almachius heard of this, he commanded that she should be beheaded in that very bath. The executioner struck her three times on the neck, but could not cut off her head; and since the law decreed against a fourth stroke for decapitation, the executioner left her there bleeding half alive and half dead. During the next three days she gave all her possessions to the poor, and continually preached the faith all that while. And all those whom she converted to the faith she commended to bishop Urban, saying: "I have asked a respite of three days, that I might commend these souls to your blessing, and that you might consecrate my house as a church." Then Saint Urban, taking up her body, with his deacons buried her among his bishops, and consecrated her house as a church, in which the service of our Lord is said to this day in memory of the blessed Cecilia. She suffered her passion about the year of our Lord two hundred and thirty-six, in the time of Alexander the emperor. However, it is read in another place that she suffered in the time of Marcus Aurelius, who reigned about the year of our Lord two hundred and twenty.

NOTES

1. Lat. *coeli lilia*.
2. Lat. *caecis via*.
3. I.e., "heaven" and Lia (or Leah, representative of the active life, according to the conventional interpretation of Gen. xxix–xxx).
4. Lat. *caecitate carens*.
5. Lat. *coelo*, "heaven," and Gk. *leos*, "people."
6. Isidore of Seville, *Etymologiae* III, 31: "Caelum philosophi rotundum, volubile atque ardens esse dixerunt."
7. See Psalm xc, 11, a basis for the Christian belief in a "guardian angel."
8. Pope Urban I (ruled 222–30). He was beheaded May 25, 230. As a martyr he became a "saint," but only after the events recorded in this legend. His own legend appears in the *Legenda aurea*, Chapter LXXVII. Cecilia has sent Valerian to the Catacombs, near Rome.
9. The old man is usually identified as St. Paul. The passage he reads is Ephesians iv, 5–6.
10. Probably a spiritual version of the "nuptial crowns" worn in Roman wedding ceremonies. The roses and lilies conventionally symbolize martyrdom and virginity.
11. The reference is to the Ambrosian *praefatio* to the Mass for St. Cecilia's day.
12. For the image, compare Matthew xx, 1–16.
13. Compare Wisdom, xv.

Giovanni Boccaccio:
from *Il Filocolo*

Chaucer used the tale of Menedon in Boccaccio's Filocolo *as the model for his Franklin's Tale. There a group of young aristocrats arrange a "Court of Love" and propose a series of "problems in love" which are gracefully solved by "Fiammetta," Boccaccio's fictional name for his idealized lady, Maria d'Aquino. Fiammetta's opinion in this case is especially interesting as an example of the way a well-informed medieval reader would analyze such a tale, and because it provides an authoritative solution to the question with which the Franklin concludes his. Particularly to be noticed is the recourse to moral authority as a basis for making literary judgments. It is clear as well that Boccaccio has arranged the narrative so as to reflect an unjudicious bias on the part of the teller.*

Boccaccio was a student of canon law when he wrote the Filocolo. *A short account of his life and work may be found on pp. 86–88.*

A new translation.

[The Question of Menedon and Fiammetta's Opinion]

IV, QUISTIONE 4 [MENEDON'S QUESTION]

Her countenance showed the gentlewoman [Fiammetta] to be satisfied, when Menedon, who sat next to her, said: Most noble Queen, now has my turn come to propose my question which, with your permission, I will present here before you. And if in my tale I go on at too great length, I apologize in advance to you and to the others. But the question I intend to propose cannot be fully understood unless it is preceded by a tale, which may, perhaps, not be a short one. And after these words he began in this way:

In the city where I was born, I remember that there was a very rich and noble knight who, loving a noble lady of the land with a most perfect love, took her to wife. Since this lady was very beautiful, another knight, named Tarolfo, became enamored of her, and loved her with so great a love that he saw nothing which he desired more than her. To gain her love, he exerted himself in many ways, perhaps by frequently passing before her house, by jousting, by tourneying, and by other deeds, and by frequently sending her messengers, perhaps promising her great gifts, to make her aware of his intent. The lady put up with this matter silently, without giving any sign or answer to the knight, saying to herself, "When this man sees that I will not favor him by word or deed, perhaps he will stop loving me and offering these enticements." But despite this, Tarolfo did not cease, following the precepts of Ovid, who says: A man ought not cease to persevere because a woman is obdurate, for with persistence soft water pierces hard rock.[1] The lady, fearing that these matters would come to the ears of her husband, and that he would think that it had all happened with her approval, decided to tell him about it. But then, upon reconsideration, she said, "If I were to tell him, I might bring about such a rift between them that I could not lead a happy life. He must be put off by some other means." And she thought up a subtle trick.

So she sent for Tarolfo and said that if he loved her as much as he pretended, she would ask of him one gift; and she swore by her gods and by that loyalty which ought to be in a gentlewoman that when she received that gift she would satisfy his every pleasure. But if he would not give her what she required, he should determine in his heart not to offer her henceforth any enticements if he did not want her to reveal them to her husband. And the gift which she asked for was this: she said that she would have, in the month of January, in that city, a spacious and beautiful garden filled with herbs and flowers and trees and fruits, just as if it were the month of May, saying to herself, "This is an impossibility, and in this way I will get this fellow off my back." Although it seemed to him impossible and though he knew very well why the lady had made this demand, Tarolfo, hearing this, answered that he would never rest or come again into her presence, until he might give her the gift she had demanded.

Then he departed from the city with such company as it pleased him to take. He searched through all the lands to the west for means to accomplish his desire; but not finding the answer, he searched through the warmer regions, and arrived in Thessaly,[2] to which he had been directed by a knowing man. And after he had stayed there many days, not yet having found out what he came seeking, it happened that, almost despairing of ever finding what he sought, he arose one morning before the sun was ready to enter the east, and he began to wander all alone across the wretched plain which once had been soaked in Roman blood.[3] When he had traveled a great distance, he saw before him at the foot of a mountain a man, not young nor yet extremely aged, bearded, dressed in a manner which showed that he was probably poor, short in stature and very thin, who went about gathering herbs and digging up with a little knife different roots, with which a flap of his robe was filled. When Tarolfo saw him, he marveled, and wondered whether what he saw was something else; but his reason quickly told him it was certainly a man, and he approached him, greeted him, and asked him who he was, whence he came, and what he went about doing in that place at such an hour.

The little old man answered him, "I am from Thebes, and my name is Tebano. I go about this plain gathering these herbs so that from their juices I can make necessary and useful things for various infirmities. I earn my livelihood this way, and it is necessity, not delight, which constrains me to come at this hour.[4] But who are you, who appear to me to be noble; and what are you doing here all alone?" Tarolfo replied, "I am from the farthest parts of the west, a very rich knight, possessed and driven by concern for a task I have undertaken but not been able to achieve: on which account, in order the better and more freely to lament, I am walking here alone in this way." Tebano asked him, "Do you not know the nature of this place? Why did you not take another way? Here you could easily be assailed by vengeful spirits."[5] Tarolfo answered, "God is everywhere equally powerful, here as elsewhere; He holds my life and my honor in His hands. Let Him rule me according to His pleasure. Death would truly be a rich treasure to me."

Then Tebano asked, "What is the undertaking, for which you grieve that you cannot achieve it?" And Tarolfo answered, "It is something which it seems to me now impossible to accomplish, since heretofore I have not found help." Tebano asked, "Can you say what this is?" Tarolfo replied, "Yes, but what use can it serve? Perhaps none!" "But what can you lose by telling me?" asked Tebano. Then Tarolfo said, "I am seeking to find out how, in the coldest month of the year, it is possible to make a garden full of flowers and fruits and herbs, as beautiful as if it were in the month of May, but I haven't found anyone to teach me or to tell me that it is possible." Tebano stood for a while as if in doubt, without answering, and then said, "You and many others judge the knowledge and ability of a man by his garments. If my robe was such as yours is, or if perchance you had found me beside some rich prince, rather than gathering herbs, you would not have delayed so long in telling me your need. But often under the shabbiest garments lie hidden great treasures of learning. And therefore let no one conceal his needs from one who offers advice or help, unless he might prejudice his case by doing so. But what would you give the man who could bring about what you have been searching for?"

Tarolfo gazed attentively at the fellow's face as he spoke these words, and wondered whether he was mocking him, judging it incredible that this man could have such ability, unless he were a god. Notwithstanding, he answered him thus: "I have seigniory over many castles in my country, and many treasures besides, and I would give half of them all to him who would do me such a favor." "Truly," said Tebano, "if you should do this, I would no longer need to go about gathering herbs." "I assure you," said Tarolfo, "that if you can really bring about the things you have promised, and give them to me, you will never again need to trouble yourself to become rich. But how and when can you provide this for me?" Tebano said, "The time when will be for you to determine. Do not bother yourself as to how. I will go with you, trusting in the words of the promises you have made me, and when we arrive where you want to be, command whatever you wish, and I will provide everything without fail."

Tarolfo was so well pleased with this development that he would scarcely have been happier if he had held his lady in his arms at that moment; and he said, "My friend, it will seem an eternity to me before you provide what you have promised. So let us depart without delay, and go where this is to be performed." Tebano cast away his herbs, and took up his books and other things necessary to his art, and journeyed with Tarolfo. And in a short time they arrived at the desired city, very close to the month in which the garden had been demanded. There they remained, in secret and silence, until finally the proper time arrived. And when the month had begun, Tarolfo commanded that the garden be prepared, so that he could give it to his lady.

When Tebano received this command, he waited for the night, and, when it had come, observed that the horns of the moon formed a perfect circle, and that it shone brightly over all the inhabited earth. Then he went out of the city all alone, leaving behind his garments, barefooted, with his disheveled hair hanging on his bare shoulders. The charming hours of the night passed; birds, wild beasts, and men took their rest without a sound; on trees the unfallen leaves hung motionless; and the dewy air rested in peace. Only the stars shone down[6] when he, having circled the city many times, came at length to a place beside a river, which it pleased him to choose for his garden. Here, turning to the stars, he stretched out his arms three times towards them, and turning as many times he bathed his white locks in the running water, as many times requesting their aid with a loud voice.[7] Then, kneeling on the hard earth, he began to pray in this way: "O night, who most faithfully hold the secrets of high things; and you, O stars, who together with the moon follow the resplendent day; and you, O most high Hecate,[8] whom I pray to come as a helper in this enterprise we have begun; and you, O holy Ceres, renewer of the wide face of the earth;[9] and all you verses or arts or herbs, and all you powerful plants which the earth produces; and you, O breezes, winds, mountains, rivers and lakes; and all you gods of the woods and of the secret night: through whose aid I have reversed the running of streams, making them return to their sources,[10] and have made moving things stand still and still things to move, and who have given my verses the power to dry up the seas and to search out their depths without impediment, and to make cloudy weather clear and to fill the clear sky with dark clouds as I wished, making the winds cease or come at my pleasure, and with them breaking the hard jaws of terrible dragons, and making the standing woods to move and the lofty mountains to tremble, and to make their shades return to the bodies of the dead from the Stygian marsh and come forth from their sepulchres alive,[11] and at such times, O moon, to draw you from your fullness (to which [fullness] the sounding basins formerly helped you to attain),[12] also making the clear face of the sun turn pale[13]—may you all be present now, and grant me your aid. At this time I have need of the juices of herbs[14] with which I may make a part of the dry earth, despoiled of its flowers, fruits, and herbs first by the

Autumn and then by the bitter cold of Winter, return to its flowering state, appearing as if it were Spring before its due time."

And having said these things, he silently added many other things to his prayers. And when he ceased, the stars did not shed their light in vain, but more swiftly than the flight of any bird a chariot drawn by two dragons appeared before him. He mounted it and gripped the reins attached to the bridles on the two dragons, and was carried up into the air. And, making his way through the upper regions, he left Spain and all Africa behind, and sought out the isle of Crete, and after that he sought out Pelion, Othrys and Ossa, Mount Nerius, Pachinus, Pelorus, and Appennine. In each place he uprooted or cut with a sharp sickle what roots and herbs he wanted, not forgetting those which he had when he was found by Tarolfo in Thessaly. He gathered stones from Mount Caucasus and from the sands of the Ganges, and from Libya he brought the tongues of venomous serpents. He searched the watery banks of the Rhône, of the Seine in Paris, of the great Po, of the Arno, of the imperial Tiber, of the Don and the Danube, taking from each of them whatever herbs seemed to him necessary, and these he added to others gathered from the summits of savage mountains. He sought out the island of Lesbos, and that of Colchis, and Patmos, and whatever others which he thought contained anything useful for his enterprise.[15]

With these things he returned to the place from which he had departed, before the end of the third day, and the dragons, which had cast off skin many years old simply by smelling the odors of the herbs he had gathered, were renewed and restored to youth. There he dismounted, and he built two altars out of the grassy earth, the one to his right that for Hecate, and the one to his left that for the goddess of renewal.[16] When he had done this, having kindled devout fires upon them, he began to circle about them, with his disheveled hair over his old shoulders, murmuring quietly; and he often stained the burning brands with blood he had collected. Then, replacing them on the altar, he at times sprinkled with them the soil which he had prepared for the garden. And after this, he moistened the same soil again three times with fire, water, and sulphur. And after that, he placed a great vessel on the blazing flames, filled with blood, milk, and water, which he boiled for a long time, and to which he added the herbs and roots he had gathered from faraway places;[17] and he also put in with them various seeds and flowers of unknown herbs, and added stones found in the far East, and hoar-frost gathered on previous nights, along with the flesh and wings of infamous witches, the essential part of the testicles of a wolf, the slough of a chelydra[18] and the skin of a tortoise, and finally a liver and the lungs of an ancient stag. Along with these he put a thousand things, so strange and nameless that I cannot remember what they were called.[19]

Then he took the branch of a dry olive tree, and began to mix all these things together. And as he stirred them, the dry branch began to become green and quickly to put forth leaves and, dressed with these, not long after one could see it loaded with black olives. When Tebano saw this, he took the boiling liquors and poured them on the ground he had selected, in which he had planted as many and as varied sticks as he wished trees to grow there. And he began to scatter and sprinkle the liquors upon them everywhere. And the soil had no sooner begun to feel this change than it put forth flowers on all sides, producing lovely new lawns; and all the dry slips which he had planted became green and fruitful plants.[20]

This done, Tebano returned to the city to Tarolfo. He found him, as if fearing to be thought a fool on account of Tebano's long delay, preoccupied with his thoughts. And he said to him: "Tarolfo, that which you have required has been accomplished, according to your wishes." This news was very pleasing to Tarolfo, and since he had to attend a very important occasion in the city the next day, he went before his lady, who had not seen him for a long time, and spoke to her in this way: "My lady, after long exertions I have provided for you what you command of me, and when it should please you to see it, and accept it, is at your discretion."

The lady, seeing this fellow, wondered greatly, and hearing what he said, even more. And not believing him, she answered, "I am very pleased; you will let me see it tomorrow." On the following day, Tarolfo went to the lady and said, "Madame, may it please you to go to the garden which you required me to provide in this cold month?" So the lady, with many companions, went and, having arrived at the garden, entered into it through a pretty gateway. And the air they felt there was not cold, as it was outside, but sweet and temperate. The lady went all about the garden, gazing at the herbs and flowers, which she saw to be very plentiful, and picking them. And the power of the sprinkled liquors had worked even more wonders, so that the trees there, in that bitter time of year, brought forth lovely fruits which are usually produced in August. And many of the people who accompanied the lady ate of them. The garden appeared to the lady a most beautiful and marvelous thing, and she thought she had never seen one so lovely. And because by many proofs she knew it to be truly a garden, and that the knight had fulfilled all that she had required, she turned to Tarolfo and said, "Without doubt, sir knight, you have won my love, and I am ready to serve you in what I have promised you. But truly I would ask a favor of you: that it please you to delay asking for the reward of your desire until my lord has gone hunting, or to some place outside of the city, so that you may the more wisely and without any suspicion take your delight." This was agreeable to Tarolfo, who, content with her words, departed, leaving the garden to her.

This garden became known to all who dwelt in those parts, although no one knew, until a long while after, how it came to be. But the gentlewoman who had been given it departed from it in sorrow, returning to her chamber full of grief and melancholy. And trying to think of what way she could avoid fulfilling her promise, and finding no lawful excuse, she became more and more sorrowful. Seeing this, her husband began to wonder at it, and asked her what troubled her. The lady replied that nothing troubled her, being ashamed to reveal to her husband the promise she had made in return for the gift she demanded, and feeling sure that her husband would consider her wicked. Finally, unable to withstand the continual questioning of her husband, who always sought to find out the reason for her melancholy, she gave in and told him from beginning to end the reason for her sorrowful state.

When he had heard this, the husband thought for a long time; and since he was sure in his mind of the purity of the lady, he told her this: "Go and fulfill your oath, in secret, and liberally perform for Tarolfo that which you have promised, for he has rightfully earned it with great toil." The lady began to weep, and said, "May the gods keep me far from such a fault. In no way will I do this. I would kill myself before I would do anything that would dishonor or displease you." Then the knight said to her, "Lady, I certainly do not want you to kill yourself because of this, nor even to suffer the slightest regret. It shall in no way displease me. Go and do what you have promised; I will not cherish you any the less. But after you have done this, be more careful next time about making promises of this sort, even though the gift demanded may seem to you impossible."

Perceiving the will of the husband, the lady adorned and beautified herself, and, taking her companions with her, went to Tarolfo's home and presented herself, modestly blushing, before him. When Tarolfo saw her, he rose from the side of Tebano, with whom he was sitting, and greeted her, full of wonder and joy. He received her most honorably, asking the reason for her coming. The lady replied, "I have come to be wholly at your will; do with me whatever you please." Then Tarolfo said, "You make me marvel above measure, considering the hour and the company which has come with you. This cannot be, unless something has happened between you and your husband. Tell me about it, I pray you." Then the lady related to Tarolfo, fully and in proper order, how the whole matter stood. And when he had heard this, Tarolfo began to marvel more than at first and to think deeply; and he began to recognize her husband's great liberality, that he had sent her to him. And he said to himself that anyone who harbored villainous thoughts toward such a liberal man would be worthy of most serious reproof. So, speaking to the lady, he said this: "Gentle lady, you have faithfully performed your duty like a worthy woman,[21] and for this reason I consider that I have received that which I desired of you. And therefore when it pleases you, you may return to your husband, and thank him on my behalf for so great generosity, and ask him to excuse me for the folly I have committed in the past. I assure him that, henceforth, I will never again engage in such acts."

The lady thanked Tarolfo very much for his great courtesy, and she departed happily, returning to her husband, to whom she related in proper order all that had happened. But Tebano, returning now to Tarolfo, asked him how matters stood. And Tarolfo told him the whole story. Then Tebano said, "So, then, have I lost what you promised me, because of this?" But Tarolfo replied, "No, indeed. Whenever you please, go and take possession of half of my castles and my treasure, as I promised you; for I consider that you have served me perfectly." Tebano answered, "May it never please the gods if, where the knight was so liberal toward you with his wife, and you refrained from villainy toward him, I were to be less courteous. More than anything else in the world it pleases me that I have been of service to you. Therefore it is my will that what I was to receive as the reward for my services should remain in your hands, just as before." And he would not take anything at all from Tarolfo.

The question is now: Whose was the greatest liberality—that of the knight who permitted the lady to go to Tarolfo; or that of Tarolfo, who released from her bond and sent back to her husband the lady whom he had always desired, and for whom he had done so much in order to come to the point he had reached when the lady came to him; or that of Tebano, who, leaving his country even though he was old, and having come there to gain the reward promised him, and having toiled to bring about what he had promised, and having earned his reward, gave back everything, remaining poor as at first?

[FIAMMETTA'S OPINION]

Most excellent is the tale and the question, said the Queen, and truly each of them was very liberal, if we consider the cases—the first with respect to his honor, the second with respect to his lustful will, and the third with respect to the riches he had gained, was indeed courteous. And therefore, if we wish to understand which of them used the greatest liberality or courtesy, it is appropriate to decide which of these three things is the most valuable. When we have determined this, it is clear that we shall know who was the most liberal, for he who gives up the most is to be held the most liberal. And of these three things one is precious: that is, honor, which Paulus Aemilius, the conqueror of Perseus, desired before the treasures he had won.[22] The second is to be fled: that is, a lustful union, according to the opinion of Sophocles and Xenocrates, who said that lust is to be shunned as a mad seigniory.[23] The third is not to be desired: that is, riches, inasmuch as, in most cases, they are troublesome to a virtuous life, and it is possible to live virtuously in moderate poverty, like Marcus Curtius, Attilius Regulus, and Valerius Publicola, as they demonstrate in their deeds.[24] And so, if only honor is to be cherished among these three things, and the others not, then he used the greatest liberality who gave away the lady, although he acted less than wisely in so doing. He was also the leader in this liberality, in that the others followed him. Therefore, according to our judgment, he who gave up the lady in whom resided his honor was more liberal than the others.

I, said Menedon, agree that it may be as you say, in that it has been said by you; but it seems to me that each of the other men was more liberal, and let me tell you how. It is very true that the first man gave away the lady, but in doing so he did not exercise as much liberality as you say. Even if he had wished to deny her, he could not have done so in justice, because of the oath made by the lady, which had to be observed. And he who gives up what he cannot deny does the right thing, and thus appears liberal, but he actually gives up little. And therefore, as I have said, each of the others was more courteous.

Then, since Tarolfo, as I said before, had desired the lady a long while, and loved her more than anything else, yet had suffered a long time in order to possess her, and had devoted himself, for the fulfilment of her requirement, to search out what seemed impossibilities, then when he had attained them, he deserved to possess her because of her promise. Having this contracted pledge, there is no doubt, as we have said, that he held both her husband's honor and the means of remitting the debt in his hands. This he did. And therefore Tarolfo was liberal with respect to the honor of the husband, and to the lady's oath, and to his long-awaited pleasure. It is a great thing to have suffered thirst for a long while, and then to arrive at a fountain and not drink, but permit someone else to drink.

The third man was also very liberal, if we consider that poverty is one of the most troublesome things in the world to bear, inasmuch as it chases away both mirth and rest, flees from honors, conceals virtue, and brings on bitter cares, so that every man naturally exerts himself with an ardent desire to flee poverty. This desire is so kindled in many that they engage in dishonest gain and in shameful adventures, so that they may live very splendidly in comfort, not knowing, perhaps, or not having at their command, any other means of satisfying their desire. And because of this, men have often been justly condemned to death or to eternal exile from their land. Therefore, how much more pleasing and dear ought riches to be to one who has earned them in a lawful way? Now, who can doubt that Tebano was most poor, if he observes how he gave up his night's rest to go about gathering herbs and digging up roots in dangerous places, in order to sustain his life? And that this poverty of his did indeed conceal his true virtue we may well believe, seeing that Tarolfo believed he was being mocked when he first saw him clothed in shabby garments. And we can see that he desired to escape from that misery and to become rich, since we know that he came from Thessaly all the way to Spain, setting himself on perilous routes in uncertain climates, to fulfill the promise he had made and receive what the other had promised. Without doubt, whoever undergoes such trials in order to escape poverty knows it to be full of all miseries and suffering. And the greater the poverty one has escaped by achieving a life of riches, the more gratifying is this new life to him.

Therefore, if a man has come into riches out of poverty, and if he delights in this sort of life, how great is his kind of liberality when he gives it away and agrees to return to that state which he had sought with such toil to escape? Surely his is a very great and liberal act, and this seems to me greater than all the others. And we should consider also the age of the giver, who was an old man, inasmuch as avarice is always much more powerful in old men than in young.[25] Therefore, my opinion is that each of the two others used a greater liberality than the first, who was so commended by you, and that the third used far more than anyone.

You have defended your reasoning as well as it can possibly be defended by anyone, said the Queen, but we intend to show you briefly how our opinion rather than yours should prevail. You contend that he used no liberality at all in giving up his wife, because reason dictated that it was proper for him to do so, on account of the oath made by the lady. This might be the case indeed, if the oath were valid. But the lady, inasmuch as she was a member of her husband, or rather one body with him, could not make such an oath without the will of her husband;[26] and if she did make it, it was null, because a first oath lawfully made could not reasonably be derogated by any succeeding oath, and especially not by one which was not duly made and for an appropriate cause.[27] It is the custom in matrimonial unions to swear that the man will always remain satisfied with the lady, and the lady with the man, and that neither will ever change the one for another.[28] So then, the lady could not make such an oath, and if she did so, as we have said, she swore an unlawful matter contrary to her first oath. Therefore it could not be binding. And since it was invalid, the husband should not have sent her to Tarolfo, unless he wished to. And if he did send her, then he, and not Tarolfo as you contend, was liberal with his honor. For since the oath was invalid, he could not be liberal in releasing her from it.

Therefore Tarolfo was liberal only with respect to his lustful desire. But it is the proper duty of every man to do this, because we are all bound by reason to avoid vice and to follow virtue. Now, whoever does something which he is by reason bound to do is (as you yourself said) not at all liberal, though whatever good works done are above and beyond such moral duty may lawfully be called liberality.

But because you perhaps have mental reservations about how great and dear an honor it is for a husband to have a chaste lady, we will prolong our talk a little, showing you clearly how Tarolfo and Tebano, about whom we intend to speak next, exercised no liberality at all towards the knight.

You should know that chastity, together with the other virtues, yields no other reward to its possessor than honor: which honor, among virtuous men, makes even the less virtuous the more esteemed. If men uphold this honor with humility, it makes them friends of God,[29] and consequently able to live and die in happiness, and hereafter to possess eternal rewards. If a lady preserves this honor for her husband, he lives in joy, certain of his offspring, and he can walk openly among the people without shame, pleased to see her honored among the best ladies on account of this virtue. And in his mind this is a clear token that she is good, fears God, and loves him—a fact which should be no small pleasure to him, seeing that she has been given to him as an eternal companion, inseparable until death part them. By means of such grace he is seen to increase and multiply continually in both worldly and spiritual goods.[30]

Just so, on the contrary, he whose lady is lacking in such virtue cannot pass a single hour in true contentment. He finds nothing agreeable to him, and each desires the death of the other. He hears his name bandied about in the mouths of most detestable wretches, because of this disgusting vice, nor does it seem to him that these things should not be believed by whoever heard them. Even if he possessed every other virtue, this vice seems to have the power to contaminate and ruin them all.

Therefore the chastity which a good woman renders to her husband is a great honor, and should be cherished most dearly. He who is granted such a gift through grace may be called blessed, although we believe that there are few who may be envied for such a good.

But to return to the subject of enquiry, you can now see how much the knight gave up. It has not escaped our mind that you have said that Tebano was to be held more liberal than the others, since he went to such trouble to become rich, and did not hesitate to return to the misery of a poor life, by giving up all that he had gained. It seems clear that you are poorly acquainted with poverty, which surpasses all riches if it comes happily. Perhaps Tebano, now that he had acquired those riches, felt himself full of many bitter cares. Now he imagined that Tarolfo thought that he had done him wrong, and plotted to murder him in order to recover his castles. He lived in fear that perhaps he would be betrayed by his subjects. He had been introduced to the worries of governing his lands. He now became aware of all the deceptions practiced by his tenants. He saw himself greatly envied for his riches, and he feared that thieves would secretly steal them. He was filled with so many different worries and cares that all peace of mind had fled from him. As the result of such anxieties, he recalled his previous life, remembering how he had lived in happiness without so many cares, and he said to himself, "I desired to become rich to gain peace, but now I see that wealth brings more tribulations and worries, and puts all rest to flight." And so, desiring to return to the condition of his former life, he returned that wealth to him who had given it.

Poverty is the renunciation of riches, an unappreciated good, which puts temptations to flight—a fact which Diogenes fully understood.[31] Poverty finds sufficient whatever nature requires. Whoever lives with her in patience lives secure from any deceit. Nor is he prevented from achieving great honors, if he lives virtuously in the way we have described. Therefore, when Tebano ridded himself of this burden, he was not liberal, but wise. He was gracious to Tarolfo in that it pleased him to give his possessions to him rather than to another, since he could have given them to many others.

Therefore, the knight who gave up his honor was more liberal than either of the others. And consider this: the honor that he gave up can never be recovered. This is not true in many other cases, as in battles, or contests, and the like, for in them if honor is lost at one time it is possible to recover it at another.

Let this suffice as answer to your question.

NOTES

1. This allusion, along with the narrative context, establishes Tarolfo as an "Ovidian lover." Compare *Ars amatoria*, I, 469–70, 475–86; for example, "If she does not receive your message and sends it back unread, hope that one day she will read, and hold to your purpose. . . . What is harder than rock, what softer than water? yet soft water hollows out hard rock. Only persevere; you will overcome Penelope herself." Ovid used the figure of water and rock again in *Ex Ponto*, IV, x, 5. Compare Chaucer's transferral of the image in Franklin's Tale, 829–35.

2. District in northeastern Greece in which, according to ancient tradition, magic and witchcraft flourished. Jason brought the sorceress Medea to Thessaly, where she magically restored his old father Aeson to youth. Medea was the niece of Circe, another enchantress. See Ovid, *Remedia amoris*, 249–64.

3. Apparently the allusion is to the Battle of Pharsalia, 48 B.C., in which Julius Caesar defeated Pompey.

4. One of a number of echoes of Dante in this tale. Compare *Inferno*, XII, 85–87, where "necessity" explains the Pilgrim's presence in Hell!

5. Thessalian demons? The spirits of the Roman dead?

6. Tebano's magic rite is closely modeled on that of Medea when she restored old Aeson to youth. Compare Ovid, *Metamorphoses*, VII, 179–88.

7. Compare *Metamorphoses*, VII, 188–90.

8. Threefold goddess, associated with the moon (Luna) in heaven, Diana on earth, and Proserpine in the underworld. She was reputed to send phantoms and demons at night from the underworld, and to have taught the arts of witchcraft and sorcery. She had some power over the shades of the dead, and protected those who practiced sorcery.

9. Goddess of crops, daughter of Saturn and Cibele, mother of Proserpine.

10. Compare *Metamorphoses*, VII, 154: Medea taught Jason words "which stay the swollen sea and swift-flowing rivers." Compare the passage in note 13; and *Amores*, II, i, 26.

11. See Virgil, *Eclogue* VIII, 98–99: "I have seen him [Moeris, a werewolf] call up ghosts from deep down in the grave, and shift a standing crop from one field to another." Echoes of the magic in *Eclogue* VIII appear in both Ovid and Boccaccio. See *Remedia amoris*, 253–56. Ovid's *Amores*, II, i, 25 attributes to "songs" the power to break the hard jaws of serpents (dragons).

12. Reference to a magical ritual by which it was thought that by the proper sounds the moon's course could be hastened or restrained. See Virgil, *Eclogue* VIII, 69. The present translation of "e tal volta trar, te, o luna, alla tua ritondità" may, however, be rendered as "draw you from your sphere," in imitation of Ovid, *Heroides*, VI, 85, concerning Medea: "illa reluctantem cursu deducere lunam" ("she [strives to] draw down from its course the unwilling moon"). See *Amores*, II, i, 23.

13. See Ovid, *Remedia amoris*, 256; *Heroides*, VI, 86. With the preceding passage compare *Heroides*, VI, 83–90, where Hypsipyle laments Jason's choice of Medea as his new wife: "It is neither by her beauty nor by her merits that she wins you, but by the incantations she knows and the baneful herbs she cuts

with enchanted knife [with which compare Tebano's introduction in Thessaly]. She is the one to strive to draw down from its course the unwilling moon, and to hide in darkness the horses of the sun; she curbs the waters and stays the down-winding streams; she moves from their places the woods and living rocks. Among sepulchres she stalks, ungirded, with hair flowing loose, and gathers from the yet warm funeral pyre the appointed bones."

14. Tebano's invocation to Night closely imitates Ovid, *Metamorphoses*, VII, 191–216. Boccaccio's explicit imitation of the *Metamorphoses* equates Tebano's performance with the pagan sorcery of Medea, which was regarded in the Middle Ages as diabolic. Menedon does not appear to be aware that Tebano's model puts him in dubious company.

15. See *Metamorphoses*, VII, 217–33 (further imitation of Medea's witchcraft).

16. I.e., Ceres. In the *Metamorphoses* the left-hand altar is for Youth.

17. See *Metamorphoses*, VII, 234–48, 257–62.

18. An amphibious snake. See *Metamorphoses*, VII, 270; Isidore of Seville, *Etymologiae*, XII, iv, 24.

19. See *Metamorphoses*, VII, 257–76.

20. See *Metamorphoses*, VII, 277–84.

21. *Valorosa donna*, probably an allusion to the *mulier fortis* (see below, pp. 393–95).

22. From Valerius Maximus, *Factorum et dictorum memorabilium libri ix* ("Nine Books of Memorable Deeds and Sayings"), IV, iv ("De paupertate").

23. From Valerius, IV, iii ("De abstinentia et continentia").

24. Marcus Curtius: from Valerius, V, vi ("De pietate"); Attilius Regulus: from Valerius, I, i ("De religione"); Valerius Publicola: from Valerius, IV, i ("De moderatione").

25. A medieval truism; see Reeve's Prologue, 3883–85.

26. See Parson's Tale, 931 (below, p. 367).

27. The law respecting vows held that a vow was invalid if 1) it derogated a previous vow lawfully sworn, 2) it committed one to sin, and 3) its conditions were fulfilled by fraud.

28. See the Form of Solemnization of Marriage (below, pp. 373–84); Parson's Tale, 921.

29. See James iv, 4.

30. See the Form of Solemnization of Marriage.

31. From Valerius Maximus, IV, iii ("De abstinentia et continentia").

Francis Petrarch:
from *Letters of Old Age, XVII, 3,*
"To Giovanni Boccaccio"

Chaucer's Clerk says that he learned his tale at Padua from another "worthy clerk" (Clerk's Tale, 26–30).

> Fraunceys Petrak, the lauriat poete,
> Highte this clerk, whos rethorike sweete
> Enlumyned al Ytaille of poetrie. (31–33)

Whether or not he acquired it in "Padowe," Chaucer had before him a letter from Petrarch to his friend, another clerk, Giovanni Boccaccio. Written in 1373, the letter was collected among his Epistolae de rebus senilibus *(1363–74).*

The reputation of Francis Petrarch (1304–74) was, as the Clerk suggests, enormous—as author, critic, and scholar (see above, p. 82). His decision to translate this, the final tale in Boccaccio's Decameron *(1353), reflects a critical discrimination of great authority. Those who find the tale dull or trivial should consider as well the reaction Petrarch attributes to his friends, in this letter. Because the translators of the letter and the tale are different, the tale itself is printed here following the rest of the letter.*

Petrarch's Latin translation of Boccaccio's Italian is clearly an attempt to impart dignity and depth to the tale. The style is elevated, and Boccaccio's sparer narrative is expanded with moral reflection. Grisildis' speeches, particularly, are extended—sometimes invented. Major changes are indicated in the notes.

Chaucer also consulted an anonymous French translation of Petrarch's Latin. The notes indicate instances where the French departs significantly from the present text.

The Letter (to p. 140), trans. J. H. Robinson and H. W. Rolfe, Petrarch, The First Modern Scholar and Man of Letters *(New York: Putnam's, 1899), pp. 191–96. The* De obedientia ac fide uxoria mythologia *(pp. 140–151), trans. R. D. French,* A Chaucer Handbook *(New York: Appleton Co., 1927), pp. 291–311. © 1955. Reprinted by permission of Prentice-Hall, Inc., Englewood Cliffs, New Jersey.*

[The Story of Griselda]

Your book, written in our mother tongue and published I presume, during your early years, has fallen into my hands, I know not whence or how. If I told you that I had read it, I should deceive you. It is a very big volume, written in prose and for the multitude. I have been, moreover, occupied with more serious business, and much pressed for time. You can easily imagine the unrest caused by the warlike stir about me, for, far as I have been from actual participation in the disturbances, I could not but be affected by the critical condition of the state. What I did was to run through your book, like a traveller who, while hastening forward, looks about him here and there, without pausing. I have heard somewhere that your volume was attacked by the teeth of certain hounds, but that you defended it valiantly with staff and voice. This did not surprise me, for not only do I well know your ability, but I have learned from experience of the existence of an insolent and cowardly class who attack in the work of others everything which they do not happen to fancy or be familiar with, or which they cannot themselves accomplish. Their insight and capabilities extend no farther; on all other themes they are silent.

My hasty perusal afforded me much pleasure. If the humor is a little too free at times, this may be excused in view of the age at which you wrote, the style and language which you employ, and the frivolity of the subjects, and of the persons who are likely to read such tales. It is important to know for whom we are writing, and a difference in the character of one's listeners justifies a difference in style. Along with much that was light and amusing, I discovered some serious and edifying things as well, but I can pass no definite judgment upon them, since I have not examined the work thoroughly.

As usual, when one looks hastily through a book, I read somewhat more carefully at the beginning and at the end. At the beginning you have, it seems to me, accurately described and eloquently lamented the condition of our country during that siege of pestilence which forms so dark and melancholy a period in our century. At the close you have placed a story which differs entirely from most that precede it, and which so delighted and fascinated me that, in spite of cares which made me almost oblivious of myself, I was seized with a desire to learn it by heart, so that I might have the pleasure of recalling it for my own benefit, and of relating it to my friends in conversation. When an opportunity for telling it offered itself shortly after, I found that my auditors were delighted. Later it suddenly occurred to me that others, perhaps, who were unacquainted with our tongue, might be pleased with so charming a story, as it had delighted me ever since I first heard it some years ago, and as you had not considered it unworthy of presentation in the mother tongue, and had placed it, moreover, at the end of your book, where, according to the principles of rhetoric, the most effective part of the composition belongs. So one fine day when, as usual, my mind was distracted by a variety of occupations, discontented with myself and my surroundings, I suddenly sent everything flying, and, snatching my pen, I attacked this story of yours. I sincerely trust that it will gratify you that I have of my own free-will undertaken to translate your work, something I should certainly never think of doing for anyone else, but which I was induced to do in this instance by my partiality for you and for the story. Not neglecting the precept of Horace in his *Art of Poetry*, that the careful translator should not attempt to render word for word,[1] I have told your tale in my own language, in some places changing or even adding a few words, for I felt that you would not only permit, but would approve, such alterations.

Although many have admired and wished for my version, it seemed to me fitting that your work should be dedicated to you rather than to anyone else; and it is for you to judge whether I have, by this change of dress, injured or embellished the original. The story returns whence it came; it knows its judge, its home, and the way thither. As you and everyone who reads this knows, it is you and not I who must render account for what is essentially yours. If anyone asks me whether this is all true, whether it is a history or a story, I reply in the words of Sallust, "I refer you to the author"—to wit, my friend Giovanni. With so much introduction I begin.

[Petrarch's translation is introduced at this point.]

My object in thus re-writing[2] your tale was not to induce the women of our time to imitate the patience of this wife, which seems to me almost beyond imitation, but to lead my readers to emulate the example of feminine constancy, and to submit themselves to God with the same courage as did this woman to her husband. Although, as the Apostle James tells us, "God cannot be tempted with evil, and he himself tempteth no man,"[3] he still may prove us, and often permits us to be beset with many and grievous trials, not that he may know our character, which he knew before we were created, but in order that our weakness should be made plain to ourselves by obvious and familiar proofs. Anyone, it seems to me, amply deserves to be reckoned among the heroes of mankind who suffers without a murmur for God, what this poor peasant woman bore for her mortal husband.

My affection for you has induced me to write at an advanced age what I should hardly have undertaken even as a young man. Whether what I have narrated be true or false I do not know, but the fact that you wrote it would seem sufficiently to justify the inference that it is but a tale. Foreseeing this question, I have prefaced my translation with the statement that the responsibility for the story rests with the author; that is, with you. And now let me tell you my experiences with this narrative, or tale, as I prefer to call it.

In the first place, I gave it to one of our mutual friends in Padua to read, a man of excellent parts and wide attainments. When scarcely half-way through the composition, he was suddenly arrested by a burst of tears. When again, after a short pause, he made a manful attempt to continue, he was again interrupted by a sob. He then realised that he could go no farther himself, and handed the story to one of his companions, a man of education, to finish. How others may view this occurrence I cannot, of course, say; for myself, I put a most favorable construction upon it, believing that I recognise the indications of a most compassionate disposition; a more kindly nature, indeed, I never remember to have met. As I saw him weep as he read, the words of the Satirist came back to me:

Nature, who gave us tears, by that alone
Proclaims she made the feeling heart our own;
And 'tis our noblest sense.[4]

Some time after, another friend of ours, from Verona (for all is common between us, even our friends), having heard of the effect produced by the story in the first instance, wished to read it for himself. I readily complied, as he was not only a good friend, but a man of ability. He read the narrative from beginning to end without stopping once. Neither his face nor his voice betrayed the least emotion, not a tear or a sob escaped him. "I too," he said at the end, "would have wept, for the subject certainly excites pity, and the style is well adapted to call forth tears, and I am not hard-hearted; but I believed, and still believe, that this is all an invention. If it were true, what woman, whether of Rome or any other nation, could be compared with this Griselda? Where do we find the equal of this conjugal devotion, where such faith, such extraordinary patience and constancy?" I made no reply to this reasoning, for I did not wish to run the risk of a bitter debate in the midst of our good-humored and friendly discussion. But I had a reply ready. There are some who think that whatever is difficult for them must be impossible for others; they must measure others by themselves, in order to maintain their superiority. Yet there have been many, and there may still be many, to whom acts are easy which are commonly held to be impossible. Who is there who would not, for example, regard a Curtius, a Mucius, or the Decii, among our own people, as pure fictions; or, among foreign nations, Codrus and the Philaeni; or, since we are speaking of a woman, Portia, or Hypsicratia, or Alcestis, and others like them? But these are actual historical persons. And indeed I do not see why one who can face death for another, should not be capable of encountering any trial or form of suffering.

DE OBEDIENTIA AC FIDE UXORIA MYTHOLOGIA ("A LEGEND OF WIFELY OBEDIENCE AND FAITH")

In the chain of the Apennines, in the west of Italy, stands Mount Viso, a very lofty mountain, whose summit towers above the clouds and rises into the bright upper air. It is a mountain notable in its own nature, but most notable as the source of the Po, which rises from a small spring upon the mountain's side, bends slightly toward the east, and presently, swollen with abundant tributaries, becomes, though its downward course has been but brief, not only one of the greatest streams but, as Vergil called it, the king of rivers. Through Liguria its raging waters cut their way, and then, bounding Aemilia and Flaminia and Venetia, it empties at last into the Adriatic sea, through many mighty mouths. Now that part of these lands, of which I spoke first, is sunny and delightful, as much for the hills which run through it and the mountains which hem it in, as for its grateful plain. From the foot of the mountains beneath which it lies, it derives its name; and it has many famous cities and towns.[5] Among others, at the very foot of Mount Viso, is the land of Saluzzo, thick with villages and castles. It is ruled over by noble marquises, the first and greatest of whom, according to tradition, was a certain Walter, to whom the direction of his own estates and of all the land pertained. He was a man blooming with youth and beauty, as noble in his ways as in his birth; marked out, in short, for leadership in all things,—save that he was so contented with his present lot that he took very little care for the future. Devoted to hunting and fowling, he so applied himself to these arts that he neglected almost all else; and—what his subjects bore most ill—he shrank even from a hint of marriage. When they had borne this for some time in silence, at length they came to him in a company; and one of their number, who had authority and eloquence above the rest and was on more familiar terms with his overlord, said to him, "Noble Marquis, your kindness gives us such boldness that we come separately to talk with you, with devoted trust, as often as occasion demands, and that now my voice conveys to your ears the silent wishes of us all; not because I have any especial privilege, unless it be that you have shown by many signs that you hold me dear among the others. Although all your ways, then, justly give us pleasure and always have, so that we count ourselves happy in such an overlord, there is one thing in which we should assuredly be the happiest of all men round about, if you would consent to it and show yourself susceptible to our entreaties; and that is, that you should take thought of marriage and bow your neck, free and imperious though it be, to the lawful yoke; and that you should do this as soon as possible. For the swift days fly by, and although you are in the flower of your youth, nevertheless silent old age follows hard upon that flower, and death itself is very near to any age. To none is immunity against this tribute given, and all alike must die; and just as that is certain, so is it uncertain when it will come to pass. Give ear, therefore, we pray you, to the entreaties of those who have never refused to do your bidding. You may leave the selection of a wife to our care, for we shall procure you such an one as shall be truly worthy of you, and sprung of so high a lineage that you may have the best hope of her. Free all your subjects, we beseech you, of the grievous apprehension that if anything incident to our mortal lot should happen to you, you would go leaving no successor to yourself, and they would remain deprived of a leader such as their hearts crave."[6]

Their loyal entreaties touched the man's heart, and he made answer: "My friends, you constrain me to that which never entered my thoughts. I have had pleasure in complete liberty, a thing which is rare in marriage. Nevertheless, I willingly submit to the wishes of my subjects, trusting in your prudence and your devotion. But I release you from the task, which you have offered to assume, of finding me a wife. That task I lay on my own shoulders. For what benefit can the distinction of one confer upon another? Right often, children are all unlike their parents. Whatever is good in a man comes not from another, but from God. As I trust to Him all my welfare, so would I entrust to Him the outcome of my marriage, hoping for His accustomed mercy. He will find for me that which shall be expedient for my peace and safety.[7] And so, since you are resolved that I should take a wife, so much, in all good faith, I promise you; and for my part, I will neither frustrate nor delay your wishes. One promise, in your turn, you must make and keep: that whosoever the wife may be whom I shall choose, you will yield her the highest honor and veneration; and let there be none among you who ever shall dispute or complain of my decision. Yours it was that I, the freest of all men that you have known, have submitted to the yoke of marriage; let it be mine to choose that yoke; and whoever my wife may be, let her be your mistress, as if she were the daughter of a prince of Rome."

Like men who thought it hardly possible that they should see the wished-for day of the nuptials, they promised with one accord and gladly that they should be found in nothing wanting; and with eager alacrity they received the edict from their master, directing that the most magnificent preparations be made for a certain day. So they withdrew from conference; and the marquis, on his part, laid care upon his servants for the nuptials and gave public notice of the day.

Not far from the palace, there was a village, of few and needy inhabitants, one of whom, the poorest of all, was named Janicola. But as the grace of Heaven sometimes visits the hovels of the poor,[8] it chanced that he had an only daughter, by name Grisildis, remarkable for the beauty of her body, but of so beautiful a character and spirit that no one excelled her. Reared in a frugal way of living and always in the direst poverty, unconscious of any want, she had learned to cherish no soft, no childish thoughts; but the vigor of manhood and the wisdom of age lay hidden in her maiden bosom. Cherishing her father's age with ineffable love, she tended his few sheep, and as she did it, wore her fingers away on the distaff. Then, returning home, she would prepare the little herbs and victuals suited to their fortune and make ready the rude bedchamber. In her narrow station, in fine, she discharged all the offices of filial obedience and affection. Walter, passing often by that way, had sometimes cast his eyes upon this little maid, not with the lust of youth, but with the sober thoughts of an older man; and his swift intuition had perceived in her a virtue, beyond her sex and age, which the obscurity of her condition concealed from the eyes of the common throng. Hence it came about that he decided, at one and the same time, to take a wife—which he had never before wished to do—and to have this woman and no other.[9]

The day of the nuptials drew on, but no one knew whence the bride should come, and there was no one who did not wonder. Walter himself, in the meanwhile, was buying golden rings and coronets and girdles, and was having rich garments and shoes and all necessities of this kind made to the measure of another girl, who was very like Grisildis in stature. The longed-for day had come, and since not a word about the bride was to be heard, the universal bewilderment had risen very high. The hour of the feast arrived; and already, the whole house was in a great ferment of preparation. Then Walter came out of the castle, as if he were setting out to meet his approaching bride, and a throng of noble men and matrons followed in his train.

Grisildis, ignorant of all the preparations which were being made on her account, had performed what was to be done about her home; and now, with water from the distant well,[10] she was crossing the threshold of her father's house, in order that, free from other duties, she might hasten, with the girls who were her comrades, to see her master's bride. Then Walter, absorbed in his own thoughts, drew near and, calling her by name, asked her where her father was; and when she had replied reverently and humbly, that he was within, "Bid him," he said, "come hither."

When the old man was come, Walter took him by the hand and drew him a little aside; and lowering his voice, he said, "Janicola, I know that I am dear to you. I have known you for my faithful liegeman, and I believe you wish whatever suits my pleasure. One thing in particular, however, I should like to know: whether you would take me, whom you have as your master, for a son-in-law, giving me your daughter as a wife?"[11]

Stupefied at this unlooked-for matter, the old man went rigid. At length, hardly able to stammer out a few words, he replied, "It is my duty to wish or to deny nothing, save as it pleases you, who are my master." "Let us, then, go in alone," said the marquis, "that I may put certain questions to the girl herself in your presence." They entered the house, therefore, while the populace stood expectant and wondering, and found the maiden busying herself about her father's service and abashed by the unexpected advent of so great a throng of strangers. Walter, approaching her, addressed her in these words: "It is your father's pleasure and mine that you shall be my wife. I believe that this will please you, too. But I have one thing to ask you: when that is done which shortly shall take place, will you be prepared, with consenting mind, to agree with me in all things; so that you dispute my wish in nothing, and permit me, with mind consenting, and without remonstrance of word or look, to do whatever I will with you?"

Trembling at this marvelous thing, the girl made answer: "I know myself unworthy, my lord, of so great an honor; but if it be your will, and if it be my destiny, I will never consciously cherish a thought, much less do anything, which might be contrary to your desires; nor will you do anything, even though you bid me die, which I shall bear ill."[12]

"It is enough," said he; and so, leading her out before the throng, he showed her to the people, and said, "This is my wife, this is your lady; cherish her and love her; and if you hold me dear, hold her most dear of all." Then, lest she carry into her new home any relic of her former fortune, he commanded her to be stripped, and clad from head to heel with new garments; and this was done, reverently and swiftly, by matrons who stood around her and who embraced her each in turn.[13] So this simple peasant girl, new clad, with her dishevelled tresses collected and made smooth, adorned with gems and coronet, was as it were suddenly transformed, so that the people hardly knew her. And Walter solemnly plighted her his troth with a precious ring, which he had brought with him for that purpose; and having placed her on a snow-white horse, he had her conducted to the palace, the populace accompanying her and rejoicing. In this way, the nuptials were celebrated, and that most happy day was passed.

Shortly thereafter, so much did God's favor shine upon the lowly bride, it seemed she was reared and bred, not in a shepherd's cottage, but in the imperial court; and to all she became dear and venerable beyond belief. Even those who had known her from her birth could hardly be persuaded she was Janicola's daughter; such was the graciousness of her life and of her ways, the gravity and sweetness of her speech, by which she had bound the hearts of all the people to her with the bond of a great love. And already her name, heralded by frequent rumor, had spread abroad, not only within the confines of her fatherland, but through every neighboring province; so that many men and matrons, with eager desire, came flocking to see her. So, graced by a marriage which, however humble, was distinguished and prosperous, Walter lived in the highest peace and honor at home; and abroad he was held in the highest esteem; and because he had so shrewdly discovered the remarkable virtue hidden under so much poverty, he was commonly held to be a very prudent man. Not only did his wife attend adroitly to those domestic matters which pertain to women; but when occasion demanded, in her husband's absence, she undertook state affairs, settling and composing the country's law-suits and disputes among the nobles, with such weighty opinions and so great a maturity and fairness of judgment, that all declared this woman had been sent down from heaven for the public weal.

Not long time had passed ere she became pregnant; and after she had held her subjects for a time in anxious expectation, at length she bore the fairest of daughters. Though they had preferred a son, nevertheless she made both her husband and her country happy by this proof of her fertility they longed for. In the meanwhile, it so happened, when this little daughter had been weaned, that Walter was seized with a desire more strange than laudable—so the more experienced may decide—to try more deeply the fidelity of his dear wife, which had been sufficiently made known by experience, and to test it again and again. Therefore, he called her alone into his chamber and addressed her thus, with troubled brow: "You know, Grisildis—for I do not think that amid your present good fortune you have forgotten your former state—you know, I say, in what manner you came into this house. To me, indeed, you are dear enough and well-beloved; but to my nobles, not so; especially since you have begun to bear children. For they take it most ill that they should submit to a low-born mistress. Since, therefore, I desire peace with them, I must follow another's judgment, not my own, in the case of your daughter, and do that which is most grievous to me. But I would never do it without letting you know, and I wish you to accommodate your will to mine and to show that obedience which you promised at the outset of our married life."

She listened without a protesting word or glance. "You are our master," she said, "and both this little girl and I are yours. Do, therefore, as you will with your own; for nothing can please you which would displease me. There is absolutely nothing which I wish to have or fear to lose, save you. This is fixed in the very center of my heart, and never, either by lapse of years or by death, will it be torn away. Anything can happen ere I shall change my mind."

Happy in her reply, but feigning sadness in his looks, he left her; and a little later, he sent to her one of his underlings,[14] a most faithful man, whose services he was wont to use in his most weighty affairs, and whom he intrusted in the task before him. The fellow, coming to Grisildis by night, said to her, "Spare me, my lady, and do not lay to my blame what I am forced to do. You are right knowing, and you understand what it is to be subject to a master; nor is the harsh necessity of obedience unknown to one endowed with so much sense, though inexperienced. I am bidden to take this little baby girl, and—" Here, breaking off his speech, he ceased, as if he would indicate his cruel business by his silence. Suspect was the reputation of the man, suspect his face, suspect the hour, suspect his words. By these tokens, she clearly knew her sweet daughter was to be killed; yet she shed no tear, she breathed no sigh,—a thing most hard, even for a nurse, much more so for a mother. But taking up the little girl, with tranquil brow, she looked at her a little, and kissing her, blessed her and made the sign of the Holy Cross upon her. Then she gave the child to the fellow, and said, "Go;

and whatever our lord hath laid upon you, see that you perform it. One thing I beg of you: take care lest beasts or birds tear her little body; and this, only if no contrary orders have been laid upon you."

The fellow returned to his master and told him what he had said and how Grisildis had replied; and when he had given him his daughter, paternal pity touched the marquis to the heart. Nevertheless, he did not relax the rigor of his purpose. He ordered his slave to wrap the child in cloths, to place it in a wickerwork basket upon a beast of burden, and carry it, secretly and with all the diligence he could command, to Bologna, to Walter's sister, who had married the Count of Panago. He should hand the child over to her, to be cherished with maternal care, to be reared in gentle ways, and to be concealed, moreover, with so much care that no one could know whose daughter she was. The slave journeyed thither and fulfilled with care what had been laid upon him.

Walter, in the meanwhile, though he often studied his wife's face and words, never detected any sign of a change of feeling: equal alacrity and diligence, her accustomed complaisance, the same love, no sadness, no mention of her daughter! Never did the girl's name fall upon her mother's lips, either by design or by chance. In this way, four years went by; and being again with child, behold she brought forth a most excellent son, a great delight to his father and all their friends. But when after two years, this child had been weaned, the father fell back into his former caprice. And again he said to his wife, "Once before you have heard that my people bear our marriage ill, especially since they knew you capable of bearing children; but it has never been so bad as since you gave birth to a son. For they say—and the murmur of it comes often to my ears,—'So, when Walter dies, Janicola's grandson shall rule over us, and so noble a land will be subject to such a master.' Each day many things of this tenor are current among my people; and I, eager for peace and—to say sooth—fearing for myself, am therefore moved to dispose of this infant as I disposed of his sister. I tell you this beforehand, lest the unexpected and sudden grief disturb you."

To which she made answer: "I have said, and I say again, that I can have no wishes save yours. In these children, indeed, I have no share, beyond the pangs of labor. You are my master and theirs: use your power over your own. Nor seek my consent; for when I entered your house, as I put off my clothes, so I put off my wishes and desires, and put on yours. Whatever you wish to do, therefore, about anything whatsoever, that is what I wish, too. Nay, if I could foresee your future wishes, I should begin beforehand, whatever it might be, to wish and desire what you wish. Now I gladly follow your desire, which I cannot anticipate. Suppose it pleased you that I should die, I would die gladly; nor is there any other thing—not death itself—to equal our love."

Marvelling at the steadfastness of the woman, he took his departure, his face agitated with emotion; and straightway he sent to her the servant whom he had sent before. The latter, with many a plea of the necessity of obedience, and with many an entreaty for forgiveness, if he had done or was doing her a wrong, demanded her child, as one who is about to commit a monstrous crime. But she, with unchanged mien, whatever might be passing in her mind, took up in her arms the son who was so well beloved, not only by his mother but by everyone, for the beauty of his body and his disposition; and she made upon him the sign of the Cross, blessing him, as she had blessed her daughter, clinging to him just a little while with her eyes, and bending down to kiss him; but she gave absolutely no other sign of grief. Then she gave him to the fellow who had come to seek him, and she said, "Take him, too, and do what you are bidden. But one thing I beg of you: that if it can be done, you will protect the tender limbs of my beautiful baby against the ravages of birds and beasts."

The man, returning to his master with these words of hers, drove him to yet greater wonder, so that if he had not known her for the most loving of mothers, he might have had some faint suspicion that the strength of the woman came from a certain hardness of heart; but while she was strongly attached to all that were hers, she loved no one better than her husband. The servant was then bidden to set off for Bologna and to take the boy where he had taken his sister.

These trials of conjugal affection and fidelity would have been sufficient for the most rigorous of husbands; but there are those who, when once they have begun anything, do not cease; nay, rather, they press on and cling to their purpose. Keeping his eyes upon his wife, therefore, Walter watched continually for any change in her behavior toward him, and he was not able to find any at all, save that she became each day more devoted and more obedient to his wishes; so that it seemed there was but one mind between them, and that not common to them both, but, to say truth, the husband's alone; for the wife had declared, as has been said, that she had no wishes of her own.

Little by little, an ugly rumor about Walter had begun to spread abroad; namely, that with savage and inhuman cruelty, out of regret and shame for his humble marriage, he had ordered his children slain; for neither did his children appear, nor had anyone heard where in the world they were. Wherefore, he who had once been a man of spotless reputation, dear to his people, had become in the eyes of many men infamous and hateful. Not on that account, however, was his stern purpose altered, but he persevered in the severity which he had assumed and in his harsh caprice of testing his wife. And so, when twelve years had passed since the birth of his daughter, he sent envoys to Rome to bring back thence documents bearing the appearance of a papal bull, which should cause the rumor to circulate among the people that licence had been granted him by the Roman pontiff, with a view to his own peace and that of his people, to annul his first marriage and to take another wife; nor was it difficult, in fact, to convince those untutored Alpine folk of anything you pleased. When this rumor reached Grisildis, she was sad, I think; but as one who had made her decision, once and for all, about herself and her destiny, she stood unshaken, awaiting what should be decreed by him to whom she had submitted herself and all that was hers.

Walter had already sent to Bologna and had asked his kinsman to send him his children, spreading the story in every quarter that this maiden was to be Walter's bride. His kinsman faithfully performed these orders and set out upon his journey on the appointed day, bringing with him, amid a brilliant throng of noblemen, the young maiden, who was now of marriageable age, of excellent beauty, and adorned with magnificent attire; and with her he brought her brother, who was now in his seventh year.[15]

Walter, in the meanwhile, with his accustomed inclination to try his wife, even to the heights of grief and shame, led her forth before the multitude and said, "I have been wont to take ample delight in our marriage, having regard for your character, not your lineage; but now, since I perceive that great place is always great servitude, it is not permitted me to do what any peasant may. My people compel me—and the Pope consents—to take another wife. Already my wife is on her way, and presently she will be here. Therefore, be of stout heart, and yielding your place to another, take back your dowry and return to your former home with equal mind. No good fortune lasts forever."

She made answer: "My lord, I have always known that there was no proportion between your greatness and my lowly station. I have never considered myself worthy to be—I will not say, your wife, but your servant; and in this house, in which you have made me mistress, I call God to witness that I have remained in spirit as a handmaid. For these years, therefore, that I have dwelt with you in honor far beyond my deserts, I give thanks to God and you. For the rest, I am ready, with good heart and peaceful mind, to return to my father's house, to pass my age and to die where I have passed my youth, always happy in the honorable estate of widowhood, since I have been the wife of such a man. I readily yield place to your new bride—and may her coming bring you joy!—and I will not take away any ill feeling from this place, where I was wont to live most happily, while it so pleased you. But as for my dowry, which you bid me take back with me, I see of what sort it is, and it has not been lost; for as I came to you long since, stripped at my father's threshold of all my clothes and clad in yours, I had no other dowry but nakedness and devotion. Lo, therefore, I strip off this dress and restore this ring, with which you wed me. And the other rings and finery, with which your gifts have enriched me to the point of envy, are in your chamber. Naked I came from my father's house, and naked shall I return again,[16]—save that I think it unseemly that this belly, in which the children you begot were shaped, should appear naked before the people. Wherefore, if it please you—but not otherwise—I pray and beseech you, as the price of the maidenhood which I brought hither and do not take hence, bid me keep one shift, out of those I have been wont to wear, that I may cover therewith the belly of her who was once your wife."

The tears welled into her husband's eyes, so that they could no longer be restrained; and so, turning his face aside, "Take your one shift," he said, and his voice trembled so that he could scarcely say it. So, weeping, he took his departure. Before them all, she stripped off her clothes, keeping upon her only her shift; and covered with that alone, she went forth before them with feet and head quite bare. Followed by many, who wept and railed at fortune, she alone dry-eyed and to be honored for her noble silence, returned to her father's house. The good man, who had always held his daughter's marriage in suspicion and had never allowed himself high hopes, ever expecting it to turn out that so high-born a husband, proud after the fashion of noblemen, would one day be sated with so lowly a bride and send her home, had kept her coarse and well-worn gown hidden away in some corner of his narrow dwelling. Hearing the uproar, not of his daughter, who returned in silence, but of the accompanying throng, he ran to meet her at the threshold and covered her, half-naked as she was, with the old gown. She remained with her father a few days, showing marvelous equanimity and kindness; for she gave no sign of the sadness of her heart and showed no trace of her more favorable lot, since, forsooth, she had always dwelt amid riches with a lowly and humble spirit.

Now the Count of Panago was drawing near; and, on every hand, rumors of the new nuptials were rife. Sending forward one of his train, he announced the day on which he would arrive at Saluzzo. The day before, therefore, Walter sent for Grisildis, and when she had come with all fidelity, he said to her, "It is my desire that the maiden who is coming on the morrow to dine with us should be received sumptuously, as well as the men and matrons who come with her and such of our own people as are present at the feast, so that honor of place and welcome may be preserved unspotted, according to the dignity of each and all. But I have no women in the house who are suited to cope with this task; therefore, though your garments are but poor, you may best assume the duty of receiving and placing my guests, for you know my ways."

"I will do this," said she, "and whatever else I see will please you, not only willingly, but eagerly. Nor shall I grow weary or sluggish in this labor, so long as the least remnant of my spirit shall last." And when she had said this, straightway she caught up the implements of servant's toil and set to work, sweeping the house, setting the tables, making the beds, and urging on the others, like the best of handmaids.[17]

At the third hour of the next day, the count arrived; and all the people vied in commending the manners and the beauty of the maiden and her youthful brother. There were those who said that Walter had been fortunate and prudent in the change he made, since this bride was more delicate and of nobler breeding, and had so fine a kinsman into the bargain.[18] So, while the preparations for the feast went feverishly on, Grisildis, who had been present everywhere and solicitous of all—not cast down by so grievous a lot nor confused with shame for her old-fashioned clothing, but serene of countenance—came to meet the maiden as she entered. Bending the knee before her, after the manner of servants, with eyes cast reverently and humbly down, she said, "Welcome, my lady." Then she greeted others of the guests with cheerful face and marvelous sweetness in her words, and she managed the vast household with great skill; so that everyone greatly wondered—especially the newcomers—whence came that dignity of manner and that discretion beneath such a dress. She, in her turn, could not grow weary of praising the maiden and the boy: now she extolled the maiden's beauty, now the boy's.

Just as they were to sit down at the tables, Walter turned toward her and said before them all, as if he were making game of her, "What think you, Grisildis, of this bride of mine? Is she pretty and worthy enough?"

"Surely," said she, "no prettier or worthier could be found. Either with her or with no one, can you lead a life of tranquillity and happiness; and that you may find happiness is my desire and my hope. One thing, in all good faith, I beg of you, one warning I give you: not to drive her with the goads with which you have driven another woman. For since she is younger and more delicately nurtured, I predict she would not be strong enough to bear so much."

Walter, seeing the cheerfulness with which she spoke, and turning over in his mind the steadfastness of the woman, who had been so often and so bitterly injured, took pity on the unworthy fate that had befallen her so unjustly. Able to bear it no longer, he cried out, "It is enough, my Grisildis! Your fidelity to me is made known and proved; nor do I think that under heaven there is another woman who has undergone such trials of her conjugal love." And saying this, with eager arms he embraced his dear wife, who stood all overcome with stupor and as if waking from a troubled sleep. "And you," he said, "are my only wife. I have no other, nor ever shall have. This maiden, whom you think to be my bride, is your daughter; and he, who is thought to be my kinsman, is your son. They whom you believed you had lost, each in turn, you get back both together. Let all know, who thought the contrary, that I am curious and given to experiments, but am not impious: I have tested my wife, not condemned her; I have hidden my children, not destroyed them."

Almost out of her wits for joy and beside herself with maternal love, on hearing these words, Grisildis rushed into her children's arms, shedding the most joyous tears. She wearied them with kisses and bedewed them with her loving tears. And straightway the ladies gathered about her with alacrity and affection; and when her vile apparel had been stripped off her, they clothed her in her accustomed garments and adorned her. The most joyous plaudits and auspicious words from all the throng resounded all about; and the day was the most renowned that ever was for its great joy and sorrow,—more renowned, even, than the day of her nuptials had been.

Many years thereafter they lived in great peace and concord; and Walter, who had appeared to neglect his father-in-law, lest he should stand in the way of the experiment he had conceived, had the old man move into his palace and held him in honor. His own daughter he gave in noble and honorable marriage, and his son he left behind him as his heir, happy in his wife and in his offspring.

[*Petrarch's statement concerning the "moral" to be drawn from this story, appearing in the Clerk's Tale 1142–62, is printed above, pp. 138–39, at the beginning of the second part of the letter to Boccaccio.*]

NOTES

1. *Ars poetica*, 133–34.
2. Petrarch seems to have written *stilo nunc alio* ("in another style"); Chaucer's text apparently read *stilo nunc alto* ("in the high style"); see Clerk's Tale, 1148.

3. James i, 13 (King James version). The full context in the Douay Bible reads: "Blessed is the man that endureth temptation; for when he hath been proved, he shall receive the crown of life, which God hath promised to them that love him. Let no man, when he is tempted, say that he is tempted by God. For God is not a temptor of evils, and he tempteth no man. But every man is tempted by his own concupiscence, being drawn away and allured" (James i, 12–14). The passage is conventionally related to Job v, 17–18: "Blessed is the man whom God correcteth: refuse not therefore the chastising of the Lord: For he woundeth, and cureth: he striketh, and his hands shall heal."

4. Juvenal, *Satire* XV, 131–33.

5. This introductory matter is Petrarch's addition to Boccaccio. The French version eliminates the geographical preface. Petrarch was familiar with and fond of the area.

6. The speech is Petrarch's invention.

7. Moralizations concerning character, more soberly presented than in Boccaccio, are omitted in French version.

8. Transferred from the very end of Boccaccio's version, where it appears as a kind of "moral." Chaucer heightened the effect by using the image of the "oxes stalle" (207), an allusion to the Nativity. See Luke ii, 7.

9. The description of Grisildis is Petrarch's.

10. Allusion to Rebecca; see Genesis xxiv, 15–20.

11. Boccaccio's Gualtieri arranged beforehand with the father, Giannucolo. Petrarch heightened the suspense and justified Grisildis' surprise.

12. The interrogation is considerably expanded from Boccaccio, and put into direct discourse. Grisildis' speech, in particular, is Petrarch's addition. Walter's "It is enough" ("*Satis est*") is echoed at the conclusion of Grisildis' trials. Grisildis' obedience suggests that of the Virgin at the Annunciation: Luke i, 38, "Behold the handmaid of the Lord; be it done to me according to the word." Compare also Luke xxii, 42.

13. The French version mentions the "shame" of the ladies regarding her poor clothes.

14. Petrarch's Latin: *unum suorum satellitum*; the French: *un sien serviteur et sergent*.

15. We learn that Boccaccio's Gualtieri sends for the children after the "divorce." Petrarch thus suggests that Walter here foresees the denouement he produces.

16. Petrarch reduces Boccaccio's casual allusion to conform more precisely with the text of Job i, 21: "Naked came I out of my mother's womb, and naked shall I return thither: the Lord gave, and the Lord hath taken away: as it hath pleased the Lord so is it done: blessed be the name of the Lord." Compare Ecclesiastes v, 14; 1 Timothy vi, 7.

17. *Ancilla in morem fidelissime*; compare Luke i, 38.

18. In Boccaccio it is the nobles, not the populace, who make this judgment.

four

THE THREE
ESTATES

Chaucer's friend John Gower was referring to the most conventional medieval theory of society when he wrote in his Vox clamantis that "We recognize that there are three estates. In his own way, everyone in the world lives under them and serves them" (III, Prologue). He went on to explain that "there are the cleric, the knight, and the peasant [Clerus, Miles, Cultor], the three carrying on three different affairs. The one teaches, the other fights, and the third tills to fields" (III, i). To knighthood was assigned the task of governing the temporal order of society, while to the clergy was entrusted the governance of the spiritual order. These two authorities made up what would today be called the Establishment. The third Estate comprised the whole body of "providers" (the populus) who perform the great variety of tasks connected with society's subsistence. The Plowman, certainly ideally represented by the "brother" of Chaucer's Parson (General Prologue, 529–41), symbolized those whose manual labor produced the material goods for the commonwealth. In addition, we often hear of a separate sovereign "estate," namely, that of wives.

Traditional "offices" for each Estate described the ideals which they should theoretically serve in a Christian society. Thus Chaucer's idealized Knight dedicates his strength and blood to the just rights of Church and State; and his Parson, Clerk, and Second Nun learn and teach, and provide living models in their "work." The obligations of these offices, as they were popularly regarded, are often most colorfully presented in a vast literature of complaint and satire, which takes as its subject departures from these ideals. Gower, for example, is quite conventional in accusing knights of lechery, vainglory, or a failure to serve the common weal—all vices contrary to their official oath, and all illustrated in different ways by knights and squires in Chaucer's work. The errant ecclesiastical pilgrims in the Canterbury Tales are to be measured similarly by their offices. Complaint against the "providers" usually emphasizes the sins of dishonesty or rebellious presumption, matters in which Chaucer's Miller can be contrasted with his Plowman. Complaint against women, finally, is basic to the antifeminist literature which fills such a large shelf in the library of medieval authority (see below, pp. 399ff.).

THE ESTATE OF TEMPORAL RULERS: CHIVALRY

As a court poet Chaucer wrote for an aristocratic audience whose way of life was obliquely pictured in "courtly" literature, such as the chivalric romance. Records indicate that by 1357, when he was about twelve years old, he was serving as page in the household of Prince Lionel of Antwerp, first Duke of Clarence, the third son of Edward III; and he lived among knights and ladies throughout his life. Thus he was familiar with the actual concerns and activities of those who made up the Estate of Temporal Rulers.

Despite the recreancies and follies of individual members, some of which become the subject of romances, a sober sense of obligation to the Christian community seems to have informed the chivalric code of those dedicated to the defense of Christendom, the kingdom, and the civil law (or lex positiva, as in the Knight's Tale, 1165–68, where Arcite's devotion to "lawe" takes a surprising turn). The ordination to knighthood and the right to bear the sword had, as early as the tenth century, acquired a religious character which was, as chivalric manuals and the ritual of ordination testify, still present in Chaucer's day.

But it must be stressed that the office of chivalry was regarded as a secular, not a spiritual, occupation. Though spiritual models, such as St. Michael (Apocalypse xii, 7–9) and Christ Himself (Apocalypse xix, 11–15), are often held up for imitation, the knight as the "armed hand of the state" was expected to exercise virtues consistent with the "active" life. These differ essentially, for instance, from those defined by the clerical vows of poverty, chastity, and humility. The knight is required to be poor in the sense that he properly evaluate the uses of material wealth. He is expected to have certain possessions: the virtue of "fredom" or "largesce" is predicated upon this expectation. Similarly, the knight is enjoined to practice "marital chastity"—fidelity and

156

"*trouthe*" *within the state of marriage. Thus Theseus serves "Dyane"
in the Knight's Tale, 1682. While they consistently condemn lechery,
the "Arts of Chivalry" exhort the knight to preserve his marriage and
household as a model for the commonalty, and to educate his sons
properly in the parts of chivalry. The humility of the knight, again, is
typically a lay virtue—absence of undue pride, and obedience to the
"higher powers" described in Romans xiii. His accoutrements are hon-
orific, he is accorded the aristocratic privileges which accompany rule,
he is set high on his horse to symbolize his relationship to the common-
wealth, and he is expected to achieve honor and a good name.*

*The following texts repeatedly stress the virtues of "Trouthe and
honour, fredom and curteisie" (General Prologue, 46) with which
Chaucer endowed his ideal Knight. The standards, moreover, provide a
sober perspective on the comic deficiencies of characters like Palamon
and Arcite, Januarie, the Squire's Cambyuskan, and even the Squire
himself. Particularly interesting is the treatment of lechery, as back-
ground to the element of romantic love in chivalric literature. One of
the knight's "duties" is indeed to "serve women," but it is doubtful
that the code envisioned the kind of service practiced by literary lovers
such as Troilus or Aurelius. If the conventions of romantic love, illus-
trated separately in this volume (see below, pp. 271ff.), are reviewed
in this light, they may appear to be less desirable than they do to prac-
ticing "servants of love."*

Eustache Deschamps:
"Du Bachelier d'Armes"

*Eustache Deschamps (c. 1346–1406) was born in Vertus, in the province
of Champagne. He is known to have been a pupil (perhaps the nephew) of
the poet Guillaume de Machaut. Like Chaucer, he moved in courtly cir-
cles, holding a number of civil-service positions and traveling on diplomatic
missions for the French Court. Deschamps was a prolific writer: over 1,000
ballades, 171 rondeaux, 84 virelays, and 84 lais have been attributed to him.
In addition, he wrote longer didactic poems, of which one—Le* Miroir de
mariage, *a matrimonial satire of 12,113 lines—greatly influenced Chaucer
(see below, pp. 388–90). His prose treatise on poetics,* L'Art de dictier
(1392), is the first to have been written in French.

*Although Chaucer seems never to have met Deschamps, many echoes
of Deschamps' ballades have been detected in his poetry, and the* Miroir de
mariage *is a major source for the* Wife of Bath's Prologue *and the* Mer-
chant's Tale. *His familiarity with the French poet's work may be traced to
a gift volume which Deschamps sent c. 1393 to "Grand translateur, noble
Gieffroy Chaucier."*

*The following ballade is a highly conventional summation of the quali-
ties a medieval courtly society expected of the chivalric man.*

A new translation by Diane Bornstein.

Figure 5. Perseus and Andromeda: Christian knight rescues damsel from
dragon. British Library MS Harley 4431, fol. 98.

Ballade: "The Bachelor at Arms"

You who desire the order of chivalry
Must lead a new life,[1]
Lie awake in prayer devotedly,
Flee sin, pride, and villeiny,
Must defend the Church,
The widow also, support the orphan,
Be brave and guard the people,
A valiant, loyal man
   who takes nothing from others.
Thus must a knight govern himself.

You must have a humble heart, always must labor in
And pursue deeds of chivalry,
Fight in just wars, be a great crusader,
Engage in tournaments, and joust for your lady,
Must always act honorably
So that no man can find fault with you
Nor find cowardice in your deeds,
And among all people you must
   hold yourself to be least.
Thus must a knight govern himself.

You must cherish your lord's rights,
And above all guard his lordship,
Show generosity, be a true judge,
Follow the company of valiant men,
Listen to and learn from their sayings,
And comprehend the brave deeds of heroes,
So that you can achieve great exploits,
As Alexander the Great did
   in former times.
Thus must a knight govern himself.

NOTE

1. *Nouvelle vie:* compare the theme of Christian renovation in the Ceremonial of Ordination (below, pp. 169–73). Many details of this ballade are clearly drawn from some version of the Ceremonial. The address to the squire is similar to that in the Lullian *Order of Chivalry*, as well (see below, pp. 180–83).

Scriptural Authority

The Estate of Temporal Rulers had, in theory, absolute authority in the administration of secular justice, for which it was established. This authority was ordained by God, and delegated down through the ranks of the feudal hierarchy, from Emperor to the poorest knight. An important text often cited in support of this theory is Romans xiii, in which St. Paul defines not only the duty of subjects, but the responsibility of those who bear the sword of justice, in a Christian society. Chaucer's Knight, who engages "in his lordes werre" (General Prologue, 47), may be seen as properly serving both his temporal and his heavenly lord, according to this view; and Theseus, the model prince in his tale, invokes the "Firste Moevere of the cause above" (Knight's Tale, 2987) and seeks to subject his kingdom to its law. We may wonder, on the other hand, what "higher power" the Squire serves, when he bears his sword "In hope to stonden in his lady grace" (General Prologue, 88).

Lessons of Obedience to Superiors, and Mutual Charity

ROMANS XIII

1. Let every soul be subject to higher powers:[1] for there is no power but from God: and those that are, are ordained of God.

2. Therefore he that resisteth the power, resisteth the ordinance of God. And they that resist, purchase to themselves damnation.

3. For princes are not a terror to the good work, but to the evil. Wilt thou then not be afraid of the power? Do that which is good: and thou shalt have praise from the same.

4. For he is God's minister to thee, for good. But if thou do that which is evil, fear: for he beareth not the sword in vain. For he is God's minister: an avenger to execute wrath upon him that doth evil.

5. Wherefore be subject of necessity, not only for wrath, but also for conscience' sake.

6. For therefore also you pay tribute. For they are the ministers of God, serving unto this purpose.

7. Render therefore to all men their dues.[2] Tribute, to whom tribute is due: custom, to whom custom: fear, to whom fear: honour, to whom honour.

8. Owe no man any thing, but to love one another. For he that loveth his neighbour, hath fulfilled the law.

9. For *Thou shalt not commit adultery: Thou shalt not kill: Thou shalt not steal, Thou shalt not bear false witness: Thou shalt not covet:*[3] and if there be any other commandment, it is comprised in this word, *Thou shalt love thy neighbour as thyself.*[4]

10. The love of our neighbour worketh no evil. Love therefore is the fulfilling of the law.

11. And that knowing the season; that it is now the hour for us to rise from sleep. For now our salvation is nearer than when we believed.

12. The night is passed, and the day is at hand. Let us therefore cast off the works of darkness, and put on the armour of light.[5]

13. Let us walk honestly, as in the day: not in rioting and drunkenness, not in chambering and impurities, not in contention and envy:[6]

14. But put ye on the Lord Jesus Christ,[7] and make not provision for the flesh in its concupiscences.[8]

NOTES

1. See Wisdom vi, 1–6; 1 Peter ii, 13–17.
2. Matthew xxii, 21.
3. Exodus xx, 13–17; Deuteronomy v, 17–21.
4. Leviticus xix, 18; Matthew xxii, 39; Mark xii, 31; Galatians v, 14; James ii, 8.
5. Such imagery is echoed and developed in medieval dawn-hymns such as Prudentius' *Ales diei nuntius* (below, pp. 304–6). It appears in the ritual and ceremony of ordination of knights (see below, pp. 167–68, 171–73). By assuming a spiritual "chivalry" it provides an ironic counterpart to the secular chivalric *alba* in which the Christian knight condemns the day (see below, pp. 307–8).
6. Luke xii, 34.
7. Galatians v, 16–17; 1 Peter ii, 11.
8. Putting off the old and putting on the new like clothing is a repeated Pauline image (see, e.g., Ephesians iv, 22–32; Colossians iii, 9–16) which is significantly imitated in the ceremony of ordination (see below, p. 172).

Saint Augustine:
from *The City of God*

In The City of God *St. Augustine projected the form of the new Christian community which was to supplant the "City of Man," typified by Rome. New political virtues, exercised always with reference to God rather than simply to the state, were to replace even the undeniable virtues of Roman polity. In this remarkably compact chapter he describes the "princes" envisioned by St. Paul in Romans xiii, establishing an ideal for future rulers to emulate.*

Trans. Marcus Dods, The City of God *by Saint Augustine (Edinburgh: T. & T. Clark, 1872: rept. New York: Hafner, 1948), I, 222–23. Copyright 1948 by Hafner Publishing Company. Reprinted by permission of Macmillan Publishing Co., Inc.*

[Virtues of the Christian Ruler]

V, 24

Neither do we say that certain Christian emperors were therefore happy because they ruled a long time, or, dying a peaceful death, left their sons to succeed them in the empire, or subdued the enemies of the republic, or were able both to guard against and to suppress the attempt of hostile citizens rising against them. These and other gifts or comforts of this sorrowful life even certain worshipers of demons have merited to receive, who do not belong to the kingdom of God to which these belong; and this is to be traced to the mercy of God, who would not have those who believe in Him desire such things as the highest good. But we say that they are happy if they rule justly; if they are not lifted up amid the praises of those who pay them sublime honors, and the obsequiousness of those who salute them with an excessive humility, but remember that they are men; if they make their power the handmaid of His majesty by using it for the greatest possible extension of His worship; if they fear, love, worship God; if more than their own they love that kingdom in which they are not afraid to have partners; if they are slow to punish, ready to pardon; if they apply that punishment as necessary to government and defence of the republic, and not in order to gratify their own enmity; if they grant pardon, not that iniquity may go unpunished, but with the hope that the transgressor may amend his ways; if they compensate with the lenity of mercy and the liberality of benevolence for whatever severity they may be compelled to decree; if their luxury is as much restrained as it might have been unrestrained; if they prefer to govern depraved desires rather than any nation whatever; and if they do all these things, not through ardent desire of empty glory, but through love of eternal felicity, not neglecting to offer to the true God, who is their God, for their sins, the sacrifices of humility, contrition, and prayer. Such Christian emperors, we say, are happy in the present time by hope, and are destined to be so in the enjoyment of the reality itself, when that which we wait for shall have arrived.

Geoffroi de Charny:
from *The Book of Chivalry*

What little is known of Geoffroi de Charny may be gathered from Frois-sart's account of the Battle of Poitiers, September 19, 1356, in which Ed-ward the Black Prince overwhelmed King John II of France:

> During the whole engagement the Lord de Chargny, who was near the King, and carried the royal banner, fought most bravely; the English and Gascons, however, poured so fast upon the King's division, that they broke through the ranks by force, and in the confusion the Lord de Chargny was slain, with the banner of France in his hand.

Since this knight, entrusted with the oriflamme *on that day, is probably as good an authority as any for the actual chivalric ideals and customs in France around 1350, this account in his* Le Livre de chevalerie *of the ritual of initiation into the "order of chivalry" is of particular interest, as is his description of "chivalric love" (below, pp. 207–9).*

A new translation by Margaret Ehrhart.

166

[The Making of a Knight]

So that it might be better understood why the order of chivalry was created and established, it is good to review [the ritual of ordination].

You ought to know that when it is desired to create a new knight, it is customary right at the first that he be confessed and repentant of all his sins, and that he prepare himself to receive the body of Our Lord. And then, on the eve of the day on which he is to become a knight, he should get into a bath and remain there for a long while, thinking that he ought to wash and cleanse henceforth his body of all filth of sin and immoral living, and ought to leave all such filth within that water. Then, all clean of conscience, he should leave the water of that bath and should go lie down in a completely new bed, with clean, white linen sheets, and there he should rest like those who have emerged from the great anguish of sin and from the great peril of the devils' torment. This bed signifies the tranquillity of goodness, of conscience, of reconciliation between himself and Our Lord with respect to everything by which he may have angered Him in times past.

Then the knights should come to the bed to dress him, and they should dress him in new linens and everything necessary—all new—signifying that just as his body should be cleansed of all filth of sin, so he is reclothed in white, new, and clean linen as a sign that henceforth he should keep himself pure and without sin. Then the knights should dress him in a red tunic, signifying that he is obliged to shed his blood to defend and uphold the faith of Our Lord and the rights of Holy Church, and all the other duties described above that a knight is obliged to perform.[1] And then the knights should bring him black shoes, and put them on him as a sign that he should remember that from earth he has come, and to earth he must return, because of the death which he must expect,[2] whose hour he knows not; and because of this he should put all pride beneath his feet. And then the knights should bring him a belt, all white, and gird him with it, and put it around him as a sign that his body should be completely enclosed in chastity and fleshly purity. Then the knights should bring him a red mantle, and place it on his shoulders as a sign of very great humility, because mantles thus made were in ancient times made in true humility.

Then the knights should lead him with great joy into the church, and he should remain in the church and keep vigil all night until morning, in very great devotion, praying to Our Lord that He be willing to pardon him the vain slumbers and wakings in which he has engaged in times past, and that He should help him keep vigil in His grace and in His service henceforth.

The next morning the knights lead him to mass to hear the service very devoutly, praying Our Lord that He give him grace to enter and to fulfill this order in His service. And when the mass has been sung and said, then the knights lead him to that one or to those knights who are to bestow on him the order. Then the knight who bestows the order gives two golden spurs to two knights, one to each, and those two knights put the spurs on his feet, as a sign that, as gold is the most coveted metal there is, it is placed on his feet because he removes from his heart all evil desire for possession.

Then that knight who is to bestow on him the order of chivalry takes up a sword, because the sword cuts in two parts. So he should guard and uphold and maintain right, reason, and justice everywhere without contradicting for anything the Christian faith and the rights of Holy Church. And then the knights who bestow the order on him should kiss him as a sign of confirming the order that they bestow and which he receives, so that peace and love and loyalty be in him, and that he may thus obtain them and keep them wherever he can. And then those knights should give him the *colée*,[3] as a sign that he should forevermore remember the order of chivalry that he has received, and perform the deeds which pertain to that order.

These things should be performed in this way. And they are indeed happy who conduct and maintain themselves just as their station requires. And as for anyone who would do the contrary, it would be better had he never been made a knight.

NOTES

1. The duties include: to shed his blood honorably for his lord (his soul will be saved if he does); to preserve the honor and heritage of poor girls and of poor widows, and to battle for their bodies and souls; to protect poor orphans; to maintain the rights of Holy Church.
2. See Genesis iii, 19.
3. A slap upon the cheek.

from the *Ceremonial of Ordination*

Elements of the initiation ritual for the new knight are documented as early as the twelfth century and are found throughout Europe. These include the ritual bath, awakening from sleep, revestment in new garments, vigil and prayer, and the actual cincture which "makes" a knight. Such formalities enact the Christian mystery of renovation, to "put off the old man, and put on the new man" in newness of life, as it is expressed, for instance, in Ephesians iv, 22–32, and Colossians iii, 8–15. For the Pauline sense of "awakening" see especially Ephesians v, 8–14 (and see below, pp. 305–6).

Ceremonial blessings of arms appear as early as the tenth century. By the twelfth century more elaborate Church services had been developed. The following ceremony, translated from the Pontifical of William Durand, *bishop of Mende (c. 1295), became the official rite for Christian practice in the fourteenth century.*

A new translation.

Figure 6. Knight receives sword from King. Durham Cathedral MS A. II. 3, fol. 225 (Latin Bible).

[The Blessing of The New Knight]

1. *The blessing of the new knight proceeds in this manner. The Bishop, before the reading of the Gospel, blesses his sword, saying:*

2. *Blessing of the sword.* Grant, we pray, O Lord, our prayers, and see fit to bless with the hand of your majesty this sword with which your servant desires to be girt, to the end that he may be a defender of the Church, of widows, of orphans, and of all the servants of God, against the cruelty of the pagans, and that he may be the terror and dread of his other enemies, ensuring for him the performance of equitable prosecution and just defense. *Response:* Amen.

3. *Another blessing.* ✠ Holy Lord, Father Almighty, Eternal God, through the invocation of your holy name and through the coming of Christ your son, our Lord, and through the gift of the Holy Spirit, the Paraclete, bless this sword, so that this man, your servant, who is girt today with it, by favor of your benevolence, may trample underfoot his invisible enemies and, gaining victory in all things, always remain safe and sound.

4. *At this point other blessings of arms may be recited. Then, the arms having been blessed, before he girds him with the sword, he first says:*

5. Blessed be the Lord my God, who teacheth my hands to fight, and my fingers to war. / [My mercy, and my refuge: my support, and my deliverer: My protector, and I have hoped in him: who subdueth my people under me. / Lord, what is man, that thou art made known to him? or the son of man, that thou makest account of him?][1] *And after the first three verses, with* Gloria Patri, *he says:* Keep safe your servant. Be to him, O Lord, a tower.[2] Hear our prayers, O Lord. The Lord be with you. Let us pray.

6. O Lord, omnipotent father, eternal God, who alone establish and lawfully rule the order of all things: who to put down the malice of reprobates and to defend justice have, by your beneficent disposition, permitted men on earth the use of the sword, and have willed to institute a Chivalric Order for the protection of the people: and who said by way of the blessed John to the soldiers who came to him in the desert that they should do violence to no man, but be content with their pay:[3] we humbly pray that, just as you granted to your child David the power to vanquish Goliath,[4] and as you caused Judas Machabeus to triumph over the nations who did not call upon your name,[5] so grant, through your heavenly bounty, to this your servant, who comes

as a new recruit to put his neck under the military yoke, the power and valor to defend the faith and justice, increase in him faith, hope and charity, the fear as well as the love of God, humility, perseverance, obedience and good patience, and direct him lawfully in all things, so that he will never injure anyone unjustly with this or any other sword, and so that he will defend with it all just and lawful causes, and so that, just as he is raised from an inferior station to the new honor of chivalry, so, putting off the old man with his deeds, he will put on the new man,[6] to fear you and render you just worship, to avoid the society of the wicked, to pour out his charity upon his neighbor, to obey the articles of his oath lawfully in all things, and to fulfill his office justly at all times. Through Jesus Christ our Lord. *Response:* Amen.

7. *After this the Bishop takes up the unsheathed sword from the altar, and puts it in the knight's right hand, saying:* Receive this sword, in the name of the Father, and of the Son, and of the Holy Spirit, and use it for your defense and that of the holy Church of God, and for the confusion of the enemies of the Cross of Christ and of the Christian faith and of the crown of the kingdom of England (or other), and, insofar as human frailty permits you, injure no man unjustly with it. May He consider you worthy of honor, who with the Father and the Holy Spirit lives and reigns now and forever, ✠ *Response:* Amen.

8. *Next, when the sword has been sheathed, he girds him with the sword and its sheath, saying:* Gird thy sword upon thy thigh, O thou most mighty,[7] in the name of our Lord Jesus Christ, and remember that the saints have conquered kingdoms not with the sword, but by faith. ✠

9. *When the sword has been thus girt, the new knight draws it from its sheath, and manfully brandishes it unsheathed three times and, after wiping it on his arm, returns it quickly to its sheath.*

10. *Which done, as a sign of the knight's chivalric character, the Bishop gives him the kiss of peace, saying:* As a knight, be peace-loving, active, faithful, and dedicated to God. ✠

11. *Then he slaps him lightly on the ear,[8] saying:* Awake from the sleep of malice, and be vigilant in the faith of Christ, and keep a praiseworthy name. ✠ Amen.

12. *Then the nobles present put on his spurs, where this is the custom, and the antiphon is sung:* Thou art beautiful above the sons of men;[9] gird thy sword upon thy thigh, O most mighty.[10]

13. *Prayer.* Omnipotent God eternal, pour out the grace of your blessing upon this your servant N[ame], who desires to be girt with an honorable sword, strengthen him with trust in the power of your right

hand, and protect him with heavenly hosts against every adversary, that he never be disturbed by the tempests of war in this world.

14. *Finally, the Bishop gives him his standard, where it is the custom to do so.*

NOTES

1. Psalm cxliii, 1–3. See also 2 Kings, xxii, 33–43; Psalm xvii, 33–41.
2. Psalm, lx, 4.
3. Luke iii, 14.
4. 1 Kings xvii.
5. 1 and 2 Machabees.
6. Colossians iii, 9–10; Ephesians iv, 22–24.
7. Psalm xliv, 4.
8. *Alapa.* This is in French the *colée,* which implies that the neck is struck. According to Roman custom, the *alapa* was delivered by a master upon the manumission of a slave. The *colée* is sometimes explained as a symbolic reminder of the blows suffered by Christ.
9. Psalm xliv, 3.
10. Psalm xliv, 4.

[The Blessing of Arms]

1. *For the spurs.* Bless, O Lord, these spurs, that he to whose feet they are fitted, who is honored today with the chivalric office, may, by treading evil underfoot, attain eternal life.

2. *For the shield.* O Lord, we pray of your mercy, that your servant, who receives this shield in honor of chivalry, may pass through this temporal world without losing the eternal one.

3. *For the sword.* O Lord, hear my prayer, and grant your servant, who is girt with this sword, that, in his defense of justice for the Church, for orphans, and for widows, he may so please you that on the Day of Judgment he will be found among the company of the just.

John of Salisbury:
from the *Policraticus*

John of Salisbury (1115–80) was secretary to Thomas Becket, Archbishop of Canterbury, and is known to have been with Becket on the day of his assassination by the knights of King Henry II in 1170. Educated under the leading scholars of France, including Peter Abelard, he was first appointed secretary to Theobald, Archbishop of Canterbury, in 1154, apparently through the helpful offices of Bernard of Clairvaux. In this capacity he engaged in numerous diplomatic missions to France and Italy, as well as in England. John continued as secretary to Theobald's successor, Thomas Becket, in 1161, joining him in his exile (1164–70) and rejoining him on his fatal return to England. In 1176 he was appointed Bishop of Chartres by King Louis VII, a position he held until his death.

The best known of John's writings are the Metalogicon, an important educational treatise sometimes known as "A Defense of the Trivium," and the Policraticus ("The Statesman's Book"), the first full treatise on politics in the middle ages. Both of these works were addressed to Thomas Becket, then Chancellor of England under Henry II, in 1159. His account of the soldier's oath and dedication illustrates the Christian adaptation of principles practiced by the Roman legions, and indicates the high ideals expected of one who, like Chaucer's Knight two centuries later, engaged in "his lordes werre." The continuity of these traditions can be seen by comparison with the Ceremonial of Ordination printed above, pp. 169–73.

Trans. John Dickinson, The Statesman's Book of John of Salisbury (New York: Knopf, 1927), pp. 196–200, 203–4. © 1955. Reprinted by permission of Prentice-Hall, Inc., Englewood Cliffs, New Jersey.

[Chivalric Duties]

VI, 7

By ancient law no one was presented with the soldier's belt without the binding sacrament of an oath. As may be read in Julius Frontinus, it was during the consulship of Lucius Flacus and Gaius Varro that an oath was first required to make a man a soldier;[1] before that time only an oath of allegiance was administered by the tribunes, but the soldiers swore to one another that they would not run away for fright, not leave the line of battle except for the purpose of getting a weapon or striking an enemy or to save a comrade. And this was called the military oath; and the practice was confirmed by the authority of the most Christian emperors and by usage.

On the testimony of Vegetius the formula of this oath is as follows:[2] The soldiers swear by God and His Christ and by the Holy Ghost and the prince's majesty, which according to God's commandment is to be loved and worshiped by the human race. For when anyone receives lawful princely power, faithful devotion is to be accorded to him and ever watchful service as to God present and manifest in the flesh. Both the private citizen and the soldier serve God when they loyally love him who reigns by the authority of God.[3] They swear, I say, that they will do to the best of their ability all things which the prince shall enjoin upon them; that they will never desert from military service nor refuse to die for the commonwealth, of which they are the enlisted soldiers. After they have taken this oath, they are presented with the soldier's belt and become entitled to the soldier's privileges. . . .

VI, 8

Turn over in your mind the words of the oath itself, and you will find that the soldiery of arms not less than the spiritual soldiery is bound by the requirements of its official duties to the sacred service and worship of God; for they owe obedience to the prince and ever-watchful service to the commonwealth, loyally and according to God. . . . The name of soldier is one of honor, as it is one of toil. And no man can take honor upon himself, but one who is called of God glories in the honor which is conferred upon him.[4] . . .

The sacred Gospel narrative bears witness that two swords are enough for the Christian *imperium*;[5] all others belong to those who with swords and cudgels draw nigh to take Christ captive and seek to destroy His name.[6] For wherein do they partake of the character of the true soldier who, although they may have been called, yet do not obey the law according to their oath, but deem the glory of their military service to consist in bringing contempt upon the priesthood, in cheapening the authority of the Church, in so extending the kingdom of man as to narrow the empire of Christ, and in proclaiming their own praises and flattering and extolling themselves with false commendations, thus imitating the braggart soldier to the amusement of all who hear them?[7] Their valor shines forth chiefly in stabbing with swords or tongues the clergy and the unarmed soldiery.

But what is the office of the duly ordained soldiery? To defend the Church, to assail infidelity, to venerate the priesthood, to protect the poor from injuries, to pacify the province, to pour out their blood for their brothers (as the formula of their oath instructs them), and, if need be, to lay down their lives. The high praises of God are in their throat, and two-edged swords are in their hands to execute punishment on the nations and rebuke upon the peoples, and to bind their kings in chains and their nobles in links of iron.[8] But to what end? To the end that they may serve madness, vanity, avarice, or their own private self-will? By no means. Rather to the end that they may execute the judgment that is committed to them to execute;[9] wherein each follows not his own will but the deliberate decision of God, the angels, and men, in accordance with equity and the public utility. I say "to the end that they may *execute*"; for as it is for judges to pronounce judgment, so it is for these to perform their office by executing it. Verily, "This honor have all His saints."[10] For soldiers that do these things are "saints," and the more loyal to their prince in proportion as they more zealously keep the faith of God; and they advance the more successfully the honor of their own valor as they seek the more faithfully in all things the glory of their God.

VI, 10

Though some soldiers do not regard themselves as bound to the Church by a solemn oath, because today by general custom no such oath is actually taken, yet there is none who is not in fact under an obligation to the Church by virtue of a tacit oath if not of an express one. And perchance the solemnity of the oath has been given up for precisely the reason that the requirements of their office and the sincerity of their faith are a sufficient inducement and guarantee of the same result. Whence the solemn custom has now taken root, that on the day on which a man is girt with the belt of a soldier he goes solemnly to the church, and placing his sword on the altar like a sacrificial offering, and making as it were a public profession, he dedicates himself to the service of the altar and vows to God the never-failing obedience of his sword, that is to say, of his performance of the duties of his office.[11]

Nor is it needful that this profession should be made expressly and in so many words, since the lawful profession of a soldier seems implicit in this act. Who would demand of an illiterate man whose duty is to know arms rather than letters, that he should make a profession in writing? Bishops and abbots are visibly bound to fidelity and obedience by a written or spoken profession; and they are truly bound, for it is not lawful to break faith with God. But it is surely an act of even greater, or at least of equal solemnity, which soldiers perform when they offer up not a parchment but their sword, and as it were redeem from the altar the first-fruits of their office; whereby they enter into the perpetual service of the Church; for as they must lawfully do all that in them lies for the Church, so it is not lawful for them to do aught against the Church. Luke relates that the soldiers came to John to be baptized, asking him, "Master, what must we do?" And he said unto them, "Extort from no man by violence, neither accuse anyone wrongfully, and be content with your wages."[12] A faithful saying worthy of all acceptance, and befitting the forerunner of grace, the herald of the Truth, the precursor of the Lord. For he knew that the military arm is only too prone to commit outrages, is practiced and hardened in rapine, and seldom or never is so satisfied with its own that it does not lust after that which belongs to others. Therefore by forbidding extortion he closed the door to outrages, and by excluding false accusations he banished rapine. Also he condemned avarice when he bade each to be content with his own wages. For, as has been said, a soldier is never permitted to be in actual want, since, as long as he is in the service, he is paid the wages of his service, and, after he has been honorably discharged, he is provided from the public funds with land or such other support as his need requires.

NOTES

1. Sextus Julius Frontinus, the Roman governor of Britain (75–78 A.D.). John of Salisbury may be referring to his lost treatise on the theory of military science, *De re militari*.

2. Flavius Vegetius Renatus (4th century A.D.) was long regarded as an essential authority on military tactics, because of his *Epitoma rei militaris*. Vegetius' manual codifies the practices of the Roman legions, yet it was used extensively by John of Salisbury in his discussion of the military arm of the state, was literally translated by Jean de Meun as *L'Art de chevalerie*, and was adapted by Christine de Pisan in *Le livre des fais d'armes et de chevalerie* (1408–9), a work translated in 1489 by William Caxton as *The Boke of Fayttes of Armes and of Chyualrye*. The oath quoted is recorded by Vegetius in Book II, chapter v of his work.

3. Compare Romans xiii (above, p. 162).

4. Hebrews v, 4; compare Knight's Tale, 2406.

5. Luke xxii, 38. Compare Alanus de Insulis, *De arte praedicatoria*, xl ("ad milites"): "External knighthood is a figure for internal knighthood, and without the internal, the external is vain and empty. And just as there are two parts of a man, corporal and spiritual, so there are two swords proper to defense against the various enemies of man: the material, with which injuries are repelled, and the spiritual, with which those things which injure the mind are repelled. Whence it is said, 'behold, here are two swords' (Luke xxii, 38). The knight should gird on the temporal one to keep temporal peace safe from violence, and the internal one, which is the sword of the Word of God, to restore peace to his own breast." Compare the Ceremonial of Ordination, above pp. 169–74, and the spiritual armor defined in Ephesians vi, 11–18.

6. Luke xxii, 52.

7. For example, like Thraso, the *miles gloriosus* in Terence, *Eunuchus*.

8. Psalm cxlix, 6–8.

9. See Psalm cxlix, 9.

10. Psalm cxlix, 5.

11. See Ceremonial of Ordination, above, pp. 169–74.

12. Luke iii, 14.

Ramón Lull:
from *The Book of the Order of Chivalry*

The most important chivalric manual in the late Middle Ages was a fourteenth-century French treatise known as Le livre de l'ordre de chevalerie, *of which numerous copies survive. This manual was probably translated from a Latin version (perhaps a* Liber militiae secularis, *reported but now lost) of* Le libre del orde de cauayleria *(c. 1276) written by the Catalan mystic and missionary, Ramón Lull.*

Lull was born on the island of Majorca c. 1232. He is said to have spent a dissolute youth as a courtier and accomplished troubadour, but he was educated as a knight and became seneschal, in charge of the household of the prince of Majorca. In 1257 he married, but c. 1263 he experienced conversion as the result of a repeated vision of Christ crucified. The rest of his life was dedicated to the conversion of Islam. To this end he learned Arabic, wrote an incredible variety of books and treatises, engaged extensively in missionary disputation with Mohammedans, and pressed for the founding of missionary schools for the teaching of Arabic. A tradition which has recently been questioned holds that in 1314, while preaching against the errors of Mohammedanism outside the walls of Bougie in North Africa, he was stoned to death. His writings—philosophical, encyclopedic, mystical— deal with virtually every area of medieval thought. Over 250 works survive, of which Liber contemplationis, Ars generalis ultima, *and* Arbor scientiae *are considered the most important. Lull's mystical poems are among the best in Catalan. It has recently been demonstrated that the influence of Lullism, the philosophical system expounded in his* Art, *was considerable in fourteenth-century France.*

The Book of the Order of Chivalry treats such matters as the theory of chivalry and the duties expected of the office of chivalry, the inquisition of the bachelor, and the symbolic meanings of the knight's military appurtenances. Perhaps no other contemporary work expresses so clearly the feelings associated with the code to which Chaucer dedicated his Knight. Its continuing popularity is indicated by two fifteenth-century translations into Scots and the faithful translation by William Caxton (1484) which is given here in modernized form.

[The Origins and Purpose of Chivalry]

When charity, loyalty, truth, justice, and verity failed in the world, then cruelty, injury, disloyalty and falseness arose. Therefore there was error and trouble in the world in which God had created man with the intention that He be known, loved, feared, served, and honored by man. When the world had fallen into wickedness, it was through fear that justice first returned to the honor which had been customary. And therefore the people were divided into groups of one thousand. And from each thousand was chosen one man who more than all the others was most loyal, most noble in courage, best instructed, and best mannered.[1]

After that they sought for the most fitting animal—the most handsome, most courageous, strongest to bear up in travail, and best able to serve this man. And they found that the horse was the most noble and most fitting to serve him. And because men chose the horse above all the other beasts and gave him to the man chosen among a thousand, that man is named after the horse, which is called *cheval* in French, a *chevalier*, which in English is a *knight*. Thus to the most noble man was given the most noble beast. After this it was most proper that there should be chosen such arms as be most noble, and most fitting for battle and to protect this man from death. And these arms were assigned and given to the knight.

Whoever wishes to enter into the order of chivalry, therefore, must remember the noble origin of chivalry. It is incumbent upon him that the nobility of his heart and his good behavior accord with the origin of chivalry. If he did not do so, he would behave contrary to his order and its origins. Therefore it is not proper for the order of chivalry to grant honors to its enemies, or to them who act contrary to its origins. And therefore the knight should be loved and feared by the people because of his noble heart, and his noble behavior and bounty, and the great and high honor granted him by his election, and because of his horse and his arms. Through love he should restore charity and learning, and through fear he should restore verity and justice.

Insofar as a man has more reason and understanding and has a stronger nature than a woman's, to that degree is he better than a woman. For if he were not more powerful and differently endowed to be better than the woman, it would follow that the bounty and strength of nature were not given to provide for a bountiful heart and for good works. But just as a man by his nature is created so as to have a noble heart and to be better than the woman, so he has a greater capacity for vice than a woman has. If this were not so, he would not be worthy of his greater capacity to be good. . . .

You, O Squire, who wish to enter into the order of chivalry, be careful what you do. For when you become a knight you will receive the honor and the service that must be accorded to the friends of chivalry. And insofar as you will have a more noble origin and more honor, so much more are you sworn and bound to be good and pleasing to God, and also to the people. And if you are wicked, you are an enemy of chivalry, and contrary to its commandments and honors.

So high and noble is the order of chivalry that it is not enough that knights be chosen as the most noble persons, nor that they should be given the best and most noble beast and the best and most noble arms. It is fitting and necessary that he be made lord over many men. For in lordship is as much nobility as in servitude there is subjection. So if you enter the order of knighthood, and are a vile and wicked man, you will do great injury to all your subjects and to all your peers who are good. Because of your baseness and wickedness you should be put under a serf or bondman. And considering the nobility of knights who are good, you will be unworthy to be called a knight.

Neither election, nor horse, nor armor, nor authority yet suffice for the high honor which is proper for a knight, but he should also be given a squire and a servant who can care for his horse.[2] And it is also proper that the common people work the land to bring forth fruits and goods to sustain the knight and his beasts, and that the knight rest and dwell in keeping with his nobility, and that he exercise upon his horse either by hunting or in other ways that may please him, and that he find ease and delight in things which his men provide with labor and pain.

Clerks study doctrine and knowledge to learn how to know God and love Him in order to teach the lay and bestial people by good examples how to know, love, serve, and honor God, our glorious Lord. And so that they may do these things in a proper manner, they attend the schools. Then just as clerks, by their honest life, by good example, and by learning, have achieved their status and office to direct the people to devotion and a good life, so likewise knights, by their noble hearts and by force of arms, maintain the order of chivalry, and hold this order so that the common people may be deterred, by fear, from doing wrong to one another.

As for the school and learning of the order of chivalry, the knight should have his son learn to ride in his youth, for if he does not learn when young he will not learn how in his old age. And the son of a knight, during the time he is a squire, should learn to take care of horses. And it is proper that he first serve and be subject before he become a lord. Otherwise he would not understand the nobility of his authority when he became a knight. And therefore every man who aspires to knighthood should learn in his youth to carve at the table,[3] to serve, to arm, and to equip a knight. . . .

So high and so honored is the order of chivalry that it is not enough that he care for horses, and learn to serve a knight, and go with him to tourneys and battles, but it is necessary that a school of the order of knighthood be held for him, and that the science be written in books, and that the art be demonstrated and read in the way other arts are read.[4] The sons of knights should learn first the science that pertains to the order of chivalry, and after they become squires they should ride through divers countries with the knights.

If clerks and knights were without error, there should hardly be any in other people. For from the clerks they should learn devotion and the love of God, and because of the knights they should fear to commit wrong, treason, or strife with one another.

NOTES

1. This idea of "election" was widespread. Isidore of Seville's *Etymologiae* IX, iii, 32, reports: "The knight [*miles*] is so called because he is one elected from a thousand [*mille*]."
2. Chaucer's Knight is thus properly attended.
3. See General Prologue, 100. This detail is a French addition to Lull.
4. This treatise is presented as a book to be read in the "school of chivalry."

[The Office of Knighthood]

The office of a knight is defined by the end and purpose for which the order of chivalry was instituted. . . .

The office of a knight is to maintain and defend the holy Catholic faith, according to which God the Father sent His Son into the world, who took upon Himself the flesh of man in the glorious Virgin, our lady Saint Mary, and who in this world suffered many labors, despites, and painful death, to bring honor to the faith and to multiply it.[1] So just as our Lord God has chosen clerks to maintain the holy Catholic faith against unbelievers, with Scripture and reasoning, just so the God of glory has chosen knights to vanquish the unbelievers who labor daily to destroy Holy Church, with the force of their arms. Such knights [who so defend the Catholic faith] God regards as His honored friends in this world, and also in the other world, when they maintain the faith by which we expect to be saved. . . .

The emperor ought to be a knight and the lord of all knights, but because the emperor may not govern all knights by himself, he should have under him kings who are knights, so that they may help to uphold the order[2] of chivalry. And the kings should have under them dukes, earls, viscounts, and other lords.[3] And under these barons there should be knights. . . .

The office of a knight is to uphold and defend his earthly lord [in the administration of justice]. . . . Justice ought to be upheld and preserved by the knights, for as it is the office of judges to judge, so it is the office of the knights to protect them from violence in their administration of justice. If chivalry and clergy could work together in such a way that knights should be made learned, so that they were sufficient in knowledge to become judges, no office would be better suited to assume judgeship than chivalry. . . .

Knights ought to joust upon their coursers and go to tournaments,[4] to hold open table,[5] to hunt after harts, boars, and other wild beasts, for in doing these things knights exercise themselves for arms, to maintain the order of knighthood. So, to undervalue or to abandon the manner in which a knight can best serve his office amounts to despising the order. And just as all these matters refer to a knight with respect to his body, so justice, wisdom, charity, loyalty, truth, humility, strength, hope, swiftness, and all other similar virtues refer to a knight with respect to his soul. And therefore the knight who practices those things which pertain to chivalry with respect to the body, but has none of the virtues which pertain to chivalry with respect to his soul, is not a friend of the order of chivalry. . . .

The office of a knight is to govern the land, for because of the dread which the common people have of knights, they labor and cultivate the earth, for fear lest they be destroyed.[6] And because of their dread of the knights, they fear the kings, princes, and lords, from whom knights receive their power. But the wicked knight who does not aid his earthly lord and native country against another prince is a knight without office, and is like faith without works,[7] or heresy which is against the faith. . . .

Nothing is so pleasing to chivalry as the noble heart, and no man may more honor and love chivalry, nor do more for it, than he who dies for the love of the order of chivalry, to honor it.

Chivalry and courage may not exist together without reason and discretion. If folly and ignorance were acceptable to it, then reason and discretion would be contrary to the order of chivalry, and that is impossible. By this is openly signified to you, O knight, that you have great love for the order of chivalry. For just as chivalry by nobility of heart has endowed you with bravery, so that you fear no peril nor death because you wish to honor chivalry: just so it is appropriate that chivalry endow you with a love of wisdom with which to love and honor the order of chivalry, standing against the disorder and default in those who think to follow the order of chivalry in folly and ignorance and without understanding.

The office of a knight is to uphold and defend women, widows and orphans, and men who are in distress and not strong. . . . So to wrong or to oppress women, widows who are in need of aid, and orphans in need of guidance, or to rob and destroy the weak who have need of strength, and to take away from them what they have been given—these acts are not in accordance with the order of chivalry. For this is wickedness, cruelty, and tyranny; and when a knight is full of such vices, both he and his order are contrary to loyalty, and to justice, and especially to the nobility of chivalry.

Just as God has given eyes to artisans so that they may see to work, so He has given eyes to sinners so that they may weep for their sins. And just as God has given the knight a noble heart to make him brave, so he ought also to have mercy in his heart. His heart should be inclined to the works of compassion and pity: that is, to help and aid all those who, weeping, request aid and mercy of the knights, and who place their hope in them. . . .[8]

The office of a knight is to have a castle and horses with which to protect the ways and to defend those who work the lands. . . .

The office of a knight is to search out thieves, robbers and other wicked folk, and to bring them to punishment. . . .

Because God and chivalry are in concord, those who uphold the order of chivalry should not engage in false swearing and untrue oaths.[9] And if lechery could agree with justice, then chivalry, which is founded on justice, would agree with lechery. And if lechery were proper for chivalry, chastity, which is contrary to lechery, would be contrary to the honor of chivalry. . . . [But] lechery and justice are contrary, and chivalry is ordained in order to maintain justice.[10]

NOTES

1. Christ was often thought of as the prototype of the Christian knight. See, e.g., Apocalypse xix, 11–16.
2. "Ordre" in the sense of Latin *ordo* (status, rank).
3. Fr.: "Counts, Viscounts, Dukes, Princes, and Vavasors [or Barons]." Caxton regards all these ranks as "barons."
4. General Prologue, 96. The Squire's other accomplishments, except perhaps his "horsemanship," are not recommended in this manual, though they are recommended for lovers by the God of Love in the *Roman de la rose* 2051–534.
5. See General Prologue, 339–54. The Franklin, a pretender to the chivalric estate, observes only this aspect of the rule, and that extravagantly.
6. The Third Estate was conventionally typified by *cultores*, or "plowmen."
7. James ii, 20.
8. In Knight's Tale, 893–974, Theseus does just this, responding as well to the chivalric duty to aid widows. This passage in Lull goes on to relate mercy to the "eyes of the heart," which see the needs of the unfortunate.
9. This is the virtue of "trouthe," as in General Prologue, 46. The idea is rudely tested in Franklin's Tale, 1479.
10. An important and repeated view in the literature of chivalry, which has profound implications for "courtly lovers" who are knights or squires. See below, pp. 271ff.

Honoré Bonet:
from *The Tree of Battles*

*As members of the feudal system, medieval knights and their lords were
subject to a kind of international military law. The most famous compila-
tion of this code was the* De bello, de represaliis, et de duello *("On War,
Reprisals, and the Duel"), published in 1360 by the respected Bolognese
legist John of Legano (see Clerk's Prologue, 34–35). This treatise, highly
regarded by jurists, was the major source for the* Arbre des Batailles *by Hon-
oré Bonet (1387), a work which brought the code to the layman by pre-
senting it in a less formal manner and in the vulgar tongue. Copies have
been found in libraries in France, Burgundy, England, and Spain.*

*Honoré Bonet was born in Provence c. 1340. Educated for the Church,
by 1382 he had been ordained, had taken his vows as a Benedictine monk,
and had assumed the Priorate of Salon. He became attached to the Univer-
sity of Avignon, from which he was awarded the degree of Doctor of
Decretals in 1386. The Tree of Battles, issued in 1387, was dedicated to
King Charles VI of France. After 1390 Bonet performed various admin-
istrative and ambassadorial duties for the royal court, moving in the com-
pany of knights and lords, and observing first-hand the results of war and
unjust administration. In 1394 he wrotè* Somnium super materie schismatis
*("Dream of the Matter of Schism") dealing with the politics connected
with the Great Schism.*

*The code compiled by John of Legnano and popularized by Honoré
Bonet is based primarily on the Canon Law contained in the Decretals of
the Church, and represents a juridical solution to the dilemma raised by the
Church's need for a military arm which necessarily conflicted with the
Commandment against killing, God's own Law. The argument, basically,
sanctifies violence in the cause of God's justice; the code seeks to regulate,
by a kind of elaborate etiquette, the brutality inherent in time of war, and*

Trans. G. W. Coopland, The Tree of Battles of Honoré Bonet (*Liverpool at the
University Press, 1949), pp. 121, 131, 156, 158–59. Reprinted by permission of
Liverpool University Press.*

stresses the high moral obligations of knighthood. Bonet wrote the Tree of Battles, he says, because the schism threatened the Church's existence unless God and the King of France could resolve the issue, and because all Christendom was "so burdened by wars and hatreds, robberies and dissensions, that it is hard to name one little region, be it duchy or county, that enjoys good peace."

The Tree of Battles *speaks of such matters as the definition of war, provides ancient history, examines feudal rights and obligations, defines the law regarding virtually any circumstance that could arise in military service or actual battle, and describes the rules regarding trial-by-combat (of which he disapproves). Bonet's effort to reach the secular arm of the state seems to have borne fruit. Not only do the libraries of nobles contain this work; his book was extracted in Christine de Pisan's* Livre des fais d'armes et de chevalerie *("Feats of Arms and Chivalry") and in the* Boke of Noblesse *(attributed to William Worcester) in England.*

The following excerpts illustrate the moral character officially expected of the knight under this code. The last examines the specific problem faced by Palamon in Theseus' prison, in the Knight's Tale.

[Laws of Chivalry]

FROM PART IV
Chapter viii. *The duties of a good knight*

Now we must see what are the qualities of all good knights, and what their duties are.

And I tell you that the first and principal thing is that they should keep the oath which they have made to their lord to whom they belong, and to whom they have sworn and promised to do all that he shall command for the defence of his land, according to what is laid down by the laws. He is no true knight who, for fear of death, or of what might befall, fails to defend the land of his lord, but in truth he is a traitor and forsworn. A knight must be obedient to him who is acting in place of his lord as governor of the host, and if he is not obedient to him he is no good knight but is overbearing and insolent. And knights, especially those who are in the king's service, or in a lord's, should in thought and deed be occupied only with the practice of arms, and with campaigning for the honour of their lord, and for his peace, as says the law. They must always carry out the orders of him who takes the place and guards the interests of their lord, and if a knight acts contrary to such command he must lose his head.

Further, the laws say that a knight must not till the soil, or tend vines, or keep beasts, that is to say, be a shepherd, or be a matchmaker, or lawyer; otherwise he must lose knighthood and the privileges of a knight. And he should never, if he is a paid soldier, buy land or vineyards while he is in service, and what he does buy must belong to his lord. If you wish to know why this was so ordained, I tell you that it was that knights should have no cause to leave arms for desire of acquiring worldly riches.

Chapter lii. *If a knight happen to die in battle do we say that his soul is saved?*

I ask now whether the soul of a knight killed in battle is saved. It would appear not, for according to one opinion a knight cannot follow arms and war without sin. Further, if a knight die in battle he must not be buried in sacred ground, such as a church or cemetery. The chief reason on which we base this supposition or opinion is that any mortal man who is killed while in anger or evil intention is held to have died in mortal sin, and we may consider this knight to be in such state.

Notwithstanding this argument I will draw three conclusions. The first is: if a knight die in war ordained by the Church, as in the case of war against the unbelievers or the enemies of the Pope or of the Faith, and is not otherwise in mortal sin, his soul goes forthwith to Paradise, for thus the decree stands. The second conclusion is: that if a soldier die in battle in a just war and to maintain a just quarrel, he, similarly, will be saved in Paradise. The third conclusion is: if he die or be killed in unjust warfare he is in the way of damnation, for we hold according to our Faith that the souls of those who die in mortal sin go to hell.

Chapter lv. *If one knight is in the prison of another who keeps him shut up in a strong tower may he without acting against reason break prison and go?*

Now I ask your consideration of another matter which may commonly arise in case of war. A knight has captured another knight, his enemy, and has thrust him into a strong prison in his castle. I ask whether, if an opportunity present itself to escape by stratagem or subtlety, the prisoner may break prison, and his captor's arrest, without acting against reason?

It would appear that he cannot, and that this is so I prove forthwith. It is quite certain that he is bound to be in his captor's mercy, according to law; then, since law decrees this and has ordained it, why should he escape? Again, we say, according to Scripture, that we must not do to another what we would not wish done to ourselves. And no man on earth would wish that his prisoner should break his arrest. Hence the prisoner must not break prison, for his captor is his master until the ransom due or agreed is paid. Further, according to written law, when a man has pledged his faith to his enemy he is bound to keep it; and if this is so, how can he go without forswearing his faith and his oath and without incurring great guilt?

On the other hand I might bring forward reasons against what has been said above. It is beyond argument that every man desires to have his liberty and freedom, for liberty comes of the law of nature, and we assert that natural law is at all times good and just. So, if he goes, he acts according to the law of nature, and offends in no point. Again, we say that a promise or obligation made under force or violence is null. But it is common knowledge that when the prisoner surrendered and pledged his faith he did it under force or violence. Hence I say that he may go and may break his arrest.

To cut this discussion short and to avoid a long story, I say that, in my opinion, if it happens that a knight is imprisoned and has given his faith to submit to arrest or prison, and takes his oath accordingly, then if he cannot depart without agreement with his master, and without obtaining leave, he offends against our Lord God and against man. This is on the assumption, however, that his master does not use any extraordinary harshness towards him; for if he were kept in such close imprisonment that he was in danger of falling into languor, or mortal sickness, or any grievous ill of body, and for that reason took his opportunity to escape, he would commit no offence. Again, if his master refused to accept due and reasonable ransom, in keeping with the prisoner's estate, goods, and riches, and if it seemed plain that he was asking ransom beyond his condition, then the prisoner would commit no offence if he took himself off, since, within the limits of his ability, he had offered reasonable ransom. And if his master were so cruel as to be in the habit of killing or causing the death of his prisoners in his prisons, and if, on opportunity arising, he quitted such a host, I would blame him not at all, for commonly a man fears for his own house when he sees his neighbour's burning. I mention another possibility. In the case of a master so fierce and hard that he was not in the habit of putting his prisoners to ransom, but in preference inflicted death on them in his prisons, if the prisoner escaped when he could, he would act well and wisely. If the master were not a man of this kind, and did nothing unfitting, I hold that, notwithstanding the reasons urged above on the other side, according to right he would break faith if he went off without his master's leave, and would be accounted perjured if he had taken his oath to remain a prisoner.

John Gower:
from *Vox clamantis*

Chaucer's dedication of Troilus and Criseyde (c. 1386) publicly affirmed his respect for John Gower:

> O moral Gower, this book I directe
> To the and to the, philosophical Strode,
> To vauchen sauf, ther nede is, to correcte,
> Of youre benignities and zeles gode. (V, 1856–59)

There is much to recommend the tradition that Gower and Chaucer were personal friends. After 1377 Gower lived in the Priory of St. Mary Overy, on the south side of London Bridge in Southwark, close to the Tabard Inn, where we can imagine them, together with Ralph Strode and other legal and literary acquaintances, discussing poetry and the reign of Richard II. In 1378 Chaucer gave Gower a power-of-attorney during his trip to Italy. The first version of Gower's Confessio Amantis (1390) complements Chaucer as a love poet—although he makes Venus the speaker. Venus requests that he "make his testament of love" as Gower has done (Confessio, VIII, 2941–57). Some critics feel that Gower deleted this passage in his 1393 recension because Chaucer, in the Introduction to the Man of Law's Tale, 77–89, had characterized as "abhomynacions" tales Gower related in the Confession. These are the story of Canace and Macareus (Confessio, III, 143–360) and that of Apollonius of Tyre (Confessio, VIII, 271–2008), both involving incest.

After Chaucer, John Gower (1330–1408) was for several centuries the most highly praised English author of his time. Before moving to Southwark he was a wealthy "purchasour" of lands, probably a lawyer, living in Kent. He seems to have known Richard II, although from 1393 onwards he became disenchanted with his reign and supported Henry of Lancaster,

Trans. Eric W. Stockton, The Major Latin Works of John Gower (Seattle: University of Washington Press, 1962), pp. 196–208. Reprinted by permission of University of Washington Press.

later Henry IV. Royal grants to Gower in 1399 and 1400 indicate a better relationship with the Crown than that enjoyed by Chaucer, whose "Complaint to his Purse" is often interpreted as a plea to Henry for funds. As a writer Gower was industrious, conservative, and trilingual. He became blind in 1400.

Gower's earliest work, Cinkante balades *(there are actually 52), is composed of light, conventional love lyrics in the French fashion. In line 27340 of his next work, the* Mirour de l'omme *("The Mirror of Man"), he referred to them as foolish love-songs, the "fols ditz d'amour" of his youth. The* Mirour, *or* Speculum hominis *(1378), a mammoth French poem of over 30,000 lines, is a combination of a penitential manual treating the seven deadly sins and their opposing virtues, an extended complaint against the three Estates of society, and a life of the Virgin. This was followed (c. 1386) by the* Vox clamantis *("The Voice of One Crying"), which in 10,265 lines describes a dream-vision of the Peasant's Rebellion (1381) and proceeds to picture social corruption under Richard by cataloguing conventional "complaints" against the Estates. The title of this work in Anglo-Latin is taken from Isaias xl, 3: "The voice of him that crieth in the wilderness," i.e., in England. The first version of his English poem,* Confessio Amantis *("The Lover's Confession," 1390), was dedicated to Richard II, but in the 1393 version Henry received the honor. Gower, who was sixty when the poem was published, plays the part of a woeful Lover who is made by Venus to "confess" to her priest, Genius—a character drawn from the* Roman de la rose. *In 34,000 lines the Lover learns about the seven deadly sins and the three Estates through a huge collection of* exempla *designed to help him recognize his cupidity. At the end, Venus releases him, and he returns to his books. In 1397, at about the time he was himself married, he wrote the* Traitié pour essampler les amantz *("Examples of Married Lovers"), a series of poems on the virtue of married love which are added in some manuscripts to the* Confessio. *Finally, about 1400 Gower completed the* Cronica tripartita *("Tripartite Chronicle"), a poetic account of the deposition of Richard II and Henry IV's assumption of the crown. Its 1,062 lines cover the years 1387–99. Gower appended it to the* Vox clamantis *in its final form. Though distorted by political bias, it is interesting as a contemporary document expressing attitudes of at least one political faction.*

The present text, drawn from the Vox clamantis, *stresses the often-repeated view that the greatest enemy of chivalry was lechery. Gower mentions vainglory, avarice, and woman-service, but stresses the last. His combination of conventional topics is interesting, for as he passes from praise of the good woman (most knights were expected to marry), we encounter a full-fledged antifeminist tirade. This, along with the* De amore *of Andreas Capellanus, is one of the clearest indications of a medieval connection between Antifeminism and Courtly Love.*

[Complaint against Chivalry]

V, 1. [THE AUTHOR WILL NOW] SPEAK OF THOSE IN THE ESTATE OF KNIGHTHOOD, WHO ARE UNDER OBLIGA TION TO ASSIST AND UPHOLD TEMPORAL AFFAIRS.

I shall speak . . . of how the knights' ancient order used to be appro priate for them. In the beginning, knighthood was endowed with great honor. It was first established for three reasons: first, it is to protect the rights of the Church; second, it fosters the common good; third, it is to uphold the right of the needy orphan and defend the widow's cause with its power. In such ways does the law will that the knight in arms be ever ready to enter into battle. Indeed, not long ago the knight did conquer his enemies in such fashion, for which reason his fame in the world lives on. A knight did not bear arms for fame, however, but instead performed his deeds for the sake of justice. The worthy knight who preserves the order's way of life ought to receive due praise for it. But if a knight makes war for the sake of vain praise, his praise is un warranted, if it is granted under such a circumstance.

Now tell me . . . : what honor shall a conqueror have if a woman's love can conquer him? I don't know what the world will reply to me about that. I do know he will have no praise from Christ. If a man wishes to enjoy honor, let him protect his honor, and let him perform the work that his responsibility urges upon him. The end will bring nothing but inevitable folly upon the man for whom Venus initially leads the way to arms. It is not right that lead be mixed with shining gold, nor that Venus prescribe the deeds of a doughty knight. A woman does not often release a man whom she has ensnared so that he may escape. Instead, she envelops him with her silly love. The man who is once free and subjugates himself voluntarily ought to be reckoned more idiotic than an idiot. It is practical for a knight to avoid battles in which he might be made captive, when he cannot win. It is not for the wise man to enter a ford in which he could be drowned, but rather to check his course away from the destruction, once he has seen it.

V, 2. *HERE HE SPEAKS OF HOW THE KNIGHT WHO EN-*
GAGES IN THE USE OF ARMS WHEN HE IS BURNING
WITH LUST FOR A WOMAN'S AFFECTION CERTAINLY
DOES NOT DESERVE THE HONOR OF PRAISE FOR IT AT
ALL. HE ALSO DESCRIBES THE INCONSTANCIES OF SUCH
LOVE, THE PASSIONS OF WHICH ARE HIGHLY AT VARI-
ANCE WITH EACH OTHER, BECAUSE OF THEIR MIXED
EMOTIONS.[1]

O, if a knight were to think of the ways of love, which are changed so suddenly, he would not suffer them. Love is not of one hue, but is conflicting within itself; it tempers its vicissitudes intemperately. Love conceals and reveals, disunites and reunites, and often drives happy hearts mad with grief. Love is an unjust judge; marrying opposites, it makes the very natures of things deteriorate. In love, discord is harmonious, learning is ignorant, anger makes jests, honor is base, a poor man has plenty, joys grieve, praise reproves, despair hopes, hope is afraid, harms are helpful, assets are harmful. In love, anguish is tasteful, bitterness becomes sweet, winter is springlike, chills perspire, sickness is strengthening. So take greater heed, knight, of the dangers you see. Read what forms love's sickness takes.

Love is sickly health, troubled rest, pious sin, warlike peace, a pleasant wound, a delightful calamity, anxious happiness, a devious path, dark light, gentle harshness, a light lump of lead, both a flowery winter and a withered, flowerless spring, a thorny rose, a capricious law without justice, weeping laughter, laughing lamentation, intemperate temperance, a hostile ally and a gracious enemy, fickle constancy, a wish opposed to itself, hope despairing of itself, doubting faith, black whiteness, bright blackness, bitter honey, delicious gall, a prison offering pleasures, irrational reason, foolish discretion, an untrustworthy judge, an ignorant person reflecting upon everything, food never digestible and drink ever thirsty, an insatiable mental hunger, a living death, a dying life, harmonious discord, a garrulous mind, mute speech, a secret fever, poor prosperity, prosperous poverty, a slavish prince, a subject queen and a destitute king, drunken sobriety, demented clemency, the port of Scylla, a pestilential cure, a way of health; love is a delightful serpent, a ferocious lamb, a gentle lion, a timid hawk and a rapacious dove, a fatuous school turning out an even more fatuous pupil, whose mind applies itself the more diligently as a result.

V, 3. *HERE HE DESCRIBES THE BEAUTY OF A COMELY WOMAN, FOR LUST OF WHOM KNIGHTS' HEARTS ARE ENSNARED AND VERY OFTEN LEFT DESTITUTE OF RATIONAL JUDGMENT.*

When the trembling lover admires a woman endowed with radiant beauty, the blush of the rose is in her face.[2] [He admires her] golden hair, her well-shaped ears, the smoothness of her brow which is gleaming white, her youthful cheeks, her eyes which shine like the sun and which a well-composed countenance graces, her straight nose and delicately opened nostrils, her honeyed lips—and the breath of her mouth is sweet—her even teeth, whiter than milk, and the beauty of her mind, which is in keeping with her. The radiance from her face brightens her ivory neck,[3] together with her throat of crystal; and the luster of her breast glistens whiter than snow, as if two dazzling apples were affixed to it.

He beholds her long arms, just the least bit roundly plump, and he thinks their embrace is a heavenly kingdom. And he sees her hands and bejewelled fingers glitter—no soft wool is softer than they. He perceives her youthful shoulders, unaccustomed to burdens; no boniness shows in them, so he marvels at them the more. From aside he sees her extend her graceful figure, and no line is straighter than she. He observes her steps treading in the dance and notes the measure of her paces. The singing sirens compare not at all with her voice, and the voice of an angel sounds scarcely like hers.

And he sees her head encircled and glittering with jewels, and the splendor of her clothes, which are highly becoming to her. She approaches, decked out beyond measure, and wishes to appear beautiful, so that her lover may be more than half carried away with wonder. All her limbs seem to be in such array that God [must] have fashioned that handiwork in heaven. Delightful are the part in her hair, her serene brow, her milk-white neck, her mouth, her little lips, her blush, and the bright light of her eyes. Beautiful are the crown of her head, her brow, eyes, nose, teeth, mouth, cheeks, chin, neck, hands, breast, and perfect foot.[4] The girl's beauty transcends humankind; she possesses a kind of divinity which surpasses the race of man.[5] Fortunate above all others whom grace of form adorns, she becomes a phoenix without peer.[6] Splendid is her raiment, her head bound round with flowers, and a modest blush encompasses her pink cheeks.[7] Her figure pleases, and her snowy hue and flaxen hair; and her sparkling grace is artlessly achieved.[8] A man scarcely glances at her without being charmed by her to the point that, kneeling on the ground, he would offer his devotion. If she shows regard for the lover with her countenance, the man stands transfixed before her open eyes.

When a man sees her womanly beauty—so sweet, elegant and fine, but more like an angel's—he thinks her a goddess, and puts his fate of life and death in her hands. As he turns such marvellous beauty over in his mind, having been turned by it, he withdraws without turning around. Outwardly, he does not show what the sight of her means to him; inwardly, the sting of love pierces his heart. He stands motionless as a stone and does not move from her sight, as if he were in a trance. His mind's eye grows dull, blind from the darkness of lust, and he sinks down to his own destruction. He does not know what he sees, but he is consumed with what he sees. So he goes blindly mad because of his blind love. Colder than ice and hotter than burning fire, he both freezes with fire and burns with cold.[9] Just as a bird envelops itself with birdlime by rolling about in it,[10] so does he grow the more ardent with love while defending himself against it.

Thus love conquers everything[11]—whatever nature has created—yet love itself remains unconquered throughout everything. It imprisons and sets free, it fetters and unfetters, it subjugates everything to itself yet is unrestricted to all. It constrains and appeases nature, it undermines and rebuilds it. And nature grieves because of love, yet is joyless without it. It militates against everyone; its rule excepts scarcely anyone, for it often causes even saintly people to be sinful. There is no one who can calmly go against its laws, but love itself bears everything calmly. Discretion fails the man whom virtue could not fail, and no man alive is safe in going against these things. Love with its pains[12] is not equal to the pain of retaliation. Love wounds the whole human race, but suffers no wound itself. So when love is brandishing its piercing dart, fly a safe distance away from it. There are no arms which prevail in combat with love, nor does anyone have a treaty of lasting peace with it.

Love is a trusting thing, suddenly smitten with grief,[13] and the beginner does not know what end there will be for him. The knight does not lack for a battle who says within himself, "O how I keep silent, even while knowing that love burns me!"[14] The lover's mind is stirred in countless ways, as a rock is struck on every side by the waters of the sea.[15] One of noble birth [may] lie prostrate under the effects of love and often recover,[16] yet more often he does not know what the noble course of action should be. Continually shifting into uncertainties in his imagination, love now lifts up the inner heart and now agitates it. Thus does blind love lead blind, foolish lovers,[17] so that no lover sees what is proper for himself. Tell me, what does not dare to rush into the madness of love? When one longs for embraces, he knows nothing of which he is afraid. He doesn't see the leaf for the trees, nor the grass for the open field, nor the waters for the brimming river.[18] Instead he brings profits and losses upon himself as if he were blind, because impulse forces his mind to love. Neither heaven, earth, nor hell, neither sea, sky, nor air can hinder his undertakings by force. He will often lie freezing on the bare ground, suffering the heavy rain sent from a cloud in the sky.[19] Night and winter, long journeys and bitter sorrows are the rewards love offers foolish lovers.[20] There are as many sorrows in love as the groans you make; its madness and pity are equal on this earth. The lover feels his injuries but nevertheless fervently assists in them, and pursues the source of his suffering.

Alas, that love is not curable by any herbs![21] Neither brawn nor brain can escape its burden. No one can avoid this innate disease, unless it be that divine grace alone watch over him. O how grievous is the nature of man! Driven to his own destruction by it, it forces him to love. O the nature of man, which no one could bear! It does not even absolve him from the evil which it commits itself. O the nature of man, which contains a mixture of two opposites, yet does not allow him to follow the promptings of both! Lust of the flesh wages battles with chastity; what the body wants, the spirit forbids. O the nature of man, which is fashioned in such a way, and cannot shun that which ought not to be done![22] O the nature of man, which frustrates the feeble power of reason, and possesses wickedness like a beast's! Arts are of no help; the wound rages incurable.[23] The wiser a man is, the madder he becomes as a result. And if anyone should wish to curb his passion,[24] let him provide a means before he falls. In the meantime, until the seas grow calm and until love moderate its ways,[25] one should seize upon his salvation. You will conquer if you shun love, and you will be conquered if you resist it. Lest you be conquered like a lion, you must flee like a hare.[26] Nor does a woman escape the flames of love or its sharp arrows.[27] The weaker she is, the keener will be her passion. Just as a woman deceives men, so does a man deceive women, for love, foxlike, sings with the words of a wolf. To beguile a trusting girl is not a praiseworthy honor,[28] but a deed of character. No art of man is more subtle than Venus'; by her art love long continues to demand its rights.[29]

V, 4. HERE HE SAYS THAT WHEN LUSTFUL LOVE FOR WOMEN DOMINATES A KNIGHT, IT VERITABLY EXTINGUISHES ALL CHIVALROUS VIRTUE IN HIM.

A knight does not rightly have to fear a bodily wound, since he should receive the world's praises for it. But he should fear the wounds of the spirit, which blind, incurable lust inflicts with fiery darts. Bodily wounds are to be healed, but not even Galen will make a man well who is sick with love.[30] If the knight holds with womanish behavior, his honor dies, bereft of his noble lineage. When a wise knight falls, his fame forsakes him, as though he were fatuous and foolish. When carnal love holds the mind ensnared, an intelligent man's reason becomes irrational. When the brightness of human intelligence is clouded over by the shadow of the flesh, and the spirit of reason withdraws into the flesh, man's reason stands utterly scorned. It is a slave to the flesh, and scarcely retains the post of handmaiden.

Nevertheless, blind love does not weigh equally in the balance for all men, nor deal out appropriate rewards to all. It often drives trustworthy people out of office for no reason and puts unreliable ones in their place. It will refuse me a gift even when I deserve it, which it will give to you without a trace of deservedness. Love blindly imposes its obligations upon men, just as if you were to have to recognize different colors in the dark.[31] But almost every knight is a slave to love now, and waits at its doors to receive his fate.

V, 5. HERE HE SPEAKS OF THOSE KNIGHTS OF WHOM ONE WILL ENGAGE IN FEATS OF ARMS FOR THE SAKE OF A WOMAN'S LOVE AND ANOTHER FOR THE SAKE OF WORLDLY FAME. IN THE END, HOWEVER, BOTH THINGS PASS AWAY IN VAIN, WITHOUT THE REWARD OF DIVINE COMMENDATION.

One part of the knightly estate seeks after woman's love, and another, what the world's lofty praise may extol to it. Everywhere the knight aspires to and tries for new favor so that he may have fame. But God knows by what right he desires honor, if the world or woman's love will bestow it. If he wishes worldly praise, then he pours out the wealth of Croesus in order that his lofty praises may be sounded, because of his gifts. Then he sows gold, clothes, gems, and horses like grain, in order that a crop of praises may grow in his ear. But if a knight chooses a woman's love for himself, then will he pay for it more dearly than with his wealth. He will give up so many good things for it—his body, his soul, his property, everything that Nature or God has imparted to him. Nevertheless, when he shall have done with his troublesome doings, yet at the same time every fickle compliment deceives him; and when neither the prattling talk of the world reaches his ears nor virtuous love bestows its treasures upon him, then the dupe will say, "Alas, how wicked Fortune is! For all my labor turns out fruitless after such a long time." The man who laments for himself in this foolish way is too late, for he himself is the cause of his suffering, and not another.

The world brings heavy burdens, but woman brings heavier ones. It moves along, while she rushes; it buffets, while she kills. When a knight thinks he has vanquished a woman's power, and with tender affection she grants everything he has asked, then he himself is thoroughly defeated, just when he thinks he is thoroughly victorious, and the conquered woman reconquers him. And even if the knight chooses worldly fame, surely it passes away vainly in a short time.

O why does a knight whose worldly honor remains without God's esteem seek such honors for himself? Why does he believe that the words of the prattling mob are an honor, and wish to possess them at the price of death? Then, too, he fears nothing when he is overcome by a woman, whereby he, guilty before God, loses a wealth of honor. So why does a knight's undaunted courage wish in vain for things which are senseless? His praises are sung in vain, unless God is the author of them. And that honor which is noised about apart from God is a disgrace. A knight is eager for any kind of praise or honor, when God knows he is unworthy of it.

V, 6. HERE HE SPEAKS FOR THE MOMENT IN COMMEN-
DATION OF THE GOOD WOMAN: TRIED AND TRUE VIR-
TUE OF HER SORT TRANSCENDS ALL EARTHLY DE-
LIGHTS. HE ALSO SPEAKS OF THE BAD WOMAN, WHOSE
WILES A WISE MAN CAN HARDLY RESIST.[32]

There was one woman through whom God on high came down, and was made flesh of her flesh. Because of her honor, there are those most praiseworthy women to whom the honor of praise ought deservedly be paid. All good things come from a good woman, whose chaste love provides love's riches. A good woman is worth more than silver or gold; no fit value can be set upon her. Tongue cannot recite nor pen describe the worth of her whom utter goodness properly distinguishes. Her noble husband dwells revered within his gates, and her household contains all that is good. Her servants are fittted out with garments which her hand, busy in its activities, fashions of double strength. No idleness attempts to run through her thoughts; womanly modesty effectively protects them at all times. For her merits, such a good woman should receive everlasting praise which no wicked, gossiping tongue can take away.[33]

The woman who has acted just the opposite, however, does not thereby dishonor the others who are good. Although we may be speaking of a foolish man, his actions are nothing to the righteous one, nor do a thief's dishonest crimes involve honest men, but are as nothing to the good. Granted that the reputation of a harlot is inglorious, the woman whom a sense of decency watches over suffers nothing from it. Granted that a harlot is infamous, that shameful woman does not disgrace virtuous women by her own ill repute. One angel is good and another is bad, yet the sin of the bad cannot harm the good one. The reputation of an infamous woman should not injure an honest one, nor have the power to take away her honor. While a foul, noxious weed may mingle with a rose, the rose is not otherwise than it was before.[34] When open guilt makes known its crimes, people cry out that this kind of conduct always has been and always will be just as they now observe it. But let what I may write here always be to the inviolate honor of those whose deeds a sense of honor watches over. Accordingly, what is of concern here [is that] the blame find out blameworthy women, whereby greater praise may be duly bestowed upon the praiseworthy. It is helpful to know of evil, so that we can the more ably avoid it and beware of the slippery course before us.

All evils have usually proceeded from an evil woman; indeed, she is a second plague to men.[35] With her blandishments, a cunning woman gently touches upon a man's evil inclination and breaks down his manly honor. Through her various wiles she destroys his feelings, his riches, his virtues, his strength, his reputation, and his peace. She deceives in a thousand ways and sets a thousand snares in order to catch one man. Such a woman comes adorned with radiant jewels, gold and finery so that she can deceive. Her clothes are well arranged, her rising breast is bound up, and the pattern of her bosom extends her neckline. She adorns her head with tinted hair and veils, and the golden splendor of gems decorates her handiwork. In order to sharpen the eyes of the frenzied man upon herself, there is one ring after another on her fingers. It is not her task to soften wool by spinning it,[36] but to be able to catch men when she is all decked out. A showy woman lets herself be seen by people;[37] perhaps there will be one out of many whom she can allure.

Ah, how many times a lover is inflamed by false words[38] when the cunning tongue of some worthy beauty tempts him! If the woman does not possess pleasing words to incite foolish men, there is charm in her very defect:[39] with hands folded, she emits heavy sighs, and her words do not lack their promised effect. Often a woman sounds somewhat raucous, but she laughs pleasantly,[40] and forces her hesitant tongue to sound with a lisp.[41] What can art not do? She learns to weep becomingly,[42] so that by her look she deceives men whom her talk does not attract. She deludes with her false expression and with tears falling down her cheeks, and she pretends that she can hardly speak. And as often as is necessary the sly mistress falls sick, and outwardly her face suffers with pain. The Sirens were wondrous creatures of the sea, who with melodious voice detained whatever vessels were sent to them.[43] Similarly, one who habitually listens to feminine blandishments cannot safely retreat one foot from his downfall. Just as one hand can paint many figures, and will vary its work in different ways, so one sole woman adds to the number of her various lovers; and Venus forces them to believe in her foolish influence. She alters what Nature has sensibly endowed her with, and her cunning tongue charms with its lispings.[44] Her fluency certainly torments a good many foolish men, as she pleases now by laughing and now by crying. She likewise adorns every part of her delicate body, and adds to the beauty which God gave her. I abhor relating the wickedness of this discourse, which another and more experienced one has previously reported. Rest assured, I am going to repeat verses which the poet Ovid set forth, and the words do not belong to me. . . .

[Omitted is a long catalogue of conventional antifeminist clichés, drawn mainly from Ovid's *Ars amatoria*, III.]

The world is false but woman is falser, for Paradise perceived her to be unfaithful. Behold, the world is a wolf in sheep's clothing; where it first caresses, it finally bites. Yet it at least is outside, but the serpent-like "turtledove"[45] causes harms closer to home, in the very bedchambers. For she is indeed a serpent who deceives through a thousand meanderings and stings peaceful hearts. The man who remains strong and wise after having been struck by her is of heavenly nature, but earth itself cannot prevail against her. Neither the strength of Samson nor the sword of David nor the wisdom of Solomon is of any worth against her. So why does the knight of today try to such an extent to overcome what so many men have not been able to conquer? There is not a man whom past perils make cautious, but instead he falls into the traps he sees. Who would forbid lesser men to adopt examples for their actions from the great? But our [kind of love] does not allow of this. The rash soldier takes up arms and enters the fray, unmindful of his former wound.

V, 7. HERE HE SAYS THAT A PROPERLY CONSTITUTED KNIGHTHOOD IS RESPONSIBLE FOR THE GENERAL ESTABLISHMENT OF SECURITY FOR ALL OTHER CLASSES OF SOCIETY.

O how knighthood stands out in the land as brave and noble, if it behaves well! If he does not labor for worldly praise or gain, and if an untamable lust does not vanquish his heart of steel, then a knight will conquer with the glory of everlasting praise, and his eternal fame will make him renowned.

If knighthood were worthy, God would dwell within it, so that the knight might triumph with his unvanquished sword. If knighthood were worthy, its good repute, which now lies in bed overcome with sleep, would be wide awake. If knighthood were worthy, then the husband would prepare himself for his ventures together with his wife, with peace being restored. If knighthood were worthy, then the Church's enemy would be overthrown by it, and the Church itself would grow in faith. If knighthood were worthy, then the harsh estimate [of it] which is noised about in the land would be of no importance. If knighthood were worthy, then peace, with which all prosperity would return, would not be slow in coming.

The knight who is worthy is ignorant of experiencing fear, nor does he suffer the inner vexations of a lukewarm spirit.[46] The knight who is worthy wipes out all worldly pride and fiercely conquers evil with a humble heart. The knight who is worthy battles in behalf of Christ's name and defends the common cause with his valor. The knight who is worthy knows well and demonstrates that the beginning of peace in the world comes from the ending of war. Whatever esteem his code has in this world, such a knight is deserving of genuine praise.

V, 8. HERE HE TELLS HOW WICKEDNESS ON THE PART OF THE KNIGHTLY ESTATE HARMS AND OFFENDS ALL OTHER CLASSES OF SOCIETY BY ITS UNSEEMLINESS.

If, however, the knight were to bear his arms in just the opposite way, many evil and fearful misfortunes would result. If knighthood is bad, its shield is as nothing, its lance is as nothing, and its hand upon the sword would not shine with honor. If the knight is bad, who in arms will defend us? If he is soft, he will cause hardships for us. If knighthood is bad, what can the cleric and peasant do for themselves when war looms at their doors? If knighthood is bad, then the fierce enemy who ordinarily is law-abiding renews his activities. Thus the good knight who carries our defenses in his hands brings good things, and the bad knight brings on fearful evils. The clean hand strikes blows of wondrous worth, while the one that is stained with its own filth flies from the field. Conscious of himself as he ponders his evil deeds, [the bad knight] hesitates, and his performance is untrustworthy because of his wavering spirit. Feats of arms thrive upon good morals; otherwise, good fortune vanishes. No virtue endures for long in company with vices.

Therefore, knight, be zealous for virtues. And resist vices, O warrior, and strongly cherish your public duties. To conquer all the hosts of the earth is not a bit to my advantage so long as I am conquered, defenseless, by a single vice. And what is not more severely at fault than a knight slow to take up arms, yet eager for assize money?[47] When a knight stands before nearby enemies like a partridge does [before] a hawk, his action is shameful. The man whom Mars' glorious feats of arms do not delight cannot be worthy of Rachel's embraces. The handsome woman who yields her love to such a man makes a mistake, and does not know what honorable love is. Rather, the infamous Leah is more suitable for such a husband as has little use for deeds of valor. Let such men go to Leah and attach her to themselves; let the timid fellow who cannot be Rachel['s] be Leah['s].[48] Let no man be loved who is unworthy of love, and let the man lack love who refuses its responsibility. When Jacob was smitten with love, he did not possess Rachel's embraces without the anxious labor of seven years' time.

But the knight whom the sake of gain moves to enter into battle will have no righteous honor. It is the vulture's ghastly nature to want [to eat] men, and to follow the camps of war in order to seize upon its food. Those who want war and who follow the camps and are eager for spoils and thirsting for loot are similar.[49] This bird is terrifying, since it plunders like the swift hawk, and every flock of them is like a cruel wolf. O knight, you who prefer pleasures and abandon your arms and seek to have rest at home and plunder spoils from the poor like a lion: you seek the fat of the land for yourself, thereby causing others to waste away. Sluggishness motivates you and voluptuous lust urges you on, together with money and the driving force of avarice. Undertake the awesome duties of bloody warfare and I believe that your vices will flee you once again. A knight should prefer honor to money, and in offering his prayers to God he will thereby conquer everything. But alas! I see that honor is now neglected for gold, and the world and the flesh are preferred to God. The number of knights increases but their activity decreases. Thus their honor is empty, since it is without responsibility.

NOTES

1. The oxymorons and paradoxes in this chapter are Gower's adaptation of a literary convention used to describe the discordant nature of carnal concupiscence. The categories can in part be understood in terms of the conflicting views of the flesh and the spirit. The trope was elaborated by Alanus de Insulis in his *De planctu Naturae* ("The Complaint of Nature," c. 1270?), meter v, in which Nature describes this infraction against her law; it was further popularized by Jean de Meun in the *Roman de la rose*, 4293–334, where Reason is the speaker.
2. What follows is a rhetorical *effictio*, the formula by which a woman's beauty was described (see above, pp. 66–68). Gower links the beauty so described with external *visibilia* which capture the soul, and thus condemns "love at first sight." Compare The Book of the Duchess, 848–960.
3. This passage contains details drawn from Ovid's *Metamorphoses*, III, 422 (the image with which Narcissus falls in love).
4. Imitated from Peter Riga's verse commentary on the Bible, *Aurora* (c. 1200), "II Kings," 47–48 (description of Absalom).
5. From Peter Riga, *Aurora*, "Evangelium," 131–32 (description of the Virgin Mary).
6. Compare Peter Riga, *Aurora*, "II Kings," 43–44 (description of Absalom); The Book of the Duchess, 981–84.
7. Taken from Ovid, *Heroides*, iv, 71–72 (Phaedra's description of her stepson Hippolytus, with whom she has fallen in love).
8. Adapted from Ovid, *Fasti*, II, 763 ff.
9. Compare Troilus and Criseyde, I, 420. Petrarch had popularized such paradoxes: see his Sonnet lxxxviii, or *Rima* clxxxii, 5.
10. From Ovid, *Ars amatoria*, I, 391.
11. Gower wrote *amor omne domat* instead of the more usual *amor vincit omnia*, the Prioress's emblem (General Prologue, 162). The motto appears in the *Roman de la rose*, 21327–39, where Courteisie refers to Virgil's *Eclogue X*, 69, to justify the Lover's plucking the Rose. The *Roman* makes it clear that false and carnal "Courtesy" adduces this emblem.
12. *Non amor in penis est . . .* may involve an obscene pun.
13. From Ovid, *Metamorphoses*, VII, 826 (Procris credulously believes a rumor that Cephalus has a secret lover; her credulity leads to her death).
14. From Ovid, *Heroides*, IV, 52 (Phaedra concealing her illicit passion for her stepson).
15. From Ovid, *Remedia amoris*, 691–92.
16. From Ovid, *Heroides*, IV, 161 (Phaedra's condition).
17. See Matthew xv, 14; Luke vi, 39.
18. From Ovid, *Tristia*, V, iv, 9–10.
19. From Ovid, *Ars amatoria*, II, 237–38 (below, p. 280).
20. From *Ars amatoria*, II, 235 (below, p. 280).
21. From Ovid, *Heroides*, V, 149 (Oenone to Paris).
22. See Galatians v, 17; Romans vii, 15–24.

23. From Ovid, *Metamorphoses*, X, 189 (the story of Hyacinthus).
24. From Ovid, *Heroides*, XVI, 231 (Paris to Helen: he claims he cannot).
25. From *Heroides*, VII, 179 (Dido to Aeneas: neither came to pass for her).
26. See 1 Corinthians vi, 18; compare The Parliament of Fowls, 140.
27. From Ovid, *Ars amatoria*, III, 29.
28. From Ovid, *Heroides*, II, 63–64 (Phyllis to Demophöon).
29. From Ovid, *Ars amatoria*, III, 42. The numerous allusions in this chapter suggest that Gower, in the tradition of Jean de Meun, considered the conventions of aristocratic romantic love to be of Ovidian extraction.
30. From Ovid, *Ex Ponto*, I, iii, 21–22.
31. Compare Troilus and Criseyde, II, 21.
32. For other instances of this conventional topic, see below, p. 387. The ideal, of course, is for the knight to marry a "good woman" (see pp. 391–95).
33. See Proverbs xxxi, 10–31, below, pp. 393–95.
34. From Ovid, *Ex Ponto*, II, iv, 14–15.
35. Compare Ovid, *Tristia*, III, vi, 17. The following section makes use of antifeminist conventions (see below, pp. 399ff). Gower's adoption of this convention here implies his association between "chivalric love" and the conventions of antifeminist literature.
36. From Ovid, *Metamorphoses*, II, 411.
37. From Ovid, *Ars amatoria*, I, 99; see *Roman de la rose*, 9029–30, and the Wife of Bath's Prologue, 552.
38. From *Ars amatoria*, III, 481.
39. From *Ars amatoria*, III, 295 (below, p. 283).
40. From *Ars amatoria*, III, 281–90 (below, pp. 282–83); see *Roman de la rose*, 13351–66.
41. From *Ars amatoria*, III, 294 (below, p. 283).
42. From *Ars amatoria*, III, 291–92 (below, p. 283); see *Roman de la rose*, 13367–84.
43. From *Ars amatoria*, III, 311–12.
44. Compare Ovid, *Ars amatoria*, I, 598; III, 294.
45. Symbolic of marital faith.
46. From Peter Riga, *Aurora*, "Deuteronomy," 199–200 (on the *militia Christi*).
47. With the addition of avarice as a corrupt motive, Gower seems to have completed the pattern which sets World (avarice), Flesh (love), and Devil (vain praise) as enemies to true chivalry.
48. From Peter Riga, *Aurora*, "Deuteronomy," 201–4. See Genesis xxix, 16–28.
49. From *Aurora*, "Leviticus," 655–58 (on the vulture).

Geoffroi de Charny: from *The Book of Chivalry*

An interesting complement to Gower's puritanical strictures concerning "chivalric love" occurs in Geoffroi de Charny's treatise on chivalry. What Geoffroi means by a "secret" love par amour *in practice is unclear. He appears to have absorbed the idealistic aspect of love celebrated by the troubadours, purging the insistent Ovidian strain which characteristically complicated this idealism in their songs. Geoffroi's treatise is consistently devout, as his account of the ritual of ordination indicates (above, pp. 167–68); he praises the "order of marriage"; and he concludes with a virtually mystical profession of faith. It would thus probably be wrong to attribute to the* amour *he speaks of the carnal motives which his phrasing sometimes suggests.*

A new translation by Margaret Ehrhart.

[Chivalric Love]

There is another kind of chevalier: those who are at first so foolish that they are completely ignorant of the great honor that they can gain by doing deeds of arms. But things nevertheless turn out well for them because they devote their hearts to loving *par amour*. And from this good befalls them, because their ladies themselves, out of their excellent honor and goodness, do not at all want to permit them to remain [at home] or to lose the time they could use to earn such honor as honor at arms. Thus they inform them of this, and they command them that they go to work to win the great honors where good men seek them. Thus they make them ride out, despite the fact that they had no will to do so before. But nevertheless they have such good adventures that everyone thinks well of their exploits and of the merit that they gain in many fine places and travels where these are found. And they are rightly to be praised and honored, as well as the excellent ladies who have so directed them and by whom they are formed. It is right to honor, serve, and love these excellent ladies. . . . And because of this, all good chevaliers are properly bound to guard and defend the honor of all ladies against those who might try to impugn or attack it in any way. But I should return to chevaliers and their deeds, and as I said before I say again: *He who performs better is better esteemed.* . . .

Thus those folk ought to live loyally and happily, and, along with the other things, honorably love *par amour*; this is the right life for those who want to gain such honor. But take care that the loves and the lovers be of the sort that you hold dear. As you ought to love your honors and your good names, look that you hold the honor of your ladies above all and that you keep secret all the good, honor, and love that you find in your ladies, without bragging in any way nor making it apparent, as might suit others, lest many notice it; because in the end, if it is widely known, no good at all comes of it, but many cruel difficulties can occur on account of it, which then result in great unpleasantness. Saying "She is the one I love" is not in the least the greatest enjoyment that one can obtain from a love affair, nor is wanting to act in such a way that everyone is bound to say "He loves that lady very much *par amour*." Many say that they would not want to love Queen Guenivere if they could not talk about it or if it was not known. Those people would like it better that everyone said and thought they loved very much *par amour*, and there was nothing to the story, than that they loved and that the affair went well and they profited by it, and it was a well-kept secret. And this is not good at all, because one has more perfect joy being in the company of his lady secretly than one could have in a year in a case where the affair was known and observed by many. We ought certainly to know that the most secret love is the most joyous, and the most lasting, and the most loyal, and this is the kind of love one should wish to engage in.

Just as one should want to guard the honor of his lady, insofar as it has anything to do with him, so on account of the love he bears her, one ought to guard his own honor for the honor of his lady and for the love she shows him. This means that you should arrange it in such a way that the renown of your manners, your positions, and your physical prowess is of such a quality and so good, so great, and so honorable, that you must be held in great account for your excellences both indoors and afield, and especially for deeds of arms in peace and deeds of arms in war, wherever great honors are recognized. Thus your ladies will be more honored, and rightly so, since they will have formed a good knight or a good chevalier. And if it could be said that a good knight or a good chevalier loves such a lady, in the case that it could be known, certainly there would be greater honor for the lady who loved such a one, than for a lady who devoted her time to an unfortunate scoundrel who would not arm himself, neither for peaceful nor for warlike deeds of arms, and who would not want to join the company of those who know how and are able to do such things well. What honor do they, who would like to love in this way, bring to their ladies, when it can be said of them that they love a wretch?

Which of two ladies should have greater joy on account of her friend, when they are at a feast in a great company of people, and each knows where the other's love is placed? She who loves a good knight and who sees her friend enter the dining hall, and sees him honored, greeted, and celebrated by all manner of people, and introduced to ladies and damsels, knight and squires, with the good name everyone gives him and considers him to have? —that excellent lady rejoices in her heart exceedingly, because she has devoted her heart and her intention to loving and forming such a good knight. . . . But what of the other lady?—if there is one who loves a wretched scoundrel who does not want to arm himself and has no excuse. When she sees him enter that same room, and observes and realizes that no one pays any attention to him, no one celebrates him nor even pretends to, few people recognize him and those who do so hold it of no account, and he remains behind the others because no one invites him forward, . . . she must indeed have an uneasy heart.

THE ESTATE OF SPIRITUAL RULERS: CLERGY

Just as Chaucer cast his chivalric characters against the conventional ideals of the Estate of Temporal Rulers, so he made use of the official expectations concerning the Estate of Spiritual Rulers in his depiction of the clerical members of the Canterbury Pilgrimage. These expectations appear in the various Rules which governed the regular clergy, in accounts of the different "offices" within the Church, and, by implication, in the literature of complaint and satire, which turned such figures as the hunting monk into stereotypes.

Chaucer's inclusion of churchmen as tale-tellers who risk exposing their own ignorance or venality would not have been interpreted as blasphemous. Medieval satire of the ecclesiastical establishment was always directed at the officer, not the office he held within the Church of Christ. In his portraits, in the tales he writes for individual clerics, and in the characterizations within different tales, Chaucer subtly probes the religious mentality, as he does the chivalric mentality when that Estate is his subject. But he never questions the doctrine or the mission of the Church itself.

Hugh of St. Victor:
from *On the Sacraments of the Christian Faith*

Hugh of St. Victor composed the De sacramentis Christianae fidei *about
1134. It is an encyclopedic compendium of Church authority which sets an
account of the sacraments in the broad context of the creation and end of
the world. The first excerpt identifies the two ruling powers, from the
point of view of the Church. The second is Hugh's introduction to the
"clerical" office.*

A brief account of Hugh's life and works appears above, p. 58.

Trans. Roy J. DeFerrari, Hugh of Saint Victor: On the Sacraments of the Christian Faith (Cambridge, Mass.: Mediaeval Academy, 1951), pp. 256, 259–60. Reprinted by permission of the Mediaeval Academy.

[The Two Powers]

For there are two lives, the one earthly, the other heavenly; the one corporeal, the other spiritual; one by which the body lives from the soul, the other by which the soul lives from God. Both have their own good by which they are invigorated and nourished, so that they can subsist. The earthly life is nourished by earthly goods; the spiritual life is nurtured by spiritual goods. To the earthly life pertain all things that are earthly, to the spiritual life all goods that are spiritual. Now, that in both lives justice may be preserved and utility flourish, at first those have been distributed on each side who would acquire the goods of each according to necessity or reason by zeal and labor.

Then there are others who by the power of the office committed to them dispense according to equity, that no one may step over his brother in business but justice may be preserved inviolate. On this account powers were established in both peoples distributed according to both lives. Indeed, among the laics, to whose zeal and providence those things which are necessary for the earthly life belong, is earthly power. But among the clerics to whose office look those things which are the goods of the spiritual life, is divine power. Thus the one power is said to be secular; the other is called spiritual. In both powers are diverse grades and orders of powers; yet in both they are distributed under one head and, as it were, deduced from one beginning and referred to one. The earthly power has as its head the king. The spiritual power has the highest pontifex. To the powers of the king pertain all things that are earthly and made for the earthly life. To the power of the highest pontifex pertain all things that are spiritual and attributed to the spiritual life. Now the more worthy the spiritual life is than the earthly and the spirit than the body, so much does the spiritual power precede the earthly or the secular in honor and in dignity.

For spiritual power has also to establish earthly power in order to exist, and it has to judge it, if it has not been good. Indeed, it itself was established first by God and when it goes astray it can be judged by God alone, just as it is written: "The spiritual man judgeth all things; and he himself is judged by no man."[1] Now, it is manifestly declared among that ancient people of the Old Testament where the priesthood was first established by God that spiritual power, in so far as it looks to. divine institution, is both prior in time and greater in dignity; afterwards indeed royal power was arranged through the priesthood at God's order. Wherefore, in the Church sacerdotal dignity still consecrates regal power, but sanctifying it through benediction and forming it through institution. If then, as the Apostle says, "He who blesses is greater, and he who is blessed less,"[2] it is established without any doubt that earthly power which receives benediction from the spiritual is thought inferior by law.

NOTES

1. 1 Corinthians ii, 15.
2. See Hebrews vii, 7.

[On Clerics]

Spiritual power in the cleric is arranged with different grades and orders of dignity. The first sign of the cleric is the crown by which he is marked for a part of the lot of the divine ministry, serving in which is ruling. The crown indeed signifies kingly dignity. Thus the blessed apostle Peter says: "You are a chosen generation, a kingly priesthood."[1] On this account, therefore, the hair of the head of a cleric is cut in the manner of a crown and the very top of the head is made bare from above and is uncovered so as to grant as understood through this that it is assumed unto kingly power in Christ, and that between him and God then there should be no veil, so that with face revealed and with mind pure he may contemplate the glory of his Lord. The top of the head is the top of the mind. The baring of the head signifies the illumination of the mind.

A cleric indeed should not be ignorant of the secrets of God, because he is His messenger to the people. For the hairs of the head are shorn even to the opening and unveiling of the senses, that is, of the eyes and of the ears, that occupation with earthly things, which are signified by the hair, may not impede him from hearing and understanding the words of God. Now after one has been made a cleric, he should then be sustained by the stipends of the Church and be taught in the divine science and ecclesiastical discipline under the tutelage and custody of spiritual masters, in order that, when reason demands, he may be able worthily to enter upon the sacred orders of the divine ministry.

NOTE

1. 1 Peter ii, 9.

John Gower:
from *Vox clamantis*

[The Clergy: Ideal and Complaint]

John Gower's praise and complaint concerning the chivalric Estate in his
Vox clamantis *(see above, pp. 194–205) is matched by a detailed survey of
the clerical Estate. The following passages provide conventional stereo-
types such as Chaucer's audience would have recognized in his Parson,
Clerk, Monk, Prioress, and Second Nun.*

Trans. Eric W. Stockton, The Major Latin Works of John Gower (*Seattle:* Uni-
versity of Washington Press, 1962), pp. 161–68, 171–73, 178–79, 181. *Reprinted
by permission of the University of Washington Press.*

[A Parson]

III, 27. HERE [THE AUTHOR] SPEAKS OF THE SPIRITUAL WORTHINESS OF PRIESTS, AND OF HOW THEY ACCOMPLISH MORE THAN OTHERS, IF THEY PERFORM THEIR DUTIES WELL. OTHERWISE, THEY FURNISH MORE OPPORTUNITY FOR TRANSGRESSION THROUGH THEIR OWN BAD EXAMPLES.

A priest's honor is great, and his power is even greater, if he remains pious and good, and far removed from vices. With their hands they perform the rites of the highest sacrament, through which the flesh is made one with God by a word. And they can take away the sin for which our first parent fell, by the sacred purification of baptism. They also celebrate our marriages according to the new law, and if they seek after righteousness, they will not engage in anything idle. They also offer pardon to those confessing they have fallen, and they provide an erring man a return to God. They also give us to partake of the heavenly host, and afterwards on our deathbed their unction awaits us. They also must assist the dead and buried, and offer up pious prayers in their masses.[1]

They are the salt of the earth, by which we on earth are seasoned; without their savor man could scarcely be seasoned.[2] Elisha healed the waters with the salt he cast into them, and no bitter taste remained in them.[3] The salt signifies the knowing discretion of the just man, whereby the man of discretion may season his people. They are the light of the world.[4] For this reason, if they are in darkness, we in the world stand blind and uncertain. As God has declared, he shall be cursed who puts any stumbling block before a blind man that is hurt by it. He who has placed obstacles before a blind man shall, by his cursed deeds, show the pathway to sin.[5]

They are Jacob's ladder with its many steps, reaching to the heights of heaven;[6] by them the pathway will lie revealed. They are a holy mountain; through them every man of faith must mount the peak of virtues. They are our counsel, the right way to on high, the teachers of the law, and our new way of salvation. These good men close heaven and open it wide to people, and they can subject everything to themselves. It was said unto them, "Multiply, and yield much fruit." These words have reference to good morals. It was said unto them, "Replenish the earth." Note what is said unto you: be full of good fruits in the Church.[7]

No worthless person should come before God, for no one lacking in virtue should be near God. So the priest should reconcile both the righteous and the sinful to God, and pour forth the frankincense of prayers to heaven. Let him pray lest the just man fall away from justice, and let him pray that the dissolute man may rise up and weep over his extreme wickedness. O what a shameful thing it is when a priest is like an ass, unversed in morals and lawlessly wild! Priests are like the stars of the sky in number, but scarcely two out of a thousand shine with light. They neither read the Scriptures nor understand them. Nevertheless, being tonsured, these men are apart from the common herd, and they think this is enough. There are some like this; and there are others whom an ardent virtue distinguishes in the Church, and who do many good works. Noah sent forth a raven and it did not return. He sent forth a dove and it did return.[8] Similarly, in the Church there are ravens and doves. The good ones are without gall, while the bad ones are full of gall. "Tomorrow at prime," they sing, since they are slow to reform themselves; but the day of judgment often does away with such people. Such are the black ones whom the bonds of this world shackle, and who are unwilling to thirst after the promised kingdom of God. [As for] the priest who upholds the laws of his order and who imparts holy teachings by both action and example, no esteem is too high for him, even when he is not held in honor by his order. Praise from the people is not enough for him, but God's praise is. I maintain that among the clergy, for those whom an ardent virtue shows to be good and true, their thanks shall be larger than they deserve.

[A Clerk]

*III, 28. NOW THAT HE HAS SPOKEN OF THE WAYWARD-
NESS OF THOSE AMONG THE SECULAR CLERGY WHO
HAVE USURPED THE OFFICE OF THE PRIESTHOOD FOR
THEMSELVES, HE INTENDS TO SPEAK A SECOND TIME
OF THE WAYWARDNESS OF SCHOLARS, WHO ARE
CALLED THE LITTLE SCIONS OF THE CHURCH.*

We know that under the name of the clergy there are scholars, whom
God calls the scions of the Church. The good scholar is a scion from
the divine garden, and makes the fruits of the Church good. The cleric
who is zealous for virtue and not for vice, and who reckons not the
world but God for himself, is consequently thought of as belonging to
God. And what he begins is brought to a good conclusion. The just
authority of a teacher outstanding in virtues rightly encourages the apt
students. Those who stick to their studies and lift up their hearts and
fix them on high are true offerings to God.

But I think that nowadays although many among them are called,
few are chosen as being upright in their ways.[9] For a long time in their
behavior they have left off the virtue of study, and now they apply
their studies vigilantly to vices. Scarcely a one studies for the sake of
the necessary subject matter; instead the mere shadow of its outline is
enough. A cleric used to go to school with a patient spirit, but now
worldly glory is his master. He rambles here and there, a lazy, wander-
ing drunkard, wayward and given to lust. A fruitful tree will not grow
out of a barren plant, nor will a bad tree bring forth good fruit.[10] Old
age often holds to what it held to as a youth. If a youth is evil, he will
scarcely be good when old. It is the good root which brings forth seeds
of goodness; utter badness sprouts forth from a bad root. Therefore
everyone should punish his boys, seeing that the rod does not disturb
the mind's proper activities. The youth who has a master of flowering
virtue should learn what things are righteous, and he will become well
versed in them. But the man whom a dissolute teacher has instructed
will rarely bear fruit.

III, 29. HERE HE INQUIRES OF THE CAUSE WHICH PER-
SUADES THE MINDS OF SCHOLARS TO ADOPT THE
PRIESTHOOD. HE ALLEGES THAT THERE ARE THREE
CAUSES IN PARTICULAR. HE ALSO DISCUSSES A FOURTH,
WHICH RARELY OBTAINS AT PRESENT.

There are some nowadays who persist in zealous study, but I do not
know what cause is responsible for this. Their intention judges all
men, no matter what they do. God himself grasps what is in the heart.
Now that I have made these remarks, explain the truth to me, scholar.
Tell me what the underlying reason for your study is, when you first
strengthen yourself for holy orders, when you first come to make your-
self a priest. O what motive was then uppermost in your mind? Was
this for love of the world or love of God? Either you tell me the particu-
lar source of your reason, or I want to tell you what I know to be true.

"As you may now observe, there are several reasons for which our
order is widely esteemed throughout the world. In the first place, I es-
cape the everyday scourgings of the common law, which deals harshly
with men.[11] Furthermore, I see that I do not have to sweat with toil,
and so I can have the idleness I desire. The third reason [is that it] pro-
vides my food and clothing; and so I quietly persist in my pleasures.
All my devotion is due to these things; for this reason the shaven ton-
sure can be seen as mine. This is the reason for going to school, which
makes me study civil law and which skillfully teaches its logic. The
school lets me progress upward to its highest levels, and in this way I
try to rise into a good church. For I think that if his reputation pros-
pers, a prebend·will prosper, and so it is an easy task to devote some
time to books. I like holy orders, and clerical learning is useful, as long
as I get a fat profit from my study. Now I have told you the reasons
that the position of a scholar is agreeable, so I confess I am guilty [of
being one] for the sake of this world. For I don't think there is any-
thing better for me than to enjoy the pleasures of the world while there
is sufficient opportunity."

But there is nevertheless a still better reason than all those, namely,
that a school rejoices in having a good student. This reason, which vir-
tuously embraces the work of a school, used to hold good in days of
old but does not in our own. There used to be saints who disdained
worldly pomp and longed for the highest good. And since becoming
acquainted with schools incited their spirits to be holy, they gave
themselves over to the pious study of Scripture. Ambition and love of

possession did not move them, but they rightly went out of eagerness for virtue. In contemplating heaven they shunned the earth, and no lascivious purpose drew them aside. Nor did they wish to be in the service of a king, nor to have the name of rabbi among the people.[12] Nor did vain, sumptuous adornment, nor indulgence in wine, nor woman's love overcome them. Well versed in good morals, they furnished examples for those to come which the student ought to adopt for his own instruction. Today, however, virtue has been changed into vice, and what were once morals now bring on great disgrace. Their greed for worldly preferment now turns into worldly glory the writings which they say they are learning for the glory of God. What an astounding state of affairs! The scholar reads and studies about virtue, while his own actions become more and more vicious. So, because the clergy without the light of virtue is blind, we errant laymen wander about in darkness.[13]

[A Monk]

IV, 1. SINCE HE HAS DISCUSSED THE WAYWARDNESS OF THE CLERGY, TO WHOM HE LOOKS ESPECIALLY FOR GUIDANCE FOR OUR SOULS, HE NOW INTENDS TO DISCUSS THE WAYWARDNESS OF MEN IN MONASTIC ORDERS. AND HE WILL SPEAK FIRST OF MONKS AND OTHERS WHO GET POSSESSION OF TEMPORAL GOODS. WHILE COMMENDING, TO BE SURE, THE SANCTITY OF THEIR ORDER, HE REBUKES IN PARTICULAR THOSE WHOSE ACTIONS ARE JUST THE CONTRARY.

There are also cloistered men of diverse kind, concerning whom I wish to write the little I know. As their actions show, some of them are noted for property and some for poverty, but the poverty is feigned to too great an extent. A monastic order is good in itself, but we say that those who betray it are evil. I believe that those who live faithfully in their cloister and who cannot be held guilty of worldly love are blessed. A religious order will recognize as holy men those who put their hand to the plow without looking back.[14] God is present among the monks who are willing to enter monasteries apart from mankind, and the fellowship of heaven is theirs. When a man undertakes to love two opposing things equally, the one love will detract from the effectiveness of the other.[15] I accordingly direct my words to those who presume to mask their faces under the shadow of a religious order, yet inwardly commit worldly sins. And no one else is going to be hurt by what I have written; instead, every man shall bear his own burden.[16] Nothing that I write is my own opinion; rather, I shall speak what the voice of the people has reported to me.

There are certainly monks whom ownership of property has made a claim on, men whom no religious order can hold in check through moral precepts. For some men of property seek the leisure of an order so that they cannot suffer any hardships. They avoid being hungry, and slake their thirst with wine. They get rid of all cold with their warm furred cloaks. Faintness of the belly does not come upon them in the hours of night, and their raucous voice does not sing the heights of heaven in chorus with a drinking cup. A man of this kind will devour no less than several courses at table, and empties a good many beakers in his drinking. Then he believes he has grown sick and demands to be made well again; and in such fashion does he devote himself to his sports. Indeed, it is only with difficulty that this man of professed vows is to be worn out from drinking; thus, master monk is willing to appear before God while in his cups. And while you are bringing him wine, he allures women to himself; wanton monasteries now furnish these two things together. If he can get to heaven after being inflamed with passion even while in his vestments; and if his gluttony can gain a place among those above, then I think that the monk distinguished on these two counts will stand as Peter's fellow-citizen in the vault of the skies.

IV, 2. HERE HE SPEAKS OF THE MONKS WHO, CONTRARY TO THE DECREES OF THEIR ORDER, ARE THE FIRST TO ABANDON THE VIRTUE OF SELF-RESTRAINT AND PARTAKE AGAIN AND AGAIN OF THE DELIGHTS OF THE FLESH.

Things which are dead by no means belong with the living; and one who renounces the world does not return to worldly behavior. No matter how much he seems to be a sheep, neither tonsure nor the humblest garb is any help at all to him, if he is a wolf. For men can be deceived, but no one can deceive Christ, Who deceived no man. Indeed, He condemns the pretense of feigned religion and reckons its work as nothing. Nevertheless, a monk withdraws from the world nowadays only in respect to his dress, and thinks that a religious order is sufficient for him in outer appearance alone. The vestments will be the monk himself, and his thoughts will wander about in the world, heeding nothing beyond the material wealth of his order. Since he knows that bodies seldom thrive properly on slender rations for the belly, such a monk demands plentiful sustenance for his gullet. And the more food he eats the more he craves, so that his belly may enjoy its pleasures, with the help of his gullet. Unmindful of his father, who used to bear burdens on his shoulders, the monk lugs the finest wines about in his belly. Such a man pours the fruit of the vine into his stomach as if it were a flagon, and he is not one to allow any place in his swelling paunch to be empty.

A monk ought to shun wine for many reasons, one of them being lest his flesh yearn for debauchery. A man should not spoil the good works of his brothers in religion, or sit around in a drunken state or have a fever from it. Nevertheless, the monk cares about nothing except stuffing his worthless body, yet his soul goes hungry every day. In these times snow-white bread, delicate wine, and meats provide monks with daily feasts. Just see how the cook bakes and roasts, freezes and

melts, grinds and presses, strains and tests his performances. If a glut-
tonous monk can fatten his paunch, he thinks there is nothing in Holy
Writ to the effect that one should work. Scorning manna, this kind
of people demands that its cooking pots be black [with constant use],
and prefers its vices to virtues. Lest hunger might weaken these fat fel-
lows, their belly's harlot gluttony crams their faint stomachs full. A
monk does not know what ought to be honored, but what ought to be
esteemed for the belly. This, he says, is the way, the life, the salvation.
When the bell rings for the dinner pot, he runs at a fast clip, and not
one crumb from the table escapes him. But when the sluggard gets up
at night and comes to prayers at a slow pace, he tries to be last.

When their order began, monks' homes were caves; now a grand
marble palace sets them off. They used to have no steaming kitchen,
and no cook served them delicacies roasted or baked by the fire. In
former times no boiled food or dishes loaded with meat made monks
fat. Bodily gluttony did not afflict their souls, nor were they inflamed
by lust of the flesh to seek out debauchery on the sly. They who used
to cover their bare bodies with the skins of animals now cover them
more comfortably with wool. Herbs used to furnish their food, a spring
their drink, and a base hair shirt their clothing, yet there was no grum-
bling in those days. There was no envy or splendor in a monastery then;
he who was the greater served as did the lesser. There was no great
quantity of silver or chain of gold that could corrupt their holy state
then. Money did not touch their pockets, nor wine their palates, and
no carnal flame burned in their loins. They had a holy spirit which
served their resolution well, and which persevere successfully in the
work it undertook.

They were righteous men who shunned the world and who were
burdened with no love of sins. The world did not draw them away
from the right path, and the flesh did not beckon them toward heinous
evils. They put aside all the vanities which the world affords, and
yearned only for the God of heaven. It was no disgrace then to take
one's rest upon straw or to put hay under one's head.[17] The forest
was their home, herbs were their food, and leafy boughs were their
bedding,[18] which the earth furnished without their even asking.[19] The
hazel then flourished among them in high esteem, and the sturdy oak
yielded splendid treasures.[20] They gathered the fruits of the arbutus
and mountain [strawberries],[21] which were seasoned neither with salt
nor with spices. And although they partook of acorns from Jove's
spreading tree,[22] they grew strong from these foods. Contented with
the modest things produced by Nature of her own accord,[23] they sent
forth their humble prayers to God on high. Admirable sowers of the

seeds of justice then, now they reap their fruits eternally a hundred-fold.[24] But that ancient salvation of souls, which religious orders once possessed, has perished, undermined by the weakness of the flesh.

IV, 5. HERE HE SPEAKS OF HOW MONKS OUGHT NOT TO WANDER AROUND OUTSIDE THE MONASTERY.

The sea is the proper habitat of a live fish, and the monastery is the right home for a monk. Just as the sea will not keep dead fish, so the monastery casts out evildoing monks. A fish ought not to be out of the water, nor ought a monk to be away from his cloisters, unless you return to them, O monk in holy orders.[25] If there were a fish that forsook the waters of the sea to seek its food on land, it would be highly inappropriate to give it the name of fish; I should rather give it the name of monster. Such shall I call the monk who yearns for worldly delights and deserts his cloister for them. He should not rightly be called a monk but a renegade, or what God's wrath brands as a monster of the Church. As for those who still remain within the monastery, yet with wandering minds look back on the world with new love in their hearts, their transgression disgraces such men in the eyes of God. Because of this they lose their cloister's rightful rewards. It is not a wise man who amasses goods for himself for several years and dissipates them in only one day. The monk who makes the rounds of town and country quite frequently commits a fault for which he perishes as a sinner. In spite of this, there are only a few at present who do not give their errant hearts to sensual pleasures. Solomon said that a man's foolish attire, which is outwardly visible, tells what is within.[26] But although a monk should array himself with humble garb, nevertheless you now see many sumptuous things on his back.

IV, 7. HERE HE SPEAKS OF HOW PATIENCE TOGETHER WITH OTHER VIRTUES HAVE BETAKEN THEMSELVES AWAY FROM CERTAIN CLOISTERS, WITH VICES SUPERSEDING THEM.

Abbot Patience is dead, and the monk Grumbler lives on, and there can be no peace in his cloisters. Abbot Chastity is also now dead, and Lust has succeeded him and is ruining the religious houses. And Abbot Inconstancy has refused Constancy the monasteries that Hatred occupies and claims as his. Abbot Hypocrisy links up with Abbot Deceit, while Fraud aspires to achieve high rank. Monks of old used to plant the fruits of love; the modern monastic order now bears the fruits of Envy.

The rule of St. Bernard or St. Maure[27] is of no use to our modern fellow monks; on the contrary, it displeases them. A greedy fellow sets himself against St. Bernard and St. Maure, as does another, proud and envious; they now refuse to carry out the precepts of their order. Thus Malediction has driven Benedict out of the monasteries, Gluttony has driven out Temperance, and Guile has driven out Faith. Gone is the Abbot Gentle whom gentle cloisters obey. The religious order's false shadow now conceals false men. What was once spirit is now a lifeless body, and Abbot World governs the whole undertaking.

[A Nun]

IV, 13. HERE HE GOES ON TO SPEAK ABOUT WOMEN WHO, IN A NUN'S GARB, ENTER UPON THE PROFESSION OF VOWS UNDER THE VEIL OF HOLY RELIGION AND DO NOT OBSERVE THE CONTINENCE OF THEIR ORDER.

I have now left off writing of the sins of the errant monk, and shall sing to you of woman veiled in religion. A monastic order is appropriate for men as long as they live virtuously, whereby they, apart from the world, may reach the kingdom of heaven. It is also appropriate for virtuous women to fulfill their vows of chastity to God under the veil. Just as a holy order binds monks, it also binds nuns, so that both may shine in their merits for God. Nevertheless, if weak women in the cloisters go astray, their unchastity does not militate against them equally with men. For a woman's foot cannot stand as steady as a man's can, nor can it make its steps firm. Neither learning nor understanding, neither constancy nor virtue such as men have flourishes in woman. But you often see women's morals change because of their frail nature, rather than by conscious choice. Quite frequently we perceive the very women whom their order thinks most sensible to be full of foolish behavior. And above all, those who know the Scriptures often fall because of an indiscreet secular crime. They think the Scriptures permit them to do as they do, because frequently they simply read the text and are not concerned about the gloss. The reading of Scripture teaches them to approve everything, and so, since they read about everything, they wish to make proof of everything.[28] Nature's laws, which God in the beginning wrote down from her own lips, are to be fruitful and multiply.[29] And these are the Scriptures of God they wish to obey, and the regular laws of Nature which they wish to administer in dutiful spirit.

Woman strives for what is forbidden,[30] but she rarely does what is permissible without mentally grumbling. But nuns are made more perfect by the Scriptures [if] they patiently do what the Scriptures command them. It is written that the seeds which good earth will not receive do not bear any fruit at all, but lie dying.[31] And yet a nun should be the kind of earth which lies in readiness, for there the seeds are multiplied tenfold. And since frail women sustain such a heavy burden, sometimes they rightly seek rest and quiet. Therefore it happens that on Venus' days[32] they eat meat because of their weak stomach. For to Genius, Venus entrusts for her worthy foster daughters[33] the pork dishes which he should prepare for his own nymphs. But when sated, their maw often grows too heavy and swells up because it is in pain, troubled by the weight of the food. The swelling is too burdensome, and being tainted with poison, it is toxic to the stomach, and will bring on a fear of death. On the other hand, the food which is eaten secretly in the dark is injurious, and often causes heavy illnesses.

IV, 15. HERE HE SPEAKS IN PRAISE OF CHASTITY, WHICH IS MOST HIGHLY IN KEEPING FOR WOMEN WHO HAVE MADE PROFESSION OF VOWS IN A RELIGIOUS ORDER.

O how the virginity which follows the Lamb through all the vaults of heaven[34] shines above every glory! Wedded to the Godhead, it is radiant on earth, forsaking the actions to which the nature of the human body prompts it. Just as the unchaste woman is fetid, the untainted chaste one is sweet-scented. The one possesses God, the other a corpse. Flowery garlands heaped three-fold with a hundred fruits decorate the head of the virgin in God's presence. The rank of virgin transcends bands of angels and abides more in heaven than even the Triple Crown.[35] As John is my witness, the spirit of a virgin, imitating the prerogative of the eagle and yearning for the heights, flies up before God.[36] Just as a rose springing from thorns rises above them, so the status of a virgin surpasses others. Just as a white pearl is pleasing, being highly valuable, so a virgin in a cloister is pleasing, having professed her vows to God. Such a nun is indeed highly worthy of the cloister and holy in merit, so long as she keeps her vows. But no matter what woman seeks the cloister under the veil, the rule which she obeys will sanctify her. If she has been a good woman, it will make her better, and at all times add more morals to her good character. If she were defiled before she took the veil and live chastely from now on, her previous sin shall be as nothing. Therefore it is not permitted for men to violate consecrated nuns, for the sacred veil carries the mark of chastity. How heavy a crime in our judgment does a man commit who takes it upon himself to violate another's bride! But be assured that the man who destroys nunneries and takes it upon himself to violate the bride of God sins even more heavily.

NOTES

1. Gower lists the sacraments entrusted to the clergy.
2. See Matthew v, 13; Mark ix, 49; Luke xiv, 34.
3. See 4 Kings ii, 21–22.
4. See Matthew v, 14.

5. See Leviticus xix, 14.
6. See Genesis xxviii, 12.
7. See Genesis i, 28. Compare the interpretation in the Wife of Bath's Prologue, 26–29.
8. See Genesis viii, 6–9.
9. See Matthew xxii, 14.
10. See Matthew vii, 16–20. Compare Matthew iii, 10; xii, 33; Luke vi, 43–44.
11. See Psalm lxxii, 5–6.
12. See Matthew xxiii, 8. Compare James iii, 1.
13. See John viii, 12. Compare 1 John ii, 11.
14. See Luke ix, 62: the scriptural basis for the widely used image of the "plow-man," symbolic of the good Christian.
15. See Matthew vi, 24; Luke xvi, 13.
16. See Galatians vi, 5.
17. See Ovid, *Fasti*, I, 109 ff.
18. See Ovid, *Ars amatoria*, II, 475, and context; Chaucer's "The Former Age."
19. See Ovid, *Fasti*, IV, 396.
20. See *Fasti*, IV, 400.
21. From Ovid, *Metamorphoses*, I, 104 (the Golden Age).
22. See *Metamorphoses*, I, 106.
23. See *Metamorphoses*, I, 103.
24. See Matthew xix, 29.
25. See General Prologue, 179–82.
26. See Ecclesiasticus xix, 27.
27. See General Prologue, 172–76. St. Maure was a disciple of St. Benedict.
28. See 1 Thessalonians v, 21.
29. See Genesis i, 28.
30. See Ovid, *Amores*, III, iv, 17.
31. See Matthew xiii, 3–8; Mark iv, 3–8; Luke viii, 5–8.
32. That is, Fridays. See Nun's Priest's Tale, 3341–46.
33. The figure of Genius, drawn from Alanus de Insulis' *De planctu Naturae*, appears in the *Roman de la rose* as Venus' priest. Compare his function in Gower's own *Confessio Amantis*. Genius seems to correspond to "natural instinct" of Nature after the Fall.
34. See Apocaplypse xiv, 4.
35. The crown of the Pope.
36. Compare Apocalypse xii, 14.

A Pardoner's License

The following form letter, issued on June 20, 1400, by Richard le Scrope, Archbishop of York, would have been like the documents exhibited by Chaucer's Pardoner.

Trans. Arnold Williams, "Some Documents on English Pardoners, 1350–1400," Mediaeval Studies in Honor of Urban Tigner Holmes, Jr. (Chapel Hill: University of North Carolina Press, 1965), p. 204. Reprinted by permission of The University of North Carolina Press.

[A Pardoner's License]

On the twentieth day of the month of June in the year of Our Lord MCCCC at Thorp near York the lord by his letters conceded a license to run two years from the present date to the proctors or messengers of the hospital or chapel of the most blessed Virgin Mary of Roncesvalles near Charing Cross in the city of London to publish indulgences and privileges conceded to the benefactors of the same hospital or chapel and to collect and receive alms given or to be given by any of the faithful of Christ to the said hospital or chapel throughout the archdeaconries of York, Cleveland, and Nottingham.

THE ESTATE OF
PROVIDERS: PLOWMEN

The theory of the Three Estates assumed that all citizens shared the condemnation of Adam: "cursed is the earth in thy work; in labor and toil shalt thou eat thereof all the days of thy life" (Genesis iii, 17). Ideally, the peasant accepted his lot like the Plowman in the General Prologue:

A trcwe swynkere and a good was he,
Lyvynge in pees and parfit charitee.
God loved he best with al his hoole herte
At alle tymes, thogh him gamed or smerte,
And thanne his neighebor right as hymselve. (531–35)

The reign of Richard II, however, was marked by civil unrest, particularly in the Peasants' Revolt of 1381, and the kind of belligerent contempt for the ruling Estates exhibited by Chaucer's Miller was apparently common.

John Gower:
from *Vox clamantis*

In the following brief excerpt Gower expresses conventional attitudes to-
ward those members of society subject to the ruling Estates. In this section
of the Vox clamantis *he goes on to discuss the role of merchants and*
lawyers in the commonwealth.

From John Gower, Vox clamantis, *trans* Eric W. Stockton, The Major Latin
Works of John Gower (Seattle, University of Washington Press, 1962), *pp.* 208–9.
Reprinted by permission of the University of Washington Press.

[Complaint against Plowmen]

V, 9. NOW THAT HE HAS SPOKEN OF THOSE OF KNIGHTLY RANK WHO OUGHT TO KEEP THE STATE UNHARMED, IT IS NECESSARY TO SPEAK OF THOSE WHO ARE UNDER OBLIGATION TO ENTER INTO THE LABORS OF AGRICULTURE, WHICH ARE NECESSARY FOR OBTAINING FOOD AND DRINK FOR THE SUSTENANCE OF THE HUMAN RACE.

Now you have heard what knighthood is, and I shall speak in addition of what the guiding principle for other men ought to be. For after knighthood there remains only the peasant rank; the rustics in it cultivate the grains and vineyards. They are the men who seek food for us by the sweat of their heavy toil, as God Himself has decreed. The guiding principle of our first father Adam, which he received from the mouth of God on high, is rightly theirs. For God said to him, when he fell from the glories of Paradise, "O sinner, the sweat and toil of the world be thine; in them shalt thou eat thy bread."[1] So if God's peasant pays attention to the plowshare as it goes along,[2] and if he thus carries on the work of cultivation with his hand, then the fruit which in due course the fertile field will bear and the grape will stand abundant in their due seasons. Now, however, scarcely a farmer wishes to do such work; instead, he wickedly loafs everywhere.

An evil disposition is widespread among the common people, and I suspect that the servants of the plow are often responsible for it. For they are sluggish, they are scarce, and they are grasping. For the very little they do they demand the highest pay. Now that this practice has come about, see how one peasant insists upon more than two demanded in days gone by. Yet a short time ago one performed more service than three do now, as those maintain who are well acquainted with the facts. For just as the fox seeks his hole and enters it while the woods are echoing on every side of the hole, so does the servant of the plow, contrary to the law of the land, seek to make a fool of the land. They desire the leisures of great men, but they have nothing to feed themselves with, nor will they be servants. God and Nature have ordained that they shall serve, but neither knows how to keep them within bounds. Everyone owning land complains in his turn about these people; each stands in need of them and none has control over them. The peasants of old did not scorn God with impunity[3] or usurp a noble worldly rank.

Rather, God imposed servile work upon them, so that the peasantry might subdue its proud feelings; and liberty, which remained secure for freemen, ruled over the serfs and subjected them to its law.

The experience of yesterday makes us better informed as to what perfidy the unruly serf possesses.[4] As the teasel harmfully thins out the standing crops if it is not thinned out itself, so does the unruly peasant weigh heavily upon the well-behaved ones. The peasant strikes at the subservient and soothes the troublesome, yet the principle which the old order of things teaches is not wrong: let the law accordingly cut down the harmful teasels of rabble, lest they uproot the nobler grain with their stinging. Unless it is struck down first, the peasant race strikes against freemen, no matter what nobility or worth they possess. Its actions outwardly show that the peasantry is base, and it esteems the nobles the less because of their very virtues. Just as lopsided ships begin to sink without the right load, so does the wild peasantry, unless it is held in check.[5]

God and our toil confer and bestow everything upon us. Without toil, man's advantages are nothing. The peasant should therefore put his limbs to work, as is proper for him to do so. Just as a barren field cultivated by the plowshare fails the granaries and brings home no crop in autumn, so does the worthless churl, the more he is cherished by your love, fail you and bring on your ruin. The serfs perform none of their servile duties voluntarily and have no respect for the law. Whatever the serf's body suffers patiently under compulsion, inwardly his mind ever turns toward utter wickedness. Miracles happen only contrary to nature; only the divinity of nature can go against its own powers. It is not for man's estate that anyone from the class of serfs should try to set things right.

NOTES

1. Expansion of Genesis iii, 19.
2. See Luke ix, 62.
3. See Ovid, *Metamorphoses*, VI, 318.
4. Probably a reference to the Peasants' Rebellion, 1381. See Nun's Priest's Tale, 3394–96.
5. See Ovid, *Metamorphoses*, II, 163.

five

ANTIFRATERNAL
TEXTS

One branch of the clergy was singled out from the rest for particularly caustic treatment in the thirteenth and fourteenth centuries. Papal recognition of the mendicant fraternal orders early in the thirteenth century led almost immediately to friction within the Church between the established secular clergy and the friars (who were called "regulars" because they lived under a regula, or "rule") and among the orders themselves. Of the "ordres foure" (General Prologue, 210), the first to achieve papal recognition (in 1216) were the followers of St. Dominic, who became known as the Preaching Friars (ordo praedicatorum) or Black Friars. In 1223 the Franciscan Order was officially approved, though St. Francis and eleven followers had received verbal authorization to pursue a life of poverty and to preach penance as early as 1209. This order became the Minorites, or Grey Friars. The Carmelites, or White Friars, who claimed to derive from the prophet Elijah (see Summoner's Tale, 1890; 3 Kings xix, 8 ff.), received papal approval in 1226; while the Austin Friars, who sought to trace their lineage to St. Augustine, were recognized in 1256.

Tension between these regular orders and the secular clergy arose when the former were granted papal license, or "privilege," to preach, to hear confession, and to bury the dead. In each of these activities the alien friar competed for the revenues of the parish priest, or curate, and hence threatened the entire secular establishment. Smoldering resentment toward the mendicants flared into open conflict in Paris after 1254, when the strong support given the friars by the newly elected Pope Alexander IV challenged secular control of the University. Spokesman for the University and the bishops was William of Saint-Amour, who developed the main charges against the friars in a series of sermons delivered in 1254 and 1255. These charges were given definitive expression in 1256 with the publication of the De periculis novissorum temporum ("The Perils of the Last Times"), a treatise which became the standard reference in antifraternal writings for the next two centuries.

In England, the most outspoken defender of the secular Church against the proliferating mendicants was Richard FitzRalph, whose Defensio curatorum ("Defense of the Curates," 1356) was widely disseminated and became a central document in the intensified attacks against the fraternal orders during the 1380s.

Literary artists generally sided with the secular masters in this dispute. Jean de Meun defended William of Saint-Amour with deft irony in the Romance of the Rose. As Fals-Semblant, a scandalous figure in fraternal habit, says in the Romaunt of the Rose, a translation attributed to Chaucer:

. . . William Seynt Amour wolde preche,
And ofte wolde dispute and teche

Of this matere all openly
At Parys full solempnely.
And, also God my soule blesse,
As he had, in this stedfastnesse,
The accord of the universite
And of the puple, as semeth me. (6763–70)

The character of Fals-Semblant in this poem reflects a large number of the standard antifraternal charges (see below, pp. 000-00). Among Chaucer's immediate predecessors, Petrarch and Boccaccio are noteworthy supporters of the secular clergy, and among his contemporaries, John Gower.

Chaucer's companion-pieces, the Friar's Tale and Summoner's Tale, contain the most devastating satire on the fraternal establishment in all literature. The friar in the Summoner's Tale, particularly, epitomizes a surprising number of the traditional complaints. Thus, for example, he preaches for personal gain (1713 ff.); claims the superiority of the fraternal over the secular clergy (1719–23; 1727–28, etc.); boasts of the great humility of friars (1873–1928); begs, contrary to Biblical injunction, "with scrippe and tipped staf" (1737: compare Luke ix, 3); hears confessions in the houses of the rich; shows a sophisticated taste for fine foods, despite pretending temperance (1838–50); engages in "glosing" where the Biblical text does not actually support him (1791–94; 1919 ff.); accepts the title maister (see Matthew xxiii, 10) in Thomas' house (1781, 1800), but hypocritically protests the name in the lord's (2185–88). The Summoner, furthermore, provides an excellent parody in his friar's "sermon" on ire, replete with vapid generalizations and exempla to which are given obviously inappropriate "applications." The degree to which Chaucer's Pardoner, who is largely modeled on Fals-Semblant, reflects his antimendicant attitude, has not yet been made clear. The friendly fox in the Nun's Priest's Tale, however, should probably be admitted to the fraternity, as Reynard's son Daun Russel is identified in French versions of the Reynard cycle as a Franciscan friar (compare Romaunt, 6795, where Fals-Semblant's "foxerie" translates French renardie).

Figure 7. Friar greets woman outside tavern. British Library MS Yates Thompson 13, fol. 177 (Taymouth Hours). Note the "Nicholas approach" (Miller's Tale, 3276).

Scriptural Authorities

The claim of the mendicants to be the "new apostles," replacing an apostolic succession which began according to Scripture with Christ's instructions to his disciples, led the secular clergy to stress these very instructions, as well as the Epistles of the Apostle Paul, in disputing such claims. The following passages, among the most frequently cited, provided Chaucer with many telling details. Other scriptural passages important to the secular adherents are indicated in the notes to their texts.

[Apostolic Instruction]

FROM *MATTHEW* X

5. These twelve Jesus sent: commanding them, saying: Go ye not into the way of the Gentiles, and into the city of the Samaritans enter ye not.

6. But go ye rather to the lost sheep of the house of Israel.

7. And going, preach, saying: The kingdom of heaven is at hand.

8. Heal the sick, raise the dead, cleanse the lepers, cast out devils: freely have you received, freely give.[1]

9. Do not possess gold, nor silver, nor money in your purses:[2]

10. Nor scrip for your journey, nor two coats, nor shoes, nor a staff;[3] for the workman is worthy of his meat.[4]

11. And into whatsoever city or town you shall enter, inquire who in it is worthy, and there abide till you go thence.

12. And when you come into the house, salute it, saying: Peace be to this house.[5]

13. And if that house be worthy, your peace shall come upon it; but if it be not worthy, your peace shall return to you.[6]

14. And whosoever shall not receive you, nor hear your words: going forth out of that house or city shake off the dust from your feet.

NOTES

1. Compare Summoner's Tale, 1765–69; 1851–78; General Prologue, 240–50; Summoner's Tale, 1832–33.
2. See Mark vi, 8; Luke ix, 3; x, 4.
3. See Summoner's Tale, 1737.
4. See Luke x, 7; 1 Timothy v, 18; Summoner's Tale, 1972–73.
5. As in Summoner's Tale, 1770?
6. Luke x, 7 adds: "And in the same house, remain, eating and drinking such things as they have." Compare Summoner's Tale, 1838 ff.

[Condemnation of the Pharisees]

FROM *MATTHEW XXIII*

1. Then Jesus spoke to the multitudes and to his disciples,

2. Saying: The scribes and the Pharisees have sitten on the chair of Moses.

3. All things therefore whatsoever they shall say to you, observe and do: but according to their works do ye not; for they say, and do not.

4. For they bind heavy and insupportable burdens, and lay them on men's shoulders; but with a finger of their own they will not move them.[1]

5. And all their works they do for to be seen of men. For they make their phylacteries broad, and enlarge their fringes. ·

6. And they love the first places at feasts, and the first chairs in the synagogues.[2]

7. And salutations in the market place, and to be called by men, Rabbi.

8. But be not you called Rabbi. For one is your master; and all you are brethren.

9. And call none your father upon earth; for one is your father, who is in heaven.[3]

10. Neither be ye called masters; for one is your master, Christ.[4]

11. He that is the greatest among you shall be your servant.

12. And whosoever shall exalt himself shall be humbled: and he that shall humble himself shall be exalted.[5]

13. But woe to you scribes and Pharisees, hypocrites; because you shut the kingdom of heaven against men, for you yourselves do not enter in; and those that are going in, you suffer not to enter.

14. Woe to you scribes and Pharisees, hypocrites: because you devour the houses of widows, praying long prayers. For this you shall receive the greater judgment.[6]

15. Woe to you scribes and Pharisees, hypocrites; because you go round about the sea and the land to make one proselyte; and when he is made, you make him the child of hell twofold more than yourselves.

25. Woe to you scribes and Pharisees, hypocrites; because you make clean the outside of the cup and of the dish, but within you are full of rapine and uncleanness.[7]

26. Thou blind Pharisee, first make clean the inside of the cup and of the dish, that the outside may become clean.

27. Woe to you scribes and Pharisees, hypocrites; because you are like to whited sepulchres, which outwardly appear to men beautiful, but within are full of dead men's bones, and of all filthiness.[8]

28. So you also outwardly indeed appear to men just; but inwardly you are full of hypocrisy and iniquity.

29. Woe to you scribes and Pharisees, hypocrites; that build the sepulchres of the prophets, and adorn the monuments of the just,[9]

30. And say: If we had been in the days of our Fathers, we would not have been partakers with them in the blood of the prophets.

31. Wherefore you are witnesses against yourselves, that you are the sons of them that killed the prophets.

32. Fill ye up then the measure of your fathers.

33. You serpents, generation of vipers, how will you flee from the judgment of hell?

NOTES

1. See Luke xi, 46; Romaunt of the Rose, 6889–904.
2. See Mark xii, 39; Luke xi, 43 and xx, 46; Romaunt, 6905–20.
3. See Malachias i, 6.
4. See James iii, 1. This text was frequently cited against the friars' desire to be known as "masters." See General Prologue, 261; Friar's Prologue, 1300; Summoner's Tale, 1781, 2184–88.
5. See Luke xiv, 11; xviii, 14.
6. See Mark xii, 40; Luke xx, 47.
7. See Luke xi, 39.
8. See Luke xi, 44.
9. See Luke xi, 47–48.

[The Last Times]

1. Know also this, that, in the last days, shall come dangerous times.[1]

2. Men shall be lovers of themselves, covetous, haughty, proud, blasphemers, disobedient to parents, ungrateful, wicked,

3. Without affection, without peace, slanderers, incontinent, unmerciful, without kindness,

4. Traitors, stubborn, puffed up, and lovers of pleasures more than of God:

5. Having an appearance indeed of godliness, but denying the power thereof. Now these avoid.

6. For of these sort are they who creep into houses, and lead captive silly women laden with sins, who are led away with divers desires:

7. Ever learning, and never attaining to the knowledge of the truth.

8. Now as Jannes and Mambres resisted Moses,[2] so these also resist the truth, men corrupted in mind, reprobate concerning the faith.

9. But they shall proceed no farther; for their folly shall be manifest to all men, as theirs also was.

NOTES

1. See 1 Timothy iv, 1; 2 Peter iii, 3; Jude i, 18–19.
2. See Exodus vii, 11.

William of Saint-Amour:
from *The Perils of the Last Times*

Leader of the antimendicant clergy at the University of Paris, William of Saint-Amour was a Professor of Theology and the Procurator of the University when the conflict developed. In 1255 and 1256 he preached a series of sermons against the friars, whom he identified as "false apostles," precursors of Antichrist, who preached without episcopal authority. In 1256, with the tacit approval of Louis IX of France, the archbishops of Sens, Rheims, Bourges, and Rouen reached an accord with the University which severely limited the activities of the mendicants. The text of the De periculis novissorum temporum (1256) was designed as a defense and justification of this decision. Pope Alexander IV condemned the book in 1256, ordered it burned, and exiled William from France (see Romaunt of the Rose, 6777–78). The text, nevertheless, was widely propagated, and William died in Saint-Amour, in 1272.

The title of the De periculis is based on 2 Timothy iii, 1: "Know also this, that, in the last days, shall come dangerous times" (see above, p. 244). This was a text used by certain Franciscans to support their claim to be the "new apostles" of the last age of the world. The De periculis, in effect, provides a parody of this claim. The words of the Apostle are necessarily true, but it is the friars themselves who are the false apostles ushering in the last days in league with Antichrist.

The following excerpts are drawn from the last chapter (XIV) of the treatise, in which William catalogues forty-one "signs" by which "True Apostles" may be distinguished from those he calls false, or "Pseudo." His repeated citation of Saint Paul is a constant reminder of the true and original apostolic tradition. The Gloss referred to is the Glossa ordinaria, attributed to Walafrid Strabo, a collection of commentary on the Scriptures which was usually written in the margins of Biblical manuscripts. William thus satirizes the friars' custom of "glosing" Scriptural texts which did not clearly support their "traditions" (see Summoner's Tale, 1788–94, 1918–23), by turning the Gloss itself against them.

A new translation.

[Signs of the True and Pseudo Apostles]

Since these Seducers have repeatedly claimed to be Apostles, or men sent by God to preach, and to save souls through their ministry according to the words of the Apostle: "For such false apostles are deceitful workmen, transforming themselves into the apostles of Christ,"[1] therefore we shall set forth signs, some infallible, others very probable, by which Pseudo-Apostles can be distinguished from the true Apostles of Christ.

The first sign is, that *True Apostles do not creep into houses, nor lead captive silly women laden with sins.*[2] Those Preachers, therefore, who creep into houses, and lead captive silly women laden with sins, are not true Apostles, but Pseudo.

The second sign is, that *True Apostles do not deceive the hearts of simple folk with studied speech with which they praise their own teachings,*[3] as do the Pseudo. "By pleasing speeches and good words, they seduce the hearts of the innocent";[4] *Gloss:* "With studied words they commend their own teachings, with which they deceive the hearts of simple men." Those men seduce the hearts of simple folk so well that they make them enter their order, a way of life which they call *Religion*; and then they who lived before in simple honesty, after entering, become crafty, hypocrites, pseudo, and creepers into houses, just like those men, and sometimes they become even worse. Concerning whom Matthew xxiii, 15, states: "Woe to you scribes and Pharisees, hypocrites; because you go round about the sea and the land to make one proselyte; and when he is made, you make him the child of hell twofold more than yourselves."[5] Those, therefore, who do these things are not true Apostles, but Pseudo.

The third sign is, that *True Apostles, if they are rebuked, bear themselves patiently.* "The signs of my apostleship have been wrought on you, in all patience";[6] *Gloss:* "He commends patience in relation to the conduct of preachers." Those, therefore, who do not take correction patiently are not true Apostles; in fact, they show that they are not even Christians. "No man can speak of Jesus Christ our Lord, except in the Holy Spirit."[7] Also, such men show that they are carnally minded, even though they pretend to be spiritual. "Am I then become your enemy, because I tell you the truth?"[8] *Gloss:* "No carnal man wishes to be rebuked for error." Those Preachers, therefore, who will not bear correction, seem to be not true Apostles, but Pseudo.

The fourth sign is, that *True Apostles do not commend themselves.*

"For we preach not ourselves."[9] "For we dare not match, or compare ourselves with some, that command themselves";[10] *Gloss:* "As do the Pseudo, who commend themselves with certain arts, while God does not commend them." Also, true Apostles through good works render themselves commendable to every man's conscience, not so much to their eyes, as the Apostle says: "Commending ourselves to every man's conscience, in the sight of God";[11] yet they do not commend themselves in comparison with others. Whence the *Gloss:* "Making ourselves commendable without comparison with others." Rather, indeed, they value the virtues of others above their own. Thus 2 Peter iii, 15: "As also our most dear brother Paul, according to the wisdom given him, hath written to you." . . . Those, therefore, who do the opposite, declaring their order or their teachings to be better than others, as do the Preachers, are not true Apostles, but Pseudo.

The sixth sign is, that *True Apostles do not preach unless they are sent.* "How shall they preach unless they be sent?"[12] *Gloss:* "They are not true Apostles unless they are sent, for no signs of virtue provide testimony for them." Who may be sent has been dealt with earlier.[13] Those, therefore, who preach without being sent, are Pseudo.

The eleventh sign is, that *True Apostles preach only for the sake of God and the salvation of souls, not for temporal profit.* "We preach not ourselves";[14] *Gloss:* "We do not preach for our own glory, or for personal gain, but for the glory of Christ." But the preaching of the Pseudo aims at the contrary; as the *Gloss* to Philippians i, 18, "Whether by occasion,[15] or by truth, Christ be preached," says: "The Pseudo preach the Gospel by occasion, seeking their own advantage either in money, or in honors, or in praise of men, and willing to accept favors from anyone; seeking in him to whom they preach not so much the salvation of his soul as his favors." . . . Those Preachers, therefore, who preach for temporal profit, or for worldly honor, or for the praise of men, are not true Apostles, but Pseudo.

But how can we know "when they preach for their own glory"? We answer, when those preach who have not been called. "He that glorieth, let him glory in the Lord";[16] *Gloss:* "Because he cannot glory, who has not received the power from the Lord." And he has not received the power from the Lord, who has not been called by God, that is, by the Church. "Neither doth any man take the honor to himself, but he that is called by God, as Aaron was";[17] *Gloss:* "He is called by God, who is lawfully chosen by the Church."

The twentieth sign is, that *True Apostles do not receive the temporal goods of those to whom they preach,* by which they are distinguished from wolves, that is, from the Pseudo. Thus Acts xx, 33: "I have not coveted any man's silver, gold, or apparel"; *Gloss:* "By this the Wolves can be recognized, because they covet these things." And also: "For such things as were needful for me and them that are with me, these hands have furnished";[18] *Gloss:* "Example of labor for Bishops, and a sign by which they are distinguished from Wolves." . . .

But someone may say: "Cannot a Preacher ask those to whom he preaches for his expenses, even by begging?"

We answer: If he preaches by authority (if as the good Shepherd he feeds his flock with the food of the Word) he may receive his necessities. But then, it is not begging, but his due. "The husbandman, that laboureth, must first partake of the fruits";[19] *Gloss:* "He sees to it that the chaste preacher of the Gospel is without material care, and holds that receiving necessities provided by his flock, just like those provided for him who feeds his sheep, is not begging, but his due." But that it is proper for a Preacher to beg is nowhere to be found in sacred writings. Rather, the Apostle forbids all Christians to beg; begging was abhorrent to Solomon, and it was disapproved of by Saint Augustine and many other holy expositors of the Bible, as we have shown earlier.[20] It is clear, therefore, that true Apostles do not covet the temporal goods of those to whom they preach, nor do they beg. Those, therefore, who seek goods from them to whom they preach, or who assign others to do so, do not appear to be true Apostles, but Pseudo.

The twenty-first sign is, that *True Apostles are patient in tribulation, and do not render evil for evil.* "Behold I send you as sheep in the midst of wolves";[21] *Gloss:* "Whoever undertakes to preach, ought not to stir up evil, but to suffer patiently." And the Lord Himself offered an example of this, according to Saint Peter: "Who when he was reviled, did not revile: when he suffered, he threatened not: but delivered himself to him that judged him unjustly."[22] Those, therefore, who do not patiently suffer evils, but rather incite them, are not true Apostles, but Pseudo.

The twenty-sixth sign is, that *True Apostles are content with the food and drink offered them, and do not ask for more elegant dishes.* "Eating and drinking such things as they have";[23] *Gloss:* "[Christ] conceded necessities as the preacher's due, so long as they were content with the food and drink offered them." Those Preachers, therefore, who, even though they preach without authority, are offended when they are not served more elegant meals, are not true Apostles, but Pseudo.

The thirty-eighth sign is, that *True Apostles do not speak boastfully, and do not attribute to themselves anything except that which God performs through them.* "For I dare not speak of any of those things which Christ worketh not by me";[24] *Gloss:* "That is, I speak only of those things which Christ works through me, that is, by my ministry." Those, therefore, who speak many things boastfully, and attribute many things to themselves which have not been done through them, are not true Apostles, but Pseudo.

The forty-first sign is, that *True Apostles do not acquire for themselves friends of this world.* "Whoever desires the friendship of this world is the enemy of God."[25] Those preachers, therefore, who acquire for themselves friends of this world, are not true Apostles, but Pseudo.

NOTES

1. 2 Corinthians xi, 13, a text used by Franciscans to describe the secular clergy, in order to justify their claim to be "true apostles."
2. 2 Timothy iii, 6. William discusses this important text in detail in chapters II and V. The "houses" are identified as the consciences of confessants; "silly women" are interpreted to be any persons of weak rationality. Chaucer's close linking of the Friar with his Wife of Bath may reflect this significant text. It is certainly clear that the Wife is "laden with sins."
3. *Traditiones,* translated as "teachings," carries the secondary suggestion of "betrayals." The charge that friars substitute "eloquence" for "wisdom" is traditional, and important in understanding Chaucer's "fraternal" speakers.
4. Romans xvi, 18; see xvi, 17.
5. See above, pp. 242–43 for context.
6. 2 Corinthians xii, 12. This charge is repeated by Richard FitzRalph (below, p. 256), and is obviously illustrated in the Summoner's Tale.
7. The reference is to 1 Corinthians iii, but it is more likely that William draws on the general sense of 1 Corinthians ii.
8. Galatians iv, 16.
9. 2 Corinthians iv, 5.
10. 2 Corinthians x, 12.
11. 2 Corinthians iv, 2.
12. Romans x, 15.
13. Chapter II of the *De periculis* explains the Biblical text to authorize only those preachers who are "called" by the bishops into their sees. The friars' authorization was granted by the Pope.
14. 2 Corinthians iv, 5.
15. I.e., by pretense.
16. 2 Corinthians x, 17.
17. Hebrews v, 4.

18. Acts xx, 34.
19. 2 Timothy ii, 6. See Summoner's Tale, 2277–88.
20. Chapter XII of the *De periculis* challenges the right of any able-bodied servant of Christ to beg. The "poverty" of the mendicants is a major issue in the controversy. See Romaunt of the Rose, 6545–614.
21. Matthew x, 16.
22. 1 Peter ii, 23.
23. Luke x, 7; Summoner's Tale, 1838–50.
24. Romans xv, 18.
25. James iv, 4.

Jean de Meun:
from the *Romance of the Rose*

Fals-Semblant in the Roman de la rose *appears as a friar enlisted in the army of Amours, the god of love. Jean de Meun gave him a long "confession" into which are worked most of the antimendicant charges in the works of William of Saint-Amour. Of special interest in the excerpt printed here is the claim against friars that they engaged in all kinds of secular "business." Suggestions of this sort also creep into the General Prologue portrait of the Friar. Fals-Semblant's hypocritical confession is also extensively adapted by Chaucer for his Pardoner's Prologue. The influence of Jean de Meun and the* Roman de la rose *are indicated on pp. 452–53. This section of the* Roman *is translated in the Romaunt of the Rose, 6801–922, 6971–7007.*

Trans. Charles Dahlberg, The Romance of the Rose *(Princeton: Princeton University Press, 1971), pp. 202–5. The passage translates lines 11528–636, 11679–718. Copyright © 1971 by Princeton University Press. Reprinted by permission of Princeton University Press.*

[Fals-Semblant Describes the Friars' Life]

"The man who wants to fear God can hardly attain anything great in this world, for the good, who avoid evil, live legitimately on what they have, and keep themselves according to God, scarcely get from one loaf to the next. Such people drink too much discomfort; there is no life that displeases me so much.

"But consider how usurers, counterfeiters, and loan sharks have money in their storehouses. Bailiffs, beadles, provosts, mayors, all live practically by rapine. The common people bow to them, while they, like wolves, devour the commoners. Everybody runs over the poor; there isn't anyone who does not want to despoil them, and all cover themselves with their spoil. They all snuff up their substance and pluck them alive without scalding. The strongest robs the weakest. But I, wearing my simple robe and duping both dupers and duped, rob both the robbed and the robbers.

"By my trickery I pile up and amass great treasure in heaps and mounds, treasure that cannot be destroyed by anything.[1] For if I build a palace with it and achieve all my pleasures with company, the bed, with tables full of sweets—for I want no other life—my money and my gold increases. Before my treasure can be emptied, money comes to me again in abundance. Don't I make my bears tumble? My whole attention is on getting. My acquisitions are worth more than my revenues.[2] Even if I were to be beaten or killed, I still want to penetrate everywhere. I would never try to stop confessing emperors, kings, dukes, barons, or counts. But with poor men it is shameful; I don't like such confession. If not for some other purpose, I have no interest in poor people; their estate is neither fair nor noble.

"These empresses, duchesses, queens, and countesses; their high-ranking palace ladies, these abbesses, beguines,[3] and wives of bailiffs and knights; these coy, proud bourgeois wives, these nuns and young girls; provided that they are rich or beautiful, whether they are bare or well turned out, they do not go away without good advice.[4]

"For the salvation of souls, I inquire of lords and ladies and their entire households about their characteristics and their way of life; and I put into their heads the belief that their parish priests are animals in comparison with me and my companions. I have many wicked dogs among them, to whom I am accustomed to reveal people's secrets, without hiding anything; and in the same way they reveal everything to me, so that they hide nothing in the world from me.

"In order that you may recognize the criminals who do not stop deceiving people, I will now tell you here the words that we read of Saint Matthew, that is to say, the evangelist, in the twenty-third chapter: 'Upon the chair of Moses' (the gloss explains that this is the Old Testament), 'the scribes and pharisees have sat.' These are the accursed false people that the letter calls hypocrites. 'Do what they say, but not what they do. They are not slow to speak well, but they have no desire to do so. To gullible people they attach heavy loads that cannot be carried; they place them on their shoulders, but they dare not move them with their finger.' "[5]

"Why not?" asked Love.

"In faith," replied False Seeming, "they don't want to, for porters' shoulders are often accustomed to suffer from their burdens, and these hypocrites flee from wanting to do such a thing. If they do jobs that may be good, it is because people see them. They enlarge their phylacteries and increase their fringes; since they are haughty, proud, and overbearing, they like the highest and most honorable seats at tables and the first in the synagogues. They like people to greet them when they pass along the street, and they want to be called 'master,' which they shouldn't be called, for the gospel goes against this practice and shows its unlawfulness.[6] . . .

"I also undertake brokerage commissions, I draw up agreements, I arrange marriages, I take on executor's duties, and I go around doing procurations.[7] I am a messenger and I make investigations, dishonest ones, moreover. To occupy myself with someone else's business is to me a very pleasant occupation. And if you have any business to do with those whom I frequent, tell me, and the thing is done as soon as you have told me. Provided that you have served me well, you have deserved my service. But anyone who wanted to punish me would rob himself of my favor. I neither love nor value the man by whom I am reproved for anything. I want to reprove all the others, but I don't want to hear their reproof, for I, who correct others, have no need of another's correction.

"I have no care either for hermitages. I have left the deserts and woods, and I leave desert manors and lodgings to Saint John the Baptist, for there I was lodged much too far away. I make my halls and palaces in towns, castles, and cities, where one can run with a free rein. I say that I am out of the world and immerse myself in it; I take my ease and bathe and swim better than any fish with his fin.

"I am one of Antichrist's boys, one of the thieves of whom it is written that they have the garment of saintliness and live in pretense; we seem pitiful sheep without, but within we are ravening wolves."

Figure 8. Franciscan and Dominican Friars with Devils. Corpus Christi College MS 180, fol. 1 (Richard FitzRalph, *De pauperie Salvatoris*).

NOTES

1. A parody of Matthew vi, 19–21.
2. See General Prologue, 256.
3. One of a sisterhood, devoted to a religious life, but not bound by formal vows.
4. Reflecting the charge that friars preyed particularly on simple women; see 2 Timothy iii, 6 (above, p. 244).
5. See above, p. 242.
6. See above, p. 242.
7. Technically, acting as attorney or agent for another; also, "procuring," i.e., pimping. The Friar in Chaucer's General Prologue engages in such "public services."

Richard FitzRalph:
from *Defense of the Curates*

The most ardent English spokesman against the fraternal orders was Richard FitzRalph (c. 1295–1360). Educated at Oxford, he was widely admired as a teacher, preacher, and theologian. In 1347 he was made Archbishop of Armagh and Primate of Ireland.

From 1349 until his death FitzRalph pressed the complaints of the English clergy against the friars, in the Papal Court at Avignon. In 1350 four of his sermons on this issue, delivered in London, provoked the Pope's displeasure. The Defensio curatorum (1357) is a long Latin sermon originally presented in his own defense before the Papal Court. FitzRalph seems to have died at Avignon before his case was decided.

The Defensio enjoyed a wide circulation during Chaucer's lifetime, both in its original Latin form and in the English translation by John Trevisa, on which the present text is based.

[Charges against Friars]

These men in the orders of beggars multiply contrary to the wisdom of the law of Almighty God; they fleece the people and the clergy, and burden them everywhere. For now no man, whether in high station or low, learned or not, can sit down to a morsel of meat but such beggars appear unbidden, and they beg not as poor men should at the gate or door, meekly asking alms as Saint Francis taught and requires in his Testament, but unasked they come right into houses and courts, where they are sheltered and given food and drink. And even though they bring with them grain, meal, bread, meat, or cheese, they will take something more away with them even if there are but two in the house.[1] If they are reproved, they feel no natural shame. It is a wonder that they do not fear the judgment of Pope Gregory, who wrote in an open letter to the prelates of Holy Church: "Satan often disguises himself as an angel of light. We bid and command you, by our authority, that if any, who profess to be of the order of Preachers, preach in your districts and then turn to begging money, so as to bring discredit on those whose order has made a profession of poverty, treat them as hypocrites and condemn them." They have become so subtle in this craft of begging that poor vicars and parsons, and all people, complain against them almost everywhere. It is a strange way of life for those who say that they profess the Gospel, and yet act contrary to the very words of Christ, who when he sent out his disciples to preach the Gospel, said: "Remove not from house to house."[2] They also act contrary to another scripture, which states: "[Evil has made men] to go from place to place."[3] But yet they go about from court to court, and from house to house, so that their cloister will not be their prison. Is this not damaging to the clergy and to the people as well? It certainly seems so to many men. And the misuse of privileges is the cause of all this, for they claim that they have the privilege of preaching and hearing confession, and almost no one will reprove them or put them off.

These privileges do much harm to the friars, for it seems that they infect them with many different sins: with the sins of injury and of wrong, with arrogance, with avarice, and with the sin of pride. . . . It seems that the procuring of these privileges infects friars with the sin of injury and wrong toward the curates, for that procuring is against God's commandment that says: "Thou shalt not covet thy neighbor's house: neither shalt thou desire his wife, nor his servant, nor his handmaid, nor his ox, nor his ass, nor any thing that is his."[4] These privileges that friars have acquired were, in truth, the rights of curates; therefore it was contrary to the commandment of God to covet those rights. Avarice precedes acquisition in every procurer. Since it is not lawful to covet the curate's ox or his ass, as it is against God's commandment, it is more wrongful to covet those things which are of more profit to the curates, and such are these rights. Such procuring is also against the commandment to love thy neighbor, which says: "Thou shalt love thy neighbor as thyself."[5] Every man so loves himself that he does not want others wrongfully to covet his goods. Since the rights of curates were not formerly due to friars, they were wrongfully procured by them, and so against the commandment of God. . . .

Procuring of such privileges also infects them with the sin of disobedience, for these privileges are contrary to the rules of their profession. They claim that their four orders are ordained by Holy Church and founded on begging and voluntary poverty. Can the right to preach and to baptize be consistent with this foundation in beggary, when the means of gaining a living pertain to this privilege, as it does according to law, if the friars compete for these means with those who preach the Gospel? . . .

The same may be said of the privilege of burial, of hearing confession, of taking the offerings which are offered to God. For God has commanded: "Thou shalt not appear before the Lord empty-handed"[6] when you go into the church to partake of the sacraments. They fall into the sin of disobedience, for they use their office contrary to the will of the Apostle, who says: "And how shall they preach unless they be sent, as it is written: *How beautiful are the feet of them that preach the gospel of peace, of them that bring glad tidings of good things!*"[7] And "Neither doth any man take the honor to himself, but he that is called by God."[8] They also disobey Christ's word, which says: "Neither be ye called masters; for one is your master, Christ."[9] Thus [these friars], who promise in their profession to keep Christ's Gospel, are disobedient and arrogant.

NOTES

1. See Summoner's Tale, 1738–53; General Prologue, 252–55.
2. Luke x, 7; see Summoner's Tale, 1736–39, 1765.
3. Ecclesiasticus xxix, 24.
4. Exodus xx, 17; Deuteronomy v, 21.
5. Matthew xix, 19.
6. Exodus xxiii, 15; xxxiv, 20; Deuteronomy xvi, 16.
7. Romans x, 10. See Isaiah lii, 7; Nahum i, 15. The Ordinary Gloss to this text

explains it as a warning against all new teachers, who usurp to themselves the ministry without the lawful mission derived from the Apostles, to whom Christ said: "As my Father hath sent me, I also send you" (John xx, 21).

8. Hebrews v, 4.

9. Matthew xxiii, 10; see James iii, 1.

Richard de Bury:
from the *Philobiblon*

As a friend of Richard FitzRalph (see above p. 255) and other secular scholars, Richard de Bury was involved in the antifraternal attacks in the middle of the fourteenth century. In this chapter of his Philobiblon (1345) his charges are general, but typical. Against the friars' profession of "evangelical poverty" he charges a love "of the stomach, of dress, and of houses"—all of which reappear in Chaucer's treatment of friars. Since these charges are brought by "books," the implication is that the fraternal orders, despite pretensions to great learning, neglected serious study.

The term "Mendicants" conventionally designates the Franciscan order of friars, whose "Spiritual" wing originally provoked the first antifraternal attacks, especially as a result of their applications of the mystical works of Joachim of Fiore (see n. 16, below). But allusions to the other orders, indicated in the notes, suggest that Richard had in mind more generally the "ordres foure," all of which were technically "mendicants"—i.e., beggars.

The notes also indicate something of Richard's facility at Scriptural allusion, not unusual in his day, and the degree to which it characterizes his rhetoric. These allusions not only demonstrate his own learning, but they are often chosen from the very texts used by the friars to justify themselves. References to the apostolic tradition allude to the friars' claim to be inheritors of that tradition or even, in the case of the Joachimite faction of the Franciscans, to be the new apostles of the third and last age of the world. Elijah is cited to show how far the friars are from true spiritual ideals—in this case of the prophet claimed by the Carmelite order as their founder.

Trans. E. C. Thomas, The Love of Books: The Philobiblon of Richard de Bury (London: Kegan, Paul, Trench, 1888: rept. New York: Cooper Square Publishers, 1966), pp. 38–45.

[The Complaint of Books against the Mendicants]

CHAPTER VI

Poor in spirit,[1] but most rich in faith, off-scourings of the world[2] and salt of the earth,[3] despisers of the world and fishers of men,[4] how happy are ye, if suffering penury for Christ ye know how to possess your souls in patience![5] For it is not want, the avenger of iniquity, nor the adverse fortune of your parents, nor violent necessity that has thus oppressed you with beggary, but a devout will and Christ-like election, by which ye have chosen that life as the best, which God Almighty made-man, as well by word as by example, declared to be the best. In truth, ye are the latest offspring of the ever-fruitful Church, of late divinely substituted for the Fathers and the Prophets, that your sound may go forth unto all the earth,[6] and that instructed by our healthful doctrines ye may preach before all kings and nations the invincible faith of Christ. Moreover, . . . the faith of the Fathers is chiefly enshrined in books . . . , from which it is clearer than light that ye ought to be zealous lovers of books above all other Christians. Ye are commanded to sow upon all waters,[7] because the Most High is no respecter of persons,[8] nor does the Most Holy desire the death of sinners,[9] who offered Himself to die for them, but desires to heal the contrite in heart, to raise the fallen, and to correct the perverse in the spirit of lenity.[10] For which most salutary purpose our kindly Mother Church has planted you freely, and having planted has watered you with favors, and having watered you has established you with privileges, that ye may be co-workers with pastors and curates in procuring the salvation of faithful souls.[11] Wherefore, that the order of Preachers was principally instituted for the study of the Holy Scriptures and the salvation of their neighbors, is declared by their constitutions, so that not only from the rule of Bishop Augustine, which directs books to be asked for every day, but as soon as they have read the prologue of the said constitutions, they may know from the very title of the same that they are pledged to the love of books.[12]

But alas! a threefold care of superfluities, *viz.*, of the stomach, of dress, and of houses,[13] has seduced these men and others following their example from the paternal care of books, and from their study. For, forgetting the providence of the Savior (who is declared by the Psalmist to think upon the poor and needy),[14] they are occupied with

the wants of the perishing body, that their feasts may be splendid[15] and
their garments luxurious, against the rule, and the fabrics of their build-
ings, like the battlements of castles, carried to a height incompatible
with poverty. Because of these three things, we books, who have ever
procured their advancement and have granted them to sit among the
powerful and noble, are put far from their hearts' affection and are
reckoned as superfluities; except that they rely upon some treatises of
small value, from which they derive strange heresies and apocryphal
imbecilities,[16] not for the refreshment of souls, but rather for tickling
the ears of the listeners.[17] The Holy Scripture is not expounded, but is
neglected and treated as though it were commonplace and known to
all, though very few have touched its hem,[18] and though its depth is
such, as holy Augustine declares, that it cannot be understood by the
human intellect, however long it may toil with the utmost intensity of
study.[19] From this he who devotes himself to it assiduously, if only He
will vouchsafe to open the door who has established the spirit of
piety,[20] may unfold a thousand lessons of moral teaching, which will
flourish with the freshest novelty[21] and will cherish the intelligence of
the listeners with the most delightful savors. Wherefore the first profes-
sors of evangelical poverty, after some slight homage paid to secular sci-
ence, collecting all their force of intellect, devoted themselves to labors
upon the sacred scripture, meditating day and night on the law of
the Lord. And whatever they could steal from their famishing belly,
or intercept from their half-covered body, they thought it the highest
gain to spend in buying or correcting books.[22] Whose worldly contem-
poraries observing their devotion and study bestowed upon them for
the edification of the whole Church the books which they had collected
at great expense in the various parts of the world.

In truth, in these days as ye are engaged with all diligence in pursuit
of gain, it may be reasonably believed, if we speak according to human
notions, that God thinks less upon those whom He perceives to distrust
His promises, putting their hope in human providence, not considering
the raven, nor the lilies, whom the Most High feeds and arrays.[23] Ye
do not think upon Daniel and the bearer of the mess of boiled pot-
tage,[24] nor recollect Elijah who was delivered from hunger once in the
desert by angels,[25] again in the torrent by ravens, and again in Sarepta
by the widow,[26] through the divine bounty, which gives to all flesh their
meat in due season. Ye descend (as we fear) by a wretched anticlimax,
distrust of the divine goodness producing reliance upon your own
prudence, and reliance upon your own prudence begetting anxiety
about wordly things, and excessive anxiety about worldly things taking
away the love as well as the study of books; and thus poverty in these

days is abused to the injury of the Word of God, which ye have chosen only for profit's sake. . . .

NOTES

1. See Matthew v, 3; Luke vi, 20: a text frequently cited by the friars to justify their existence. See Summoner's Tale, 1923. Their profession of "evangelical poverty" is often refuted by secular writers, as in the present text.
2. See 1 Corinthians iv, 13: "We are made as the refuse of this world, the off-scouring of all even unto now." St. Paul is referring to the life of the apostles.
3. See Matthew v, 13.
4. See Matthew iv, 19: again in reference to the apostolic tradition.
5. See Luke xxi, 19.
6. See Psalm xviii, 5; Romans x, 18.
7. See Isaias xxxii, 20: that is, they are to serve all men, not just the rich and influential.
8. See Acts x, 34: that is, a person's position in life does not affect God's justice. Compare Deuteronomy x, 17; 2 Paralipomenon xix, 7; Job xxxiv, 19; Wisdom vi, 8; Ecclesiastes xxxv, 15; Romans ii, 11; Ephesians vi, 9; Colossians iii, 25; 1 Peter i, 17. Galatians ii, 6, which also uses the formula, appears in the context of the "false brothers" (*falsi fratres:* Galatians ii, 4) who are taken to represent the friars in condemnations of the fraternal orders; this text may therefore have been foremost in Richard's mind.
9. See Ezechiel xxxiii, 11.
10. See Galatians vi, 1.
11. See 1 Corinthians iii, 6.
12. The Order of Preachers (*fratres praedicatores*), the order instituted by St. Dominic in 1216, received papal sanction from Honorius III, on condition that it adopt the Rule of St. Augustine. The Austin friars claimed St. Augustine as their founder.
13. See Summoner's Tale, 2108, where the friar says that his cloister will have to sell their books, in order to build their house.
14. See Psalm xxxix, 18.
15. See Matthew xxiii, 6: an important context in antifraternal polemic.
16. Apparently a reference to Pseudo-Joachimite treatises such as the *Liber introductorius in evangelium aeternum* (1254) by Gherardo da Borgo San Donnino, produced by the rigorist (or "Spiritual") wing of the Franciscan order. Gherardo claimed that the eternal sense of Holy Writ—the "Eternal Gospel" which was to be the foundation of the third and last age of the world—had been entrusted to the Franciscan order, and that this order in fact realized the spiritual ideals of the "third age." This treatise, denounced by the secular masters at the University of Paris, was condemned and ordered destroyed by a commission of Pope Alexander IV in 1255. Richard's "books" may have resented particularly the thesis of Joachim of Fiore that the second age was an age of reading, while the third age was to be devoted to prayer and song. See Romaunt of the Rose, 7089–212.
17. See 2 Timothy iv, 3.
18. See Matthew xiv, 36.
19. St. Augustine, *Epistle* CXXXVII.
20. See Colossians iv, 3.
21. See Romans vii, 6.
22. Chaucer's Clerk abides in this tradition (General Prologue, 293–303).

23. See Luke xii, 24, 27.
24. See Daniel i, 12–16. Daniel and Elijah were true prophets and visionaries.
25. Elijah: called Elias in the Vulgate Bible. The Carmelite order of friars claimed Elijah as their founder. See Summoner's Tale, 1890. Elijah is fed by an angel in 3 Kings xix, 5–8.
26. See 3 Kings xvii, 6, 9–16.

John Gower:
from *Vox clamantis*

This selection from the work of Chaucer's friend illustrates the contemporary vitality of the conventions of invective against the mendicants. It can be used as a yardstick to measure the artistic grace with which Chaucer makes similar points. Gower and the Vox clamantis *are discussed above, pp. 192–93.*

Trans. Eric W. Stockton, The Major Latin Works of John Gower (Seattle: University of Washington Press, 1962), pp. 182–84. Reprinted by permission of the University of Washington Press.

[On Friars]

IV, 16. NOW THAT [THE AUTHOR] HAS DISCUSSED THOSE IN PROPERTY-OWNING RELIGIOUS HOUSES WHO BREAK THEIR VOWS, IT IS NECESSARY TO SPEAK OF THOSE IN THE ORDER OF MENDICANT FRIARS WHO GO ASTRAY. AND HE WILL SPEAK FIRST OF THOSE WHO CONSPIRE UNDER THE SHADOW OF FEIGNED POVERTY FOR WORLDLY RICHES, AS IF THEY WOULD BRING ALL THE EARTH UNDER THEIR DOMINION.

. . . I grant that the functions of the original order were holy, and that in the beginning its founders were pious. A friar remains blessed who follows after them, who in renouncing the world seeks to reach God, who adopts monastic poverty for himself and bears it voluntarily,[1] and who patiently undertakes the work of his order. Such a man is indeed to be praised for his high merits, for the earth is restored through his prayers. But he who disguises his outer appearance in the order and lacks its true essence, he who preaches outwardly yet inwardly yearns for riches—to such men of the present this book offers its message, since the voice of the people furnished the things for it to say.

The throng of friars overflows the mendicant order; the original rule is dead, inundated by them.[2] These men, who used to bear hardships pleasing to God in accordance with the vow of their order, are becoming soft. For the first time they are giving themselves a name which must be described as "headless"; those upon whom everyone confers opulence call themselves "inopulent." The friars maintain that they are disciples of Christ and that they are pursuing all their duties after His example. Their false faith claims this, but this is sufficient unto them, as those who know the Scriptures say.[3] They are now acting like people who have no property, yet under a pauper's guise they grab everything. I do not know whether it is a sign of favor or doom for these friars, but all the world abounds with them. They hold the Pope in their hands; he mitigates the hardships of their order and decrees that more and more things are now permissible. And if the papal authority rejects their suits, their perverse order will secretly make them lawful. There is no king nor prince nor great man in the world who should not confess his secrets to them.

And so the mendicants are mightier than lords, and from the world they secretly usurp what their order plainly forbids. I would say that these men are not disciples but rather gods: both life and death bring money to them. For a friar demands that he himself bury the dead bodies of those to whom he attached himself as confessor, if they were dignitaries. But if it should be a poor [man's] body, he makes no claim at all, since his piety takes no cognizance of anything unless there is money in it.[4] They refuse to baptize mere faith, since a matter of business with no money in it will not be esteemed or performed at their hands. Just as a merchant buys every kind of goods in order that he can make a great deal for himself out of a great many people, so the greedy friar embraces every worldly cause in order that he may enjoy his various gains. They are men whom the grasping world has not frightened away; on the contrary, it shows a high regard for them, and has surrendered up its affairs to them. It is obvious that these converted men are subverted, so they should derive their true reputations from their deeds. Thus the pharisaical branch has cut itself off from its source of life, and its fruit is pungently bitter to the taste.[5]

IV, 17. HERE HE SPEAKS OF THE FRIARS WHO HYPOCRITI-CALLY REBUKE THE PEOPLE'S SINS WHEN PREACHING IN PUBLIC, BUT NEVERTHELESS PROMOTE THEM ZEAL-OUSLY IN PRIVATE WITH BLANDISHMENTS AND SATIS-FACTION.

A friar's assiduous hypocrisy sows his words[6] in order that his harvest of profit in the world may thrive through them. He thunders out fearful sermons as he publicly damns the practice of sin, like a very servant of God. But like a servant of Satan, he furnishes glosses for them when he comes to sit down for a while in private chambers. His gentle blandishment is soothing to the ear [of] those whom his deep, resounding voice has goaded before. And thus does this sinner cater to sins for others, for by encouraging vice he gets a profit from it. A friar knows well that when sin dies, then his revenue dies for all time. Tell me where a friar will come three times, unless he may take away money. He does not return by the road where his lot is unprofitable. If you took away crime from the friars' foundations their house which was lofty for so long would fall without a struggle.

O how the words of the prophet Hosea are now verified! Thus did he speak the truth: "A certain tribe will arise on earth which will eat up the sin of my people and know much evil."[7] We perceive that this prophecy has come about in our day, and we give credit for this to the friars. No matter what is necessary for their sustenance, fate provides everything for them through sins. There are no such sensuous pleasures as sometimes fail to yield a crumb to friars, if they are confessors. Notice that doves come to spotless quarters, and that an unclean tower does not harbor such birds. Similarly, no house except those of tycoons provides friars of today with guest accommodations where they wish to stay on. Ants never make their course toward empty granaries, and a wandering friar will not come near when one's wealth is lost.[8] With no thought of the blooms which it bore before, they disdain the thorn when the roses have fallen off.[9] In this way do the friars scorn the favors of friendship from a man formerly rich, when he can give no more. Many are friars in name but few by rights. As some say, Falseness is their prophet. Their cloak's appearance is poor, but their money box is rich. They hide their shameful deeds under sanctimonious words. Poor without poverty and holy without Christ, thus does a man who is lacking in goodness stand out as eminently good. They call upon God with their lips, yet they venerate gold in their hearts, and on every side they seek to learn the way to it. The Devil has placed everything under their foot, but their pretended sanctity does not teach them how to hold on to anything. Thus does one who "scorns" the world grasp in turn at the things of this world, while his sheep's clothing conceals a hostile wolf.[10] And thus the people, deluded by pretenses, will think of men whom deceitfulness inwardly rules as outwardly holy. There is scarcely a one who repoaches the falseness of another; rather, each contributes to the trickery so that they may be the more deceiving. Driven by the same vice, they are thus tainted the more, and they taint all the earth with their dishonesties. In any event, may the Lord repress those whom He knows to be sinning at this time against the age-old faith. I do not ask that they be destroyed, but that the weak be strengthened, and that they submit to the original way of life which their order imposed.

NOTES

1. The distinction between voluntary poverty (a virtue) and involuntary poverty (a source of sinful discontent) was a commonplace. See Pardoner's Tale, 439–42; Wife of Bath's Tale, 1178–1206.
2. See Wife of Bath's Tale, 864–81; a standard complaint.
3. Compare Matthew vi, 1–7, 16–18.
4. Burial fees claimed by friars would otherwise go to the secular clergy; another repeated grievance.
5. See Matthew xii, 33.
6. *Sermones* means both "words" and "sermons." The friars' license to preach was a standard grievance; see Summoner's Tale, 1711–34, 1788–96, 2281–86.

7. See Osee iv, 8, and context.
8. See Ovid, *Tristia,* I, ix, 9–10.
9. See Ovid, *Fasti,* v, 354.
10. See Matthew vii, 15.

six

MODES OF LOVE

Many of Chaucer's poems are concerned in some way with actions arising from romantic love. Such works as Troilus and Criseyde and the Knight's Tale are directly modeled on the medieval romance, in which love in a courtly setting traditionally plays a part. Elements of this tradition appear in tales like those of the Franklin and Merchant, and are the basis for some earthy humor in the Miller's Tale. Even the Wife of Bath's discourse on marriage strikes tangentially at ideas characteristically involved in the typical medieval formula for romantic love affairs: for example, in her insistence on the "obedience" of husbands.

According to this formula, the golden arrow of Cupid, entering the lover's eye, stimulates secret yearning and causes the "lover's malady" which only the "mercy" or "grace" of the lady can cure. After complaining against his misfortune, the lover engages in good works and service "in hope to stonden in his lady grace" (General Prologue, 88). The lady, on her part, also has an assigned role: to exhibit "daunger," or coy disdain, until she has proved the lover's worth. The man who succeeds may be accepted, like Troilus, into her "grace" as a clandestine lover, or she may "take hym for hir housbonde and hir lord" as does Dorigen in the Franklin's Tale, 742. The climax of the ritual is thus a "union" with the lady whose beauty entered the lover's eye.

This ritual, or "code," it must be emphasized, is primarily a literary artifice, like the pastoral convention, which could be employed for different purposes, ranging from sentiment to satire and even obscenity. Its literary predecessors and popularizers include Ovid, whose Art of Love purported to be a "handbook for lovers"; the French troubadours; Andreas Capellanus, who modeled his Treatise on Love on Ovid's work; and the long, amatory allegory of love, the Romance of the Rose, which Chaucer translated. Ovid wrote for the equestrian class of Augustan Rome, and his medieval imitators address themselves to a literate, courtly audience. Medieval literary lovers who follow the formula are usually knights and squires, or parodies of courtiers; only in courtly circles could there be such leisure as seems to be needed for this behavior. The code, sometimes referred to as "chivalric love," receives much attention in chivalric texts (see above, pp. 199–203, 208–9).

What Ovid, posing as a "master" (magister amoris) of the subject, described as a "system" (ratio) contained many elements of parody of the civic and military obligations of his day. In the Middle Ages these obligations were assumed by a chivalric class whose "code" provided terms and standards against which the loyalties of lovers must be seen. Furthermore, the Church had promulgated new, spiritual standards for the understanding of human love. Both Church and State, in fact, regarded with extreme disfavor romantic passion which irrationally replaced officially sanctioned obligations. As Ovid had drawn on the language of Roman politics, the medieval language of love, we find, *draws on the more complex lexicons of authority in the Middle Ages.*

The idea of "service," for example, is both a Christian and a chivalric ideal. The lover's service of the lady thus takes on possible resonances which Ovid could not have known. As the texts above indicate, the chivalric duty to "serve" women meant protecting the weak from injustice. Servitude like that practiced by the lover is not officially envisioned, nor is "bed-service," sometimes implied in more cynical texts which, in Ovidian fashion, turn the "worth" of the knight into sexual prowess. Church doctrine, on the other hand, offered its own dimension for interpreting the behavior of conventional lovers. In one sense, the "lover's malady"—sleeplessness, loss of appetite, loneliness—can be seen as an analogy to the act of religious contemplation (waking, fasting, solitary isolation). Andreas Capellanus' insistence that "love" demands "excessive meditation" may, indeed, contemplate just such an analogy for the "religion of love" (which would, in such terms, automatically become idolatry). In another sense, these symptoms coincide with what appear repeatedly in clerical discussions of "the incommodities of lust (luxuria)." The account attributed to Vincent of Beauvais in the Speculum morale *(1310–25) provides a good instance of such terms. To show that the vice of* luxuria *is to be avoided, he lists its "pains":*

> Who is able to record how many labors and days without food, how many poor meals, how many sleepless nights (since lovers pass many nights without sleeping), how many fears and imagined perils, how many anxieties and distresses, how much "bad weather"—that is, hot spells and cold, thunderstorms, snow and ice, and many such—these wretched people bear: in order to experience the shortest and most vile delight; who, if they bore them for God and for the health of their souls, would truly be martyrs before God.

Although these miseries are listed to dissuade the reader from indulging in luxuria, *it is evident that the author (who here consciously echoes the Ovidian "system") recognizes a parallelism between sensual and spiritual love. His lover is a "martyr" whichever "God of Love" he follows. So he can conclude, substituting "malice" for "love":*

> Whence it is clear that their "malice" has so blinded them, that that which is truly foul seems to them fair, and that which is truly harmful seems to them delightful.

The lady's "mercy" or "grace" sought by the lover is symptomatic of a Christianizing of Ovidian language. To explain the high percentage of locutions drawn from the religious system of the day, some cultural historians have stressed the influence of the cults of Mary and the growing "Mariolatry" in the twelfth and thirteenth centuries. It is true that the figure of Mary stands in the medieval iconographical system as a standard antithesis to the figure of Eve. Eve offered the apple which subjugated the rational man to the temptations of the flesh; Mary brought forth Christ who redeemed the spirit from its fleshly bondage. Eve is the prototype of the woman described so colorfully in the antifeminist treatises of Chaucer's day (see below, pp. 399ff.); Mary is the prototype of the Church, the nun, and the good wife who offers true "saving grace" (see below, pp. 365ff.). Eve's power is over the flesh, and she opens up the gates to a sensual paradise; the spiritual man hopes to "stand in the grace" of Mary, who makes him worthy of heaven. Writers need not have turned to specific hymns and liturgies to Mary for language in which to express the sentiments of secular love. The analogy between Eve and Mary arises from a deeply ingrained habit of thought which sees things in terms of contraries—that is, in the light of charity or of cupidity. A language conventional to secular love is commonplace in the expression of religious sentiments from a very early date; it becomes most daring, perhaps, in the relation of mystics, such as Richard Rolle, to their divine "lover" (see below, pp. 345–48). Saint Paul stressed that he had to speak of spiritual matters "after the manner of men because of the infirmity of your flesh" (Romans vi, 19), the result being an elaborate correspondence between divine and secular terminology. Canticles (as it was then interpreted) uses the full range of sensuous imagery to express what was interpreted as the love between Christ and the Church, or between the pure soul and its celestial Bridegroom. It is to be expected that the reverse should also occur—that the vocabulary of theology should be drawn into the service of secular love.

For a sense of the variety possible in the application of the medieval conventions of love, one might compare the accounts of "chivalric love" by John Gower (above, pp. 195–203) and the pious Geoffroi de Charny (above, pp. 208–9), the bourgeois account of courtship by Bartholomaeus (below, pp. 386–87), and the rejection of carnal delights by Andreas Capellanus (below, pp. 357–59).

Figure 9.   The Triumph of Venus. Maternity tray, the Louvre. Photo Giraudon. The adoring heroes in the love garden are identified, from left to right, as Achilles, Tristan, Lancelot, Samson, Paris, and Troilus.

Ovid:
from *The Art of Love*

Ovid's contribution to the code of romantic love, which medieval courtly lyrics and romances tirelessly repeat, is enormous. Particularly in the Loves, The Art of Love, *and* The Remedies of Love, *he developed a "doctrine" or "system," referred to amusingly as an* ars *or* ratio, *which he as a* magister *("master") teaches. Virtually all of the salient characteristics of the medieval convention are already present in Ovid's system. Rules for duping the husband (who becomes the medieval* jaloux *or* gilos—*the "jealous one") establish this "love" as adulterous, in conflict with the social order. Such Ovidian topics as advice on writing letters, the use of a go-between, secrecy, the "lover's malady" of Hereos (or ereos), and above all an extravagant ritual of woman-service, become the conventional lore of medieval literary lovers. Ovid even recommends, to wives who wish to dupe their suspicious husbands, the* adultera clavis *("forged key," Ars amatoria, III, 643–44) which shows up in the Merchant's Tale, 2116–24, with the pun left implied.*

Allusions, imitations, and adaptations of Ovid by medieval authors occur so often that we must conclude that they thought of themselves as writing fundamentally in the Ovidian tradition. How that tradition was then interpreted has thus an immediate bearing on our understanding of the love practiced by knights and squires in medieval fiction. Readers can draw their own conclusions from the numerous instances of Ovidian usage annotated in this volume. One possibility is plainly suggested by the comment on the Wife of Bath, whom Chaucer presents as an "experienced teacher," that

Of remedies of love she knew per chaunce,
For she koude of that art the old daunce.

(General Prologue, 475–76)

Trans. J. H. Mozley, Ovid: The Art of Love, and Other Poems, Volume II (Cambridge, Mass.: Harvard University Press, 1929: Loeb Classical Library), pp. 63, 77, 79–83, 101–3, 123–25, 139, 149, 157–61, 171–73. Reprinted by permission of the publishers and The Loeb Classical Library.

275

Her own experience, it seems, has been refined by Ovid's Remedia amoris *and* Ars amatoria. *Chaucer provides her with a source by including "Ovides Art" in the "book of wikked wyves" read by her fifth husband (Wife of Bath's Prologue, 680, 685), though as a literary fiction she inherits this knowledge from la Vieille, a great quoter of Ovid, in the* Roman de la rose *(see below, pp. 469–72).*

Ovid's influence can be felt, furthermore, in literary technique. His shimmering wit was appreciated and imitated by writers deeply versed in his Latin. His critique of Augustan Rome was a model for social satire based on irony rather than invective. Perhaps most important, he worked out a structure in which the poet set up a persona, *or substitute of the same name, who turns out to be, in many ways, foolish. Thus the* love *the* persona *magisterially systematizes is utterly incompatible with* Romanitas *such as Virgil celebrated; in fact, his ratio provides a series of jocular inversions of Roman virtues and Augustan morality. In the Middle Ages, the technique of the first-person* persona *is found everywhere, notably in the* Romance of the Rose, *in Boccaccio's romances, and in all of Chaucer's longer works.*

For a resume of Ovid's literary career, see above, pp. 106–7.

[Advice to Men]

I, 723–38

White is a shameful colour in a sailor; swarthy should he be, both from the sea-waves and from heaven's beams; shameful too in a husband-man, who ever beneath the sky turns up the ground with curved ploughshare and heavy harrows. Thou too who seekest the prize of Pallas' garland art shamed if thy body be white.[1] But let every lover be pale; this is the lover's hue. Such looks become him; let fools think that such looks avail not. Pale did Orion wander in Dirce's glades, pale was Daphnis when the naiad proved unkind.[2] Let leanness also prove your feelings; nor deem it base to set a hood on your bright locks. Nights of vigil make thin the bodies of lovers, and anxiety and the distress that a great passion brings. That you may gain your desire be pitiable, so that whoso sees you may say, "You are in love."[3]

II, 143–68, 177–250

Come then, trust but timidly, whoever you are, to treacherous beauty; or possess something worth more than outward shape. Chief above all does tactful indulgence win the mind; harshness causes hatred and angry wars. We hate the hawk because he ever lives in arms, and the wolves that are wont to go against the timorous flock. But the swallow is free from men's attack because he is gentle, and the Chaonian bird has towers he may inhabit.[4] Keep far away, quarrels and bitter-tongued affrays; with soft words must love be fostered. With quarrels let wives pursue husbands and husbands wives, and deem that they are ever at issue with each other; this befits wives; the dowry of a wife is quarrel-ing: but let your mistress ever hear welcome sounds. Not by the law's command have you come into one bed; for you love performs the work of law.[5] Bring soft blandishments and words that soothe the ear, that your coming may make her glad. I come not to teach the rich to love: he who will give has no need of my art; he who when he pleases says "Accept" has wit enough of his own; I give place: my devices will not please so much as he. I am the the poet of the poor, because I was poor when I loved; since I could not give gifts, I gave words. Let the poor man love with caution; let the poor man fear to speak harshly; let him bear much that the rich would not endure. . . .

Should she be neither kindly nor courteous to your wooing, persist and steel your resolve; one day she will be kind. By compliance is the curved bough bent away from the tree; you will break it if you try your strength. By compliance are waters swum; nor can you conquer rivers if you swim against the current's flow. Compliance tames tigers and Numidian lions; little by little the bull submits to the rustic plough.[6] What could be more stern than Nonacrian Atalanta? yet stubborn as she was she yielded to a hero's prowess. Often, they say, beneath the trees Milanion bewailed his lot and the maiden's cruelty; often did he bear the crafty nets on his obedient neck, often with ruthless spear transfixed the grisly boars; from the bow too that Hylaeus strung did he feel the wound—and yet another bow was still more known than this.[7] I do not bid you arm and climb the forests of Maenalus, nor carry nets upon your neck; nor do I bid you offer your breast to flying arrows; easy will be the precepts of my cautious art. Yield if she resists; by yielding you will depart the victor; only play the part she bids you play. Blame if she blames; approve whatever she approves. Affirm what she affirms and deny what she denies. If she laughs, laugh with her; if she weeps, remember to weep; let her impose her laws upon your countenance. If she be gaming, and throwing with her hand the ivory dice, do you throw amiss and move your throws amiss; or if it is the large dice you are throwing, let no forfeit follow if she lose; see that the ruinous dogs often fall to you; or if the piece be marching under the semblance of a robbers' band, let your warrior fall before his glassy foe.[8] Do you yourself hold her parasol outstretched upon its rods, yourself make room for her in the crowd, where she is coming. Nor hesitate to place the footstool for her trim couch; take off her slipper from her dainty foot, or put it on. Often too when she is cold, though you are shivering too, you must warm your lady's hand in your own lap. Nor think it base (though base, it will give pleasure) to hold a mirror in your freeborn hand. He who won the heaven which first he bore himself, when his step-mother was wearied of sending monsters, is believed to have held a basket among Ionian maidens, and to have spun fine the unworked wool. The Tirynthian hero obeyed a mistress' command: go, shrink [not] from enduring what he endured![9] Bidden meet her at the Forum, go earlier than the hour of bidding, nor leave till it be late. She

---

Figure 10. The Month of May. British Library MS Roy. 2 B. VII, fol. 75 (Queen Mary Psalter). From a medieval calendar: compare General Prologue, 92. The youth on horseback carries a falcon because May is a season for "hunting"—an Ovidian metaphor for "girl-chasing." (See figure 11.)

has told you to join her somewhere: put off everything, run! let not the crowd delay your passage. At night she will return to her house, the banquet finished: then too come in the slave's stead, if she calls. You are in the country, and she says "Come!" Love hates the sluggish: if wheels fail, make the journey on foot. Let neither the fatal heat and the thirsty Dogstar delay you,[10] nor a road made white by fallen snow.

Love is a kind of warfare; avaunt, ye laggards! these banners are not for timid men to guard. Night, storm, long journeys, cruel pains, all kinds of toil are in this dainty camp. Oft will you put up with rain from melting clouds of heaven, and oft will you lie cold on the bare ground. The Cynthian is said to have pastured the kine of Admetus king of Pherae, and to have made a humble cot his lodging.[11] Whom does that not become which became Phoebus? put off your pride, whoever you are that care for an enduring love. If it is denied you to go by a safe and easy road, and if the door be held by a fastened bolt, yet slip down headlong through an opening in the roof; or let a high window afford a secret path. She will rejoice, and know herself the cause of peril to you; this will be a pledge of your lady's sure affection. Oft was it in your power, Leander, to be absent from your mistress: you swam across that she might know your passion.[12]

II, 511–34

Whoso loves wisely will be victorious, and by my art will gain his end. Not always do the furrows repay their trust with interest, not always does the wind assist perplexed vessels; what aids lovers is but little, more there is to thwart them; let them make up their minds to many a trial. As many as the hares that feed on Athos, or the bees on Hybla, as many as the berries that the blue-grey tree of Pallas bears,[13] or the shells that are on the shore, so many are the pains of love; the darts that wound us are steeped in much poison. She will be said to have gone abroad, though you perchance will see her: believe she has gone, and that your eyes deceive you. On the promised night her door will be shut against you: endure to lay your body even on unclean ground. Perhaps some lying, proud-faced maid will say, "Why does this fellow besiege our door?" Supplicate and coax both door and cruel damsel, take the roses from your head and hang them on the doorpost. When she is willing, go to her; when she shuns you, depart; the well-bred man should not bear to become a bore. Why should your mistress be able to say, "I cannot escape from this fellow"? the senses are not always present to aid.[14] Think it not shameful to endure a woman's abuse or blows, nor to give kisses to her tender feet.

NOTES

1. The athlete, whose prize was a crown of olive.
2. For his excessive efforts in wooing Merope, Orion the hunter was blinded by Merope's father. Daphnis, son of Mercury, was actually himself faithless to the Naiad, who punished him with blindness. Ovid's mythological examples often imply ironies which belie their superficial applications.
3. Ovid's version of the "loveris maladye" of *Hereos* (see Knight's Tale, 1355–79) is a part of the deliberate role he urges his lovers to play. It becomes an actual "disease" needing his "remedies" only if the lover fails in his program which reduces love to an "art."
4. The dove, associated here with the oracle of Dodona in Chaonia.
5. The Ovidian contrast between lawful marriage and illicit love becomes an amusing medieval commonplace.
6. "Compliance" translates Latin *obsequium*, which also means "submission," "obedience."
7. The bow of Hylaeus, a Centaur who attempted to rape Atalanta, marked the extreme point of Milanion's endurance on her behalf. The "other bow" is that of Cupid.
8. Ovid refers here to various Roman games; his advice is, of course, to lose. It should be noted that this, and such precepts as those quoted above, are in many ways a parody of the Roman ideal of victory through endurance, espe·cially as it is celebrated in the *Aeneid*.
9. Hercules, the son of Zeus and Alcmene, was persecuted by Hera, Zeus' wife. It was as penance for having murdered his friend Iphitus that Hercules was made to serve Omphale, queen of Lydia, spinning wool while she took up his heroic weapons. Ovid's mythological example of "lover's heroism" is a typical ex-ample of his "master's" sophistry.
10. Sirius, the dog star, signals the hot, dry weather in July and August.
11. Apollo tended the flocks of Admetus (a mortal) for nine years as penance for having killed the Cyclops.
12. Leander swam the Hellespont each night to visit Hero, priestess of Venus. He drowned one night in a storm, proving his love.
13. The olive.
14. I.e., you cannot always count on your physical attractiveness.

[Advice to Women]

III, 59–98

Now already be mindful of the old age which is to come; thus no hour will slip wasted from you. While you can, and still are in your spring-time, have your sport; for the years pass like flowing water; the wave that has gone by cannot be called back, the hour that has gone by cannot return. You must employ your time: time glides on with speedy foot, nor is that which follows so good as that which went before. These plants, now withering, I saw as violet-beds; from this thorn was a pleasing garland given me. That day will come when you, who now shut out your lovers, will lie, a cold and lonely old woman, through the night; nor will your door be broken in a nightly brawl, nor will you find your threshold strewn with roses in the morning. How quickly, ah, me! is the body furrowed by wrinkles, and the colour fled that once was in that lovely face! And the white hairs that you swear have been there since maidenhood will suddenly be scattered over all your head. Serpents put off their age with their frail skins, nor are stags made old by casting their horns: our charms flee without our aid; pluck the flower, which save it be plucked will basely wither.[1] Besides, childbirth shortens the period of youth: a field grows old by continual harvesting. Latmian Endymion brings no blush to thee, O Moon, nor is Cephalus a prize that shames the roseate goddess; though Adonis, whom she mourns, be granted to Venus, whence has she her Aeneas and Harmonia?[2] Study, ye mortal folk, the examples of the goddesses, nor deny your joys to hungry lovers. Though they at last deceive you, what do you lose? those joys abide; though they take a thousand pleasures, naught is lost therefrom. Iron is worn away, and flints are diminished by use; that part endures, and has no fear of loss. What forbids to take light from a light that is set before you, or who would guard vast waters upon the cavernous deep?[3] And yet does any woman say to a man, "It is not expedient"? tell me, what are you doing, save wasting the water that you will draw? Nor do my words make you vile, but forbid you to fear unreal loss; there is no loss in your giving.

III, 281–98

Who would believe it? women learn even how to laugh; here too seemliness is required of them. Let the mouth be but moderately opened, let the dimples on either side be small, and let the bottom of the lip cover the top of the teeth. Nor should they strain their sides with continuous laughter, but laugh with a feminine trill. One woman will distort her face with a hideous guffaw, another, you would think, was weeping, while she is laughing happily. That one's laugh has a strident and unlovely harshness, as when a mean she-ass brays by the rough millstone. How far does art not go? they learn to weep becomingly, and can wail when and how they choose.[4] What, when they defraud letters of their rightful utterance, and the tongue is compelled to lisp at their command? The defect has charm—this uttering some words amiss; they learn the power to mar their power of speech.[5] Give attention to all these things, because they are useful: learn to carry yourself with womanly step.

III, 417–32

Profitable to you, beauteous damsels, is a crowd; oft let your wandering feet stray o'er the threshold. The wolf draws nigh to many sheep that she may prey on one, and the eagle of Jove swoops down on many birds. Let the beautiful woman also offer herself to the people to be seen; out of many there will be one, perchance, whom she may attract. Let her that is eager to please be always everywhere, and give all her mind's attention to her charms. Chance everywhere has power; ever let your hook be hanging; where you least believe it, there will be a fish in the stream. Often do hounds stray in vain through mountain glens, and a stag, without any driving it, falls into the nets. What had fettered Andromeda less to hope for than that her tears could e'er find favour?[6] Often a husband is sought at a husband's funeral;[7] it is becoming to go with dishevelled hair, and to mourn without restraint.

III, 553–94

Yet dissemble, and carry not greed on your open countenance; a new lover will take fright if he sees the net. But a rider would not use the same bridle for a horse who but lately felt the reins and for one who knows his paces; nor must the same path be taken to catch discreet age and tender youth. This raw recruit, now first known to Love's campaigning, who has come, a new prey,[8] to your chamber door—let him know none but you, let him cling to you alone; high is the fence that must guard that tender crop. Avoid a rival: you will prevail, so long as you alone have power; in partnership neither thrones nor love stand sure. . . . Pluck with quick hand the fruit that quickly passes.

Let all be revealed: we have flung our gates open to the foe, and in faithless treason let us keep faith. What is easily given ill fosters an enduring love; let an occasional repulse vary your merry sport. Let him lie before your gate; let him cry, "Ah, cruel door!" and play the suppliant oft, and oft the threatener. We cannot bear sweetness; let us be refreshed by bitter juices; oft is a vessel sunk by favouring winds; 'tis this which prevents wives from being loved: to them their husbands come whenever they will; add but a door, and let a doorkeeper say to you with stubborn mouth, "You cannot"; once shut out, you too, sir, will be touched by love. Throw down the foils now, and fight with sharpened swords; nor do I doubt that I shall be attacked with my own weapons. While a lover lately ensnared is falling into the toils, let him hope that he alone has the right to your chamber; later on let him be aware of a rival and of the shared privilege of your couch; neglect these devices and his love will wane.

III, 749–68

Anxiously are you expecting me to lead you to the feast; here too do you await my counsels. Come late, and make a graceful entrance when the lamp has been set: delay will enhance your charm: a great procuress is delay. Though plain, to the tipsy you will seem fair: and night herself will hide your faults. Help yourself with your fingers: manners in eating count for something; and smear not all your face with a soiled hand. And do not take your meal beforehand at home, but stop short of your appetite; eat somewhat less than you are able; if Priam's son saw Helen eating greedily, he would hate her and say, "My prize is a foolish woman."[9] Better suited is drinking, and were more becoming in a woman: not badly goest thou, Bacchus, with Venus' son. This too note, when the head endures, the mind and feet are also firm; do not see double where there is but one. A woman lying steeped in wine is an ugly sight; she deserves to endure any union whatever.[10] Nor is it safe when the table is cleared to fall asleep; in sleep much happens that is shameful.

NOTES

1. This exercise in the theme of *carpe diem*, really self-serving "advice" to women, was cynically elaborated by Jean de Meun's la Vieille in the *Roman de la rose* (see below, pp. 469–72).
2. Selene, the moon-goddess, had fifty daughters by Endymion. Cephalus rejected

Aurora's love, as did Adonis the love of Venus. Venus, however, though the wife of Vulcan, did bear Aeneas (son of Anchises) and Harmonia (son of Mars). Aeneas was Virgil's founder of Augustan Rome but was thus, like the social ideal of "harmony," a bastard, according to Ovid's *magister*.

3. See Wife of Bath's Prologue, 331–36; Matthew v, 15–16.
4. Chaucer's Prioress has learned this, and many other tricks, probably by way of the *Roman de la rose:* see General Prologue, 142–50.
5. A technique perhaps ironically attributed to the Friar (General Prologue, 264–65). Ovid the rhetorician would have abhorred the corruption of language, here in the name of "art."
6. Andromeda was saved by Perseus from a sea monster, though not because she wept or deliberately exposed herself.
7. See Wife of Bath's Prologue, 593–602; 543–62.
8. Latin, *praeda novella,* can also mean new "plunder," or "spoils of war."
9. Source of la Vieille's advice adopted by the Prioress (General Prologue, 127–36). See below, pp. 469–70.
10. See Wife of Bath's Prologue, 464–68.

Ovid:
from *Amores*

The wit with which Ovid attacked the subject of love is well illustrated in the following elegy. In it the life of the lover is compared to that of the knight in extended detail, very much like a metaphysical conceit. The metaphor of a militia amoris *("love's warfare") becomes an intimate part of the medieval language of love; courtly lovers explore the full range of military terminology to express their struggle to "win" the lady, a technique which often produces delightful Ovidian double-entendres. Ovid's trope is more than merely witty, however. The* persona *is engaging in a characteristic boast, raising his nighttime forays to the level of the military* virtus *and Roman* pietas *(loyalty to the gods, state, and family) cherished by the Emperor Augustus and Virgil, his propagandist The comparison, though witty, can only make the speaker appear ridiculous. An equivalent effect occurs when the medieval lover transfers the language of chivalry to his amatory adventures, for we are constantly reminded of the conflict between his private desire and public duty. Furthermore, since medieval chivalry incorporates the idea of the* militia Christi *("Christian warfare," in imitation of Christ), the metaphor takes on possibilities of irony undreamed of by Ovid. In effect, we now have two "Loves" (Christ and Cupid), each with his* militia *and an identical terminology of service and struggle.*

Trans. Grant Showerman, Ovid: Heroides and Amores, Volume I (Cambridge, Mass.: Harvard University Press, 1914: Loeb Classical Library), pp. 355–59. Reprinted by permission of the publishers and The Loeb Classical Library.

[The Lover's Warfare]

Every lover is a soldier, and Cupid has a camp of his own; Atticus, believe me, every lover is a soldier. The age that is meet for the wars is also suited to Venus. 'Tis unseemly for the old man to soldier, unseemly for the old man to love.[1] The spirit that captains seek in the valiant soldier is the same the fair maid seeks in the man who mates with her. Both wake through the night; on the ground each takes his rest—the one guards his mistress's door, the other his captain's. The soldier's duty takes him a long road; send but his love before, and the strenuous lover, too, will follow without end. He will climb opposing mountains and cross rivers doubled by pouring rain, he will tread the high-piled snows, and when about to ride the seas he will not prate of swollen East-winds and look for fit stars ere sweeping the waters with his oar. Who but either soldier or lover will bear alike the cold of night and the snows mingled with dense rain? The one is sent to scout the dangerous foe; the other keeps eyes upon his rival as on a foeman. The one besieges mighty towns, the other the threshold of an unyielding mistress; the other breaks in doors, the one, gates.

Oft hath it proven well to rush on the enemy sunk in sleep, and to slay with armed hand the unarmed rout. Thus fell the lines of Thracian Rhesus, and you, O captured steeds, left your lord behind.[2] Oft lovers, too, take vantage of the husband's slumber, and bestir their own weapons while the enemy lies asleep. To pass through companies of guards and bands of sentinels is ever the task both of soldier and wretched lover. Mars is doubtful, and Venus, too, not sure; the vanquished rise again, and they fall [who] you would say could never be brought low.

Then whoso hath called love spiritless, let him cease. Love is for the soul ready for any proof. Aflame is great Achilles for Briseis taken away—men of Troy, crush while ye may the Argive strength![3] Hector from Andromache's embrace went forth to arms, and 'twas his wife that set the helmet on his head.[4] The greatest of captains, Atreus' son, they say, stood rapt at sight of Priam's daughter, Maenad-like with her streaming hair.[5] Mars, too, was caught, and felt the bonds of the smith; no tale was better known in heaven.[6] For myself, my bent was all to dally in ungirt idleness; my couch and the shade had made my temper mild. Love for a beautiful girl has started me from craven ways and bidden me take service in her camp. For this you see me full of action, and waging the wars of night. Whoso would not lose all his spirit, let him love![7]

NOTES

1. "Unseemly" translates *turpe* ("dishonorable," "base," "filthy"), suggesting an attitude like those in medieval fabliaux toward January-May marriages (see Miller's Tale, 3221–32; the *Distichs* of "Catoun" contain no such advice). When the Merchant's old knight Januarie becomes her "knyght" (Merchant's Tale, 1723–26), Venus laughs.
2. Ulysses and Diomedes invaded the camp of King Rhesus of Thrace while he slept, killed him, and stole his white horses which, according to an oracle, might have preserved Troy. Ovid is engaging in mock-heroic comparison of small things with great.
3. "The wrath of Achilles" in Homer's *Iliad* was occasioned by Agamemnon's depriving him of Briseis—but Achilles' motive was not the erotic passion assumed by Ovid's *persona*; rather it was "heroic" pride in his martial honor.
4. Andromache, in fact, attempted to dissuade Hector from battle on the day he was killed on the plains of Troy.
5. Agamemnon on seeing Cassandra, the prophetess. The Maenades were the Bacchae, frenzied followers of Bacchus.
6. See Ovid, *Ars amatoria*, II, 561–92; *Metamorphoses*, IV, 171 ff. All of the preceding examples actually rendered the lovers "spiritless," at least for martial exercise.
7. The irony of the concluding passage is picked up by Guillaume de Lorris, who makes Oiseuse ("Idleness") the portress to the Garden of Love in the *Roman de la rose*. Compare Second Nun's Tale, 1–7.

Boethius:
from *The Consolation of Philosophy*

The most important philosophical treatise in the Middle Ages was The
Consolation of Philosophy *by Anicius Manlius Boethius (c. 480–524). This
was the last work of one who had distinguished himself as both statesman
and scholar in a relatively brief lifetime. In government service he rapidly
rose to the highest state offices under the Ostrogoth king Theodoric in
Rome, only to be accused of treason in 522, imprisoned, and executed
in 524.*

*As a scholar Boethius translated many of Aristotle's treatises on logic;
wrote commentaries on logical works by Aristotle, Porphyry, and Cicero;
and composed at least three treatises of his own on the subject. In addition,
he wrote treatises on the four arts of the medieval* quadrivium: *arithmetic,
music, geometry, and astronomy. He was also the author of five theological
works. The* De consolation Philosophiae, *written in prison, is his only
known work in moral philosophy.*

In the Consolation *Boethius confronts his own misfortunes by creating
the allegorical figure* Philosophia *who engages in dialogue with the prisoner,
leading him from dark, narrow-minded self pity to an enlightened, rational
view of the human condition in a providentially governed universe. The
discussion deliberately excludes any reference to Christian revelation, thus
preserving a purely "philosophical" rationale. Its treatment of Fortune,
Fate, Divine Providence, and the relationship between Free Will and God's
Foreknowledge was the standard authority on such matters, so important
that the* Consolation *was translated by King Alfred, Jean de Meun, Geof-
frey Chaucer, and Queen Elizabeth, among others.*

The five Books of the Consolation *alternate passages of prose and poetry.
In the poem below,* Philosophia *celebrates the cosmic Love with which
God guides the universe. The concept is applied in Theseus' Boethian lec-
ture in the Knight's Tale, 2987–3089, and the poem is the source of
Troilus' hymn to Love in* Troilus and Criseyde, *III, 1744–71.*

Trans. Richard Green, The Consolation of Philosophy (New York: Bobbs-Merrill,
1962: Library of Liberal Arts), p. 41. Copyright © 1962 by The Bobbs-Merrill
Company. Reprinted by permission of the publisher.

[Cosmic Love]

That the universe carries out its changing process in concord and with
stable faith, that the conflicting seeds of things are held by everlasting
law, that Phoebus in his golden chariot brings in the shining day, that
the night, led by Hesperus, is ruled by Phoebe,[1] that the greedy sea
holds back his waves within lawful bounds, for they are not permitted
to push back the unsettled earth—all this harmonious order of things is
achieved by love which rules the earth and the seas, and commands the
heavens.

But if love should slack the reins, all that is now joined in mutual
love would wage continual war, and strive to tear apart the world which
is now sustained in friendly concord by beautiful motion.

Love binds together people joined by a sacred bond;[2] love binds
sacred marriages by chaste affections; love makes the laws which join
true friends. O how happy the human race would be, if that love which
rules the heavens ruled also your souls![3]

NOTES

1. *Phoebus*—the sun; *Hesperus*—the evening star; *Phoebe*—the moon.
2. That is, in political federations, or alliances.
3. Compare these effects with the resolutions at the end of the Knight's Tale.

Andreas Capellanus:
from *The Treatise on Love*

Of Andreas Capellanus, author of the De amore (c. 1185), practically noth-
ing is known. As he refers to himself in the work as "chaplain of the royal
court," it is probable that he served as chaplain (capellanus) in the court
of Marie de Champagne at Troyes, where the Arthurian romances of Chré-
tien de Troyes (fl. 1170) were composed.

Andreas makes his De amore a kind of repository for the premises, pos-
tures, and problems in love which the troubadours had made fashionable.
Adopting the Ovidian pose of a magister amoris, he offers a certain friend
named Walter two Books of advice on how to gain and how to retain love,
and, in a third Book, reasons for rejecting carnal in favor of spiritual love.
The division between the "art" and the "remedy" is Ovidian, although the
ultimate Christian concerns of the chaplain are not.

As a medieval "master" he organizes his treatise into scholastic "distinc-
tions," and writes in the Latin of the schools. In the first two Books
Andreas explores the sophistry and folly of the love he treats, in a manner
not unlike Ovid's in the Art of Love. In the third Book he abandons irony
for what becomes, at the end, a statement of Christian love like that in the
concluding stanzas of Chaucer's Troilus and Criseyde. The alternate title of
this work, De arte honeste amandi, is translated by J. J. Parry as "The Art
of Courtly Love." Since Latin honestus can mean either "honorable" or
"spuriously honorable," Andreas' ambiguous title might be appropriately
rendered "The Art of Loving Respectably."

At the end of Book II of the De amore Andreas provides thirty-one
"rules" to be kept faithfully "under threat of punishment by the King of
Love." They were to be given out "to all lovers in all parts of the world."

Trans. J. J. Parry, The Art of Courtly Love (New York: Columbia University Press,
1941), pp. 28–32, 184–86. Reprinted by permission of Columbia University Press.

[Distinctions concerning Love]
Book One: Introduction to the Treatise on Love

We must first consider what love is, whence it gets its name, what the effect of love is, between what persons love may exist, how it may be acquired, retained, increased, decreased, and ended, what are the signs that one's love is returned, and what one of the lovers ought to do if the other is unfaithful.

CHAPTER I. *WHAT LOVE IS*

Love is a certain inborn suffering derived from the sight of and excessive meditation upon the beauty of the opposite sex, which causes each one to wish above all things the embraces of the other and by common desire to carry out all of love's precepts in the other's embrace.

That love is suffering is easy to see, for before the love becomes equally balanced on both sides there is no torment greater, since the lover is always in fear that his love may not gain its desire and that he is wasting his efforts. He fears, too, that rumors of it may get abroad, and he fears everything that might harm it in any way, for before things are perfected a slight disturbance often spoils them. If he is a poor man, he also fears that the woman may scorn his poverty; if he is ugly, he fears that she may despise his lack of beauty or may give her love to a more handsome man; if he is rich, he fears that his parsimony in the past may stand in his way. To tell the truth, no one can number the fears of one single lover.[1] This kind of love, then, is a suffering which is felt by only one of the persons and may be called "single love." But even after both are in love the fears that arise are just as great, for each of the lovers fears that what he has acquired with so much effort may be lost through the effort of someone else, which is certainly much worse for a man than if, having no hope, he sees that his efforts are accomplishing nothing, for it is worse to lose the things you are seeking than to be deprived of a gain you merely hope for. The lover fears, too; that he may offend his loved one in some way; indeed he fears so many things that it would be difficult to tell them.

That this suffering is inborn I shall show you clearly, because if you will look at the truth and distinguish carefully you will see that it does not arise out of any action; only from the reflection of the mind upon what it sees does this suffering come. For when a man sees some woman fit for love and shaped according to his taste, he begins at once to lust after her in his heart;[2] then the more he thinks about her the more he burns with love, until he comes to a fuller meditation. Presently he begins to think about the fashioning of the woman and to differentiate her limbs, to think about what she does, and to pry into the secrets of her body, and he desires to put each part of it to the fullest use. Then after he has come to this complete meditation, love cannot hold the reins, but he proceeds at once to action; straightway he strives to get a helper and to find an intermediary. He begins to plan how he may find favor with her, and he begins to seek a place and a time opportune for talking; he looks upon a brief hour as a very long year, because he cannot do anything fast enough to suit his eager mind. It is well known that many things happen to him in this manner. This inborn suffering comes, therefore, from seeing and meditating. Not every kind of meditation can be the cause of love, an excessive one is required; for a restrained thought does not, as a rule, return to the mind, and so love cannot arise from it.[3]

CHAPTER II. *BETWEEN WHAT PERSONS LOVE MAY EXIST*

Now, in love you should note first of all that love cannot exist except between persons of opposite sexes. Between two men or two women love can find no place, for we see that two persons of the same sex are not at all fitted for giving each other the exchanges of love or for practicing the acts natural to it. Whatever nature forbids, love is ashamed to accept.[4]

Every attempt of a lover tends toward the enjoyment of the embraces of her whom he loves; he thinks about it continually, for he hopes that with her he may fulfill all the mandates of love—that is, those things which we find in treatises on the subject. Therefore in the sight of a lover nothing can be compared to the act of love, and a true lover would rather be deprived of all his money and of everything that the human mind can imagine as indispensable to life rather than be without love, either hoped for or attained.[5] For what under heaven can a man possess or own for which he would undergo so many perils as we continually see lovers submit to of their own free will? We see them despise death and fear no threats, scatter their wealth abroad and come to great poverty.[6] Yet a wise lover does not throw away wealth as a prodigal spender usually does, but he plans his expenditures from the

beginning in accordance with the size of his patrimony;[7] for when a man comes to poverty and want he begins to go along with his face downcast and to be tortured by many thoughts, and all joyousness leaves him.[8] And when that goes, melancholy comes straightway to take its place, and wrath claims a place in him; so he begins to act in a changed manner toward his beloved and to appear frightful to her, and the things that cause love to increase begin to fail. Therefore love begins to grow less, for love is always either decreasing or increasing. I know from my own experience that when poverty comes in, the things that nourished love begin to leave, because "poverty has nothing with which to feed its love."[9]

But I do not tell you this, my friend, with the idea of indicating by what I say that you should follow avarice, which, as all agree, cannot remain in the same dwelling with love, but to show you that you should by all means avoid prodigality and should embrace generosity with both arms. Note, too, that nothing which a lover gets from his beloved is pleasing unless she gives it of her own free will.

CHAPTER III. *WHERE LOVE GETS ITS NAME*

Love gets its name (*amor*) from the word for hook (*amus*), which means "to capture" or "to be captured,"[10] for he who is in love is captured in the chains of desire and wishes to capture someone else with his hook. Just as a skillful fisherman tries to attract fishes by his bait and to capture them on his crooked hook, so the man who is a captive of love tries to attract another person by his allurements and exerts all his efforts to unite two different hearts with an intangible bond, or if they are already united he tries to keep them so forever.[11]

CHAPTER IV. *WHAT THE EFFECT OF LOVE IS*

Now it is the effect of love that a true lover cannot be degraded with any avarice. Love causes a rough and uncouth man to be distinguished for his handsomeness; it can endow a man even of the humblest birth

---

Figure 11. The Month of May from a medieval calendar. British Library MS Add. 16975, fol. 4 (Psalter). As in figure 10, this youthful figure of the "Month of May" carries a hunting falcon. He also has his hunting hound and a chaplet of flowers on his head reminiscent of lovers in the *Roman de la rose* and other works.

with nobility of character; it blesses the proud with humility; and the man in love becomes accustomed to performing many services gracefully for everyone. O what a wonderful thing is love, which makes a man shine with so many virtues and teaches everyone, no matter who he is, so many good traits of character![12] There is another thing about love that we should not praise in few words: it adorns a man, so to speak, with the virtue of chastity, because he who shines with the light of one love can hardly think of embracing another woman, even a beautiful one. For when he thinks deeply of his beloved the sight of any other woman seems to his mind rough and rude.

I wish you therefore to keep always in mind, Walter my friend, that if love were so fair as always to bring his sailors into the quiet port after they had been soaked by many tempests, I would bind myself to serve him forever. But because he is in the habit of carrying an unjust weight in his hand, I do not have full confidence in him any more than I do in a judge whom men suspect. And so for the present I refuse to submit to his judgment, because "he often leaves his sailors in the mighty waves."

NOTES

1. Compare Ovid, *Ars amatoria*, II, 517–19 (above, p. 280); *Heroides*, I, 12. In Book III Andreas explains: "The man who is in love is bound in a hard kind of slavery and fears that almost anything will injure this love of his, and his soul is very much upset by a slight suspicion. . . ."
2. Compare Matthew v, 27–28: "You have heard that it was said to them of old: Thou shalt not commit adultery. But I say to you, that whosoever shall look on a woman to lust after her, hath already committed adultery with her in his heart."
3. See Troilus and Criseyde, I, 358–71; Merchant's Tale, 1594–1606.
4. The meaning depends upon whether Andreas refers to human nature before the Fall or to the depraved nature of man after the Fall.
5. The object of this love thus becomes the equivalent of Boethius' *Summum Bonum* (the Highest Good, that is, God). The idea echoes such principles as that in Matthew xiii, 45–46.
6. Compare Ovid, *Ars amatoria*, II, 225–50 (above, pp. 279–80); *Amores*, I, ix (above, pp. 287–88).
7. Compare Ovid, *Ars amatoria*, I, 399–436; II, 261–62.
8. In Book III Andreas comments: "From love comes hateful poverty, and one comes to the prison of penury. . . . What renders a man more contemptible to other men than for him to be compelled to suffer the obscurities of poverty for the love of a woman?" Compare Ovid, *Ars amatoria*, II, 161–68.
9. Ovid, *Remedia amoris*, 749. Andreas the chaplain would mean here that his vow of poverty helped him overcome the love of worldly things.
10. The definition is from Isidore of Seville's *Etymologiae*, X, i, 4–5. Isidore distinguishes between the true friend (*amicus*) and the lover of turpitude (*amator turpitudinis*). The latter is like a hook (*hamus*) because "he is bent by the love of lechery." The friend is like a hook because he is bound by the

chain of charity (*catena caritatis*). Andreas parodies Isidore's etymology by substituting "the chains of cupidity" (*cupidinis vinculis*) for the *catena caritatis*. This scholastic wit reduces the love he defines here to mere cupidity. Compare Andreas' discussion of friendship, below, p. 358.

11. The image of fishing is an Ovidian favorite: see *Ars amatoria*, I, 47–48, 393, 463–64; III, 425–26 (above, p. 283), etc.

12. See, e.g., Troilus and Criseyde, III, 1716–1806.

[The Rules of Love]

    I. Marriage is no real excuse for not loving.

    II. He who is not jealous cannot love.

    III. No one can be bound by a double love.

    IV. It is well known that love is always increasing or decreasing.

    V. That which a lover takes against the will of his beloved has no relish.

    VI. Boys do not love until they arrive at the age of maturity.

    VII. When one lover dies, a widowhood of two years is required of the survivor.

    VIII. No one should be deprived of love without the very best of reasons.

    IX. No one can love unless he is impelled by the persuasion of love.

    X. Love is always a stranger in the home of avarice.

    XI. It is not proper to love any woman whom one would be ashamed to seek to marry.

    XII. A true lover does not desire to embrace in love anyone except his beloved.

    XIII. When made public love rarely endures.

    XIV. The easy attainment of love makes it of little value; difficulty of attainment makes it prized.

    XV. Every lover regularly turns pale in the presence of his beloved.

    XVI. When a lover suddenly catches sight of his beloved his heart palpitates.

    XVII. A new love puts to flight an old one.

    XVIII. Good character alone makes any man worthy of love.

    XIX. If love diminishes, it quickly fails and rarely revives.

    XX. A man in love is always apprehensive.

    XXI. Real jealousy always increases the feeling of love.

    XXII. Jealousy, and therefore love, are increased when one suspects his beloved.

    XXIII. He whom the thought of love vexes eats and sleeps very little.

    XXIV. Every act of a lover ends in the thought of his beloved.

    XXV. A true lover considers nothing good except what he thinks will please his beloved.

    XXVI. Love can deny nothing to love.

XXVII. A lover can never have enough of the solaces of his beloved.

XXVIII. A slight presumption causes a lover to suspect his beloved.

XXIX. A man who is vexed by too much passion usually does not love.

XXX. A true lover is constantly and without intermission possessed by the thought of his beloved.

XXXI. Nothing forbids one woman being loved by two men or one man by two women.

THE ALBA

For "secret" lovers, the coming of the dawn, signaled by the call of a watchman or the sound of morning birds such as the lark or the crow, means parting. It is an event in which the medieval poet was able to weigh the conflicting loyalties of the "chivalric" lover: his private loyalty to his lady and his own desires; his chivalric duties to his lord, his companions, and the state; and his Christian obligation to "walk not in darkness" (John viii, 12) but in the light, and to be prepared for Christ's Second Coming in Judgment, conventionally symbolized by the sunrise. Although the event is only a moment in the conventional scenario of the medieval story of love, it is one which epitomizes the problems of a divided will, and which somberly portends a time when lovers must part everlastingly.

The popularity of this lyric form is attested by the survival of nineteen Provençal albas, five aubes from Northern France, and over one hundred Tagelieder in Middle High German. Chaucer's dawn-scene in Troilus and Criseyde, III, 1415–1533, is modeled in part on Boccaccio's Filostrato, III, 42–52 (see below, pp. 319–21), and is a prototype of Shakespeare's Romeo and Juliet, III, v, 1–64.

The three albas printed here suggest the strands of meaning which might be woven into the tradition of the dawn-song. Ovid's elegy pits the lover against the laws of nature and Roman civic duty. Prudentius' hymn, which is also a love-song, indicates the range of Christian meaning evoked by the rising sun. And the troubadour Giraut de Bornelh skillfully combines these concerns with an awareness of the chivalric calling professed at the courts before which he sang.

Ovid:
from *Amores*

The "lover" whom Ovid *assumes as his* persona *in the* Amores *is character-istically egotistical and rarely successful. Here his imperatives seek to stop time, so that he may lie with his "lady" (*domina, *who later appears as the troubadour's* donna*) somewhat longer. His desire thus pits the lover against the course of natural order and, as the poem unfolds, against the productive energies of the Empire (soldiers, farmers, students, lawyers, weavers). Ovid is himself a major classical authority for the idea that Venus' legiti-mate office is to defeat time through reproduction. Here Time becomes simply a foe of pleasure, not of life or the future of mankind. The "love" of the speaker is thus doomed. The opening word of the poem,* Iam *("now," "already," "certainly"), introduces a statement in the present tense, and the last word is* dies *(the "day" he has sought to deny), cast in the past tense. Yet the egotist salvages some pride by observing that at least he made Aurora "blush."*

Trans. Grant Showerman, Ovid: Heroides and Amores *(Cambridge, Mass.: Harvard University Press, 1914: Loeb Classical Library), pp. 369–73. Reprinted by permis-sion of the publishers and The Loeb Classical Library.*

[Dawn Song]

I, xiii

She is coming already over the ocean from her too-ancient husband[1]—
she of the golden hair who with rimy axle brings the day.

"Whither art thou hasting, Aurora? Stay!—so may his birds each year
make sacrifice to the shades of Memnon[2] their sire in the solemn com-
bat. 'Tis now I delight to lie in the tender arms of my love; if ever, 'tis
now I am happy to have her close by my side. Now,[3] too, slumber is
deep and the air is cool, and birds chant liquid song from their slender
throats. Whither art thou hasting, O unwelcome to men, unwelcome to
maids? Check with thy rosy hand the dewy rein!

"Before thy rising the seaman better observes his stars, and does not
wander blindly in mid water; at thy coming rises the wayfarer, however
wearied, and the soldier fits his savage hands to arms. Thou art the first
to look on men tilling the field with the heavy mattock; thou art the
first to summon the slow-moving steer beneath the curvèd yoke. Thou
cheatest boys of their slumbers and givest them over to the master, that
their tender hands may yield to the cruel stroke; and likewise many dost
thou send as sponsors before the court, to undergo great losses through
a single word. Thou bringest joy neither to lawyer nor to pleader; each
is ever compelled to rise for cases new. 'Tis thou, when women might
cease from toil, who callest back to its task the hand that works the
wool.[4]

"I could endure all else—but who, unless he were one without a
maid, could bear that maids should rise betimes? How often have I
longed that night should not give place to thee, that the stars should
not be moved to fly before thy face! How often have I longed that
either the wind should break thine axle, or thy steed be tripped by
dense cloud, and fall! O envious, whither dost thou haste? The son
born to thee was black, and that color was the hue of his mother's heart.

"I would Tithonus were free to tell of thee; no woman in heaven
would be known for greater shame. Flying from him because long ages
older, thou risest early from the ancient man to go to the chariot-wheels
he hates. Yet, hadst thou thy favored Cephalus[5] in thy embrace, thou
wouldst cry: 'Run softly, steeds of the night!'

"Why should I be harried in love because thy mate is wasting with
years? Didst thou wed an ancient man because I made the match?
Look, how many hours of slumber has Luna bestowed upon the youth

she loves!⁶—and her beauty is not second to thine. The very father of the gods, that he need not see thee so oft, made two nights into one to favor his desires."⁷

I had brought my chiding to an end. You might know she had heard: she blushed—and yet the day arose no later than its wont!

NOTES

1. Tithonus, brother of King Priam of Troy. Because of Aurora's prayers, the gods granted him immortality, but not eternal youth.
2. Memnon, son of Tithonus and Aurora and king of the Ethiopians, was slain by Achilles in the Trojan War. The *memnonides* are birds which Jupiter caused to fly from his funeral pyre to fight over the ashes. They visit his tomb each year as a memorial.
3. Repetitions of *nunc* ("now") stress the conventional desire of the lover for an eternal present, since his joys are frustrated by the fated passing of time (the theme of the poem).
4. The lover would bring a halt to many Roman occupations (including the military, which is called "savage") promoted by Augustan policy.
5. Husband of Procris (or Procne), who rejected the love of Aurora.
6. Endymion, who sleeps eternally on Mt. Latmus, so that Luna, the Moon, can kiss him.
7. Jupiter accomplished this to sleep with Alcmene, who became the mother of Hercules. The speaker fails to consider that Jupiter was not mortal.

Prudentius:
A Hymn for Cock-Crow

Aurelius Clemens Prudentius (348–c. 410) came from a noble Spanish family. Trained for the law, he became an eminent lawyer and eventually achieved high official position under the Emperor Theodosius (also a Spaniard). At the age of fifty-seven he retired to a monastery, to devote himself entirely to religion.

Prudentius is best known for three works which were among the most influential in the Middle Ages. The Cathemerinon liber, from which the present selection is drawn, is a collection of hymns for the different parts of the day. The Peristephanon contains fourteen hymns for martyrs. His best known work, the Psychomachia is an allegory pitting Christian virtues against pagan vices within the human soul.

The Hymnus ad galli cantum illustrates the new dimension brought to the tradition of the "dawn-song" by Christian perception and Biblical imagery. The notes suggest only some of the main examples of pertinent Biblical usage. In view of the chivalric setting of later medieval albas, Romans xiii, 10–14 (printed above, p. 162) is particularly interesting.

Trans. H. J. Thompson, The Poems of Prudentius, Volume I (Cambridge, Mass.: Harvard University Press, 1949: Loeb Classical Library), pp. 7–13. Reprinted by permission of the publishers and The Loeb Classical Library.

A Hymn for Cock-Crow

The bird that heralds day forewarns that dawn is at hand; now Christ, the awakener of our souls, calls us to life. "Away," He cries, "with beds that belong to sickness, sleep, and sloth. Be pure and upright and sober and awake, for now I am very near." It is late to spurn the couch after the shining sun is up, unless by adding a part of the night thou hast given more hours to toil.[1] The loud chirping of the birds perched under the very roof, a little while before the light breaks forth, is a symbol of our Judge. As we lie closed in by foul darkness, buried under the blankets of sloth, He bids us leave repose behind, for the day is on the point of coming; that when dawn besprinkles the sky with her shimmering breath she may make us all, who were spent with toil, strong to embrace the hope of light. This sleep that is given us for a time is an image of everlasting death. Our sins, like foul night, make us lie snoring; but the voice of Christ from the height of heaven teaches and forewarns us that daylight is near, lest our soul be in bondage to slumber, and to the very end of a slothful life sleep lie heavy on a heart that is buried in sin and has forgotten its natural light. They say that evil spirits which roam happily in the darkness of night are terrified when the cock crows, and scatter and flee in fear; for the hated approach of light, salvation, Godhead, bursts through the foul darkness and routs the ministers of night. They have foreknowledge that this is a sign of our promised hope, whereby being freed from slumber we hope for the coming of God. What this bird signifies the Savior showed to Peter, when He declared that ere the cock crew He should be thrice denied.[2] For sin is committed before the herald of coming day sheds light on the race of men and brings an end of sinning. So he who denied Christ wept for the wickedness that fell from his lips while his mind remained upright and his heart kept faith; nor ever after did he speak any such word by slip of tongue, and when he heard the cock crow he was made a just man and ceased to sin. Hence it is that we all believe it was at this hour of rest, when the cock crows in his pride, that Christ returned from the dead.[3] Then was the strength of death crushed, then was the law of hell subdued, then did the stronger potency of day force night to flee. Now, now let wickedness sink to rest, now let dark sin fall asleep, now let deadly guilt wither away, the victim of its own slumber; and let the spirit in its turn awake, and for the time that remains, while the night's course is drawing to a close, stand and be active at its post.[4] Let us call on Jesus with our voices, in tears and prayers and soberness; earnest supplication keeps the pure heart from slumbering. Long enough has deep forgetfulness, as we lay curled up, pressed heavily on our sense and buried it while it wandered in baseless dreams. Surely false and worthless are the things we have done because of worldly glory, as though we did them in sleep.[5] Let us awake! Reality is here. Gold, pleasure, joy, riches, honor, success, all the evil things that puff us up,—comes morning, all are naught. Do Thou burst the bonds of night. Do Thou undo our long-established [*vetus:* "old"] sin, and pour in upon us the light of the new day.

NOTES

1. The Bible frequently identifies God with light, sin with darkness. See, e.g., Psalm xxvi, 1, and xxxv, 10; Isaias lx, 1–3; John iii, 19–21, and viii, 12; 1 Thessalonians v, 4–8; Romans xiii, 10–14. The last two passages both describe a spiritual "chivalry" worthy of the "day," and both envision Christ's Second Coming in Judgment to be symbolized by the "sunrise." Ephesians v, 9–14, contains important "alba" imagery.
2. See Matthew xxvi, 69–75; Mark xiv, 66–72; Luke xxii, 55–62; John xviii, 17–27.
3. Matthew xxviii; Mark xvi; Luke xxiv; John xx.
4. Compare this use of "now" to Ovid's (above, p. 303, n. 3).
5. Compare Second Nun's Tale, 260–64.

Giraut de Bornelh: "Glorious King"

Between 70 and 80 poems are attributed to Giraut de Bornelh (c. 1145–c. 1200). Known as "maestre dels trobadors" ("Master of the Troubadours"), Giraut was apparently a professional court poet who sang for various lords in southern France and northern Spain. In his De vulgari eloquentia ("On the Eloquence of the Vernacular"), II, 2, Dante cites him as an "illustrious" poet of "moral rectitude."

"Reis glorios" has been called the most perfect troubadour alba. Certainly the complex antitheses and strain of divided loyalties inherent in the conception of the medieval alba are remarkably assimilated in this poem. The last stanza is the answer of the lover to his chivalric "companion" who has kept watch for him through the night.

Trans. Alan R. Press, Anthology of Troubadour Lyric Poetry (Austin: University of Texas Press, 1971), p. 151. Copyright © 1971 by the University of Texas Press. Reprinted by permission of the University of Texas Press, Edinburgh University Press, and the author.

[Alba]

Glorious King, true light and splendour, almighty God, Lord, if it please You, to my companion be a faithful aid, for I've seen him not since night came on, and soon it will be dawn.

Sweet friend, if you sleep or wake, sleep you no more; gently rise again for, in the East, I see the star arisen which brings the day, and I have marked it well; and soon it will be dawn.

Sweet friend, in song I call you; sleep you no more, for I hear the bird sing as it goes seeking the daylight through the woods, and I fear lest the jealous one[1] assail you; and soon it will be dawn.

Sweet friend, go to the window, and look at the stars in the sky! You'll know if I'm your faithful messenger. If you do not, then yours will be the harm; and soon it will be dawn.

Sweet friend, since I left you, I have not slept or got up from my knees, but I've prayed God, the Son of Holy Mary, that He might return you to me in loyal friendship; and soon it will be dawn.

Sweet friend, out there by the steps you begged me that I should not be sleepy, but should keep watch all night until the day. Now neither my song nor my company pleases you, and soon it will be dawn.

—Sweet, gentle friend, in such a rich dwelling am I that I would it were never more dawn or day; for the most noble woman that was ever born of mother I hold and embrace; hence I need not the jealous fool, nor the dawn.

NOTE

1. The *gilos*, the lady's husband, often the knight-lover's overlord in the convention. He becomes the French *Jaloux*.

* * *

Guido delle Colonne:
from the *History of the Fall of Troy*

For the medieval poet, lacking direct access to the Greek text of Homer, knowledge of the events of the Trojan War derived from two Latin summaries purporting to be translations of accounts by actual participants at the siege. These were the Ephemeris belli Troiani *("Diary of the Trojan War") by Dictys Cretensis, dating from about the fourth century* A.D., *and the* De excidio Troiae historia *("History of the Destruction of Troy") by Dares Phrygius, dating from about the sixth century* A.D. *Working primarily from these two texts and Virgil's* Aeneid, *Benoît de Sainte-Maure developed a long vernacular romance, the* Roman de Troie *(c. 1160), which established the guidelines for the main tradition of the Troy story.*

Chaucer's authorities for these events appear on an iron pillar in the House of Fame:

>   . . . the gret Omer;
> And with him Dares and Tytus
> Before, and eke he Lollius,
> And Guido eke de Columpnis,
> And Englyssh Gaufride eke, ywis;
> And ech of these, as I have joye,
> Was besy for to bere up Troye. (1466–72)

Here Tytus probably refers to Dictys; Lollius is the name Chaucer cites as "auctour" for his Troilus and Criseyde, though Boccaccio is really his source; and Englyssh Gaufride is Geoffrey of Monmouth, whose Historia regum Britanniae ("History of the Kings of England," c. 1147) describes the founding of Britain by Trojan survivors. Guido is Judge Guido delle Colonne of Messina, Sicily, who translated Benoît's Roman, in 1287, into the Latin of historians. In his Historia destructionis Troiae he sought, as he

Trans. Mary Elizabeth Meek, Historia Destructionis Troiae *(Bloomington: Indiana University Press, 1974), pp. 156–58. Copyright © 1974 by Indiana University Press. Reprinted by permission of the publisher.*

says, to purge poetic fictions in the interests of true history. The work be-came a popular authority, known throughout Europe. It was one of the sources for Boccaccio's Filostrato *(c. 1338; see below, pp. 314–21). John Lydgate's* Troy Book *(1412–20) is a metrical translation of the* Historia. *And the first book printed in English,* The Recuyell of the Historyes of Troye *(1475), is William Caxton's translation of the same by way of a French intermediary, Raoul le Fèvre's* Recueil des Histoires de Troie.

Despite his professed "defictionalizing," Guido's account of the exerpted event below remains close to Benoît's. He has eliminated most of the direct discourse, and has taken Troilus' outburst against women for him-self. Perhaps he concluded that the "morals" to be drawn from history were the province of the historian. Note that Briseida, a literary descendent of Homer's Briseis, has not yet become the Criseida of Boccaccio and Chaucer.

[The Exchanging of Briseida]

FROM *BOOK XIX*

Troilus, however, after he had learned of his father's intention to go ahead and release Briseida and restore her to the Greeks, was overwhelmed and completely wracked with great grief, and almost entirely consumed by tears, anguished sighs, and laments, because he had cherished her with the great fervor of youthful love and had been led by the excessive ardor of love into the intense longing of blazing passion. There was no one of his dear ones who could console him. Briseida, who seemed to cherish Troilus with no less fervor of love, revealed her grief to be no less in words of lament, and was completely drenched in floods of tears. She thus sprinkled her clothes, face, and breast with continuous showers of water distilled from the fountain of her eyes, with the result that her clothes were so drenched with the moisture of her tears that if anyone had squeezed them and wrung them out with his hands, her clothes would have poured forth a great amount of water from the wringing. She scratched her tender face with her nails, and her golden hair, released from the restraint of bands, she tore out of the milk-white skin of her head, and while with her hard nails she furrowed her cheeks tinted with ruby coloring, they seemed like torn lilies mixed with torn roses. While she was bewailing the separation from her beloved Troilus, she often swooned in the arms of those wishing to sustain her, saying that she would prefer to seek death rather than to possess life from the time when it would be necessary for her to be separated from him on whose life the pleasures of her life depended.[1]

With the coming of darkness that night, Troilus went to Briseida, and although he was likewise in tears, he advised her to moderate her grief. While Troilus thus yearned to console her, Briseida often fainted in his arms. Between sweet kisses moistened by sorrowful tears, he often tired to bring her back to her sense that night. With the approaching of the hour just before day, however, Troilus departed from Briseida in great anguish and grief, and when he had left her, he hastened to his apartment in the palace.

But oh, Troilus, what youthful credulity forced you to be so mistaken that you trusted Briseida's tears and her deceiving caresses? It is clearly implanted in all women by nature not to have any steady constancy; if one of their eyes weeps, the other smiles out of the corner, and their fickleness and changeableness always lead them to deceive men.[2] When they show signs of greater love to men, they at once at the solicitation of another suddenly change and vary their inconstant declaration of love. If perchance no seducer appears to them, they seek him themselves, secretly with furtive glances while they are walking or more frequently, while they wander through shops or while they linger in the public squares. There is truly no hope so false as that which resides in women and proceeds from them. Hence a young man can deservedly be judged foolish, and one advanced in age even more so, if he puts his trust in the flattery of women and entrusts himself to their false declarations.[3]

Briseida, accordingly, at the command of King Priam, prepared herself with great magnificence for the journey, and Troilus and many other noble Trojan nobles accompanied her for a great part of the way. When the Greeks arrived to welcome her, Troilus and the Trojans went back, and the Greeks welcomed her into their company. Among them then was Diomedes, and as Diomedes looked at her, he was immediately on fire with the flames of ardent love, and desired her with vehement longing. When he had joined Briseida and was riding at her side, he was unable to contain the flames of his ardor and revealed to Briseida the love of his burning heart. He tried humbly enough to tempt her with many affectionate and flattering speeches and also, to tell the truth, with grand promises. But Briseida, in her first impulses, as is the custom of women, refused to give her consent, but still, not wishing to deprive him of hope, she could not after his many words refrain from speaking with gentle words to Diomedes: "At present I neither refuse nor accept the offer of your love, since my heart is not so disposed that I can reply to you in any other way." Diomedes became quite happy at these words, since he perceived that he was not to be completely excluded from placing his hope in her.[4] Accordingly, he stayed with her up to the place where Briseida was to go, and when she had reached that point, he went promptly to her as she was dismounting from her horse, and, without anyone realizing it, slyly took away one of the gloves which Briseida was wearing on her hand. Although she alone perceived it plainly, she concealed the pleasing theft of the lover.

NOTES

1. A rhetorical set-piece on grief, particularly effective in view of immediately following events.
2. Imagery traditionally associated with Lady Fortune.

3. Guido's emphasis on the "youthful" nature of Troilus' love reflects the view (already in Ovid) that romantic passion is characteristic of the *juvenis. Juventus,* the period of life extending approximately to the age of thirty, was regarded as an age particularly prone to wayward error.
4. Conscious adaptation of Ovidian formulas.

Giovanni Boccaccio:
from *Il Filostrato*

In the Filostrato *(c. 1338) Boccaccio developed the love affair between Troilus and Cressida into a fully realized romance of passion, betrayal, and tragedy. The relatively brief accounts in Benoît de Sainte-Maure's* Roman de Troie *(c. 1160) and the* Historia destructionis Troiae *(1287) of Guido delle Colonne present only the parting of the lovers and Briseida's turning to Diomede. Boccaccio's version of the love affair is his own, a tapestry woven of the terms and structures (such as the* alba) *popularized in the medieval courtly version of romantic love. These included both the conventions of the troubadours, which had been assimilated in Andreas Capellanus'* Treatise on Love, *and those of the* dolce stil nuove *employed by Boccaccio's immediate Italian predecessors.*

Chaucer's Troilus and Criseyde *is a fairly close rendition of the* Filostrato. *His most obvious addition to this source, though it is one he never names, is the material drawn from the* Consolation of Philosophy, *making explicit Boccaccio's implied Boethianism. Other revisions are more subtle. Comparison of the following passage with Chaucer's version will reveal remarkably different conceptions of Cressida, of Troilus, and even of the role of Pandarus in the affair. The passage corresponds to* Troilus and Criseyde, *III, 512–1533.*

Trans. Nathaniel Edward Griffin and Arthur Beckwith Myrick, The Filostrato of Giovanni Boccaccio (Philadelphia: University of Pennsylvania Press, 1929: rept. New York: Biblo and Tannen, 1967), pp. 249–63.

[The Union of Troilus and Cressida]

23

After reaching Pandarus, [Troilus,] heard from him in full what he had to do. Thereupon he very impatiently awaited the night, which seemed to him to flee, and then quietly alone with Pandarus took his way whither Cressida was staying, who alone and in fear awaited him.

24

The night was dark and cloudy, as Troilus wished, and he advanced watching each object attentively that there might be no unnecessary disturbance, little or great, to his amorous desire, which he hoped would free him from his severe torment. And by a secret approach he made his entrance alone into the house, which was already quiet.

25

And in a certain dark and remote spot, as ordered, he awaited the lady. Nor did he find the waiting arduous or difficult or the obscurity of his whereabouts. But with a sense of courage and security he often said to himself: "My gentle lady will soon come and I shall be joyful, more than if I were the sole lord of the universe."

26

Cressida had plainly heard him come, because, as had been agreed, she had coughed to make him hear. And that he might not be sorry that he had come, she kept speaking every little while in a clear voice. And she provided that everyone should go at once to sleep, saying that she was so sleepy that she could no longer keep awake.

27

When everyone had gone to sleep and the house had become all quiet, Cressida thought it time to go at once where Troilus was in the hidden spot. When he heard her come, he stood up and with joyful countenance went to meet her, waiting in silence to be ready at her every command.

28

The lady had in hand a lighted torch and descended the stairs all alone and beheld Troilus waiting for her in suspense. She greeted him and then said as well as she could: "My lord, if I have given offense by keeping thy royal splendor confined in such a spot as this, I pray thee by the gods, forgive me, my sweet desire."

29

To her Troilus said: "Fair lady, sole hope and weal of my mind, ever have I had before me the star of thy fair visage in all its radiant splendor and of a truth more dear to me hath been this little corner than my palace. This is not a matter that requireth the asking of pardon." Then he took her in his arms and they kissed one another on the mouth.

30

They did not leave that place before they had with sweet joy and ardent dalliance embraced one another a thousand times. And as many times more did they kiss one another, as those who burned with equal fire and were very dear to one another. But when the welcome ended, they mounted the stairs and went to a chamber.

31

Long would it be to recount the joy and impossible to tell the delight they took together when they came there. They stripped themselves and got into bed. There the lady, still keeping on her last garment, said to him: "Mirror mine, the newly wed are bashful the first night."

32

To her Troilus said: "Soul of me, I pray thee remove it, so that I may have thee naked in my arms, as my heart desireth." And she replied:

"Behold, I rid myself of it." And after casting off her shift, she quickly wrapped herself in his arms, and clasping one another fervently they experienced the last delight of love.

33

O sweet and much-desired night, what wert thou to the two joyful lovers! If the knowledge that all the poets once possessed were given me, I should be unable to describe it. Let him who was ever before so much favored by Love as they, take thought of it, and he will know in part their delight.

34

They did not leave one another's arms all night. While they held one another embraced, they thought they were separated, the one from the other, and that it was not true that they were locked together, one with the other, as they were, but they believed they were dreaming of being in one another's arms. And the one often asked the other: "Have I thee in my arms? Do I dream or art thou thyself?"

35

And they beheld one another with so great desire that the one did not remove his eyes from the other, and the one said to the other: "My love, can it be that I am with thee?" "Yes, soul of my life, thanks be to the gods," replied the other. And they exchanged sweet kisses together, ever and anon clasping one another tightly the while.

36

Troilus often kissed the lovely amorous eyes of Cressida, saying: "You thrust into my heart darts of love so fiery that I am all inflamed by them. You seized me and I did not hide myself in flight, as is wont to do he who is in doubt. You hold me and ever will hold me in Love's net, bright eyes of mine."

37

Then he kissed them and kissed them yet again and Cressida kissed his in return. Then he kissed all her face and her bosom, and not an hour passed without a thousand sighs—not those grievous ones by which one loseth color but those devoted ones, by which was shown the affection that lay in their breasts and which resulted in the renewal of their delight.

38

Let now these wretched misers, who blame whoever hath fallen in love and who hath not, as they, devoted himself entirely in some way to the making of money, take thought and consider whether, when holding it full dear, as much pleasure was ever furnished by it as Love doth provide in a single moment to him to whom by good chance he is joined.

39

They will say "Yes" but they will lie. With laughter and with jests will they call this love grievous folly, without perceiving that in a single hour they will lose themselves and their money, without having known in all their lives what joy is. May the gods make them sad and give their gains to lovers.[1]

40

Reassured in their union the two lovers began to talk together and to recount to one another their laments of the past, their anguish, and their sighs. And all this talk they often interrupted with fervent kissing and abandoning their past suffering, shared delicious joy.

41

No talk was there of sleeping but they desired by keeping wide-awake to prevent the night from growing shorter. They could not have enough of one another, however much they might do or say what they believed to belong to that act. And without letting the hours run on in vain they used them all that night.

42

But when near day they heard the cocks crow by reason of the rising dawn, the desire of embracing grew warm again, not unattended by sorrow on account of the hour which was to separate them and cast them into new torment, which no one had yet felt, because of their being separated, since they were inflamed more than ever with love.[2]

43

When Cressida heard them crow she said in sorrow: "O my love, now is it time to arise, if we wish to conceal our desire. But I wish to embrace thee a little, my love, before thou arisest, that I may feel less grief at thy departure. Do thou embrace me, my sweet life."

44

Troilus well-nigh in tears embraced her and clasping her tightly, kissed her, cursing the approaching day, which so quickly separated them. Then he began saying to her: "The parting grieveth me beyond measure. How am I ever to part from thee, since the happiness I feel, thou, lady, givest me?

45

"I know not why I do not die when I consider that I must go away against my will and that I have already received banishment from life, and death hath much power over me. Nor know I how or when I shall return. O fortune, why dost thou take me afar from such pleasure, which pleaseth me more than aught else? Why dost thou take from me my consolation and my peace?[3]

46

"Alas what shall I do if at the first step the desire to return here so constraineth me that life may not bear it, wretched one that I am? Ah why, pitiless day, comest thou so soon to separate us? When wilt thou dip beneath the horizon that I may see thee bring us together again? Alas, I do not know." Then he turned to Cressida and kissed her fresh visage,

47

Saying: "If I believed, my fair lady, that I should remain continually in thy mind, as I keep thee in mine, more dear would this be to me than the realm of Troy, and I would be patient at this parting, since I come to it against my will, and would hope to return here at time and place appointed to quench, as now, our fire."

48

Cressida answered him in sighs, whilst she held him tight in her arms: "Soul of mine, I heard in conversation some time ago, if I remember correctly, that Love is a jealous spirit, and when he seizeth aught, he holdeth it so firmly bound and pressed in his claws that to free it, advice is given in vain.

49

"He hath gripped me in such wise for thee, my dear weal, that if I wished to return now to what I was at first, take it not into thy head that I could do so. Thou art ever, morn and eve, locked in my mind. If I thought I were so in thine, I should esteem myself happier than I could ask.

50

"Therefore live certain of my love, which is greater than I have ever felt for another. If thou desirest to return here, I desire it much more than thou. Nor when opportunity shall be given me, wilt thou return here sooner than I. Heart of my body, to thee I commend myself." After she said this she sighed and kissed him.

51

Troilus arose against his will when he had kissed her an hundred times. But realizing what had to be done, he got all dressed and then after many words said: "I do thy will; I go away. See that what thou hast promised be not left unfulfilled. I commend thee to the gods and leave my soul with thee."

52

Voice did not come to her for reply, so great sorrow constrained her at his departure. But Troilus set out thence with hasty steps toward his palace. He feeleth that Love vexeth him more than he did at first, when he longed for him, of so much more worth had he found Cressida than he had at first supposed.

NOTES

1. Compare stanza 42, below.
2. What follows is a version of the *alba,* or lovers' dawn-song.
3. Boccaccio's references here to *fortuna* and *solazzo* suggest a Boethian perspective on the situation.

Giovanni Boccaccio:
from the *Teseide*

For his Knight's Tale Chaucer also turned to Giovanni Boccaccio, whom he seems to have associated with courtly tastes. The Teseide *("The Book of Theseus," c. 1340–42), as the form of its title implies, presents itself as an "epic" celebration of the chivalric Theseus and the loves of Palemone and Arcita for Emilia, the young sister of Theseus' bride Hippolyta. Its over 15,000 lines of ottava rima, a stanza which Boccaccio is frequently credited with inventing, are divided into twelve books, and epic conventions are frequent, often drawn from Statius' epic, the* Thebaid *("The Book of Thebes"), as they are in the Knight's Tale. The* Teseide *was dedicated to "Fiammetta," a lady now generally believed to be only a literary convention (see above, p. 86).*

Far more than the version of Chaucer's Knight, Boccaccio's epical romance is leisurely in pace. It is also more learned, not only in its Ovidian allusions to classical story and in its rhetorical flourishes, but also in the inclusion of chiose, *explanatory "glosses" such as might accompany a classical school text. Boccaccio maintains, as well, a humorous attitude toward his subject, the pretensions of scholarship, and his own craft. The result is a kind of mock epic which yet celebrates the ordering rule of the rational faculty, personified in Theseus, over the frivolous, youthful impulses of the irascible and concupiscible appetites.*

In the following excerpt the technique of dealing lightly with philosophical truisms is illustrated. Emilia appears in her garden in the spring, as much a natural phenomenon as the flowers she gathers, and with the coming of winter she disappears. The conventional seasonal image is a Boethian favorite to illustrate the transitory nature of "partial goods," but it also permits the observation that the behavior of the characters in this scene involves, at least in part, the operation of "natural law." The corresponding passage in the Knight's Tale (lines 1033–79) provides an interesting example of Chaucer's adaptation.

Trans. Bernadette Marie McCoy, The Book of Theseus [Boccaccio's Teseide] *(New York: Teesdale, 1974), pp. 78–80, 82, 85. Reprinted by permission of Teesdale Publishing Associates.*

[Emilia Appears to Palemone and Arcita]

5

Phoebus sallying forth with his steeds was in that part of the heavens which belongs to the lowly beast that carried Europa without stopping to the place where her name still prevails.[1] Venus stepped forth with him and climbed to those lovely mansions, and for this reason all the heaven of Ammon[2] smiled, as he dallied for a time in Pisces.

6

Because of this fortunate position of the stars, the earth enjoyed charming vitality and clothed her lovely form anew with young grass and exquisite little flowers. The new shrubs adorned their limbs with boughs as the trees neared the time of their flowering and fruit-bearing to beautify the world.

7

And all the little birds began to sing about their loves, jubilant and merry among the leaves and the flowers. The animals could not conceal their love, but showed it, rather, in their outward behavior. And happy youths, ripe for love, felt passion glow hotter in their hearts than ever before.[3]

8

The beautiful Emilia, as dawn broke each morning, entered alone into the garden which opened out from her room, drawn there by her own nature, not because she was bound by any love. Barefoot and clad in her shift, she entertained herself by singing amorous songs.

9

She led this life for many days, that artless and beautiful maiden, from time to time gathering a new rose from its thorns with her white hand

323

and joining it to other flowers to weave a little garland for her blond head, until a novelty occurred one morning because of the loveliness of this child.

10

One fine morning, after she had risen and had wound her blond tresses about her head, she descended into the garden as was her custom. There, seated on the grass, singing and taking her delight, blithesome and deftly she wove her garland with many flowers, all the while light-heartedly singing charming love lyrics with her angelic voice.

11

At the sound of that pretty voice, Arcites arose, for he was in the prison adjacent to the amorous garden, without saying anything to Palaemon. Longingly he opened the window to hear that song better. Then to see more easily who was singing, he put his head out a little between the iron bars.

12

The daylight was still somewhat faint, since the horizon still hid part of the sun, but not enough to prevent him with his limited view from discovering to his supreme delight what the young maiden was doing, although he did not know her yet. Looking at her face intently he said to himself: "She is from paradise."

13

As he turned back in he said softly: "O Palaemon, come and see. Venus has truly come down here. Do you not hear her singing? O, if I mean anything to you, come here quickly. I believe for certain that it will please you to see the angelic beauty down there which has descended to us from the sovereign heights."

14

Palaemon arose, for he had already heard her with more sweetness than he believed, and he went to the window together with Arcites, and both in silence, to watch the goddess. When he saw her, he said in a bright voice: "Surely, this is Cytherea. I have never seen anything so beautiful, so charming and so lovely."

15

Meanwhile, they enjoyed themselves, breathless and attentive, keeping their eyes and ears fixed on her, and marveling much over her and over the time they had lost in their grieving, time which had passed before they saw her. Arcites said: "O Palaemon, do you see what I behold in those beautiful immortal eyes?"

16

"What?" answered Palaemon. Arcites said: "I see in them the one who wounded the father of Phaeton because of Daphne, if I am not mistaken.[4] In his hands he holds two golden arrows and now he is placing one on his bowstring as he looks at no one else but me. I do not know if it displeases him that I should look at what gives me so much pleasure."

17

"Indeed," answered Palaemon then, "I do see him. But I do not know if he has shot one arrow, for he does not have more than one in his hand now." Arcites said: "Yes, he has wounded me in such a way that pain will pierce my heart if I am not helped by that goddess." Then Palaemon, utterly astonished, cried out, "Alas, the other has wounded me."

18

At that "Alas!" the beautiful young lady turned around on her right breast and her eyes moved immediately to the little window. Then her face flushed for shame, for she did not know who they were. Becoming bold, then, she rose to her feet with the flowers she had gathered and prepared to leave.

19

And as she turned away, she was not oblivious of that "Alas!" and although she was too young for mature love, still she understood what it meant. As it seemed to her that she knew that she was indeed liked, she took pleasure in it, and considered herself more beautiful, and now adorned herself the more every time she returned to the garden.

. . . . . .

28

And she continued her walks in the beautiful garden for her recreation, sometimes alone and sometimes in company. She always secretly turned her eyes toward the window from which she had first heard Palaemon's "Alas." And she did not do this because she was urged on by love, but to see if others were looking at her.

29

If she saw that she was being observed, she began to sing and to entertain herself in her delightful and clear voice, almost as if she were unaware. She trod the grass among the shrubs with tiny, lady-like steps and clad in modesty, all the while contriving to give more pleasure to whoever was watching her.

30

She was not prompted by any thought or feeling of love, but by vanity, which women have innate in their hearts in making others see their beauty. Almost stripped of any other worth, they are satisfied to be praised for beauty, and by contriving to please by their charm, they enslave others while they keep themselves free.

. . . . . .

44

[Now] the weather altered its look and the dew-laden air wept. The grass dried, and the trees were stripped bare, and the stormy tribe of Aeolus[5] raced about, wandering here and there through the unhappy world. And so Emilia with her loving looks left the garden and stayed in her room all the while and took no notice of the weather.

NOTES

1. The sun was in the sign of Taurus (mid-April to mid-May). Jupiter took the form of a bull in order to abduct Europa: see *Metamorphoses*, II, 833–75. The myth suggests the nature of the romantic episode to follow.
2. Boccaccio's elegant term for Jupiter. *Pisces* is the sign of the "fish."
3. A similar progression through the Chain of Being appears in the General Prologue, 1–18. The passage underlines the "natural" impetus for the "youthful" passion to ensue.
4. "Phaeton was the son of Phoebus and Clymene. This Phoebus . . . was wounded by Love for a virgin called Daphne, whom he later changed into a laurel" (Boccaccio's gloss). The youth Phaeton was killed when he rashly tried to drive his father's chariot. See *Metamorphoses*, II, 1 ff.
5. "The winds" (Boccaccio's gloss).

Giovanni Boccaccio:
from the *Teseide*

In this passage Boccaccio personifies Arcita's prayer and sends her to the temple of Mars. His description of the temple is the basis for Knight's Tale, 1967–2050; Arcita's prayer occurs in lines 2373–420.

Trans. Bernadette Marie McCoy, The Book of Theseus [Boccaccio's Teseide] (New York: Teesdale, 1974), pp. 171–74. Reprinted by permission of Teesdale Publishing Associates.

[Arcita's Prayer to Mars]

24

"O strong God, you maintain your sacred dwelling in the snowy Bistonian realms, in dark places unfriendly to the sun, and brimful of the woes you devised to humble the proud brows of Earth's haughty sons.[1] For they were left on the ground, every one in mortal cold, under the attacks you and your father Jove made against them.

25

"If by the will of the Most High, my youth and my prowess merit my being called one of yours, by that compassion that Neptune had for you when you passionately enjoyed the beauty of Cytherea and were entrapped by Vulcan and made a spectacle to all the gods,[2] I humbly pray you not to deny my requests.

26

"As you see, I am a young man, and mighty Love so binds me under His lordship for youthful beauty's sake, that I need all my strength and courage if I am to take delight in what my heart most desires. Without you I have little power. In fact, I can do nothing at all.

27

"Therefore, by that holy fire which once burned you as it burns me now, help me. Honor me with your might in this coming palestral game. Such a gift certainly would not seem slight to me, but the greatest good. Perform your task here, therefore. If I am the victor in this contest, I shall have the pleasure and you shall have the honor.

28

"Your everlasting temple will be decorated with the armor of my vanquished comrade and my own will hang there too, and the reason for it will be inscribed there. Eternal fires will burn there always. I promise you my beard and those locks of my hair which remain unscathed by the sword, if you allow me to win as I have asked."

How Arcites' Prayer reached Mars, and how and where his temple is built.

29

Perhaps Mars was just then engaged in polishing the rusty places in his great and horrible dwelling place when the pious Prayer of Arcites arrived there, all tearful of countenance, to perform her assigned task. As soon as she saw the house of Mars, she became mute from fright.

30

For it is set in the Thracian fields, under wintry skies, storm-tossed by continuous tempest, with hosts of everlasting clouds which are changed, now here, now there, by various winds in various places into spring rainstorms, or are hurled down as globules of water merged together by the cold, as the snow keeps hardening little by little to form ice.

31

It is located in a barren forest of sturdy beech trees, thick clustering and very tall, gnarled and harsh, unbending and ancient, which cover the face of the sad earth with an eternal shadow. And she heard there among the ancient trunks, a great noise muffled by a thousand Furies; and there was no beast or shepherd there.

32

In this forest she saw the house of the battle-strong god, built entirely of steel, splendid and clean, from which the light of the sun, which shunned that cruel place, was deflected. The narrow entrance was all iron and the gates were re-enforced everywhere with eternal diamond.

33

And she saw the iron columns that upheld the building. It seemed to her that she saw mad Impulses coming forth proudly through the door; and Blind Sin and every Alas! appeared there too. Wrath, red as fire, and pale Fear were also to be seen in that place.

34

And she saw Betrayals with their secret weapons, and Intrigues with their fair appearance. Discord was seated there, holding bloody weapons and every Difference in her hand. All the rooms seemed clamorous with harsh Threats and Cruel Design. And in their midst sat unhappy Valor, the least to merit praise.

35

Merry Madness she saw there as well, and behind him, armed Death with his bloody looks, and Bewilderment. Every altar there was covered with blood that had been shed by human bodies only in battles. Every altar was luminous with the fire taken from flame-ravaged lands destroyed by wretched wars,

36

And the temple was all storied by a clever hand, above and roundabout. The first scenes pictured there were the depredations made day and night on ravaged lands. And anyone ever subjected to violence was here in somber garb. Enchained peoples, iron gates, and demolished fortresses could be seen here.

37

She also saw warlike ships there, and empty wagons and ravaged countenances, and weeping and unhappy wretches, and all Coercions, each with arrogant mien. Every wound was visible there, and blood, mixed with clay. And turbulent, haughty Mars with his proud bearing appeared everywhere.

38

And subtle Mulciber had built that retreat with his skill before the sun had shown him by his rays that Citherea was with Mars.[3]

NOTES

1. Earth (Gaea, or Tellus) gave birth to the Titans. Boccaccio's gloss explains that they were conquered by Jupiter and Mars through the force of arms. *Bistonian realms:* in Thrace.
2. See Ovid, *Ars amatoria*, II, 561–98, for this less than praiseworthy episode in the history of Mars.
3. Boccaccio's *chiosa* to this description is given in the following excerpt.

Giovanni Boccaccio:
from the *Teseide*

Boccaccio's "gloss" to his description of the temple of Mars is at least partly facetious, as is his chiosa to the temple of Venus. His remarks on the irascible and concupiscible appetites, however, point to an authoritative concept, reaching back to Plato and Aristotle, underlying the fiction. Similarly, the distinction between a just (i.e., reasonable) and an unjust (i.e., irrational) Mars is conventional, and explains the difference between Theseus' worship of Mars and Arcita's, hardly to Arcita's credit. A similar distinction between two Venuses is made in the following chiosa.

Trans. Bernadette Marie McCoy, The Book of Theseus [Boccaccio's Teseide] (New York: Teesdale, 1974), pp. 196–203, 206–7. Reprinted by permission of Teesdale Publishing Associates.

333

[The Temple of Mars]

In this part the author describes the house of Mars, concerning which many things must be considered minutely by whoever wants to set them forth in order. However, since it is very superficially touched on hereafter, we shall go over it with a summary explanation. And so that the exposition might be more readily understood, the author says that he intends to show four things here: The first is the kind of place where the house of Mars is situated; the second is how the house of Mars is constructed; the third is who is in the house of Mars; the fourth is with what the house of Mars is adorned. I say, therefore, first of all, that the house of Mars is in Thrace, in cold and cloudy places, full of water and of wind and of ice, wild and thronged with fruitless trees; and in shady places, unfriendly to the sun and full of confusion.

For an understanding of this it should be remarked that in every man there are two principle appetites. One of these is called the concupiscible appetite, whereby man desires and rejoices to have the things which, according to his judgment—whether it be rational or corrupt—are delightful or pleasing. The other is called the irascible appetite, whereby a man is troubled if delightful things are taken away or impeded, or when they cannot be had. This irascible appetite is found very readily in men of much blood, because blood of its nature is hot, and hot things lightly burst into flame for any small provocation. So it happens that men of much blood become angry easily although some, by very strong effort of reason, restrain and conceal their anger.

Since, as we have stated in another place, men in cold regions have more blood than elsewhere, the author says here that the temple of Mars, that is, the irascible appetite, is in Thrace, which is a province situated toward the north and very cold, and in which there are very cruel and warlike men. And they are irascible because they have much blood. He says that it is cloudy, to show that anger obfuscates the counsel of reason, which he signifies further on by the sun's rays, which he says the house of Mars thrusts away from it. By the ice, he means the coldness of the soul of the angry man, who, overcome by enkindling of his wrath, becomes cruel and intransigent and without any charity. By the water he means the tears which the enraged shed many times out of wrath. He says, likewise, that the house of Mars is in a forest. By this he means the secret schemings to do harm that angry men sometimes harbor. By the barrenness of the forest he means the effects of wrath, which are not only thieves of the fruits of men's labors, but their wasters as well. And that is why it is that in such a forest there is neither shepherd nor beast, since the angry man does not govern himself or others. And therefore the habitation of Mars in such a place has been shown, however briefly.

A look at the second matter, that is, how this habitation or house of Mars is constructed, follows. He says that it is all sparkling with steel, and has gates of diamond and columns of iron. By the steel, he means the hardness of the stubbornness of the angry man, and this shows that it is the covering of the house, because he says that the columns are of iron. And he says that when this steel reflects, it chases away from itself the light of the sun, and deservedly, because if this steel should soften so as to let the light of the sun pass through, that is, the sound advice of reason in the mind of the angry man, it would no longer be the house of Mars, that is of war and tribulation, but of peace.

Not only does this obstinacy make the divine grace which descends upon it fly away, that is, the salutary counsel of reason, but it has doors of diamond, so that no human persuasion may pass within to either bend or soften it. And it is sustained by columns of iron, that is, by unbreakable resolves. . . .

[The Temple of Venus]

GLOSS TO TESEIDE VII, 50–66

Just as he described the house of Mars earlier, so here he intends to describe that of Venus. Since he does not care to describe the kind of place where the house is located and the things that belong to the said house, in order and succession, still they can be considered in order by anyone who wants. The kind of place where the said house is, who they are who dwell in that house, what forms and functions they have, how the house is constructed, and what the adornments of this house can be readily determined.

First therefore, the kind of place will be seen. The author says that it is on Mount Cithaeron, among pines, etc., as appears in the text. To clarify this matter it must be realized that just as Mars, as was said above, consists in the irascible appetite, so Venus consists in the concupiscible. This Venus is twofold, since one can be understood as every chaste and licit desire, as is the desire to have a wife in order to have children, and such like. This Venus is not discussed here. The second Venus is that through which all lewdness is desired, commonly called the goddess of love.[1] Here the author describes the temple of this goddess, and the other things that belong to it, as appears in the text. So the author describes this temple of Venus as being on Mount Cithaeron, for two reasons. One, because it was, in fact, there, since Mount Cithaeron is near Thebes and the Thebans celebrated a solemn feast thereon in certain seasons of the year, and they offered many sacrifices to the honor of Venus. The second thing is because of the quality of the place, which is very appropriate to Venus, because it is a temperate region as regards the heat and the cold. This is seen very clearly by anyone who considers it carefully, since those parts of Greece in which Mount Cithaeron is located are not too far north nor too far south, but almost between the one and the other.

This temperance in venereal acts is much required, since, if we note well, a man who might be frigid by nature or even frigid by chance cannot, without great difficulty, arrive at that act because the active powers are impeded by the cold. Similarly, he who is too hot, either by nature or by accident, or because of too much wine, or overheated by labor, has his active powers so stimulated that he cannot exercise them in such an act. Therefore, temperance is necessary for such an exercise. For this reason, the author appropriately places the temple

336

of this goddess in a temperate place. And since various things can provoke the frigid to this act and similarly reduce those who are too hot to the required temperance, the author here describes many things in which these powers lie.[2]

He says that the place abounded in pines, the fruit of which, when used for food, has wonderful powers to provoke that appetite, as the physicists would have it. Besides this, I place Bacchus and Ceres, by which are understood drinking and eating, in the most secret part of Venus. These two items, properly used as exquisite viands and excellent wines, arouse this appetite wonderfully in one who indulges in them.[3]

Next he states that the place was very beautiful to see, and that there appeared here rabbits, stags, sparrows, doves, and lastly, ladies dancing unshod. These things, some by their effects, such as rabbits and sparrows and doves, are highly stimulating when they are seen by the lustful; and some arouse by the dress and gestures, such as ladies dancing ungirt and unshod. And besides these, he describes Venus nude in the most secret part. When this is seen, it has marvellous power. Besides this, he says that there were most beautiful flowers and myrtle. They have properties to please the sense of smell, especially the myrtle, which poets write is the tree of Venus, since its perfume is very stimulating. Songs and musical instruments are also heard, which have the power to dispel all melancholy, which is something stirred up by frigid humors and is strong against the effects of Venus.[4]

He also says that the place is shady and abounding in springs. He intends to signify two things by the shade. One is the opportune refreshment it provides against too much heat, and this applies also to the springs. The other is the kind of location which the powers of Venus require, for they want comfort and darkness, which he also indicates when he sketches the place where Venus tarries.

And after he has described those things which generally can, according to natural forces, provoke anyone to the sexual act, he sketches certain things which stimulate some whom we commonly call lovers. And he puts these things in the form of persons, and sets them in different attitudes; and he sets them forth, therefore, some as natural and some as stimulating causes. One is Yearning, which he says is the first to be found upon entering this place of Venus. By this he means that natural desire, which every man or woman has, to see and to possess or acquire some beautiful and precious things rather than other things. And this Yearning is what draws the young men to feasts and into places where ladies are gathered together, so that each youth may choose the one lady among many whom he judges most worthy of his love.[5] And among these stimulants were also: Beauty, Youth, Grace,

Nobility, Charm, and such like. He includes others that are almost strengtheners of the appetite, that is, excited by the above mentioned. Among these he places Cupid, which is commonly called Love.

It is not my intention to show how love is generated in us through the forementioned things, however much it would be fitting to do so in the present work, since the story would be too long. Whoever wishes to see this, let him read the song of Guido Cavalcanti, "The Lady implores me, etc.," and the glosses that Master Dino del Garbo wrote for it. He says, briefly, that this Love is a passion born in the soul through any pleasurable thing which makes the soul desire fervently to please the said pleasurable thing and to be able to possess it.

In describing the fervor of Love, since one cannot escape very serious wounds from Him, anyone who speaks of Him says that He is armed with arrows. Others wish to signify by these arrows His sudden and penetrating entry; these two aspects can well be taken for the swift flight and the puncture of the arrow. Then the author says that Cupid made these arrows and he includes three others who are engaged in perfecting them: that is, Voluptuousness, Idleness, and Memory. He says that Voluptuousness tempers them in a fountain. In this regard it should be explained here that Love took to wife a maiden who was called Psyche and had a daughter by her, that is, this Voluptuousness. By this Psyche the author here means Hope, for as many times as Hope comes or tarries with Love in the mind of the lover, that many times they beget this daughter, that is, Voluptuousness, which he here intends to represent the singular delight the soul feels within it when it hopes to obtain what it loves. Such a delight as this tempers the arrows of Love, that is, makes them strong to be able to impassion the heart well. And Voluptuousness tempers them in the fountain of our false esteem, when, through this delight born of Love and of Hope, we judge that the pleasurable thing is to be placed above every other thing, whether temporal or divine.

But since these matters cannot be confirmed without recollection of their cause and without an interval of time, therefore he adds Memory and Idleness to bind these arrows with iron, for these have been formed by the fervor of Love and tempered by intimate delight born of Hope. And who does not know that we could not love the pleasurable object if its form and gestures are not remembered? By the same token, even if we should remember, and were burdened by many and varied affairs, this pleasure could not be retained in the mind. On the contrary, would it not pass and give place to other matters? Therefore both Memory and Idleness bring such a passion to perfection.[6]

In addition to these, the author includes certain accidental things

Figure 12. Amant greets Wealth and her Lover. Oxford, Bodleian Library MS Douce 195, fol. 71 (*Roman de la rose*). Compare General Prologue, 81 for the Lover's hairdo. Wealth stands beneath the shade of an elm tree with her lover beside her (*Roman* 10056–57). The elm is sometimes understood to symbolize "the worldly mind."

which are inducements to the effect of the desire born from this passion, such as Elegance, since many times the lover succeeds in pleasing the beloved by the way he adorns himself. Next he includes Affability, which is a very favorable matter to understanding persons. Then he includes Courtesy, which the author says, not without reason, is completely lost, since there are very few who know how to be courteous. This Courtesy has very great powers in acquiring the love and favor of another and covers many defects without fail. He also says that there were magic Arts, which terrify by their various transformations and, by the power of diverse incantations, many times induce men and women to love what, if it were not for these, they would not love. Boldness, which helps greatly in obtaining what is desired, was there, and he calls it mad, because Boldness rarely or never can come from prudent counsel, and prudent counsel never concedes anything unless it knows its purpose. But the outcome of what a man attempts to do boldly is uncertain. It is true that the proper name for the Boldness that is meant here is Rashness.

He also says that there were Flattery and Promises and Arts.[7] These can accomplish various things at various times, as those who have experienced them know. After these, the author says that there was Patience, without which no hope could endure, and consequently no love could have any power. And he says that she was pale, and rightly, since Patience has no place except where there are pains and torments, which, as we see from experience, make the one who endures them grow emaciated and pale. He says also that Madonna Peace was there, to show that the desires that are fulfilled through force cannot be called loving, since loving desire requires harmony, equally on the one hand and on the other.

And after he has shown these things up to here without distinction, he explains what the temple of Venus was made of. He says briefly that it was all of copper, and inside he puts certain things which happen to almost anyone who enters the temple, as he will write later on. The reasons for which he says that the temple is of copper are these: primarily because copper and brass, which comprise one class of metal, although they have certain differences, are born of the planet Venus. Thus what is here called copper is to be considered copper and brass. Next it should be understood that copper or brass, whichever we want to say, has three singular properties. The first is that it solders and joins and binds every other metal, or, if not all, then most of them, as we see from experience. The second is that brass shines like gold when it is polished. The third is that it has a very sweet sound. These three things are among the effects of Venus, because it is through her influence that all conjunctions happen to be made, and especially when conjunction is needed for procreation.[8] Next, just as it appears to be gold although it is a very base metal, so it seems that when these conjunctions are effected, they afford at first the greatest delight, whereas, after the fact, they are bound to be full of heavy bitterness. Besides this, it has a very sweet sound, by which it is very well understood that if there is any sweetness in the deeds of Venus it consists more in talking about them than in performing them. And let what he has said here of the temple suffice.

Within it he places a storm of Sighs, and he says that from these are nourished the fires kindled on altars bathed in tears. And he says that these things are caused by Jealousy. By this the author wants to indicate that Sighs are not born, nor do tears come, before a man is within the temple, that is in love, and touched by Jealousy. For the sighs of one who loves without being Jealous are light and pleasant most of the time, but Jealousy introduces very bitter and unending preoccupations, which often elicit sighs and tears and anguished laments from the hearts of those who are jealous, as those who have experienced it know. These torments are the flames that burn on the altars of Venus, that is, in the hearts of those who are given over to the service of Love with little Fortune.

The author also says that in that temple Priapus, god of gardens, "held the highest place there, in such a garb," etc. . . . It should be understood here that according to what the poets write, once when many of the gods were attending a certain feast, they had set up shelters in which to lodge. Among them was a goddess called Vesta, who was a very lovely maiden. And the aforementioned Priapus, having noticed her beauty and desiring her, placed himself where she had to sleep at night. When night came and the moon was shining, Priapus got up all naked and went silently to the place where Vesta was sleeping. When he was set to get in alongside her, it happened by misfortune that an ass, on which Silenus, aged foster father of Bacchus, had come, was lying near the place where Vesta was sleeping, and he began to bray so loud that Vesta and many others awoke. When, by the light of the moon which was shining, she saw herself next to Priapus and realized what he had come for, she began to cry out. Thereupon Priapus began to flee toward his tent, but he could not flee quickly enough so as to avoid being seen naked by everyone. This is the reason why his naked figure was always placed everywhere. The author says he was portrayed naked like this in this temple, and he wants to indicate by this what the cause of love in women is, just as he shows the affection of men in describing the shape of Venus. And so he placed Priapus in a more open place than Venus, since men care less that their secret parts are seen by women than the women do.[9]

After saying this, the author proceeds to show some adornments of the temple. And first he says that he sees garlands of various flowers. By these he represents the brief delight of those who have chanced to love well according to their desire.

After this he says he sees the bows that have been removed from the choirs of Diana. It should be understood here that Diana was the goddess of chastity among the ancients and did not accept any woman into her company except virgins. The ancients used to say that her function and that of her followers belonged to the forests and to the hunt, to show that those who want to preserve their chastity intact ought to flee every human consorting as much as they can, and idleness as well. For these two things, if what has been said above is clearly understood, are very great causes of falling into the snares of Venus.

Therefore, those virgins who followed Diana used to go hunting with their bows. Now many of them were conquered by Love and, having left off following Diana, followed Venus. The author says here that the bows of those who were conquered could be seen hung here in the temple of Venus in testimony to her victories.[10] . . .

When Palaemon's Prayer had seen these stories and perhaps many others witnessing to the powers of Venus, the author says she arrived at the place where Venus was. In this part he describes very well, for anyone who considers everything carefully, the voluptuous life in which all those can be said to dwell who, after loving for a long time, have attained to their delights either by art or by cleverness or by expense, and then persevere therein. He says, therefore, that Venus was in the most secret part of that temple where Opulence sat keeping guard. By this he wants to indicate that a voluptuous life cannot be attained nor long pursued without riches.

Then he says the place is dark. This is because those who practice evil hate the light.[11]

Then he describes the beauty of Venus who he says is reclining partially nude, and partially covered with a purple cloth so fine that it scarcely conceals the parts it covers. By the reclining, he means the idleness of the voluptuous and soft living. By the beauty of Venus, which we know is something transitory and fleeting, he means the false judgment of the voluptuous, which is easily proven and shown to be vain by true reasonings.

By the naked part of Venus, the author means the appearance of things which attract the souls of those whose thought cannot penetrate reality. By that part of Venus which is shown under a thin covering, he intends to represent the hidden judgment of those who are taken in by appearance. Such persons, when they see a beautiful face on a woman, immediately hasten in their opinion to believe that the parts hidden by the garments have even more sweetness and loveliness than those of one who has a less beautiful face. And it almost seems so to them until experience later proves to them that the beautiful and the not so beautiful are all made in the same fashion.

Next he says that Bacchus, the god of wine, sat on one side, and Ceres, goddess of the grain harvest, on the other.[12] By these two he means gluttony, which the voluptuous indulge in more than others. He also says that she had Lust by the hand. By this he intends to indicate that the works of the voluptuous do not consist only in luxury, but also in Lust. By this Lust he means to indicate kissing, touching, and chattering nonsense and bantering, and the other foolishness which goes on around them.

The fact that the place is perfumed is a matter of necessity for those who persevere in such practices, since the act is of itself so fetid that if the sense of smell were not appeased by aromas, it would easily impede the stomach and the brain and consequently the whole operation.

NOTES

1. The distinction between two "Venuses" is quite traditional. In his *Commentary on Six Books of Virgil's Aeneid* (c. 1150), Bernard Silvestris wrote: "We read that there are two Venuses, a legitimate goddess and a goddess of wantonness. We say that the legitimate Venus is the music of the world, that is, the equal proportion of worldly things, whom some call Astraea [see Ovid, *Metamorphoses*, I, 149–50] and others call Natural Justice [i.e., the law of nature]. And she is in the elements, in the stars, in time, and in animate creatures. But we say that the lascivious Venus, the goddess of wantonness, is concupiscence of the flesh [1 John ii, 16], because she is the mother of all fornication." This idea goes back at least to Ovid's *Fasti*, IV, 91–108. The medieval gloss to this passage reads: "There are two Venuses. One chaste and modest, who presides over honorable loves, is held to be the wife of Vulcan. The other is the goddess of lustful pleasures, whose son is Hermaphroditus. So also there are two Loves. One is good and modest, by whom the virtues and wisdom are armed; the other is shameless and evil. To preserve the distinction for the good love [Ovid speaks of] several Loves. But it should be noted that only one Venus, who among the Romans was properly called Venus Genetrix, is according to Ovid called Mother of both Loves."
2. A clear indication that Boccaccio is not always to be taken seriously.
3. See Terence, *Eunuchus*, IV, v, 6.
4. All of the five senses are referred to in the course of this gloss. Compare this and the following description to Parliament of Fowls, 183–294.
5. See Ovid, *Ars amatoria*, I.
6. Ovid's *Remedia amoris* recommends both exercise and looking more critically at the beloved's beauties, as a "cure" for love.
7. A reference to prominent principles in Ovid's *Ars amatoria*.
8. Copper was the metal officially assigned to Venus. Boccaccio's "gloss" playfully "applies" this attribution, as Venus was commonly regarded as the "force which seeks conjunctions," not only in the elements, but in animals (animate creatures) as well. See Clerk's Tale, 1166–68; Canon's Yeoman's Tale, 829.
9. See Merchant's Tale, 2034–35.
10. There follow accounts of numerous mythical tragic victims of love: Callisto, Atalanta, Semiramis, Pyramus and Thisbe, Hercules and Iole, Byblis.
11. See John iii, 20.
12. See Terence, *Eunuchus*, IV, v, 6.

Richard Rolle:
from *The Fire of Love*

Similarities between the forms and language of carnal and spiritual love are perhaps most striking in the writings of Christian mystics. The mystic engages in a love affair with his Savior, anticipating a "union" with his heavenly Bridegroom, and experiencing anguish and joy at least verbally like those of the lover for his earthly lady.

The following selections from the Incendium Amoris *by Richard Rolle have been selected to illustrate some of these similarities. An English recluse and mystic, Rolle (c. 1300–49) was a prolific and widely read writer in both Latin and English. Educated at Oxford, he suddenly undertook the hermit's life at the age of nineteen, foregoing his University degree. His many treatises and scriptural commentaries show a wide, though not pedantic, learning and a deep personal comprehension of his subjects. He is also highly regarded as a poet.*

The Incendium Amoris *(1343), his most famous treatise (more than forty manuscripts survive), is an attempt to describe the warmth, light, sweetness, and harmony of the mystical experience. It should be noted that as a mystic lover Rolle frequently casts himself in the feminine role. We should resist the modern urge to psychoanalyse a convention which derives from the model of spiritual love in Canticles. The bride there is often glossed as the "pure soul" (anima pura) whose mutual love with Christ is celebrated. By the same token the Clerk's Griselda stands for any person whose love for the heavenly Bridegroom is perfect, and Andreas Capellanus recommended such a role for his friend Walter (see below, pp. 357–59). Rolle is simply speaking through the* persona *of his* anima.

Trans. Clifton Wolters, The Fire of Love (Bungay: Penguin Classics, 1972), pp. 52–3, 122–23, 159–60, 116, 117–19. Copyright © 1971 by Clifton Wolters. Reprinted by permission of Penguin Books Ltd.

344

[A Love Song]

O honeyed flame, sweeter than all sweet, delightful beyond all creation!
My God, my Love, surge over me, pierce me by your love, wound me
   with your beauty.
Surge over me, I say, who am longing for your comfort.
Reveal your healing medicine to your poor lover.
See, my one desire is for you; it is you my heart is seeking.
My soul pants for you; my whole being is athirst for you.
Yet you will not show yourself to me; you look away; you bar the door,
       shun me, pass me over;
You even laugh at my innocent sufferings.
And yet you snatch your lovers away from all earthly things.
You lift them above every desire for worldly matters.
You make them capable of loving you—and love you they do indeed.
So they offer you their praise in spiritual song
      which bursts out from that inner fire;
      they know in truth the sweetness of the dart of love.
Ah, eternal and most lovable of all joys,
      you raise us from the very depths,
      and entrance us with the sight of divine majesty so often!
Come into me, Beloved!
All ever I had I have given up for you;
      I have spurned all that was to be mine,
      that you might make your home in my heart,
      and I your comfort.
Do not forsake me now, smitten with such great longing,
      whose consuming desire is to be amongst those who love you.
Grant me to love you,
      to rest in you,[1]
      that in your kingdom I may be worthy
      to appear before you world without end.

NOTE

1. For Rolle's own comment on woman as a man's "blessed rest," see below,
   p. 349.

[The Sighs, Vows, and Humility of the Perfect Lover]

FROM CHAPTER 26

The voice of the soul longing with eternal love and seeking the beauty of her Maker, rings out. *Let him kiss me with the kiss of his mouth,*[1] it says; in other words, let him delight me in union with his Son. Faint with love, I long with my whole heart to see my Love in all his beauty. But meanwhile may he visit me with his sweet love as I toil and struggle on through this pilgrimage. And may he turn my heart to himself so as to delight me with the warmth of greater and greater love. Until I can see my Beloved clearly I shall sing at every remembrance of his sweet name; it is never far from mind.

He who delights to do what his Saviour wishes not surprisingly finds delights in this present world as well. Nothing is more pleasant than praising Jesus; nothing more delectable than hearing him. For hearing rejoices my mind, and praising lifts me to himself. And when I am deprived of these things I sigh in my need, for then I hunger and thirst, and know myself bereft. Yet when I feel the embrace and caress of my Sweetheart I swoon with unspeakable delight, for it is he—he whom true lovers put before all else, for love of him alone, and because of his unbounded goodness!

And when he comes, may he come into me, suffusing me with his perfect love. May he refresh my heart by his continual gifts, and by removing every hindrance to his love make me glow and expand. Who will dare to say that a man is going to fall into the foul filth of the flesh, if Christ has deigned to refresh him with the heavenly sweetness of celestial vision? This is why such a man sings sweetly something like this, "We will rejoice as we remember *your breasts that are better than wine.*"[2]

NOTES

1. Canticles i, 1.·
2. Canticles i, 1.

Figure 13. Initial "O"; Christ embracing personification of Ecclesia. Bibliothèque Nationale MS lat. 1808, fol. 1 (Jerome, *Expositio in Cantica Canticorum*).

[Love's Meditation]

Those lovers who used to sing the glorious songs of love were accustomed to say that he who is chosen primarily to love cares above all that his heart shall never depart from his Beloved, and that the recollection of Jesus may be as music at a feast, sweeter to the taste than honey and the honeycomb.[1] And the longer he exercises himself in spiritual studies the sweeter does Jesus seem. So then he withdraws his mind from silly and sinful thoughts and puts it to wanting his Creator. Everything he brings into Christ to set it in him, the fount of love. To love him only, and find joy in him alone, is his unceasing prayer.

And now there come into his soul sweet desires and wonderful meditations directed to God alone. When he has brooded on them, and given his mind to develop them, they have an unutterable effect on him, and with great delight and spiritual sweetness lead him on to the contemplation of heavenly things, purging his mind from the hunger for worldly comfort. At this time the lover of God wants nothing so much as to be alone, to attend only to the wishes of his Maker. And when he has been well exercised in all this, and is given over to prayer and meditation in great quiet, and when all wickedness and uncleanness have been destroyed, and he takes up his arduous journey with prudence, he will make wonderful progress in the virtue of eternal love. His desires rise even higher, and with the eyes of his soul he enters into, and sees, the mysteries of heaven.[2]

NOTES

1. Ecclesiasticus xlix, 2.
2. Compare Andreas Capellanus on "excessive meditation," above, p. 293.

[The Dangers of Carnal Love]

FROM *CHAPTERS* 23–24

. . . No neglect of his soul is more damnable than that of the man who looks at a woman to lust after her.[1] For when the glance of the eye excites a man, soon he will start thinking about the woman he has seen, and such thoughts cause lust in the heart, and corrupt the inner being. Then suddenly he is blinded by the smoke of a destructive fire and prevented from seeing the sentence which the strict Judge will pass. For the soul is cut off from the sight of heavenly things by this unclean and evil love, and cannot fail to show outward signs of damnation. It sets its well-being in the realization of the uncleanness it has conceived. So immediately it conceives sorrow in its grievous desire, and deservedly brings forth wickedness.[2] . . .

When a man refuses to marry out of a pure love for God and virtue and chastity, and then sets about living in continence, adorned with every sort of virtue, there can be no doubt that he acquires a great reputation in heaven. Just as here he loves God without ceasing, so there he will praise him without ceasing. Marriage, of course, is good in itself, but when men subject themselves to its bond in order to satisfy their lust, they turn what is good into something evil. And when they reckon they are making the "progress" they intended, they are by the same token going rapidly downhill. As for the man who loves wedlock merely because he fancies he will get rich as a result, undoubtedly he is trying to loosen its reins by his lasciviousness. Abounding in licence and wealth, he boasts that he has found what "helps" his vile flesh.

Moreover there are men so perverse that they are consumed by uncontrollable lust for their own wives for the sake of their beauty, and the more quickly the body is reduced by their strength, the more they give themselves to satisfy their carnal lusts. But even while they are enjoying their delights they are beginning to fail; while they flourish they perish. Busy "finding fulfilment" in voluptuous lust, they are in fact exhausting most dreadfully their mental and physical powers.[3]

There is nothing more dangerous, more degrading, more disgusting than that a man should exhaust his mind in love for a woman, and pant after her as if she were his "blessed rest." And after it is all over, small wonder that he begins to degenerate, because before it had happened he had striven for this "supreme blessedness" with such great anguish. But he knows well enough afterwards, as he thinks over his swift pleas-

349

ure and its lengthy discomfort, that he has gone wrong, shamefully and senselessly wrong, in such love. For it is clear that he was tightly held by the evil bond of weak vanity. But not wanting to turn to God with all his heart, he did not recognize his wretchedness until he experienced it. So he fell into the pit, a captive, simply because he had no thought for the Throne of Glory. If he had known even a drop of the sweetness of eternal life, carnal beauty (that false, vain grace!)[4] would not have seemed so sweet to his mind. But, alas, he does not consider how his wretched lust appears to the eyes of God Almighty, nor can he see himself as he really is in conscience, foul and revolting.

Again, no one can yield to the seductions of the flesh, without straying from the right path. For all the while the fire of earthly love inflames a man's mind, naturally enough the dew of divine grace evaporates, made useless and dry. Such love ever increases its heat, and from the fire of greed kindles the fire of sensuality, so that the crazed, enslaved soul most extraordinarily longs for nothing but carnal pleasures, and increased riches. It makes these things the purpose of its life; it burns because it must have them. It does not see the punishment which is the outcome, and to which it is rushing headlong. For the word of God, and his commandments, it cares nothing. Coveting only joys which are outward and visible, it is blind to those which are inward and invisible. And so it goes to the Fire with eyes tightly shut! And when the unhappy soul shall be free of its body, at once and for certain it will know at the Judgement how wretched it was while it lived in the flesh, though then it had thought itself to be both innocent and happy.

NOTES

1. See Matthew v, 28.
2. See 2 Corinthians vii, 10.
3. See Parson's Tale, 858–60, 903–4; Merchant's Tale, 1835–41; Nun's Priest's Tale, 3342–46.
4. Compare General Prologue, 88.

from *Harley Manuscript 2253, "The Heart of Man can Hardly Know"*

The following two lyrics appear as No. 82 and 83 in Harley 2253, a manuscript important for our knowledge of Middle English lyrics, dating from the early fourteenth century. It is not certainly known which poem preceded the other in time, but these companion pieces illustrate the manner in which the love of God and love of the lady could be opposed and expressed in similar literary forms.

Trans. Brian Stone, Medieval English Verse (*Baltimore: Penguin, 1964*), *pp.* 198–99. *Copyright* © 1964 *by Brian Stone. Reprinted by permission of Penguin Books Ltd.*

[Love of God]

The heart of Man can hardly know
    How love of us has bound
The One who on the Cross let flow
    Redemption from his wound.
His love has saved us, made us whole and sound,
And hurled the grisly Devil underground.
Continually by night and day, he keeps us in his thought;
    He will not lose what he so dearly bought.

He bought us with his holy blood;
    How could he grant us more?
He is so meek and mild and good,
    And free of sin therefore.
I say we should repent for evermore
And cry to Jesus, 'Mercy, we implore!'
Continually by night and day, he keeps us in his thought;
    He will not lose what he so dearly bought.

He saw his Father greatly wroth
    At Man's most sinful fall:
With grieving heart he swore his oath
    That we should suffer all.
But then his sweet Son made his pleading call,
And begged that he might die and save us all.
Continually by night and day, he keeps us in his thought;
    He will not lose what he so dearly bought.

He took from us the pains of death—
    Benign and gracious deed!
Sweet Jesus Christ of Nazareth,
    For heaven's reward we plead!
Of him on Cross why do we take no heed?
His freshly gaping wounds so grimly bleed.
Continually by night and day, he keeps us in his thought;
    He will not lose what he so dearly bought.

His open wounds are bleeding fast;
    We must remember him:

Through him our pains of hell are past;
    He saved us all from sin.
For love of us his cheeks are growing thin:
He gave his blood for all his earthly kin.
Continually by night and day, he keeps us in his thought;
    He will not lose what he so dearly bought.

[Love of Lady]

The heart of Man can hardly know
　　What secret love can do,
Unless a lovely woman show,
　　Who knows it through and through.
The love of such is brief, and wayward too:
She took my lover's promise once, but calls me now untrue.
Continually for love of her I grieve in heavy thought;
　　I think of her, but mostly see her not.

Today I'd call her by her name
　　If I dared begin.
Among the folk of courtly fame
　　She's fairest of her kin.
Unless she loves me she'll commit a sin:
Alas for the man who loves a girl whom he can never win!
Continually for love of her I grieve in heavy thought;
　　I think of her, but mostly see her not.

Crying, I fall before her face
　　With, 'Lady, I implore
You grant your faithful lover grace!
　　Be true to lovers' lore!
Until you are, my heart with grief is sore,
For love's affliction pains me so that I can live no more!'
Continually for love of her I grieve in heavy thought;
　　I think of her, but mostly see her not.

What bliss in that adored one's tower,
　　With knight and servant throng!
And such the pleasures of her bower,
　　With sport and courtly song.
My woe, unless she loves me, will be strong:
Alas for the man whose lover is untrue and does him wrong!
Continually for love of her I grieve in heavy thought;
　　I think of her, but mostly see her not.

Prettiest girl who breathes the air,
　　My love, I welcome you

As many many times, I swear,
 As there are drops of dew,
Or heavenly stars, or herbs of sweet or rue!
Content shall rarely come to men whose lovers are untrue;
Continually for love of her I grieve in heavy thought;
 I think of her, but mostly see her not.

Andreas Capellanus:
from the *Treatise on Love*

In the third Book of the De amore, Andreas Capellanus provides his "friend" Walter with eighteen arguments against engaging in the love he has described. One of these involves a long catalogue of women's vices, which recalls a technique recommended by Ovid in the Remedies for Love, 299 ff., adapted, however, to the antifeminist tradition of his day (see below, pp. 399ff.). Andreas' claim that this last Book only "seems" to present a point of view different from that in the first two suggests that the earlier Books should not be read too literally.

Trans. J. J. Parry, The Art of Courtly Love (New York: Columbia University Press, 1941), pp. 187:89, 210–12. Reprinted by permission of Columbia University Press.

The Rejection of Love

Now, friend Walter, if you will lend attentive ears to those things which after careful consideration we wrote down for you because you urged us so strongly, you can lack nothing in the art of love, since in this little book we gave you the theory of the subject, fully and completely, being willing to accede to your requests because of the great love we have for you. You should know that we did not do this because we consider is advisable for you or any other man to fall in love, but for fear lest you might think us stupid; we believe, though, that any man who devotes his efforts to love loses all his usefulness. Read this little book, then, not as one seeking to take up the life of a lover, but that, invigorated by the theory and trained to excite the minds of women to love, you may, by refraining from so doing, win an eternal recompense and thereby deserve a greater reward from God. For God is more pleased with a man who is able to sin and does not, than with a man who has no opportunity to sin.

Now for many reasons any wise man is bound to avoid all the deeds of love and to oppose all its mandates. The first of these reasons is one which it is not right for anyone to oppose, for no man, so long as he devotes himself to the service of love, can please God by any other works, even if they are good ones. For God hates, and in both testaments[1] commands the punishment of those whom he sees engaged in the works of Venus outside the bonds of wedlock or caught in the toils of any sort of passion. What good therefore can be found in a thing in which nothing is done except what is contrary to the will of God? Alas what an affliction it is and what bitterness to our hearts when we grieve constantly to see men reject the things of heaven for the sake of the foul and shameful acts of Venus! O wretched and insane, to be looked upon as lower than a beast, is that man who for the sake of a momentary delight of the flesh will reject eternal joys and strive to hand himself over to the flames of ever-burning Gehenna! So, Walter, you can see, and you are clever enough to understand, how much honor a man deserves who because of his fondness for some light woman scorns heaven's King and pays no attention to His commandments, and does not fear to enmesh himself in the toils of his ancient enemy. For if God had wished the act of fornication to be without blame, he would have had no reason to order the solemnization of marriage, since God's people could multiply faster without it than by marrying. We must therefore wonder at the folly of the man who because he embraces the lowest and most earthly love loses that eternal heritage which the heavenly King, with His own blood, restored to all men after it had been lost. Indeed, for a mortal man we consider it a very great disgrace and an offense against Almighty God if by following the enticements of the flesh and the pleasures of the body he slips back again into the snares of Hell, from which the Heavenly Father Himself once redeemed him by shedding the blood.of His Only-Begotten Son.

We all know, moreover, that there is a second argument against love, for by it we injure our neighbor whom, according to the divine mandate, every man is bidden to love as himself.[2] But even without the divine mandate and considering only worldly convenience, we are bound to love our neighbors, for no one can get along without neighbors even for a short time.

There is still a third thing which persuades everybody to avoid love: by it one friend is estranged from another and serious unfriendlinesses grow up between them, and these even lead to homicide or many other evils. No one is so bound to another by the bonds of affection or friendship that if he finds out that the other man is suing urgently for the love of his wife or his daughter or some near relative he will not at once be filled with a spiteful hatred toward him or conceive a venomous anger. He who neglects the honor of his friend for the sake of serving the flesh is thought to live for himself alone, and so, it seems, every man should turn from him as an enemy of human kind and should flee from him as from a venomous beast.[3] . . .

Now this doctrine of ours, which we have put into this little book for you, will if carefully and faithfully examined seem to present two different points of view. In the first part we tried to assent to your simple and youthful request and did not wish, on this subject, to give in to our indolence; so we set down completely, one point after another, the art of love, as you so eagerly asked us to do, and now that it is all arranged in the proper order, we hand it over to you. If you wish to practice the system, you will obtain, as a careful reading of this little book will show you, all the delights of the flesh in fullest measure; but the grace of God, the companionship of the good, and the friendship of praiseworthy men you will with good reason be deprived of, and you will do great harm to your good name, and it will be difficult for you to obtain the honors of this world.[4]

In the latter part of the book we were more concerned with what might be useful to you, and of our own accord we added something about the rejection of love, although you had no reason to ask for it, and we treated the matter fully; perhaps we can do you good against your will. If you will study carefully this little treatise of ours and understand it completely and practice what it teaches, you will see clearly that no man ought to mis-spend his days in the pleasures of love. If you abstain from it, the Heavenly King will be more favorably disposed toward you in every respect, and you will be worthy to have all prosperous success in this world and to fulfill all praiseworthy deeds and the honorable desires of your heart, and in the world to come to have glory and life everlasting.

Therefore, Walter, accept this health-giving teaching we offer you, and pass by all the vanities of the world, so that when the Bridegroom cometh to celebrate the greater nuptials, and the cry ariseth in the night, you may be prepared to go forth to meet Him with your lamps filled and to go in with Him to the divine marriage, and you will have no need to seek out in haste what you need for your lamps, and find it too late, and come to the home of the Bridegroom after the door is shut, and hear His venerable voice.[5]

Be mindful, therefore, Walter, to have your lamps always supplied, that is, have the supplies of charity and good works. Be mindful ever to watch, lest the unexpected coming of the Bridegroom find you asleep in sins. Avoid then, Walter, practicing the mandates of love, and labor in constant watchfulness so that when the Bridegroom cometh He may find you wakeful; do not let worldly delight make you lie down in your sins, trusting to the youth of your body and confident that the Bridegroom will be late, since, as He tells us Himself, we know neither the day nor the hour.

NOTES

1. Exodus xx, 14; Leviticus xx, 10; Deuteronomy v, 18; Matthew v, 27–28; Apocalypse xxi, 8.
2. Luke x, 27.
3. Consider the effect of love on Palamon and Arcite in the Knight's Tale.
4. These were widely regarded as "chivalric rewards."
5. Matthew xxv, 1–13.

Geoffrey Chaucer:
from *The Parson's Tale*

Of the Parson's concluding sermon on Penitence, that portion which deals
with the Seven Deadly Sins is based on the Summa de viciis ("Summa on
the Vices") by Guilielmus Peraldus (c. 1260). The present passage, how-
ever, does not occur in the Summa. Since such additions to the source of
the Parson's Tale are particularly rich in concerns and phrasing which occur
in other Canterbury Tales, it would appear that Chaucer wished to include
in the Parson's own summation materials which reflect the kind of author-
ity a parish priest would speak for, as they apply to matters spoken of earlier
by other pilgrims.

This passage occurs in the section concerning the sin of Luxuria ("Lec-
cherie"). In it the Devil's "fyve fyngres" are made to correspond to the
conventional gradus amoris, the five "steps of love"—sight, speech, touch,
kiss, and deed. The Parson's view inverts the lover's idea that by these steps
he climbs to "bliss" (see Miller's Tale, 2723–26). The Parson has described
Gluttony as the "first hand" of the Devil.

A new translation.

[The Five Fingers of Lechery]

Now, then, let us speak of that stinking sin of Lechery which is called adultery of married folk, which is to say, if one of them be married, or both. Saint John says that adulterers will be in Hell, in the pool burning with fire and brimstone[1]—in fire for their lechery, and in brimstone for the stench of their filth. Certainly, the breaking of this sacrament [of marriage] is a horrible thing. It was made in paradise by God Himself, and confirmed by Jesus Christ, as Saint Matthew witnesses in the gospel: "A man shall leave father and mother, and shall cleave to his wife, and they two shall be in one flesh."[2] This sacrament betokens the knitting together of Christ and of Holy Church.[3] And God not only forbade adultery in deed, but he also commanded that thou shalt not covet thy neighbor's wife.[4] "In this behest," says Saint Augustine, "is forbidden all lecherous desires."[5] See what Saint Matthew says in his gospel: "Whosoever shall look on a woman to lust after her, hath already committed adultery with her in his heart."[6] Here you may see that not only the commission of this sin is forbidden, but also the desire to commit that sin. This cursed sin grievously pains those whom it troubles. And first, it harms their souls, for it compels them to sin and to the pain of death that is everlasting. It grievously pains the body also, for it dries it, and wastes it, and ruins it, and of its blood makes a sacrifice to the Fiend of Hell. It wastes as well his wealth and his substance. And certainly, if it is a foul thing for a man to waste his wealth on women, it is a yet fouler thing when women, for such filth, spend their wealth and substance upon men. This sin, as the prophet says, robs both man and woman of their good name and of all their honor; and it greatly pleases the Devil, for with it he wins the greater part of world. And just as a merchant delights most in the trade which brings him most profit, so the Fiend delights in this filth.

This is the second hand of the Devil, with five fingers to drag people into his vile ways [*vileynye*]. The first finger is the fool looking of the fool woman and of the fool man, which slays, just as the basilicok[7] slays folk with the venom of his look; for concupiscence of the eyes is followed by concupiscence of the heart.[8] The second finger is vile and sinful touching. And therefore Solomon says that "he who touches and takes hold of a woman is as he who takes hold of a scorpion which stings and quickly slays with its poison";[9] just as he who touches warm pitch defiles his fingers.[10] The third is foul words, which are like fire that suddenly burns the heart. The fourth finger is kissing; truly, only a great fool would kiss the mouth of a burning oven or of a furnace. Even greater fools are they who kiss basely [*in vileynye*], for that mouth is the mouth of Hell; and especially those old lecherous dotards—they will yet kiss, though they cannot perform, and defile themselves. Certainly, they are like hounds; for a hound, when he goes past a rose-bush or any other bush, though he cannot piss, yet will he heave up his leg and make a show of pissing. And though many a man thinks that he may not sin, no matter what lechery he performs with his wife, indeed that opinion is false. God knows, a man may slay himself with his own knife, and make himself drunk out of his own wine-cask.[11] Indeed, whether it be his wife, or child, or any worldly thing, if he loves it more than he loves God, it is his idol[12] and he is an idolator. A man should love his wife with discretion, patiently and temperately, as though she were his sister. The fifth finger of the Devil's hand is the stinking deed of Lechery. The Devil puts the five fingers of Gluttony in the belly of a man, and with his five fingers of Lechery surely he gripes him by the loins, to throw him into the furnace of Hell, where he shall know the fire and everlasting worms, the weeping and wailing,[13] sharp hunger and thirst, and the cruelty of devils which shall trample him down without respite and without end.

NOTES

1. Apocalypse xxi, 8; xix, 20; xx, 9.
2. Matthew xix, 5; Genesis ii, 24; Mark x, 7; 1 Corinthians vi, 16; Ephesians v, 31. See Merchant's Tale, 1325–36; Wife of Bath's Prologue, 30–31.
3. Ephesians v, 25. Compare Franklin's Tale, 1230.
4. Exodus xx, 17.
5. Reference not traced.
6. Matthew v, 28.
7. The basilisk, a fabulous creature, originally a kind of serpent, reputed by Pliny to kill with its eye. See Isaias xi, 8; xiv, 29; lix, 5; Jeremias viii, 17. The Parson's statement strongly disapproves of romantic "love at first sight."
8. See 1 John ii, 16; and especially Matthew v, 28.
9. See Ecclesiasticus xii, 13–14; xxvi, 10.
10. See Ecclesiasticus xiii, 1.
11. Merchant's Tale, 1835–41.
12. *Mawmet*, corruption of "Mahomet" (Mohammed).
13. See Clerk's Tale, 1212, and Merchant's Prologue, 1213. The formula derives from such texts as, e.g., Matthew viii, 12; xiii, 28; xxii, 13; xxv, 30; Luke xiii, 28.

seven

MARRIAGE
AND THE
GOOD WOMAN

The ideas professed in the literature of romantic love contrast in profoundly significant ways with the official medieval view of love between man and woman as it was codified in the sacrament of marriage, and with the role of woman as it was defined in the stereotype of the "good woman." Medieval readers of courtly love stories had of course often attended weddings, or were, like Chaucer himself, married, and were familiar with Christian precepts regarding love between the sexes legitimized in that sacrament. As catechumens they had learned its premises, and as prospective spouses they would have undertaken premarital "instruction."

If we take the account of Bartholomaeus Anglicus (below, pp. 385–87) at all seriously, medieval marriage was a matter of personal choice more often than we might be led to believe by some cultural historians. Its basis was mutual consent, enacted in the exchange of vows, or trouthe (below, p. 375), a concept which Chaucer's Franklin utterly subverts in his account of Arveragus' marriage and "care" for his wife. Since marriage sacramentalized love, the Ovidian idea that "marriage is no excuse for not loving" (above, p. 298) must have seemed to many readers a witty irony; and the Wife of Bath's "doctrine" of woman's sovereignty, when we are aware of what she has consented to five times, must be seen as pure insolence.

What we are shown in the following texts are the official ideals against which the medieval literature of love is to be viewed. We can see the same sobriety of concern for the common weal in texts defining the chivalric Estate (above, pp. 156ff.). The Parson's stricture against "amorous love" (below, p. 368) succinctly epitomizes the attitude toward carnal concupiscence affirmed in Galatians v, 17, challenged by the courtly tradition, and confirmed by John Gower, among others, in his account of "chivalric love" (above, pp. 195–203).

In medieval romantic literature women appear most often only as bland objects of beauty to be wooed and won, not as human beings with an active role in the social system. The conventional picture of the "good woman" certainly removes this superficial gloss. In the devout, modest, industrious, and faithful wife described below we have a popular model against which to measure not only the flagrant derelictions of the Wife of Bath, but the less philosophical motivations of wives such as her namesake in the Miller's Tale. Yet tradition links an appreciation of the good wife with a warning against her opposite (see below, p. 387). This convention is brushed aside by the Wife of Bath in her counterblast against clerks (Wife of Bath's Prologue, 686–96).

Geoffrey Chaucer:
from *The Parson's Tale*

Although last in point of time, the comments of Chaucer's Parson on the sacrament of marriage are presented first in this section, for they succinctly summarize the formal assumptions which lie behind the marital joys and jokes in the Canterbury Tales. His terms are so conventional that they could be illustrated from innumerable authorities besides those he directly mentions. Whether or not we take his views to correspond with those of the poet Chaucer, they represent a standard body of doctrine familiar to an audience who heard it mocked in the mouths of his more worldly pilgrims. Cross references in the notes below can only suggest the many ways in which the ideas and phrasing of such a passage are echoed in the other tales.

A new translation.

[Marriage as a Remedy against Lechery]

LINES 917–43

Now you should understand that matrimony is the lawful union of a man and a woman, who receive by virtue of the sacrament the bond whereby they may not be parted during their lives, that is to say, as long as they both may live. This, as the Bible says, is a very great sacrament.[1] God made it, as I have said, in Paradise,[2] and willed that He Himself be born in marriage. And in order to sanctify marriage, He attended a wedding where He turned water into wine, and this was the first miracle which He wrought on earth before His disciples.[3] The true result of marriage is to cleanse fornication and to replenish Holy Church with a good lineage,[4] for that is the end of marriage; and it changes deadly sin into venial sin between those who are wedded, and makes one the hearts of married folk as well as their bodies. This is true marriage, which was established by God before the beginning of sin, when natural law exercised its proper power in Paradise;[5] and it was ordained that one man should have but one woman, and one woman but one man, as Saint Augustine proves by many reasons.[6]

First, because the union between Christ and Holy Church is a figure for marriage.[7] Also, because a man is the head of a woman (at any rate, it ought to be so according to God's ordinance).[8] For if a woman had more than one man, then she would have more heads than one, and that would be a horrible thing before God; also, a woman would not be able to please too many men at once. Also, there would never be peace or quiet among them, for each one would demand his own due. And furthermore, no man would know who his children were, nor who should inherit from him; and the woman would be less beloved from the time when she was joined to many men.

Now we must consider how a man should conduct himself toward his wife, and that should be in two ways, namely, in tolerance (*suffraunce*)[9] and in reverence, as Christ showed when He first made woman. For He did not make her out of the head of Adam, to show that she should not claim too great a sovereignty (*lordshipe*). For where the woman has the *maistrie*, she creates too much confusion.[10] No examples of this are needed; day-by-day experience ought to suffice. Yet God also, certainly, did not make woman out of Adam's foot, to show that she should not be kept in servitude; for a woman cannot patiently suffer. But God made woman out of the rib of Adam, to show that woman should be a companion (*felawe*) to man. A man should conduct himself toward his wife with faith, with loyalty (*trouthe*), and with love;[11] as Saint Paul says, a man should love his wife as Christ loved Holy Church, who loved it so well that He died for it.[12] So a man should for his wife, if it were necessary.

Now, how a woman should be subject to her husband, Saint Peter explains.[13] First, in obedience. As the law states, a married woman, as long as she is a wife, has no authority to swear oaths or bear witness without the permission of her husband, who is her lord (at any rate, he should be, according to reason).[14] I am sure that wives should try to please their husbands, but not by quaintness of clothing.[15] Saint Jerome says that "wives who are appareled in silk and precious purple cannot clothe themselves in Jesus Christ." And what does Saint John say on this subject?[16] Saint Gregory, also, says that "no one wears expensive array, except out of vainglory, to be more honored among men." It is a great folly for a woman to have a fair outward appearance and to be inwardly foul. A wife should also be modest in her looking, in her demeanor, and in her laughter, and discreet in all her words and deeds. She should love her husband with all her heart above every other worldly thing, and be true to him with her body. And so should a husband be to his wife. For since her body is entirely the husband's so her heart should be, or else there is, so far as that is concerned, no perfect marriage between them.

Next we should understand that a man and his wife may have carnal intercourse for three reasons. The first is the intention to conceive children for the service of God; for certainly that is the main reason for matrimony. A second reason is for each of them to render the other the debt of their bodies; for neither of them has power over his own body. The third is to avoid lechery and baseness. The fourth is truly a deadly sin. As for the first, it is meritorious. The second is also, for the law says that she preserves the merit of chastity who renders to her husband the debt of her body, even though it displeases her and is against the desire of her heart. The third is a venial sin; and truly, hardly any such unions can be without venial sin, because of original sin and the pleasure involved. The fourth occurs when a man and woman join only for amorous love and for none of the previous reasons, simply to experience that burning pleasure, no matter how often. Truly, this is a deadly sin; and yet, unfortunately, some people go to great trouble to engage in it more often than their appetites demand.[17]

NOTES

1. Ephesians v, 32. See Merchant's Tale, 1319.
2. Genesis ii, 24. See Merchant's Tale, 1325–32.
3. John ii, 1–11. See Wife of Bath's Prologue, 9–13.
4. Compare Reeve's Tale, 3981–86.
5. In the *De sacramentis*, II, xi, 1, Hugh of Saint Victor begins his discussion of marriage with this essential point: "Although all sacraments took their beginning after sin and on account of sin, we read that the sacrament of marriage alone was established even before sin, yet not as a remedy but as an office."
6. Reference untraced.
7. Ephesians v, 25.
8. Ephesians v, 23; 1 Corinthians xi, 3.
9. See Franklin's Tale, 776–88.
10. Compare Ecclesiasticus xxv, 30.
11. Compare Franklin's Tale, 1479.
12. Ephesians v, 25.
13. 1 Peter iii, 1.
14. Compare Fiammetta's view of the literary source of Dorigen's oath in the Franklin's Tale (above, p. 132).
15. 1 Peter iii, 3.
16. Apocalypse xvii, 4; xviii, 16.
17. With these four motives compare Merchant's Tale, 1441–56. For the "marriage debt" see 1 Corinthians vii, 3.

Saint Augustine:
from *The City of God*

The importance of Saint Augustine (see above, pp. 16–17) stamps this short account of "marriage in Paradise" with an authority which sarcasms like those in the Merchant's Tale, 1319–36 cannot subvert.

Trans. Marcus Dods, The City of God (Edinburgh: T. & T. Clark, 1872: rept. New York: Hafner, 1948), Vol. II, pp. 38–39. Copyright 1948 by Hafner Publishing Company. Reprinted by permission of Macmillan Publishing Co., Inc.

Of the Conjugal Union as It Was
Originally Instituted and Blessed by God

But we, for our part, have no manner of doubt that to increase and multiply and replenish the earth in virtue of the blessing of God, is a gift of marriage as God instituted it from the beginning before man sinned, when He created them male and female,—in other words, two sexes manifestly distinct. And it was this work of God on which His blessing was pronounced. For no sooner had Scripture said, "Male and female created He them," than it immediately continues, "And God blessed them, and God said unto them, Increase, and multiply, and replenish the earth, and subdue it," etc.[1] And though all these things may not unsuitably be interpreted in a spiritual sense, yet "male and female" cannot be understood of two things in one man, as if there were in him one thing which rules, another which is ruled; but it is quite clear that they were created male and female, with bodies of different sexes, for the very purpose of begetting offspring, and so increasing, multiplying, and replenishing the earth; and it is great folly to oppose so plain a fact. It was not of the spirit which commands and the body which obeys, nor of the rational soul which rules and the irrational desire which is ruled, nor of the contemplative virtue which is supreme and the active which is subject, nor of the understanding of the mind and the sense of the body,[2] but plainly of the matrimonial union by which the sexes are mutually bound together, that our Lord, when asked whether it were lawful for any cause to put away one's wife (for on account of the hardness of the hearts of the Israelites Moses permitted a bill of divorcement to be given), answered and said, "Have ye not read that He which made them at the beginning made them male and female, and said, For this cause shall a man leave father and mother, and shall cleave to his wife, and they twain shall be one flesh? Wherefore they are no more twain, but one flesh. What, therefore, God hath joined together, let not man put asunder."[3] It is certain, then, that from the first men were created, as we see and know them to be now, of two sexes, male and female, and that they are called one, either on account of the matrimonial union, or on account of the origin of the woman, who was created from the side of the man. And it is by this original example, which God Himself instituted, that the apostle admonishes all husbands to love their own wives in particular.[4]

NOTES

1. Genesis i, 27–28.
2. Augustine reviews some of the standard allegorical interpretations of the account in Genesis.
3. Matthew xix, 4–6.
4. Ephesians v, 25.

From the *Sarum Missal*

Behind the entire "debate" on marriage in the Canterbury Tales lies the fact of marriage itself. The surrounding texts in this section express a variety of views peripheral to the heart of the matter, which is crystallized in the marriage ceremony itself. Other texts, such as Boccaccio's analysis of the problem Chaucer reproduced in his Franklin's Tale, also make significant use of its terms (see above, pp. 131–32).

Chaucer's allusions to this ceremonial are so frequent, and often so subtle, that no attempt has been made to annotate them. The modern reader, however, should be attentive to the wife's vow to "obey" her husband—a matter which leads to some interesting theories by la Vieille in the Romance of the Rose (below, pp. 469–72) and her disciple, the Wife of Bath. This vow must qualify our perception of the "humble, wys accord" in the Franklin's Tale, 741–52. A fine ironic epitome of the ceremony occurs in the Merchant's Tale, 1700–1709.

In the following ceremony the ℣. stands for a versicle said by the officiating priest; the ℞. stands for the response of the congregation; and the N. refers to the name of the participant addressed.

Trans. Frederick E. Warren, The Sarum Missal in English (London: Alexander Moring Ltd., 1911).

The Form of Solemnization of Matrimony

The man and the woman are to be placed before the door[1] of the church, or in the face of the church, in the presence of God, and the priest, and the people. The man should stand on the right hand of the woman, and the woman on the left hand of the man, the reason being that she was formed out of a rib in the left side of Adam. Then shall the priest ask the banns, and afterwards he shall say in the vulgar tongue, in the hearing of all,

Brethren, we are gathered together here, in the sight of God, and his angels, and all the saints, and in the face of the Church, to join together two bodies, to wit, those of this man and this woman,

Here shall the priest look upon both persons,

that henceforth they may be one body; and that they may be two souls in the faith and law of God, to the end they may earn together eternal life; and whatsoever they may have done before this,

Then let a charge be made to the people in the vulgar tongue, thus—

I charge you all by the Father, and the Son, and the Holy Ghost, that if any of you know any cause why these persons may not be lawfully joined together in matrimony, he do now confess it.

The same charge shall be made to the man and woman; so that if aught hath been done by them secretly, or if they have made any vow, or know aught in any way concerning themselves, why they may not lawfully contract matrimony, they may then confess it. If anyone shall wish to allege any impediment, and shall give security for proving it, the marriage must be deferred until the truth of the matter be ascertained. If, however, no impediment be alleged, the priest is to enquire about the dower of the woman. The priest shall not betroth, or consent to a betrothal between a man and woman, before the third publication of banns. Banns ought to be asked on three distinct holy days, so that at least one week-day intervene between each of such holy days. After this, the priest shall say to the man, in the audience of all, in the vulgar tongue,

N[ame] wilt thou have this woman to thy wedded wife, wilt thou love her, and honour her, keep her and guard her, in health and in sickness, as a husband should a wife, and forsaking all others on account of her, keep thee only unto her, so long as ye both shall live?

The man shall answer, I will.

Then shall the priest say unto the woman,

N[ame] wilt thou take this man to thy wedded husband, wilt thou obey him, and serve him, love, honour, and keep him, in health and sickness, as a wife should a husband, and forsaking all others on account of him, keep thee only unto him, so long as ye both shall live?

The woman shall answer, I will.

Then let the woman be given by her father or a friend; if she be a maid, let her have her hand uncovered; if she be a widow, covered; and let the man receive her, to be kept in God's faith and his own, as he hath vowed in the presence of the priest; and let him hold her by her right hand in his right hand. And so let the man give his troth to the woman, by word of mouth, presently, after the priest, saying thus:

I N. take thee N. to my wedded wife, to have and to hold from this day forth, for better, for worse, for richer for poorer, in sickness, and in health, to love and to cherish, till death us depart, according to God's holy ordinance: And thereto I plight thee my troth (*withdrawing his hand*).

Then shall the woman say, after the priest,

I N. take thee N. to my wedded husband, to have and to hold from this day forth, for better, for worse, for richer, for poorer, in sickness, and in health, to love, cherish, and to obey, till death us depart, according to God's holy ordinance: And thereto I give thee my troth (*withdrawing her hand*).

Then shall the man lay gold, or silver, and a ring upon a dish or book; and then the priest shall ask whether the ring have been previously blessed or not; if it be answered not, then shall the priest bless the ring, thus,

℣. The Lord be with you.
℟. And with thy spirit.

Let us pray.

O creator and preserver of mankind, giver of spiritual grace, bestower of eternal salvation, do thou, O Lord, send thy bles+sing upon this ring, that she who shall wear it may be armed with the strength of heavenly defence, and that it may be profitable unto her eternal salvation. Through etc. ℟. Amen.

Let us pray.

Collect.

Bless, O Lord, this ring, which we bless in thy holy name; that whosoever she be that shall wear it, may abide in thy peace, and continue in thy will, and live, and increase, and grow old in thy love; and let the length of her days be multiplied. Through etc.

Then let holy water be sprinkled over the ring. If, however, the ring shall have been previously blessed, then immediately after the man has placed the ring upon the book, the priest shall take up the ring, and deliver it to the man. The man shall take it in his right hand with his three principal fingers, holding the right hand of the bride with his left hand, and shall say, after the priest,

With this ring I thee wed, and this gold and silver I thee give: and with my body I thee worship: and with all my worldly goods I thee endow.

Then shall the bridegroom place the ring upon the thumb of the bride, saying, In the name of the Father; *then upon the second finger, saying,* and of the Son; *then upon the third finger, saying,* and of the Holy Ghost; *then upon the fourth finger, saying,* Amen, *and there let him leave it, because in that finger there is a certain vein, which runs from thence as far as the heart; and inward affection, which ought always to be fresh between them, is signified by the true ring of the silver. Then, while they bow their heads, the priest shall pronounce a blessing upon them.*

Be ye blessed of the Lord, who hath made the world out of nothing.
℟. Amen.

Then shall be said this Psalm following:

Thy God hath sent forth strength for thee: stablish the thing, O God, that thou hast wrought in us.

For thy temple's sake at Jerusalem: so shall kings bring presents unto thee.

When the company of spearmen, and multitude of the mighty are scattered abroad among the beasts of the people, so that they humbly bring pieces of silver.[2]

Glory be to the Father etc. As it was etc.

> Lord, have mercy [upon us].
> Christ, have mercy [upon us].
> Lord, have mercy [upon us].

Our Father etc.

℣. And lead us not into temptation.
℟. But deliver us from evil.
℣. Let us bless the Father, and the Son, with the Holy Ghost.
℟. Let us praise and exalt him for ever.
℣. Let us praise the Lord, whom the angels praise.
℟. To whom cherubin and seraphin do cry, Holy, holy, holy.
℣. Lord, hear my prayer.
℟. And let my cry come unto thee.
℣. The Lord be with you.
℟. And with thy spirit.

Let us pray.

Collect.

The God of Abraham, the God of Isaac, the God of Jacob, be with you; and may he himself unite you, and fill you with the fulness of his blessing. Who liveth etc.

Another Collect with Let us pray.

Collect.

God the Father bl+ess you; Jesus Christ keep you, the Holy Ghost enlighten you; the Lord make his face to shine upon you, and be merciful unto you; may he turn his countenance upon you, and give you peace; and so fill you with all spiritual benediction for the remission of your sins, that ye may have life eternal, and may live for ever and ever. Amen.

Here they shall go into the church, as far as the step of the altar; and the priest, together with his ministers, shall say, as they are going, the Psalm Blessed are all they etc.[3] *without note, and with* Glory be to the Father etc. *and* As it was etc.

> Lord, have mercy [upon us].
> Christ, have mercy [upon us].
> Lord, have mercy [upon us].

Then the bridegroom and bride kneeling before the step of the altar, the priest shall ask the bystanders to pray for them, saying,

Our Father etc.
℣. And lead us not into temptation.
℟. But deliver us from evil.
℣. Save thy servant, and thy handmaid,
℟. My God, who put their trust in thee.
℣. O Lord, send them help from thy holy place.
℟. And defend them out of Zion.
℣. Be unto them, O Lord, a tower of strength,
℟. From the face of their enemy.
℣. Lord, hear my prayer.
℟. And let my cry come unto thee.
℣. The Lord be with you.
℟. And with thy spirit.

Let us pray.

Collect.

The Lord bless you out of Sion, that ye may behold Jerusalem in prosperity all the days of your life, and that ye may see your children's children, and peace upon Israel. Through etc.

Let us pray.

Collect.

O God of Abraham, God of Isaac, and God of Jacob, bless these young persons, and sow the seed of eternal life in their hearth, that whatsoever they shall profitably learn, they may indeed fulfil the same. Through Jesus Christ thy Son, the restorer of mankind. Who with thee etc. ℟. Amen.

Let us pray.

Collect.

Look down, O Lord, from heaven, and bl+ess this compact; and as thou sentest thy holy angel Raphael to Tobias, and to Sarah, the daughter of Raguel; so vouchsafe, O Lord, to send thy bless+ing upon these young person; that they abiding in thy will, and continuing under thy protection, may both live, and grow, and grow old in thy love; that they may be both worthy and peaceful, and that the length of their days may be multiplied. Through etc.

Let us pray.

Collect.

Look down, O Lord, mercifully upon this thy servant and upon thy handmaid; that in thy name they may receive heavenly bless+ing, and that they may see the sons of their sons and daughters, to the third and fourth generation, in safety, and that they may ever remain stedfast in thy will, and hereafter attain to the kingdom of heaven. Through etc.

Let us pray.

Collect.

The almighty and merciful God, who by his power did create our first parents Adam and Eve, and did knit them together by his own sanctification, himself sanctify and bless your souls and bodies, and join you together in the union and love of true affection. Through etc.

Then shall he bless them, saying thus:

God almighty bl+ess you with all heavenly blessing, and make you worthy in his sight; pour upon you the riches of his grace, and teach you with the word of truth, that ye may be able to please him both in body and soul. ℞. Amen.

These prayers being finished, they shall be brought into the presbytery, that is to say, between the quire and the altar, on the south side of the church, and the woman being placed on the right hand side of the man, that is to say, between him and the altar, there shall be begun the Mass of the Trinity.

[The introductory portions of the Mass are omitted.]

2. *Secret.*

Accede, O Lord, to our supplications, and be pleased mercifully to accept this oblation, which we offer unto thee on behalf of thy servants whom thou hast vouchsafed to bring to mature life, and to the day of their espousals.

To be concluded with one Through our Lord etc.

Preface.

Who with thy Only-begotten Son etc.

After the Sanctus *the bridegroom and bride shall prostrate themselves in prayer at the step of the altar, a pall being extended over them, which four clerks in surplices shall hold at the four corners, unless one or both shall have been previously married and blessed, because in that case the pall is not held over them, nor is the sacramental blessing given.*

Then, after the conclusion of the Lord's Prayer, before The peace of the Lord etc. *is said, after the fraction of the Eucharist in the usual manner, and having left the host on the paten in three pieces, the priest shall turn to them, and say the prayers following in reading tone, while they in the meanwhile kneel under the pall.*

℣. The Lord be with you.
℞. And with thy spirit.

Let us pray.

Collect.

Be favourable, O Lord, unto our supplications, and of thy goodness assist the ordinances whereby thou hast ordained that mankind should be increased; that they who are joined together by thy authority may be preserved by thy help. Through etc.

Let us pray.

Collect.

O God, who by thy mighty power hast made all things out of nothing, who after other things set in order in the world didst create for man, made after thine own image, the inseparable assistance of the woman; that out of man's flesh woman should take her beginning, teaching that what thou hast been pleased to make one, it should never be lawful to put asunder.

O God, who hast consecrated the state of matrimony to such an excellent mystery, that in it is signified the sacramental and nuptial union betwixt Christ and Church;

O God, by whom woman is joined to man, and the union, instituted in the beginning, is gifted with that bles+sing, which alone has not been taken away either through the punishment of original sin, or through the sentence of the deluge, look graciously, we beseech thee, on this thy handmaiden, who now to be joined in wedlock, seeketh to be guarded by thy protection. May the yoke of love and peace be upon her; may she be a faithful and chaste wife in Christ, and abide a follower of holy matrons. May she be amiable to her husband as Rachel, wise as Rebecca, long-lived and faithful as Sara. Let not the father of lies get any advantage over her through her doings; bound to thy faith and thy commandments may she remain united to one man; may she flee all unlawful unions; may she fortify her weakness with the strength of discipline. May she be bashful and grave, reverential and modest, well-instructed in heavenly doctrine. May she be fruitful in child-bearing, innocent and of good report, attaining to a desired old age, seeing her children's children unto the third and fourth generation; and may she attain the rest of the blessed, and to the kingdom of heaven. Through etc.

After this the priest shall turn to the altar, and say, The peace of the Lord etc. *and* O Lamb of God etc. *in the usual way. Then, after the pall has been removed, the bridegroom and bride shall rise from prayer, and the bridegroom shall receive the pax from the priest, and convey it to the bride, kissing her; neither the bridegroom nor the bride are to kiss any one else; but a clerk shall forthwith receive the pax from the presbyter, and offer it to others in the accustomed manner.*

Communion.

We bless the God of heaven, and we will give thanks unto him in the sight of all that live, because he hath dealt mercifully with us.[4]

In Easter-tide, Alleluya, alleluya.

Postcommunion.

May the reception of this sacrament, O Lord our God, and the confession of the everlasting holy Trinity, and of the undivided Unity of the same, be profitable to our salvation both in body and soul.

Another Postcommunion to be said under one Let us pray, *and under one* Through our Lord etc.

We beseech thee, almighty God, to accompany this institution of thy providence with thy tender love, and to preserve in old age and peace those whom thou dost join together in lawful union. Through etc.

After Mass let bread and wine, or some other good liquid in a vessel be blessed, and let them partake thereof in the name of the Lord, the priest saying:

℣. The Lord be with you.
℟. And with thy spirit.

Let us pray.

Collect.

Bl+ess, O Lord, this bread and this draught and this vessel, as thou didst bless the five loaves in the wilderness, and the six water-pots in Cana of Galilee; that all they who taste of them, may be discreet, sober, and undefiled, O Saviour of the world, Who livest etc.

On the following night, when the bridegroom and bride have gone to bed, the priest shall approach and bless the bed-chamber, saying:

℣. The Lord be with you.
℟. And with thy spirit.

Let us pray.

Collect.

Bl+ess, O Lord, this chamber and all that dwell therein, that they may be established in thy peace and abide in thy will, and live and grow in thy love, and that the length of their days may be multiplied. Through etc.

Blessing over the bed only.

℣. The Lord be with you.
℟. And with thy spirit.

Let us pray.

Collect.

Bl+ess, O Lord, this sleeping-chamber, who neither slumberest nor sleepest; thou who watchest over Israel watch over these thy servants who rest in this bed, guarding them from all phantasies and illusions of devils; guard them waking that they may meditate on thy commandments; guard them sleeping that in their slumber they may think of thee; and that here and everywhere they may ever be defended by the help of thy protection. Through etc.

Then shall this blessing be said over them in bed:

Let us pray.

Collect.

God bl+ess your bodies and souls; and bestow his bless+ing upon you, as he blessed Abraham, Isaac, and Jacob. ℟. Amen.

Another blessing over them.

Let us pray.

May the hand of the Lord be over you; and may he send his holy angel, to guard and tend you all the days of your life. ℞. Amen.

Another blessing over them.

Let us pray.

Collect.

The Father, and the Son, and the Holy Ghost bl+ess you, triune in number, and one in name. ℞. Amen.

This done, the priest shall sprinkle them with holy water, and dismissing them in peace, so depart.

NOTES

1. Thus General Prologue, 460.
2. Psalm lxvii, 29–31.
3. Psalm cxxvii.
4. Tobias xii, 6.

Bartholomaeus Anglicus: from *On the Properties of Things*

Though Bartholomaeus Anglicus was very famous in the thirteenth and fourteenth centuries as the author of the De proprietatibus rerum, *we know little about him. An English Franciscan and professor of divinity at the University of Paris, he seems to have completed this encyclopedia about 1250. On the Properties of Things, proposed as a compendium of all knowledge, proceeds in order from God, through nature, and finally through all branches of human knowledge. Book VI treats matters connected with human society.*

The popularity of this work is marked by the fact that before 1400 it had been translated into French, Italian, Spanish, Provençal, and Dutch, as well as circulating in its original Latin. The present text is based in part on the English translation (1397) by John Trevisa.

Bartholomew's treatment of marriage indicates how conventional wisdom related the stereotypes of the good woman and the antifeminist tradition to medieval standards of love and marriage.

A new translation.

[Husband and Wife]

VI, 13

A man is called *vir* in Latin, because of manly strength (*virtus*), according to Isidore.[1] For in might (*vis*) a man excels a woman. A man is the head of a woman, as the apostle says.[2] Therefore he is bound to rule his wife, as the head has charge of the whole body. And a man is called *maritus*, as it were defending the mother (*matrem tuens*), for he undertakes the care and protection of his wife, who is the mother of his children. He is also called *sponsus*, from *spondendo*, that is, from his marriage vows and obligations.[3] For in the marriage contract he plights his troth to lead his life with his wife without parting, and to pay her his debt, and to keep his marital faith, and never to put her away for another. So great is the love of a husband for his wife that he undertakes all perils for her sake, he sets his love for her before that for his mother, and to live with her he leaves both father and mother and family home, as the Lord declared, saying: "For this cause shall a man leave father and mother, and shall cleave to his wife, and they two shall be in one flesh."[4]

Before the wedding the spouse wooes his bride with presents and favors to incline her to accept his love, he makes known his desire for her with letters and messengers, he bestows many gifts and promises more, to please her he performs in public plays and sports, he engages in deeds of arms, and he dresses himself in robes and fine array.[5] And whatever he is asked to give or do out of love for her, he immediately does with all his might, and he denies nothing which is requested in her name. He speaks sweetly to her, with a charming countenance, and he gazes intently at her face with ardent eyes. When they have finally agreed, he expresses his intention openly before her parents, he weds her with a marriage ring, and he dowers her with gifts, by charter and deed, to ratify the contract of marriage.[6] He holds feasts and nuptial celebrations, gives gifts to his guests, and cheers and gladdens his friends with songs and dances and instrumental music.[7]

When the festivities are over, he takes her to his chamber, and makes her his fellow at bed and at board. He makes her mistress of his money and his household. Thenceforth he is no less careful for her than he is for himself: in his love he corrects her, he appoints a guard for her safety, he watches over her conduct, her speaking and looking, and he carefully considers her comings and goings.

No man is happier than he who has a good wife. And no man is unhappier or more miserable than he who has an evil wife, who cries and quarrels, is drunk, lecherous, changeable, contrary, costly, inquisitive, envious, lazy, wearisome, wandering, bitter, suspicious, and hateful. These matters are touched on by Fulgentius in a sermon on the marriage in Cana of Galilee, in which he compares Christ to the husband, Ecclesia to the good wife, and Synagoga to the wicked and adulterous woman. In a good wife the following conditions are necessary: that she be busy and devout in God's service, meek and obedient to her husband, gentle in word and deed with her servants, generous and liberal to strangers, merciful and friendly to the poor, mild and peaceable with her neighbors, circumspect and prudent in things to be avoided, strong and patient in things to be suffered, busy and diligent in her work, modest in her clothing, serious in her conduct, careful in her speech, chaste in her looking, honorable in her action, sober in her walking, shamefast in public, pleasant with her husband, chaste in her private life. Such a wife is worthy of praise, who studies to please her husband more with her good behavior than with her curled hair, more with her virtue than with rich clothing,[8] who engages in the goods of marriage more for the sake of offspring than for the sake of lust, and who delights more in her marriage to have children of grace than children of nature.

NOTES

1. Isidore of Seville, *Etymologiae*, XI, ii, 17.
2. See 1 Corinthians xi, 3; Ephesians v, 23.
3. Isidore, *Etymologiae*, IX, vii, 3–4.
4. Matthew xix, 5.
5. For a parody of such techniques, see Miller's Tale, 3371–84.
6. Compare, e.g., Wife of Bath's Prologue, 204–14, 812–15; Merchant's Tale, 3371–84.
7. Chaucer's most humorous account of such solemnities occurs in the Merchant's Tale, 1709–67.
8. See 1 Peter iii, 1–6.

Eustache Deschamps:
from *The Mirror of Marriage*

In his Miroir de mariage *Eustache Deschamps (see above, p. 159) devoted more than 12,000 lines to a debate on the merits of marriage. Franc Vouloir ("Free Will") is urged to marry by Désir, Folie, Serviture, and Fantise ("Hypocricy"), while the arguments against marriage are recited at length in a Theophrastian dissertation by Répertoire de Science ("Storehouse of Knowledge"), in a long letter based on his research in "books." Chaucer used the* Miroir *in the* Wife of Bath's Prologue, *and again for the debate in the* Merchant's Tale, *1469–1688.*

New translation by Margaret Ehrhart. From Miroir de mariage, lines 106–16, 217–28, 231–34, 239–44, 252–56, 275–78, 722–31, 746–73, 9063–67, 9097–100, 9107–10, 9124–25, 9135–38, 9143–44, 9150–52.

[Mock Praise of Marriage]

". . . Some hypocrites have urged me to marry, saying, '. . . He who burns in the fire of lust lives in folly and against Holy Scripture. Therefore it is better to marry than to burn,[1] because in the epistles that he addresses to us, Saint Paul tells us that marriage is a very good road for him who chooses it with the intention of propagating: by marrying, one avoids many other sins by which one could be sullied. . . . It is a very sweet union. Two bodies, which love one another both near and far, are joined together in one flesh by the law. The man should manage affairs outside the home; the woman should govern within: her speech is sweet, she serves her husband, and kisses and embraces him, and when he is in pain, she is able to calm his rage. If he is sorrowful, she watches over him, and gives him sympathetic glances. . . . She manages his home and his livestock as well; she is vigilant, wise, and efficient, and sees that nothing goes to waste. . . . She knows how to save and takes care to spend only when necessary, unlike a hired servant, who empties the coffer and the granary and thinks of nothing but stealing, doing little, and wasting time. . . . Tobias lost his sight, but his wife was useful to him, very meek, sweet, and charitable, and she took care to watch over him until God gave him back his sight.[2] . . . That Sarah of whom we tell was so loyal that she is mentioned in benedictions and in betrothals.' "[3]

[FRANC VOULOIR BECOMES CONVINCED:]

". . . I want a wife who is kind, meek, modest, quiet, hard-working, humble, young, and pure of mouth and hands, wise and graceful, and at least fifteen, sixteen, up to twenty years old. She should be refined and of a good family, with a fine body, beautiful, and sweet as a dove, obedient to me in everything. . . . And if I sire any children by her, she should love, tend, and nurture them, like a mother and sweet nurse, and economize in order to raise them and bring them into their estate. If I can find such a wife, I will love her more than anything mortal; I will live out my time in joy; I will not have bickering or contention; I will be gay and merry; I will always be very content and far from the dangers of vile harlots; no one will have such joy as I: I will live within the law. She will be the refuge of my youth; she will be the support of my old age, sustaining my frailty; and when I have gone to pay nature's debt, she will have the care of my soul and will pray for it (my friends will not), and my children who remain behind will remember me, their father. Thus my glorious light will survive, and I believe that this will be the best."

[THE "FALSE FRIENDS" REBUT THE CHARGES OF RÉPERTOIRE DE SCIENCE AGAINST MARRIAGE:]

"And yet, to tell the truth, one finds that women have been one hundred thousand times more devout and constant in their martyrdom than men. . . . I will dare to wager and bet that for one woman that can be found in books who has done evil, I will find a thousand good ones.[4] . . . What did Judith do for her town, whose blood she saved, when, with meagre weapons, she cut off the head of Holofernes?[5] . . . Is not Esther worthy of great reward for her humility? . . . she accomplished so much by her prayer that she effected the rescue of her people, who were destined to die. On account of it, Haman later came to harm. . . . Mordecai, who wisely governed himself, ruled for him.[6] . . .

"Is this not then a fine life, having a beautiful and good lady and finding such a wife?"

NOTES

1. 1 Corinthians vii, 9; Wife of Bath's Prologue, 52.
2. Tobias ii, 11–23. Tobias' wife Anna was not exactly a model of meekness and charity (see ii, 22–23). Tobias' blindness may have suggested the similar fate suffered by Januarie (Merchant's Tale, 2069–71).
3. I.e., in the Nuptial Blessing (see above, p. 381).
4. See Miller's Prologue, 3154–55.
5. Judith viii–xvi.
6. The book of Esther. See Merchant's Tale, 1362–74; Melibeus, 1098–1102.

The Good Woman in Scripture

*Scriptural praise of the "good woman" provides many of the terms conven-
tionally appropriated to describe the ideal Christian wife. The "Wisdom
Books" of the Bible, traditionally ascribed to Solomon (see below, p. 403),
are particularly rich in such praise, although the good woman is often op-
posed to her antithesis in the kind of formula which is echoed in the texts
printed above, where the "wikked wyf" is really proposed as a negation of
true womanly virtues. Two books of the Catholic Bible which are especially
important in establishing stereotypes of womanly virtue and vice—Wisdom
and Ecclesiaticus—were not accepted as canonical by the editors of the King
James Version, yet were very popular in the Middle Ages. The account of
the* mulier fortis *("the valiant woman"—or "worthy womman," as in the
General Prologue, 459), printed below, was elaborately glossed, and made
the subject of at least one separate treatise, by medieval commentators.
These interpreters saw her as a model of the Church and the Virgin Mary,
as well as of the good wife.*

*Among other authorities on good women known and used by Chaucer are
the* Liber consolationis et consilii *("Book of Consolation and Counsel") by
Albertanus of Brescia (c. 1193–1270?), chapters iv–v, which Chaucer trans-
lated, probably by way of a French intermediary, in his Melibeus, 1064 ff.,
and the account of pagan heroines in Saint Jerome's* Epistola adversus
Jovinianum *("Epistle against Jovinian"), I, 41–45, adapted in the Frank-
lin's Tale, 1360–1456. For the Epistle, see below, pp. 415–33.*

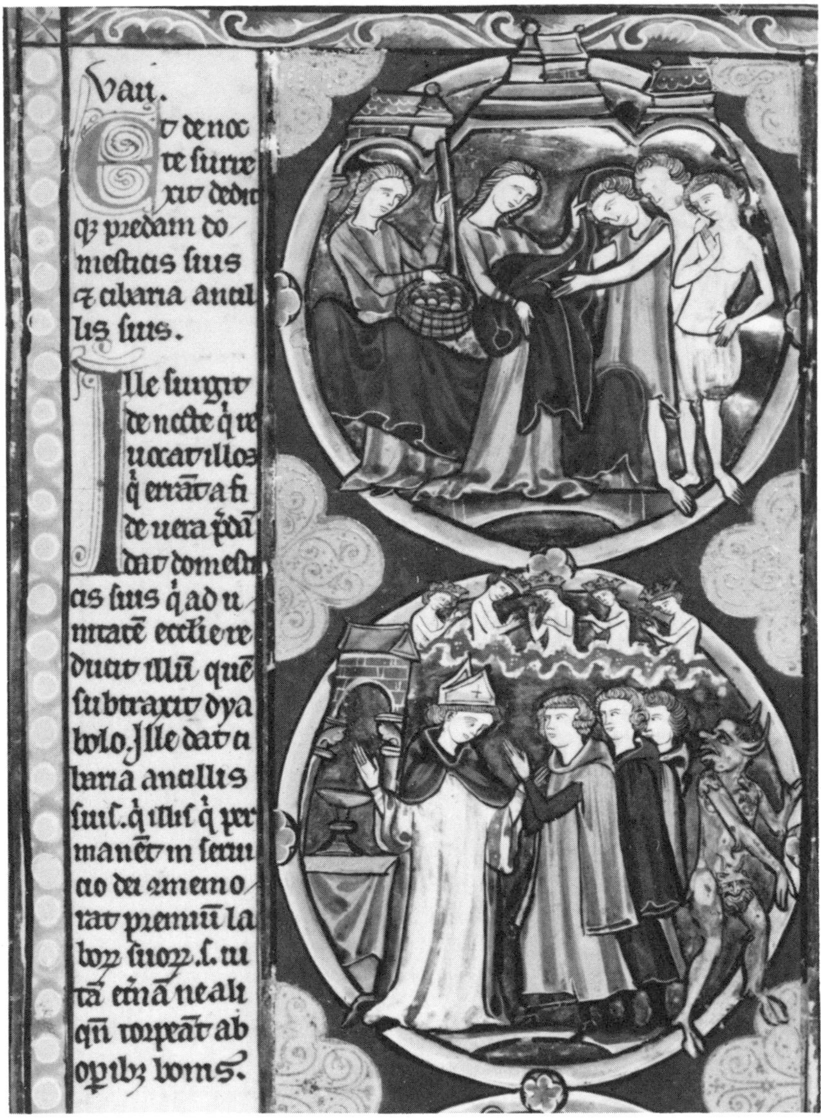

Figure 14. Mulier Fortis, with allegorical analogue. Bibliothèque Nationale MS lat. 11560, fol. 58 (Bible Moralisée). The text of Proverbs xxxi, 15 is illustrated in upper medallion. Allegorically she is said to represent those who recall to the true faith others who are wandering in sin. She "feeds her maidens" with the promise of eternal life. The allegory is represented in the lower medallion.

[The Valiant Woman]

10. Who shall find a valiant woman? far and from the uttermost coasts is the price of her.

11. The heart of her husband trusteth in her, and he shall have no need of spoils.

12. She will render him good, and not evil, all the days of her life.

13. She hath sought wool and flax, and hath wrought by the counsel of her hands.

14. She is like the merchant's ship, she bringeth her bread from afar.

15. And she hath risen in the night, and given a prey to her household, and victuals to her maidens.

16. She hath considered a field, and bought it: with the fruit of her hands she hath planted a vineyard.

17. She hath girded her loins with strength, and hath strengthened her arm.

18. She hath tasted and seen that her traffic is good: her lamp shall not be put out in the night.

19. She hath put out her hand to strong things, and her fingers have taken hold of the spindle.

20. She hath opened her hand to the needy, and stretched out her hands to the poor.

21. She shall not fear for her house in the cold of snow: for all her domestics are clothed with double garments.

22. She hath made for herself clothing of tapestry: fine linen, and purple is her covering.

23. Her husband is honorable in the gates, when he sitteth among the senators of the land.

24. She made fine linen, and sold it, and delivered a girdle to the Chanaanite.

25. Strength and beauty are her clothing, and she shall laugh in the latter day.

26. She hath opened her mouth to wisdom, and the law of clemency is on her tongue.

27. She hath looked well to the paths of her house, and hath not eaten her bread idle.

28. Her children rose up, and called her blessed: her husband, and he praised her.

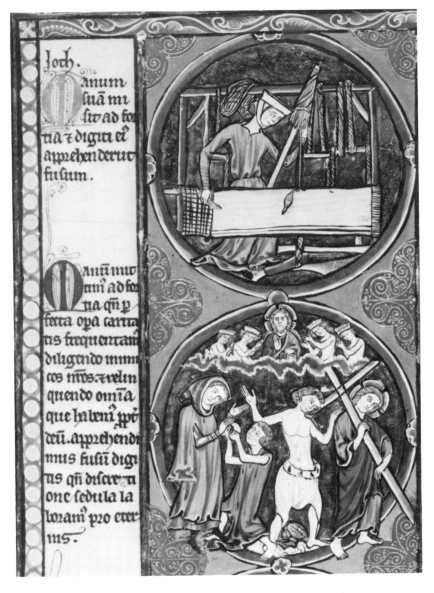

Figure 15. Mulier Fortis, with allegorical analogue. Bibliothèque Nationale MS lat. 11560, fol. 59 (Bible Moralisée). Text of Proverbs xxxi, 19 is illustrated in upper medallion. In the lower medallion, we "put our hands to strong things" when we engage in works of charity, love our enemies, and forsake our worldly goods for the sake of God. We "take hold of the spindle" when we zealously labor for eternal things.

29. Many daughters have gathered together riches: thou hast surpassed them all.

30. Favor is deceitful, and beauty is vain: the woman that feareth the Lord, she shall be praised.

31. Give her of the fruit of her hands: and let her works praise her in the gates.

[The Good Woman]

1. Happy is the husband of a good wife: for the number of his years is double.

2. A virtuous woman rejoiceth her husband, and shall fulfil the years of his life in peace.

3. A good wife is a good portion, she shall be given in the portion of them that fear God, to a man for his good deeds.

4. Rich or poor, if his heart is good, his countenance shall be cheerful at all times.

16. The grace of a diligent woman shall delight her husband, and shall fat his bones.

17. Her discipline is the gift of God.

18. Such is a wise and silent woman, and there is nothing so much worth as a well instructed soul.

19. A holy and shamefaced woman is grace upon grace.

20. And no price is worthy of a continent soul.

21. As the sun when it riseth to the world in the high places of God, so is the beauty of a good wife for the ornament of her house.

22. As the lamp sitting upon the holy candlestick, so is the beauty of the face in a ripe age.

23. As golden pillars upon bases of silver, so are the firm feet upon the soles of a steady woman.

24. As everlasting foundations upon a solid rock, so the commandments of God in the heart of a holy woman.

eight

THE
ANTIFEMINIST
TRADITION

The idea that women are a threat to the virtue and peace of men was not a medieval invention. But in the Middle Ages a great deal of parchment was devoted to treatises in which this idea was repeated, elaborated, documented, and granted the status of "authority." Such works, bound together, formed collections of the sort possessed by the Wife of Bath's fifth husband, clerk Jankyn.

He hadde a book that gladly, nyght and day,
For his desport he wolde rede alway;
He cleped it Valerie and Theofraste,
At which book he lough alwey ful faste.
And eek ther was somtyme a clerk at Rome,
A cardinal, that highte Saint Jerome,
That made a book agayn Jovinian;
In which book eek ther was Tertulan,
Crisippus, Trotula, and Helowys,
That was abesse nat fer fro Parys;
And eek the Parables of Salomon,
Ovides Art, and bookes many on,
And alle thise were bounden in o volume.

(Wife of Bath's Prologue, 669–81)

This "book of wikked wyves," or one like it, provided Chaucer and many other medieval poets with a stock of conventional images, examples, allusions, and themes.

Jankyn's book contains clerical formulations in the antifeminist tradition. In addition, stories abounded in which the wicked wiles of women were held up as warnings for the unwary. Jean de Meun adapted standard antifeminist materials into a literary context, in the tirade of le Jaloux ("the Jealous Husband") and in the figure of la Vieille ("the Old Woman") in the Romance of the Rose. *It is very likely that Chaucer modeled his own adaptations on those of Jean, who is excerpted below.*

The popularity of antifeminist materials in the Middle Ages is not necessarily proof of rampant misogyny. The tradition was inherited by way of writings of the late Roman Empire passed down as school texts. In the Fourth Book of his De rerum natura *("Of the Nature of Things," c. 57* B.C.*) Lucretius describes sexual passion which exceeds the bounds of reason, in terms which anticipate some of the language of "courtly love." To open the eyes of "blind" lovers who feed on vain "images" he recalls the dangers of such an irrational desire: "they consume their strength and kill themselves with the labor; add this, that one lives at the beck of another. Meanwhile wealth vanishes"—all of which sound very much like the standard "incommodities" cited in medieval moral treatises to discourage the sin of* luxuria (*compare Parson's Tale, 846–50). And he concludes, "Yet you can escape the danger* *even when involved and entangled, unless you stand in your own way, and begin by overlooking all faults of mind and body in her whom you prefer and desire."* By his list of female faults which lovers rationalize away, Lucretius does not mean to say that all women are monsters. What he condemns is the lover's failure to recognize reality; his words at this point are directed at men who need to be called back to their senses (De rerum natura, IV, 1121–91).

Similarly, among the "remedies" for the love whose "art" he has taught, Ovid recommends in the Remedies for Love (c. 3 A.D.) that the lover force himself to concentrate on the faults of his mistress. *"Bring often to your mind what your cursed mistress has done, and set all your loss before your eyes."* What has she plundered from you? How often has she betrayed you? *"It helped me to harp continually on my mistress's faults, and that, when I did it, often brought me relief."* He provides a long catalogue of women's less charming features, and instructs his patient in methods of observing them (lines 299–356).

Juvenal's Satire VI (c. 116 A.D.) savagely denounces the evil of women on the pretext of dissuading one Ursidius from marrying, but his real enemy is luxuria, which he saw dissolving the virile old Roman morality into "effeminacy."

The Christian community which succeeded the Roman Empire regarded the presence of death and all our woe, in what Saint Augustine called this our "penal condition," as the fatal consequence of Adam's consenting to the temptation of Eve. This also was widely understood as the dissolution of virilitas into "effeminacy" (muliebritas), whether the story was interpreted literally or allegorically. Literally, Adam the first husband abrogated his responsibility when he allowed his moral authority to be swayed by Eve. Allegorically, Reason consented to the seductions of the Flesh. In either case the natural order of Paradise was abandoned, and the descendents of Adam have been consigned to live with the weakness which he willed to them.

An emphasis on the "restoration" of the depraved image of man led to widespread asceticism in the early Christian Church, and the ascetic ideal was respected, though not always practiced, throughout the Middle Ages. To restore the image betrayed by Adam, one sought to subjugate the Flesh again to the authority of Reason. In secular circles this effort was symbolized by the good "horsemanship" of the chivalric man, who controlled the "reins of reason's rule." Among solitaries we frequently find men who, in addition to abstinence from food, drink, sleep, and the like, absolutely forbid themselves the sight of women. The lives of the early desert Fathers, the Vitae Patrum, provide many examples of this discipline. The ascetic, however, was not concerned

*with the evil of women so much as with his own evil which the sight
of a woman might arouse. He, or his spiritual directors, also sought
ways, through examples, authorities, and stories of the lives of other
hermits, to make women seem to him as repulsive as possible.*

Saint Jerome, in his famous Epistle Against Jovinian *(393 A.D.), was
working in this tradition. Buttressed with the authority of both Old
and New Testaments, he wrote a dissuasion against marriage, like
Juvenal, but only for those who could so master their flesh. Marriage,
he pointed out, is a sacrament. It is better than fornication, but inferior
to the state of virginity, which most closely approximates the state of
innocence lost through Adam's uxoriousness. Women as well as men
are called to the virgin life; in the purity of their will both can conquer
their* muliebritas, *as far as the fallen state of human nature allows. It
was in discussing the dangers of the inferior state of marriage that
Jerome became "antifeminist." The demands of a carnal partner inter-
fere with the life of the spirit (see Galatians, v, 17), one's attention is
divided, the problem of serving two masters becomes pressing (see 1
Corinthians vii, 32–34). His catalogue of "wikked wyves" and authori-
ties from all ages was directed not against women as a class, but against
the distractions which a carnal union presents to the pursuit of "phi-
losophy." His quotation of Theophrastus'* Golden Book on Marriage
*provided him with a vigorous statement from antiquity, presumably by
the disciple of Plato and Aristotle, that wives and books, the nursery
and the study, the flesh and philosophy, do not mix.*

Other chapters in Jankyn's book, such as Walter Map's Valerius to
Ruffinus *(1181), were designed along the same lines. Peter Abelard
quoted Héloise as objecting to their marriage because such a union
would distract him from his philosophical pursuits in the service of the
Church, and as citing Theophrastus as a "philosopher" who knew the
truth (see below, pp. 447–51). The conflict between the demands of
scholarship and those of the world also appeared in an amusing form
when Richard de Bury, in his* Philobiblon, IV *(1345), had books them-
selves complain that they had been expelled from the homes of the
clergy:*

> For our places are seized now by dogs, now by hawks, now by that biped
> beast (*scilicet mulier*) whose cohabitation with the clery was forbidden
> of old, from which we have always taught our nurslings to flee more than
> from the asp and the cockatrice [see Proverbs xxiii, 32]; wherefore she,
> always jealous of the love of us, and never to be appeased, at length see-
> ing us in some corner protected only by the web of some dead spider,
> with a frown abuses and reviles us with bitter words, declaring us alone
> of all the furniture in the house to be unnecessary, and complaining that

we are useless for any household purpose, and advises that we should speedily be converted into rich caps, sendal and silk and twice-dyed purple, robes and furs, wool and linen: and, indeed, not without reason, if she could see our inmost hearts, if she had listened to our secret counsels, if she had read the book of Theophrastus or Valerius, or only heard the twenty-fifth chapter of Ecclesiasticus with understanding ears.

It has been soundly suggested that this tradition should not be labeled "antifeminist," but rather "antimatrimonial," directed primarily at clerks tempted to search out the "mixed love" of the world. In the twelfth, thirteenth, and fourteenth centuries this propaganda may have been fostered by a reform movement within the Church, which opposed a married clergy. Such an intention would correspond well with the Roman antecedents earlier cited, though carnality is no longer the enemy of plain sanity or of the state, but of philosophy and of the spiritual pursuit of salvation in the service of the City of God.

If such documents were intended for the cloister, they obviously did not remain there, as Jankyn's book witnesses. When the arguments reappear in the mouths of speakers in secular works, we should be alive to the possibility of grave distortion. Le Jaloux, la Vieille, and Alice of Bath have no commitment to the interests for which these works were intended (whatever their authors' intentions), and Jankyn was surely at fault for bringing his book into the marriage chamber.

Scriptural Authorities

An immensely popular and influential section of the Bible were the so-called Wisdom Books—Proverbs, Ecclesiasticus, Canticles, Wisdom, and Ecclesiastes. Usually attributed to "Salomon" (see Wife of Bath's Prologue, 679), they are the source of innumerable images, which however popularized through repetition, continued to derive their force as literary allusions from their context in these familiar books. For example, the crown of roses adopted by Solomon's "Epicures" in Wisdom ii, 8, strongly colored the classical image of "gathering rosebuds," for it is seen as part of the "vain reasonings of the wicked." Such a value is carried over into the "rose-gathering" plot of the Romance of the Rose, and the image in Wisdom ii, 8, is the source of the rose chaplets worn by the god of Love and his followers in the text and illuminations of the Romance.

An image central to the Wisdom Books opposes the figures of good and bad women. Sometimes the image of the good woman is superficially quite literal, as in the picture of the mulier fortis (see above, pp. 393–95) to whose works are opposed those of the adulteress or harlot; more often, as in the passage below, Wisdom and Prudence are personified as women with whom the wise man will seek a union (see especially Wisdom viii, 2). The concept of Wisdom as beloved and bride undoubtedly motivates the offer of Reason in the Romance of the Rose, 5795–838 to be a lover more faithful and sure than the Rose—an offer which the Lover foolishly declines. Such Scriptural imagery influenced the development of the central trope in antifeminist literature—the conflict between philosophy and marriage, "books" versus "wives." Both Prudence and Wisdom, incidentally, appear as characters in Chaucer's Tale of Melibeus.

The antithetical woman, like the one described in the following passages, is a seducer and betrayer who ensnares foolish men, to their destruction. This figure, with her attendant imagery, was quite naturally absorbed at an early date into the antifeminist tradition.

The Love of Wisdom is the Best Preservative from Being Led Astray by Temptation

1. My son, keep my words, and lay up my precepts with thee. Son,

2. Keep my commandments, and thou shalt live: and my law as the apple of thy eye:

3. Bind it upon thy fingers write it upon the tables of thy heart.

4. Say to wisdom: Thou art my sister: and call prudence thy friend,

5. That she may keep thee from the woman that is not thine, and from the stranger who sweeteneth her words.

6. For I look out of the window of my house through the lattice,

7. And I see little ones, I behold a foolish young man,

8. Who passeth through the street by the corner, and goeth nigh the way of her house.

9. In the dark, when it grows late, in the darkness and obscurity of the night,

10. And behold a woman meeteth him in harlot's attire prepared to deceive souls; talkative and wandering,

11. Not bearing to be quiet, not able to abide still at home,

12. Now abroad, now in the streets, now lying in wait near the corners.

13. And catching the young man, she kisseth him, and with an impudent face, flattereth, saying:

14. I vowed victims for prosperity, this day I have paid my vows.

15. Therefore I am come out to meet thee, desirous to see thee, and I have found thee.

16. For I have woven my bed with cords, I have covered it with a painted tapestry, brought from Egypt.

17. I have perfumed my bed with myrrh, aloes, and cinnamon.

18. Come, let us be inebriated with the breasts, and let us enjoy the desired embraces, till the day appear.

19. For my husband is not at home, he is gone a very long journey.

20. He took with him a bag of money: he will return home the day of the full moon.

21. She entangled him with many words, and drew him away with the flattery of her lips.

22. Immediately he followeth her as an ox led to be a victim, and as a lamb playing the wanton, and not knowing that he is drawn like a fool to bonds,

23. Till the arrow pierce his liver: as if a bird should make haste to the snare, and knoweth not that his life is in danger.

24. Now therefore, my son, hear me, and attend to the words of my mouth.

25. Let not thy mind be drawn away in her ways: neither be thou deceived with her paths.

26. For she hath cast down many wounded, and the strongest have been slain by her.

27. Her house is the way to hell, reaching even to the inner chambers of death.[1]

NOTE

1. The woman envisioned here by Solomon is traditionally glossed as *caro*, "the flesh."

[The Wicked Woman]

FROM ECCLESIASTICUS XXV

23. And there is no anger above the anger of a woman. It will be more agreeable to abide with a lion and a dragon, than to dwell with a wicked woman.[1]

24. The wickedness of a woman changeth her face: and she darkeneth her countenance as a bear: and sheweth it like sackcloth. In the midst of her neighbours,

25. Her husband groaned, and hearing he sighed a little.

26. All malice is short to the malice of a woman, let the lot of sinners fall upon her.

27. As the climbing of a sandy way is to the feet of the aged, so is a wife full of tongue to a quiet man.

28. Look not upon a woman's beauty, and desire not a woman for beauty.

29. A woman's anger, and impudence, and confusion is great.

30. A woman, if she have superiority, is contrary to her husband.

31. A wicked woman abateth the courage, and maketh a heavy countenance, and a wounded heart.

32. Feeble hands, and disjointed knees, a woman that doth not make her husband happy.

33. From the woman came the beginning of sin, and by her we all die.[2]

34. Give no issue to thy water, no, not a little: nor to a wicked woman liberty to gad abroad.

35. If she walk not at thy hand, she will confound thee in the sight of thy enemies.

36. Cut her off from thy flesh, lest she always abuse thee.

NOTES

1. See Proverbs xxi, 19.
2. Genesis iii, 6; compare 1 Timothy ii, 14.

Ovid:
from *Amores*

In the Amores *Ovid plays the part of the "lover" instructed so wisely in the* Art of Love. *He presents us with a great variety of amatory episodes, ranging from virile passion to helpless impotence, with a salacious wit which modulates desire with self-mockery. Imagery in the* Art of Love *often appears in expanded form in the* Amores. *For example, the idea of "love's warfare" (the* militia amoris), *which was to become such a staple in the language of courtly love, is the subject of a whole poem (see above, pp. 287–88).*

"Dipsas" pictures the "old woman" (vetula) who communicates to a young girl the wiles she has learned through her long experience. In other antifeminist texts she will be found as the girl's mother (the disruptive mother-in-law) or the aged go-between. According to this conventional jest, the accumulated wisdom of women is passed down through the ages by such "education." Ovid here permits himself to overhear a "lesson" in this on-going endeavor. He presents the old woman as a bawd, and it is not clear whether her pupil, his "mistress," is not in reality a courtesan.

Dipsas herself is one of the chief models for la Vieille (the "Old Woman") in the Romance of the Rose *(see below, pp. 467–72);* vieille *is etymologically derived from Latin* vetula. *Chaucer's Wife of Bath, who "preaches" to "wise wyves," is strongly influenced by this literary tradition. At one point, in fact, she remarks after reporting a clever deceit, "My dame taughte me that soutilte" (*Wife of Bath's *Prologue, 576).*

Trans. Grant Showerman, Ovid: Heroides and Amores (Cambridge, Mass.: Harvard University Press, 1914: Loeb Classical Library), pp. 347–55. Reprinted by permission of the publishers and the Loeb Classical Library.

[Dipsas]

I, viii

There is a certain—whoso wishes to know of a bawd, let him hear!—a
certain old dame there is by the name of Dipsas. Her name accords
with the fact[1]—she has never looked with sober eye upon black Mem-
non's mother, her of the rosy steeds.[2] She knows the ways of magic, and
Aeacan incantations,[3] and by her art turns back the liquid waters upon
their source; she knows well what the herb can do, what the thread set
in motion by the whirling magic wheel, what the poison of the mare in
heat. Whenever she has willed, the clouds are rolled together over all
the sky; whenever she has willed, the day shines forth in a clear heaven.
I have seen, if you can believe me, the stars letting drop down blood;
crimson with blood was the face of Luna. I suspect she changes form
and flits about in the shadows of the night, her aged body covered with
plumage. I suspect, and rumor bears me out. From her eyes, too, double
pupils dart their lightnings, with rays that issue from twin orbs. She
summons forth from ancient sepulchres the dead of generations far re-
mote, and with long incantations lays open the solid earth.[4]

This old dame has set herself to profane a modest union; her tongue
is none the less [not] without a baneful eloquence. Chance made me
witness to what she said; she was giving these words of counsel—the
double doors concealed me: "Know you, my light, that yesterday you
won the favor of a wealthy youth? Caught fast, he could not keep his
eyes from your face. And why should you not win favor? Second to
none is your beauty. Ah me, apparel worthy of your person is your lack!
I could wish you as fortunate as you are most fair—for with you become
rich, I shall not be poor. Mars with contrary star is what has hindered
you. Mars is gone; now favoring Venus' star is here. How her rising
brings you fortune, lo, behold! A rich lover has desired you; he has in-
terest in your needs. He has a face, too, that may match itself with
yours; were he unwilling to buy, he were worthy to be bought."

My lady blushed.

"Blushes, to be sure, become a pale face, but the blush one feigns is
the one that profits; real blushing is wont to be loss. With eyes becom-
ingly cast down you will look into your lap, and regard each lover ac-
cording to what he brings. It may be that in Tatius' reign the un-
adorned Sabine fair would not be had to wife by more than one; but
now in wars far off Mars tries the souls of men, and 'tis Venus reigns

in the city of her Aeneas.[5] The beautiful keep holiday; chaste is she whom no one has asked—or, be she not too countrified, she herself asks first. Those wrinkles, too, which you carry high on your brow, shake off; from the wrinkles many a naughtiness will fall. Penelope, when she used the bow, was making trial of the young men's powers; of horn was the bow that proved their strength. The stream of a lifetime glides smoothly on and is past before we know, and swift the year glides by with horses at full speed. Bronze grows bright with use; a fair garment asks for the wearing; the abandoned dwelling moulders with age and corrupting neglect—and beauty, so you open not your doors, takes age from lack of use. Nor, do one or two lovers avail enough; more sure your spoil, and less invidious, if from many. 'Tis from the flock a full prey comes to hoary wolves.

"Think, what does your fine poet give you besides fresh verses? You will get many thousands of lover's lines to read. The god of poets himself attracts the gaze by his golden robe, and sweeps the harmonious chords of a lyre dressed in gold. Let him who will give be greater for you than great Homer; believe me, giving is the proof of genius. And do not look down on him if he be one redeemed with the price of freedom; the chalk-marked foot is an empty reproach. Nor let yourself be deluded by ancient masks about the hall. Take thy grandfathers and go, thou lover who art poor! Nay, should he ask your favors without paying because he is fair, let him first demand what he may give you from a lover of his own.

"Exact more cautiously the price while you spread the net, lest they take flight; once taken, prey upon them on terms of your own. Nor is there harm in pretended love; allow him to think he is loved, and take care lest this love bring you nothing in! Often deny your favors. Feign headache now, and now let Isis be what affords you pretext. After a time, receive him, lest he grow used to suffering, and his love grow slack through being oft repulsed. Let your portal be deaf to prayers, but wide to the giver; let the lover you welcome overhear the words of the one you have sped; sometimes, too, when you have injured him, be angry, as if injured first—charge met by counter-charge will vanish. But never give to anger long range of time; anger that lingers oft causes breach. Nay, even let your eyes learn to drop tears at command, and the one or the other bedew at will your cheeks; nor fear to swear falsely if deceiving anyone—Venus lends deaf ears to love's deceits. Have slave and handmaid skilled to act their parts, to point out the apt gift to buy for you; and have them ask little gifts for themselves—if they ask little gifts from many persons, there will by-and-by grow from straws a mighty heap. And have your sister and your mother, and your nurse, too, keep plucking at your lover; quickly comes the spoil that is sought by many hands. When pretext fails for asking gifts, have a cake to be sign to him that your birthday is come.

"Take care lest he love without a rival, and feel secure; love lasts not well if you give it naught to fight. Let him see the traces of a lover o'er all your couch, and note about your neck the livid marks of passion. Above all else, have him see the presents another has sent. If no one has sent, you must ask of the Sacred Way.[6] When you have taken from him many gifts, in case he still give up not all he has, yourself ask him to lend—what you never will restore! Let your tongue aid you, and cover up your thoughts—wheedle while you despoil; wicked poisons have for hiding-place sweet honey.[7]

"If you fulfil these precepts, learned by me from long experience, and wind and breeze carry not my words away, you will often speak me well as long as I live, and often pray my bones lie softly when I am dead."

Her words were still running, when my shadow betrayed me. But my hands could scarce restrain themselves from tearing her sparse, white hair, and her eyes, all lachrymose from wine, and her wrinkled cheeks. May the gods give you no abode and helpless age, and long winters and everlasting thirst!

NOTES

1. *Dipsa* in Greek means "thirst," as in "dipsomaniac." (See below, p. 445, n. 41.)
2. Aurora. Memnon, son of Aurora and Tithonis, was a king of the Ethiopians, who aided Priam toward the end of the Trojan War and was slain by Achilles.
3. Aeacus, a king of the Myrmidons, renowned for his justice, became one of the three judges in Hades after his death.
4. With Dipsas' many talents, compare the magical powers of Medea, above, pp. 134–35 nn.
5. Venus was the mother of Aeneas, whom Virgil celebrated as the founder of Rome.
6. Street where there were many shops.
7. Much of this advice can be found in Book III of Ovid's own *Ars amatoria*, a book of the kind of advice for women which may account for his inclusion in Jankyn's book (Wife of Bath's Prologue, 680).

Theophrastus:
The Golden Book on Marriage

The most popular of the antifeminist works known to the literary tradition in which Chaucer wrote was the Liber *aureolus de nuptiis, attributed to Theophrastus. It is preserved only in the excerpt contained in Jerome's* Epistle against Jovinian, *I, 47, but because it achieved an independent existence it is printed separately here. For the attribution to the Greek philosopher Theophrastus (d. 287 B.C.) there is no evidence whatever. Nevertheless, the treatise was regarded, as late as the sixteenth century, as the work of the "disciple of Aristotle"—a fact which, together with Jerome's approval, lent it unusual authority.*

"Theofraste" of the Wife of Bath's Prologue, 671, not only gave his name to Jankyn's book; this "clerk" was quoted extensively by clerical authorities such as Richard de Bury and Vincent of Beauvais. Abelard, who has Héloise cite Theophrastus as a "philosopher" in The Story of Misfortunes *(1135), had earlier quoted the* Golden Book *at length in his* Theologia Christiana *(c. 1124). In a chapter on the disadvantages of wedlock, John of Salisbury quoted it entirely, adding that the remarks of Theophrastus are "in themselves sufficient to explain the perplexities of the married state and the calamities that overtake its cherished joy" (*Policraticus, *VIII, xi).*

This authority on "wo in mariage" was comically adapted by Jean de Meun for the diatribe of his le Jaloux *(the "Jealous Husband"); Chaucer's Wife of Bath turns the accusations against her old husbands (see especially* Wife of Bath's Prologue, *235–302); and his Merchant, in what can only be the bitterest of ironies, quotes from the* Golden Book *to conclude, "Deffie Theofraste, and herke me" (*Merchant's Tale, *1293–1310). Such literary allusion suggests a deep familiarity with the text, at least among the literate members of their audience.*

Trans. W. H. Fremantle, The Principal Works of St. Jerome (*New York: Christian Literature Co., 1893: Select Library of Nicene and Post-Nicene Fathers*), *pp. 383–85.*

The Golden Book on Marriage

A book *On Marriage*, worth its weight in gold, passes under the name of Theophrastus. In it the author asks whether a wise man marries. And after laying down the conditions—that the wife must be fair, of good character and honest parentage, the husband in good health and of ample means, and after saying that under these circumstances a wise man sometimes enters the state of matrimony, he immediately proceeds thus: "But all these conditions are seldom satisfied in marriage. A wise man therefore must not take a wife. For in the first place his study of philosophy will be hindered, and it is impossible for anyone to attend to his books and his wife. Matrons want many things: costly dresses, jewels, great outlay, maid-servants, all kinds of furniture, litters and gilded coaches. Then come curtain-lectures the live-long night: she complains that one lady goes out better dressed than she: that another is looked up to by all: 'I am a poor despised nobody at the ladies' assemblies.' 'Why did you ogle at that creature next door?' 'Why were you talking to the maid?' 'What did you bring from the market?' 'I am not allowed to have a single friend or companion.' She suspects that her husband's love goes the same way as her hate. There may be in some neighboring city the wisest of teachers; but if we have a wife we can neither leave her behind, nor take the burden with us. To support a poor wife is hard: to put up with a rich one is torture. Notice, too, that in the case of a wife you cannot pick and choose: you must take her as you find her. If she has a bad temper, or is a fool, if she has a blemish, or is proud, or has bad breath, whatever her fault may be—all this we learn after marriage. Horses, asses, cattle, even slaves of the smallest worth, clothes, kettles, wooden seats, cups, and earthenware pitchers, are first tried and then bought: a wife is the only thing that is not shown before she is married, for fear she may not give satisfaction. Our gaze must always be directed to her face, and we must always praise her beauty: if you look at another woman, she thinks that she is out of favor. She must be called my lady, her birthday must be kept, we must swear by her health and wish that she may survive us, respect must be paid to the nurse, to the nursemaid, to the father's slave, to the foster-child, to the handsome hanger-on, to the curled darling who manages her affairs, and to the eunuch who ministers to the safe indulgence of her lust: names which are only a cloak for adultery. Upon whomever she sets her heart, they must have her love though they want her not. If you give her the management of the whole house, you must yourself be her slave. If you reserve something for yourself, she will not think you are loyal to her: but she will turn to strife and hatred, and unless you quickly take care, she will have the poison ready. If you introduce old women, and soothsayers, and prophets, and vendors of jewels and silken clothing, you imperil her chastity; if you shut the door upon them, she is injured and fancies that you suspect her. But what is the good of even a careful guardian, when an unchaste wife cannot be watched, and a chaste one ought not to be? For necessity is a faithless keeper of chastity, and she alone really deserves to be called pure, who is free to sin if she chooses.

"If a woman be fair, she soon finds lovers; if she be ugly, it is easy to be wanton. It is difficult to guard what many long for. It is annoying to have what no one thinks worth possessing. But the misery of having an ugly wife is less than that of watching a comely one. Nothing is safe for which a whole people sighs and longs.[1] One man entices with his figure, another with his brains, another with his wit, another with his open hand. Somehow, or sometime, the fortress is captured which is attacked on all sides. Men marry, indeed, so as to get a manager for the house, to solace weariness, to banish solitude; but a faithful slave is a far better manager, more submissive to the master, more observant of his ways, than a wife who thinks she proves herself mistress if she acts in opposition to her husband, that is, if she does what pleases her, not what she is commanded. But friends, and servants who are under the obligation of benefits received, are better able to wait upon us in sickness than a wife who makes us responsible for her tears (she will sell you enough to make a deluge, for the hope of a legacy), boasts of her anxiety, but drives her sick husband to the distraction of despair. But if she herself feels poorly, we must fall sick with her, and never leave her bedside. Or if she be a good and agreeable wife (how rare a bird she is!), we have to share her groans in childbirth, and suffer torture when she is in danger.

"A wise man can never be alone. He has with him the good men of all time, and turns his mind freely wherever he chooses. What is inaccessible to him in person he can embrace in thought. And if men are scarce, he converses with God. He is never less alone than when alone.[2] Then again, to marry for the sake of children, so that our name may not perish, or that we may have support in old age, and leave our property without dispute, is the height of stupidity. For what is it to us when we are leaving the world if another bears our name, when even a son does not all at once take his father's title, and there are countless others who are called by the same name? Or what support in old age is he whom you bring up, and who may die before you, or turn out a reprobate? Or at all events when he reaches mature age, you may seem to him long in dying. Friends and relatives whom you can judiciously love are better and safer heirs whether you like it or not. Indeed, the surest way of having a good heir is to ruin your fortune in a good cause while you live, not to leave the fruit of your labor to be used you know not how."

NOTES

1. This division between fair and foul wives is thrown back at Theophrastian thinkers in the Wife of Bath's Tale, 1219–27.
2. Compare Cicero, *De officiis*, III, i, 1; *De re publica*, I, xvii, 27.

Saint Jerome:
from *The Epistle against Jovinian*

Saint Jerome (c. 347–c. 420) was one of the most famous Latin Fathers of the Church. Like Saint Augustine, his contemporary, he studied literature and philosophy in the Roman schools before his conversion (c. 366). A scholar, linguist, ascetic, he is best known for his work on the production of the Vulgate Bible, which became the official text of the Roman Church. In addition, however, he was active in promoting monastic ideals and learning in the West, wrote many exegetical commentaries on sections of the Bible, and composed a number of influential polemical treatises.

Among these treatises his Adversus Jovinianum *enjoyed an exceptional popularity as an authority in the antimatrimonial and antifeminist library of the Middle Ages. It was written in 393 to refute the contention (among others) of a monk named Jovinian that "a virgin is no better as such than a wife in the sight of God." Jerome's arguments and citations in favor of virginity (he did not deny the legitimacy of marriage) became one of the most important sources for writers making use of the tradition. Especially noteworthy is his quotation of Theophrastus' Golden Book which, since it achieved an independent existence, has been printed separately in this collection (see above, pp. 411–14).*

As such an authority this treatise made its way into Jankyn's "book of wikked wyves":

> And eek ther was somtyme a clerk at Rome,
> A cardinal, that highte Seint Jerome,
> That made a book agayn Jovinian.

(Wife of Bath's Prologue, 673–75)

Trans. W. H. Fremantle, The Principal Works of St. Jerome (New York: Christian Literature Co., 1893: Select Library of Nicene and Post-Nicene Fathers), pp. 350–86.

Chaucer's familiarity with it is exemplified especially in the opening sec-tion of the Wife of Bath's Prologue and in Dorigen's long catalogue of "good women" in the Franklin's Tale 1364–1456. Such wholesale adapta-tion of Jerome's text presumes, for its effect, a familiarity on the part of his audience with the content and the argument of the work.

·

[Marriage and Virginity]

6. In the front rank I will set the Apostle Paul, and, since he is the bravest of generals, will arm him with his own weapons, that is to say, his own statements. For the Corinthians asked many questions about this matter, and the doctor of the Gentiles and master of the Church gave full replies. . . .

7. Among other things the Corinthians asked in their letter whether after embracing the faith of Christ they ought to be unmarried, and for the sake of continence put away their wives, and whether believing virgins were at liberty to marry. And again, supposing that one of two Gentiles believed on Christ, whether the one that believed should leave the one that believed not? And in case it were allowable to take wives, would the Apostle direct that only Christian wives, or Gentiles also, should be taken? Let us then consider Paul's replies to these inquiries. "Now concerning the things whereof ye wrote: It is good for a man not to touch a woman. But, because of fornications, let each man have his own wife, and let each woman have her own husband. Let the husband render unto the wife her due: and likewise also the wife unto the husband. The wife hath not power over her own body, but the husband: And likewise also the husband hath not power over his own body, but the wife. Defraud ye not one the other, except it be by consent for a season, that ye may give yourselves unto prayer, and may be together again, that Satan tempt you not because of your incontinency. But this I say by way of permission not of commandment. Yet I would that all men were even as I myself. Howbeit each man hath his own gift from God, one after this manner, and another after that. But I say to the unmarried and to widows, it is good for them if they abide even as I. But if they have not continency, let them marry: for it is better to marry than to burn."[1] Let us turn back to the chief point of the evidence: "It is good," he says, "for a man not to touch a woman."[2] If it is good not to touch a woman, it is bad to touch one: for there is no opposite to goodness but badness. But if it be bad and the evil is pardoned, the reason for the concession is to prevent worse evil. But surely a thing which is only allowed because there may be something worse has only a slight degree of goodness. He would never have added "let each man have his own wife," unless he had previously used the words

"but, because of fornications." Do away with fornication, and he will not say "let each man have his own wife." Just as though one were to lay it down: "It is good to feed on wheaten bread, and to eat the finest wheat flour," and yet to prevent a person pressed by hunger from devouring cow-dung, I may allow him to eat barley. Does it follow that the wheat will not have its peculiar purity, because such an one prefers barley to excrement?[3] That is naturally good which does not admit of comparison with what is bad, and is not eclipsed because something else is preferred. At the same time we must notice the Apostle's prudence. He did not say, it is good not to have a wife: but, it is good not to touch a woman: as though there were danger even in the touch: as though he who touched her, would not escape from her who "hunteth for the precious life,"[4] who causeth the young man's understanding to fly away.[5] "Can a man take fire in his bosom, and his clothes not be burned? Or can one walk upon hot coals, and his feet not be scorched?"[6] As then he who touches fire is instantly burned, so by the mere touch the peculiar nature of man and woman is perceived, and the difference of sex is understood. . . . "But, because of fornications let each man have his own wife, and let each woman have her own husband." He did not say, because of fornication let each man marry a wife: otherwise by this excuse he would have thrown the reins to lust, and whenever a man's wife died, he would have to marry another to prevent fornication, but "have his own wife." Let him, he says, have and use his own wife, whom he had before he became a believer, and whom it would have been good not to touch, and, when once he became a follower of Christ, to know only as a sister, not as a wife, unless fornication should make it excusable to touch her. "The wife hath not power over her own body, but the husband: and likewise also the husband hath not power over his own body, but the wife."[7] The whole question here concerns those who are married men. Is it lawful for them to do what our Lord forbade in the Gospel,[8] and to put away their wives? Whence it is that the Apostle says, "It is good for a man not to touch a woman." But inasmuch as he who is once married has no power to abstain except by mutual consent, and may not reject an unoffending partner, let the husband render unto the wife her due.[9] He bound himself voluntarily that he might be under compulsion to render it. "Defraud ye not one the other, except it be by consent for a season, that ye may give yourselves unto prayer." What, I pray you, is the quality of that good thing which hinders prayer? which does not allow the body of Christ to be received? So long as I do the husband's part, I fail in continency. The same Apostle in another place commands us to pray always.[10] If we are to pray always, it follows that we must never be in the bondage of wedlock, for as often as I render my wife her due, I cannot pray. The Apostle Peter had experience of the bonds of marriage. See how he fashions the Church, and what lesson he teaches Christians: "Ye husbands in like manner dwell with your wives according to knowledge, giving honor unto the woman, as unto the weaker vessel, as being also joint-heirs of the grace of life; to the end that your prayers be not hindered."[11] Observe that, as St. Paul before, because in both cases the spirit is the same, so St. Peter now, says that prayers are hindered by the performance of marriage duty. When he says "likewise," he challenges the husbands to imitate their wives, because he has already given them commandment: "beholding your chaste conversation coupled with fear. Whose adorning let it not be the outward adorning of plaiting the hair, and of wearing jewels of gold, or of putting on apparel: but let it be the hidden man of the heart, in the incorruptible apparel of a meek and quiet spirit, which is in the sight of God of great price."[12] You see what kind of wedlock he enjoins. Husbands and wives are to dwell together according to knowledge, so that they may know what God wishes and desires, and give honor to the weak vessel, woman. If we abstain from intercourse, we give honor to our wives: if we do not abstain, it is clear that insult is the opposite of honor. He also tells wives to let their husbands "see their chaste behavior, and the hidden man of the heart, in the incorruptible apparel of a meek and quiet spirit." Words truly worthy of an apostle, and of Christ's rock! He lays down the law for husbands and wives, condemns outward ornament, while he praises continence, which is the ornament of the inner man, as seen in the incorruptible apparel of a meek and quiet spirit. In effect he says this: Since your outer man is corrupt, and you have ceased to possess the blessing of incorruption characteristic of virgins, at least imitate the incorruption of the spirit by subsequent abstinence, and what you cannot show in the body exhibit in the mind. For these are the riches, and these the ornaments of your union, which Christ seeks.

8. The words which follow, "that ye may give yourselves unto prayer, and may be together again," might lead one to suppose that the Apostle was expressing a wish and not making a concession because of the danger of a greater fall. He therefore at once adds, "lest Satan tempt you for your incontinency." It is a fine permission which is conveyed in the words "be together again." What it was that he blushed to call by its own name, and thought only better than a temptation of Satan and the effect of incontinence, we take trouble to discuss as if it were obscure, although he has explained his meaning by saying, "this I say by

way of permission, not by way of command."[13] And do we still hesitate to speak of marriage as a concession to weakness, not a thing commanded, as though second and third marriages were not allowed on the same ground, as though the doors of the Church were not opened by repentence even to fornicators, and what is more, to the incestuous? . . . If you wish to know the Apostle's real mind, you must take in what follows: "but I would that all men were as I am." Happy is the man who is like Paul! Fortunate is he who attends to the Apostle's command, not to his concession. This, says he, I wish, this I desire, that ye be imitators of me, as I also am of Christ, who was a Virgin born of a Virgin, uncorrupt of her who was uncorrupt. We, because we are men, cannot imitate our Lord's nativity; but we may at least imitate His life.[14] The former was the blessed prerogative of divinity, the latter belongs to our human condition and is part of human effort. I would that all men were like me, that while they are like me, they may also become like Christ, to whom I am like. For "he that believeth in Christ ought himself also to walk even as He walked."[15] "Howbeit each man hath his own gift from God, one after this manner, and another after that."[16] What I wish, he says, is clear. But since in the Church there is a diversity of gifts, I acquiesce in marriage, lest I should seem to condemn nature. At the same time consider, that the gift of virginity is one, that of marriage, another. For were the reward the same for the married and for virgins, he would never after enjoining continence have said: "Each man hath his own gift from God, one after this manner, and another after that." Where there is a distinction in one particular, there is a diversity also in other points. I grant that even marriage is a gift of God, but between gift and gift there is great diversity. . . .

9. Then come the words "But I say to the unmarried and to widows, it is good for them if they abide even as I. But if they have not continency, let them marry: for it is better to marry than to burn."[17] Having conceded to married persons the enjoyment of wedlock and pointed out his own wishes, he passes on to the unmarried and to widows, sets before them his own practice for imitation, and calls them happy if they so abide. "But if they have not continency, let them marry," just as he said before "But because of fornications," and "Lest Satan tempt you, because of your incontinency." And he gives a reason for saying "If they have not continency, let them marry," *viz.* "It is better to marry than to burn." The reason why it is better to marry is that it is worse to burn. Let burning lust be absent, and he will not say it is better to marry. The word *better* always implies a comparison with something worse, not a thing absolutely good and incapable of comparison. It is

as though he said, it is better to have one eye than neither, it is better to stand on one foot and to support the rest of your body with a stick, than to crawl with broken legs. What do you say, Apostle? I do not believe you when you say "Though I be rude in speech, yet am I not in knowledge."[18] As humility is the source of the sayings "For I am not worthy to be called an Apostle,"[19] and "To me who am the least of the Apostles,"[20] and "As to one born out of due time,"[21] so here also we have an utterance of humility. You know the meaning of language, or you would not quote Epimenides,[22] Menander,[23] and Aratus.[24] When you are discussing continence and virginity you say, "It is good for a man not to touch a woman." And, "It is good for them if they abide even as I." And, "I think that this is good by reason of the present distress."[25] And, "That it is good for a man so to be."[26] When you come to marriage, you do not say it is good to marry, because you cannot then add *"than to burn"*; but you say, "It is better to marry than to burn." If marriage in itself be good, do not compare it with fire, but simply say "It is good to marry." I suspect the goodness of that thing which is forced into the position of being only the lesser of two evils. What I want is not a smaller evil, but a thing absolutely good.

10. . . . The same Apostle says: "A wife is bound for so long a time as her husband liveth: but if the husband be dead, she is free to be married to whom she will; only in the Lord,"[27] that is, to a Christian. He who allows second and third marriages in the Lord, forbids first marriages with a Gentile. . . . I have said this that they who compare marriage with virginity, may at least know that such marriages as these are on a lower level than digamy and trigamy.

12. Having discussed marriage and continency he at length comes to virginity and says, "Now concerning virgins I have no commandment of the Lord: but I give my judgment, as one that hath obtained mercy of the Lord to be faithful. I think therefore that this is good by reason of the present distress, namely, that it is good for a man to be as he is."[28] Here our opponent goes utterly wild with exultation: this is his strongest battering-ram with which he shakes the wall of virginity. . . . If the Lord had commanded virginity He would have seemed to condemn marriage, and to do away with the seed-plot of mankind, of which virginity itself is a growth.[29] If He had cut off the root, how was He to expect fruit? If the foundations were not first laid, how was He to build the edifice, and put on the roof to cover all! . . . The reason is plain why the Apostle said, "concerning virgins I have no commandment of the Lord." Surely; because the Lord had previously

said "All men cannot receive the word, but they to whom it is given," and "He that is able to receive it, let him receive it." The Master of the Christian race offers the reward, invites candidates to the course, holds in His hand the prize of virginity, points to the fountain of purity, and cries aloud "If any man thirst, let him come unto me and drink."[30] "He that is able to receive it, let him receive it." He does not say, you must drink, you must run, willing or unwilling: but whoever is willing and able to run and to drink, he shall conquer, he shall be satisfied. And therefore Christ loves virgins more than others, because they willingly give what was not commanded of them. . . . [Our Lord has said] some are eunuchs by nature, others by the violence of men.[31] Those eunuchs please Me who are such not of necessity, but of free choice. Willingly do I take them into my bosom who have made themselves eunuchs for the kingdom of heaven's sake, and in order to worship Me have renounced the condition of their birth. We must now explain the words, "Those who have made themselves eunuchs for the kingdom of heaven's sake." If they who have made themselves eunuchs have the reward of the kingdom of heaven, it follows that they who have not made themselves such cannot be placed with those who have. He who is able, he says, to receive it, let him receive it. It is a mark of great faith and of great virtue, to be the pure temple of God,[32] to offer oneself a whole burnt-offering,[33] and, according to the same apostle, to be holy both in body and in spirit.[34] These are the eunuchs, who thinking themselves dry trees because of their impotence, hear by the mouth of Isaiah that they have a place prepared in heaven for sons and daughters.[35] . . . "I think, therefore," he says, "that this is good for the present distress." What is this distress which, in contempt of the marriage tie, longs for the liberty of virginity? "Woe unto them that are with child and to them that give suck in those days."[36] We have not here a condemnation of harlots and brothels, of whose damnation there is no doubt, but of the swelling womb, and wailing infancy, the fruit as well as the work of marriage.[37] "For it is good for a man so to be." If it is good for a man so to be, it is bad for a man not so to be. "Art thou bound unto a wife? Seek not to be loosed. Art thou loosed from a wife? Seek not a wife."[38] Each one of us has his appointed bounds. . . . He who has a wife is regarded as a debtor, and is said to be uncircumcised, to be the servant of his wife, and like bad servants to be *bound*.[39] But he who has no wife, in the first place owes no man anything, then is circumcised, thirdly is free, lastly, is loosed.[40]

13. . . . Who are they who shall have tribulation in the flesh? They to whom he had before indulgently said "But and if thou marry, thou

hast not sinned; and if a virgin marry, she hath not sinned. Yet such shall have tribulation in the flesh."[41] We in our inexperience thought that marriage had at least the joys of the flesh. But if they who are married have tribulation even in the flesh, which is imagined to be the sole source of their pleasure, what else is there to marry for, when in the spirit, and in the mind, and in the flesh itself there is tribulation?[42] "But I would spare you."[43] Thus, he says, I allege tribulation as a motive, as though there were not greater obligations to refrain. "But this I say, brethren, the time is shortened, that henceforth both those that have wives may be as though they had none."[44] I am by no means now discussing virgins, of whose happiness no one entertains a doubt. I am coming to the married. The time is short, the Lord is at hand. Even though we lived nine hundred years, as did men of old, yet we ought to think that short which must one day have an end, and cease to be. But, as things are, and it is not so much the joy as the tribulation of marriage that is short, why do we take wives whom we shall soon be compelled to lose? "And those that weep, and those that rejoice, and those that buy, and those that use the world, as though they wept not, as though they rejoiced not, as though they bought not, as though they did not use the world: for the fashion of this world passeth away."[45] If the world, which comprehends all things, passes away, yea if the fashion and intercourse of the world vanishes like the clouds, amongst the other works of the world, marriage too will vanish away. For after the resurrection there will be no wedlock. But if death be the end of marriage, why do we not voluntarily embrace the inevitable? And why do we not, encouraged by the hope of the reward, offer to God that which must be wrung from us against our will. "He that is unmarried is careful for the things of the Lord, how he may please the Lord: but he that is married is careful for the things of the world, how he may please his wife, and is divided."[46] Let us look at the difference between the cares of the virgin, and those of the married man. The virgin longs to please the Lord, the husband to please his wife, and that he may please her he is careful for the things of the world, which will of course pass away with the world. "And he is divided," that is to say, is distracted with manifold cares and miseries. This is not the place to describe the difficulties of marriage, and to revel in rhetorical commonplaces. . . . [The Apostle] says, "The woman that is unmarried and a virgin thinks of the things of the Lord, that she may be holy in body and in spirit."[47] Not every unmarried person is also a virgin. But every virgin is of course unmarried. It may be, that regard for elegance of expression led him to repeat the same idea by means of another word and speak of "a woman unmarried and a virgin"; or at least he may have wished to give to "unmarried" the definite meaning of "virgin," so that we might not suppose him to include harlots, united to no one by the fixed bonds of wedlock, among the "unmarried." Of what, then, does she that is unmarried and a virgin think? "The things of the Lord, that she may be holy both in body and in spirit." Supposing there were nothing else, and that no greater reward followed virginity, this would be motive enough for her choice, to think of the things of the Lord. But he immediately points out the contents of her thought—that she may be holy both in body and spirit. For there are virgins in the flesh, not in the spirit, whose body is intact, their soul corrupt. But that virgin is a sacrifice to Christ, whose mind has not been defiled by thought, nor her flesh by lust. On the other hand, she who is married thinks of the things of the world, how she may please her husband.[48] Just as the man who has a wife is anxious for the things of the world, how he may please his wife, so the married woman thinks of the things of the world, how she may please her husband. But we are not of this world, which lieth in wickedness, the fashion of which passeth away, and concerning which the Lord said to the Apostles, "If ye were of the world, the world would love its own."[49] And lest perchance someone might suppose that he was laying the heavy burden of chastity on unwilling shoulders, he at once adds his reasons for persuading to it, and says: "And this I say for your profit; not that I may cast a snare upon you, but for that which is seemly, and that ye may attend upon the Lord without distraction."[50] . . . But where there is something good and something better, the reward is not in both cases the same, and where the reward is not one and the same, there of course the gifts are different. The difference, then, between marriage and virginity is as great as that between not sinning and doing well; nay rather, to speak less harshly, as great as between good and better.

14. . . . Now again he compares monogamy with digamy, and as he had subordinated marriage to virginity, so he makes second marriages inferior to first, and says, "A wife is bound for so long time as her husband liveth; but if the husband be dead, she is free to be married to whom she will; only in the Lord. But she is happier if she abide as she is, after my judgment: and I think that I also have the Spirit of God."[51] He allows second marriages, but to such persons as wish for them and are not able to contain; lest, having "waxed wanton against Christ," they desire to marry, "having condemnation, because they have rejected their first faith";[52] and he makes the concession because many had already turned aside after Satan.[53] "But," says he, "they will be happier if they abide as they are." . . . For it is better to know a single hus-

band, though he be a second or third, than to have many paramours: that is, it is more tolerable for a woman to prostitute herself to one man than to many. At all events this is so if the Samaritan woman in John's Gospel who said that she had her sixth husband was reproved by the Lord because he was not her husband.[54] For where there are more husbands than one the proper idea of a husband, who is a single person, is destroyed. At the beginning one rib was turned into one wife. "And they two," he says, "shall be one flesh":[55] not three, or four; otherwise, how can they be any longer two, if they are several? Lamech, a man of blood and a murderer, was the first who divided one flesh between two wives.[56] Fratricide and digamy were abolished by the same punishment—that of the deluge. The one was avenged seven times, the other seventy times seven. The guilt is as widely different as are the numbers. . . .

15. . . . The number of wives which a man may take is not defined, because when Christian baptism has been received, even though a third or a fourth wife has been taken, she is reckoned as the first. Otherwise, if, after baptism and after the death of a first husband, a second is taken, why should not a sixth after the death of the second, third, fourth, and fifth, and so on?[57] For it is possible, that, through some strange misfortune, or by the judgment of God cutting short repeated marriages, a young woman may have several husbands, while an old woman may be left a widow by her first husband in extreme age. The first Adam was married once: the second was unmarried. Let the supporters of second marriages show us as their leader a third Adam who was twice married. But granted that Paul allowed second marriages: upon the same grounds it follows that he allows even third and fourth marriages, or a woman may marry as often as her husband dies. The Apostle was forced to choose many things which he did not like. . . . So he allowed second marriages to incontinent persons, and did not limit the number of marriages,[58] in order that women, although they saw themselves permitted to take a second husband, in the same way as a third or a fourth was allowed, might blush to take a second, lest they should be compared to those who were three or four times married. If more than one husband be allowed, it makes no difference whether he be a second or a third, because there is no longer a question of single marriage. "All things are lawful, but not all things are expedient."[59] I do not condemn second, nor third, nor, pardon the expression, eighth marriages:[60] I will go still further and say that I welcome even a penitent whoremonger. Things that are equally lawful must be weighed in an even balance. . . .

19. What shall I say of Abraham who had three wives, as Jovinianus says, and received circumcision as a sign of his faith?[61] If we follow him in the number of his wives, let us also follow him in circumcision. We must not partly follow him, partly reject him. Isaac, moreover, the husband of one wife, Rebecca, prefigures the Church of Christ, and reproves the wantonness of second marriage.[62] And if Jacob had two pairs of wives and concubines,[63] and our opponent will not admit that blear-eyed Leah,[64] ugly and prolific, was a type of the synagogue, but that Rachel, beautiful and long barren, indicated the mystery of the Church,[65] let me remind him that when Jacob did this thing he was among the Assyrians, and in Mesopotamia in bondage to a hard master. But when he wished to enter the holy land, he raised on Mount Galeed the heap of witness,[66] in token that the lord of Mesopotamia had failed to find anything among his baggage, and there swore that he would never return to the place of his bondage; and when, after wrestling with the angel at the brook Jabbok, he began to limp, because the great muscle of his thigh was withered, he at once gained the name of Israel.[67] Then the wife whom he once loved, and for whom he had served, was slain by the son of sorrow near Bethlehem[68] which was destined to be the birthplace of our Lord, the herald of virginity: and the intimacies of Mesopotamia died in the land of the Gospel. . . .

24. . . . [Jovinianus] passes on to Solomon, through whom wisdom itself sang its own praises. Seeing that not content with dwelling upon his praises, he calls him uxurious, I am surprised that he did not add the words of the Canticles: "There are threescore queens, and fourscore concubines, and maidens without number,"[69] and those of the First Book of Kings: "And he had seven hundred wives, princesses, and three hundred concubines, and others without number."[70] These are they who turned away his heart from the Lord: and yet before he had many wives, and fell into sins of the flesh, at the beginning of his reign and in his early years he built a temple to the Lord.[71] For everyone is judged not for what he will be, but for what he is. But if Jovinianus approves the example of Solomon, he will no longer be in favor of second and third marriages only, but unless he has seven hundred wives and three hundred concubines, he cannot be the king's antitype or attain to his merit. I earnestly again and again remind you, my reader, that I am compelled to speak as I do, and that I do not disparage our predecessors under the law, but am well aware that they served their generation according to their circumstances, and fulfilled the Lord's command to increase and multiply, and replenish the earth.[72] And what is more, they were figures of those that were to come. But we to whom it is said,

"The time is shortened, that henceforth those that have wives may be as though they had none," have a different command, and for us virginity is consecrated by the Virgin Savior. . . .

28. . . . Now that he [Jovinian] may not cry out that both Solomon and others under the law, prophets and holy men, have been dishonored by us, let us show what this very man with his many wives and concubines thought of marriage. For no one can know better than he who suffered through them, what a wife or woman is. Well then, he says in the Proverbs: "The foolish and bold woman comes to want bread."[73] What bread? Surely that bread which cometh down from heaven: and he immediately adds: "The earth-born perish in her house, rush into the depths of hell."[74] Who are the earth-born that perish in her house? They of course who follow the first Adam, who is of the earth, and not the second, who is from heaven.[75] And again in another place: "Like a worm in wood, so a wicked woman destroyeth her husband."[76] But if you assert that this was spoken of bad wives, I shall briefly answer: What necessity rests upon me to run the risk of the wife I marry proving good or bad? "It is better," he says, "to dwell in a desert land, than with a contentious and passionate woman in a wide house."[77] How seldom we find a wife without these faults, he knows who is married. Hence that sublime orator, Varius Geminus, says well: "The man who does not quarrel is a bachelor." "It is better to dwell in the corner of the housetop, than with a contentious woman in a house in common."[78] If a house common to husband and wife makes a wife proud and breeds contempt for the husband: how much more if the wife be the richer of the two, and the husband but a lodger in her house! She begins to be not a wife, but mistress of the house; and if she offend her husband, they must part. "A continual dropping on a wintry day"[79] turns a man out of doors, and so will a contentious woman drive a man from his own house. She floods his house with her constant nagging and daily chatter, and ousts him from his own home, that is, the Church. . . . "The horseleech had three daughters, dearly loved, but they satisfied her not, and a fourth is not satisfied when you say Enough; the grave, and woman's love, and the earth that is not satisfied with water, and the fire that saith not, Enough."[80] The horseleech is the devil, the daughters of the devil are dearly loved, and they cannot be satisfied with the blood of the slain: *the grave, and woman's love, and the earth dry and scorched with heat.* It is not the harlot or the adultress who is spoken of; but woman's love in general is accused of ever being insatiable; put it out, it bursts into flame; give it plenty, it is again in need; it enervates a man's mind, and engrosses all thought

except for the passion which it feeds. What we read in the parable which follows is to the same effect: "For three things the earth doth tremble, and for four which it cannot bear: for a servant when he is king: and a fool when he is filled with meat: for an odious woman when she is married to a good husband: and an handmaid that is heir to her mistress."[81] See how a wife is classed with the greatest evils. But if you reply that it is an *odious* wife, I will give you the same answer as before—the mere possibility of such a danger is in itself no light matter. For he who marries a wife is uncertain whether he is marrying an odious woman or one worthy of his love. If she be odious, she is intolerable. If worthy of love, her love is compared to the grave, to the parched earth, and to fire. . . .

36. But you will say: "If everybody were a virgin, what would become of the human race?" Like shall here beget like. If everyone were a widow, or continent in marriage, how will mortal men be propagated?[82] Upon this principle there will be nothing at all for fear that something else may cease to exist. To put a case: if all men were philosophers, there would be no husbandmen. Why speak of husbandmen? there would be no orators, no lawyers, no teachers of the other professions. If all men were leaders, what would become of the soldiers? If all were the head, whose head would they be called, when there were no other members? You are afraid that if the desire for virginity were general there would be no prostitutes, no adulteresses, no wailing infants in town or country. Every day the blood of adulterers is shed, adulterers are condemned, and lust is raging and rampant in the very presence of the laws and the symbols of authority and the courts of justice. Be not afraid that all will become virgins: virginity is a hard matter, and therefore rare, because it is hard: "Many are called, few chosen."[83] Many begin, few persevere. And so the reward is great for those who have persevered. If all were able to be virgins, our Lord would never have said: "He that is able to receive it, let him receive it": and the Apostle would not have hesitated to give his advice: "Now concerning virgins I have no commandment of the Lord." Why then, you will say, were the organs of generation created, and why were we so fashioned by the all-wise creator, that we burn for one another, and long for natural intercourse?[84] To reply is to endanger our modesty: we are, as it were, between two rocks, the Symplegades[85] of necessity and virtue, on either side; and must make shipwreck of either our sense of shame, or of the cause we defend. If we reply to your suggestions, shame covers our face. If shame secures silence, in a manner we seem to desert our post, and to leave the ground clear to the raging foe. Yet it is better,

as the story goes, to shut our eyes and fight like the blindfold gladiators, than not to repel with the shield of truth the darts aimed at us. I can indeed say: "Our hinder parts which are banished from sight, and the lower portions of the abdomen, which perform the functions of nature, are the Creator's work." But inasmuch as the physical conformation of the organs of generation testifies to difference of sex,[86] I shall briefly reply: Are we never then to forego lust, for fear that we may have members of this kind for nothing? Why then should a husband keep himself from his wife? Why should a widow persevere in chastity, if we were only born to live like beasts? Or what harm does it do me if another man lies with my wife? For as the teeth were made for chewing, and the food masticated passes into the stomach, and a man is not blamed for giving my wife bread: similarly if it was intended that the organs of generation should always be performing their office, when my vigor is spent let another take my place, and, if I may so speak, let my wife quench her burning lust where she can.[87] But what does the Apostle mean by exhorting to continence, if continence be contrary to nature? What does our Lord mean when He instructs us in the various kinds to eunuchs? Surely the Apostle who bids us emulate his own chastity, must be asked, if we are to be consistent, Why are you like other men, Paul? Why are you distinguished from the female sex by a beard, hair, and other peculiarities of person? How is it that you have not swelling bosoms, and are not broad at the hips, narrow at the chest? Your voice is rugged, your speech rough, your eyebrows more shaggy. To no purpose you have all these manly qualities, if you forego the embraces of women. I am compelled to say something and become a fool: but you have forced me to dare to speak. Our Lord and Savior, Who though He was in the form of God, condescended to take the form of a servant, and became obedient to the Father even unto death, yea the death of the cross—what necessity was there for Him to be born with members which He was not going to use? He certainly was circumcised to manifest His sex.[88] Why did He cause John the Apostle and John the Baptist to make themselves eunuchs through love of Him, after causing them to be born men? Let us then who believe in Christ follow His example. And if we knew Him after the flesh, let us no longer know Him according to the flesh. The substance of our resurrected bodies will certainly be ·the same as now, though of higher glory. . . .

37. But why do we argue, and why are we eager to frame a clever and victorious reply to our opponent? "Old things have passed away, behold all things have become new."[89] I will run through the utterances

of the Apostles, and as to the instances afforded by Solomon I added short expositions to facilitate their being understood, so now I will go over the passages bearing on Christian purity and continence, and will make of many proofs a connected series. . . . Amongst other passages Paul the Apostle writes to the Romans: "What fruit then had ye at that time in the things whereof ye are now ashamed? for the end of those things is death. But now being made free from sin, and become servants to God, ye have your fruit unto sanctification, and the end of eternal life."[90] I suppose too that the end of marriage is death. But the compensating fruit of sanctification, fruit belonging either to virginity or to continence, is eternal life. And afterwards: "Wherefore, my brethren, ye also were made dead to the law through the body of Christ; that ye should be joined to another, even to him who was raised from the dead, that we might bring forth fruit unto God. For when we were in the flesh, the sinful passions, which were through the law, wrought in our members to bring forth fruit unto death. But now we have been discharged from the law, having died to that wherein we were holden; so that we serve in newness of the Spirit, and not in oldness of the letter."[91] "When," he says, "we were in the flesh, and not in the newness of the Spirit but in the oldness of the letter," we did those things which pertained to the flesh, and bore fruit unto death. But now because we are dead to the law, through the body of Christ, let us bear fruit to God, that we may belong to Him Who rose from the dead. . . . And more clearly in what follows he teaches that Christians do not walk according to the flesh but according to the Spirit: "For they that are after the flesh do mind the things of the flesh; but they that are after the spirit the things of the spirit. For the mind of the flesh is death; but the mind of the spirit is life and peace: because the mind of the flesh is enmity against God; for it is not subject to the law of God, neither indeed can it be: and they that are in the flesh cannot please God. But ye are not in the flesh, but in the Spirit, if so be that the Spirit of God dwelleth in you," and so on to where he says: "So then, brethren, we are debtors, not to the flesh, to live after the flesh: for if ye live after the flesh, ye must die; but if by the spirit to mortify the deeds of the body, ye shall live. For as many as are led by the Spirit of God, these are sons of God."[92] If the wisdom of the flesh is enmity against God,[93] and they who are in the flesh cannot please God, I think that they who perform the functions of marriage love the wisdom of the flesh, and therefore are in the flesh. . . .

40. . . . It would be endless work to explain the Gospel mystery of the ten virgins, five of whom were wise and five foolish.[94] All I say

now is, that as mere virginity without other works does not save, so all works without virginity, purity, continence, chastity, are imperfect. And we shall not be hindered in the least from taking this view by the objection of our opponent that our Lord was at Cana of Galilee, and joined in the marriage festivities when He turned water into wine.[95] I shall very briefly reply, that He Who was circumcised on the eighth day, and for Whom a pair of turtle-doves and two young pigeons were offered on the day of purification, like others, before He suffered, showed His approval of Jewish custom, that He might not seem to give His enemies just cause for putting Him to death on the pretext that He destroyed the law and condemned nature. And even this was done for our sakes. For by going once to a marriage, He taught that men should marry only once.[96] Moreover, . . . the Church does not condemn marriage, but makes it subordinate; nor does she reject it, but regulates it; for she knows, as was said before, that in a great house there are not only vessels of gold and silver, but also of wood and earthenware; and that some are to honor, some to dishonor; and that whoever cleanses himself will be a vessel of honor, necessary, prepared for every good work.[97]

[The following sections include Jerome's account of "good women" (I, 41–46), the source of Dorigen's complaint in Franklin's Tale, 1355–1456; and Theophrastus' *Golden Book on Marriage* (I, 47), given above, pp. 412–14.]

48. . . . When Cicero after divorcing Terentia was requested by Hirtius to marry his sister, he set the matter altogether on one side, and said that he could not possibly devote himself to a wife and to philosophy. Meanwhile that excellent partner, who had herself drunk wisdom at Tully's fountains, married Sallust his enemy, and took for her third husband Messala Corvinus, and thus, as it were, passed through three degrees of eloquence. Socrates had two wives, Xantippe and Myron, grand-daughter of Aristides. They frequently quarreled, and he was accustomed to banter them for disagreeing about him, he being the ugliest of men, with snub nose, bald forehead, rough-haired, and bandy-legged. At last they planned an attack upon him, and having punished him severely, and put him to flight, vexed him for a long time. On one occasion when he opposed Xantippe, who from above was heaping abuse upon him, the termagant soused him with dirty water, but he only wiped his head and said, "I knew that a shower must follow such thunder as that."[98] . . .

[Numerous examples of wicked pagan wives follow.]

We read of a certain Roman noble who, when his friends found fault with him for having divorced a wife, beautiful, chaste, and rich, put out his foot and said to them, "And the shoe before you looks new and elegant, yet no one but myself knows where it pinches."[99] Herodotus tells us that a woman puts off her modesty with her clothes.[100] And our comic poet thinks the man fortunate who has never been married.[101] Why should I refer to Pasiphaë,[102] Clytemnestra,[103] and Eriphyle,[104] the first of whom, the wife of a king and swimming in pleasure, is said to have lusted for a bull: the second to have killed her husband for the sake of an adulterer: the third to have betrayed Amphiaraus, and to have preferred a gold necklace to the welfare of her husband? In all the bombast of tragedy and the overthrow of houses, cities, and kingdoms, it is the wives and concubines who stir up strife. Parents take up arms against their children: unspeakable banquets are served: and on account of the rape of one wretched woman Europe and Asia are involved in a ten-year war.[105] . . . Chrysippus[106] ridiculously maintains that a wise man should marry, that he may not outrage Jupiter Gamelius and Genethlius.[107] For upon that principle the Latins would not marry at all, since they have no Jupiter who presides over marriage. But if, as he thinks, the life of men is determined by the names of gods, whoever chooses to sit will offend Jupiter Stator.[108] . . .

49. . . . It is disgraceful to love another man's wife at all, or one's own too much. A wise man ought to love his wife with judgment, not with passion. Let a man govern his voluptuous impulses, and not rush headlong into intercourse. There is nothing blacker than to love a wife as if she were an adultress. Men who say they have contracted marriage and are bringing up children, for the good of their country and of the race, should at least imitate the brutes, and not destroy their offspring in the womb; nor should they appear in the character of lovers, but of husbands. In some cases marriage has grown out of adultery: and, shameful to relate! men have tried to teach their wives chastity after having taken their chastity away. Marriages of that sort are quickly dissolved when lust is satiated. The first allurement gone, the charm is lost. . . . It is the saying of a very learned man, that chastity must be preserved at all costs, and that when it is lost all virtue falls to the ground. This holds the primacy of all virtues in woman. This it is that makes up for a wife's poverty, enhances her riches, redeems her deformity, gives grace to her beauty; it makes her act in a way worthy of her forefathers whose blood it does not taint with bastard offspring;

of her children, who through it have no need to blush for their mother, or to be in doubt about their father; and above all, of herself, since it defends her from external violation.[109] There is not greater calamity connected with captivity than to be the victim of another's lust. The consulship sheds luster upon men; eloquence gives eternal renown; military glory and a triumph immortalize an obscure family. Many are the spheres ennobled by splendid ability. The virtue of woman is, in a special sense, purity. . . .

NOTES

1. 1 Corinthians vii, 1–9. See Wife of Bath's Prologue (in the order of Paul's text) 87–90; 151–57; 158–60; 64–68, 73–74, 82–85; 79–81; 39, 102–4; 52. In some respects the Wife's Prologue offers a new interpretation of this text, set against Jerome's.
2. Wife of Bath's Prologue, 87–90.
3. Wife of Bath's Prologue, 142–46.
4. Proverbs vi, 26.
5. Proverbs vii, 25 (see p. 405).
6. Proverbs vi, 27–28. Proverbs vi, 29 continues: "So he that goeth in to his neighbor's wife, shall not be clean when he shall touch her."
7. Wife of Bath's Prologue, 158–60.
8. Matthew xix, 6; Mark x, 9.
9. Wife of Bath's Prologue, 152–57. The familiar concept of the "marriage debt" (*debitum*) may account for the fortune of the prosperous but unhappily married Merchant (General Prologue, 280).
10. 1 Thessalonians v, 17; Colossians iv, 2.
11. 1 Peter iii, 7.
12. 1 Peter iii, 2–4; see Wife of Bath's Prologue, 340–47. 1 Peter iii, 1, proposes the wife as a "tutor" for an unbelieving husband: "Let wives be subject to their husbands: that if any believe not the word, they may be won without the word, by the conduct of the wives." Characters like Cecilia (Second Nun's Tale) and Prudence (Melibeus) perform this office of wifely "instruction" in different ways. The Wife of Bath is one of Chaucer's wives who present themselves as "instructors" of a doctrine not envisaged by Saint Peter.
13. Wife of Bath's Prologue, 64–68, 73–74, 82–85.
14. Wife of Bath's Prologue, 79–82.
15. 1 John ii, 6.
16. Wife of Bath's Prologue, 39, 103–4.
17. Wife of Bath's Prologue, 52.
18. 2 Corinthians xi, 6. Compare Franklin's Prologue, 716–27.
19. 1 Corinthians xv, 9.
20. 1 Corinthians xv, 9.
21. 1 Corinthians xv, 8.
22. Titus i, 12.
23. 1 Corinthians xv, 33.
24. Acts xvii, 28.
25. 1 Corinthians vii, 26.
26. 1 Corinthians vii, 26.
27. 1 Corinthians vii, 39; Wife of Bath's Prologue, 84–86.
28. 1 Corinthians vii, 25–26; Wife of Bath's Prologue, 62–68.

29. Wife of Bath's Prologue, 69–74.
30. John vii, 37; Wife of Bath's Prologue, 75–76, 169–78?.
31. See Matthew xix, 10–12. The presence of this passage on "eunuchs" in a portion of Jerome's treatise clearly well known by Chaucer strengthens the likelihood that he made use of the scriptural image of eunuchry in the portrait of his Pardoner (General Prologue, 688–91). This context may, in fact, have suggested to him the Pardoner's interruption of the Wife (Wife of Bath's Prologue, 163 ff.).
32. 1 Corinthians iii, 16–17; vi, 19; 2 Corinthians vi, 16.
33. Job xlii, 8; Romans xii, 1.
34. 1 Corinthians vii, 34; Wife of Bath's Prologue, 97.
35. Isaias lvi, 3–5.
36. Matthew xxiv, 19.
37. Wife of Bath's Prologue, 113–14.
38. 1 Corinthians vii, 27.
39. 1 Corinthians vii, 18–23. Jerome's earlier discussion of this text has been omitted. See Wife of Bath's Prologue, 154–55.
40. Compare Miller's Prologue, 3151–53.
41. 1 Corinthians vii, 28; Wife of Bath's Prologue, 156–57.
42. Wife of Bath's Prologue, 3, 166–68.
43. 1 Corinthians vii, 28.
44. 1 Corinthians vii, 29.
45. 1 Corinthians vii, 30–31.
46. 1 Corinthians vii, 32–33. Compare Theophrastus, above, pp. 412–14.
47. 1 Corinthians vii, 34; Wife of Bath's Prologue, 97.
48. Wife of Bath's Prologue, 469–74.
49. John xv, 19.
50. 1 Corinthians vii, 35.
51. 1 Corinthians vii, 39–40; Wife of Bath's Prologue, 47–50.
52. 1 Timothy v, 11–12. Paul here recommends that he avoid "younger widows," and continues: "And withal being idle they learn to go about from house to house: and are not only idle, but tattlers [*verbosae*] also, and busybodies [*curiosae*], speaking things which they ought not" (v, 13). See Wife of Bath's Prologue, 547.
53. 1 Timothy v, 15.
54. John iv, 5–26; Wife of Bath's Prologue, 14–23. The Wife's five husbands make her an analogue to the Samaritan woman.
55. Genesis ii, 24. Compare Merchant's Tale, 1335–36; Parson's Tale, 920.
56. Genesis iv, 18–19, 23–24; Wife of Bath's Prologue, 53–54.
57. Wife of Bath's Prologue, 20–26, 44–45.
58. Wife of Bath's Prologue, 32–34.
59. 1 Corinthians vi, 12.
60. Wife of Bath's Prologue, 33.
61. Genesis xvii, 24. Abraham's wives were Sara, Agar, and Cetura. See Wife of Bath's Prologue, 55.
62. See Romans ix, 6–9; Galatians iv, 28; Genesis xviii, 10. The discovery of Rebecca is recounted in Genesis xxiv, of which verses 15–18 are echoed in Clerk's Tale, 274–76, 290. Rebecca and Sara are models of wifehood recalled in the Nuptial Blessing (see above, p. 381). See Merchant's Tale, 1703–5.
63. Rachel and Leah (or Lia) and their handmaidens: Genesis xxx. See Wife of Bath's Prologue, 56–58.
64. Genesis xxix, 17.
65. A conventional interpretation. Another view of Lia—as representative of the active, opposed to the contemplative, life—appears in the Second Nun's Tale, 94–98 (see above, p. 120, n. 3).

66. Genesis xxxi, 46–48.
67. Genesis xxxii, 24–28.
68. Genesis xxv, 18–19.
69. Canticles vi, 7.
70. 3 Kings xi, 3; Wife of Bath's Prologue, 35–43.
71. 3 Kings vi.
72. Genesis i, 28; Wife of Bath's Prologue, 27–29. The implication of Jerome's argument remind us that Chaucer's Wife bases her interpretations on the Old Law.
73. Proverbs ix, 17?
74. Proverbs iv, 18? Wife of Bath's Prologue, 371.
75. 1 Corinthians xv, 47.
76. Proverbs xxv, 20; Wife of Bath's Prologue, 376–77.
77. Proverbs xxi, 19, 9, conflated; Wife of Bath's Prologue, 372.
78. Proverbs xxi, 9; xxv, 24.
79. Proverbs xxvii, 15; xix, 13. Wife of Bath's Prologue, 278–80.
80. A revision of Proverbs xxx, 15–16: "The horseleech hath two daughters that say: Bring, bring. There are three things that never are satisfied, and the fourth never saith: It is enough. Hell, and the mouth of the womb, and the earth which is not satisfied with water: and the fire never saith: It is enough." See Wife of Bath's Prologue, 371–75.
81. Proverbs xxx, 21–23.
82. Wife of Bath's Prologue, 69–72.
83. Matthew xx, 16.
84. Wife of Bath's Prologue, 115–34.
85. Twin rocks at the gateway to the Black Sea, fabled to swing together and crush whatever passed between them.
86. Wife of Bath's Prologue, 121–23.
87. Compare Wife of Bath's Prologue, 333–35.
88. Wife of Bath's Prologue, 135–41.
89. 2 Corinthians v, 17.
90. Romans vi, 21–22. Compare Wife of Bath's Prologue, 113–14.
91. Romans vii, 4–6. The Pauline oppositions developed in this and the following passage—"newness" and "oldness," the "spirit" and the "letter," the "fruit of life" and the "fruit of death," the "spirit" and the "flesh"—have a general bearing on Chaucer's depiction of the Wife of Bath's age, literalism, and carnality. They may affect as well our understanding of "young" or "old" men (and women) in other contexts. For example, Jean de Meun's la Vieille, like Alice, practices the "olde daunce." And consider statements such as Wife of Bath's Prologue, 187.
92. Romans viii, 5–14.
93. 1 Corinthians iii, 19.
94. Matthew xxv, 1–13.
95. John ii, 1–10.
96. Wife of Bath's Prologue, 8–13.
97. 2 Timothy ii, 20; Wife of Bath's Prologue, 99–104.
98. Wife of Bath's Prologue, 727–32.
99. Wife of Bath's Prologue, 492; Merchant's Tale, 1553.
100. Herodotus, *Natural History*, I, vii. Wife of Bath's Prologue, 782–83.
101. Terence, *Phormio*, I, iii, 21?
102. See Ovid, *Ars amatoria*, I, 295–326; Wife of Bath's Prologue, 733–36.
103. Wife of Bath's Prologue, 737–39.
104. Wife of Bath's Prologue, 740–46.
105. I.e., the Trojan War.
106. Stoic philosopher (280–207 B.C.). Jerome's reference here probably accounts

for his inclusion in Jankyn's "book of wikked wyves" (Wife of Bath's Pro-
logue, 677).

107. Jupiter regarded as presiding over marriages and over races or families.
108. Jupiter as supporter; "Stator" means "who causes to stand."
109. Compare, ironically, the conclusion to the Wife of Bath's Tale; and, literally,
Fiammetta's opinion on the source Franklin's Tale, above, pp. 132–33.

Walter Map:
from *Courtiers' Trifles*

Walter Map (1140–c. 1209), a Welsh aristocrat and churchman, spent virtually his entire life close to the court of Henry II. From his own account we know that he traveled widely and moved freely in both aristocratic and ecclesiastical circles. He was acquainted with Thomas Becket, and a good friend of the Welsh historian Giraldus Cambrensis, who has left a number of personal reminiscences of him. In 1179 he represented Henry II at the Lateran Council under Pope Alexander III. He was appointed Archdeacon of Oxford in 1197.

The De nugis curialium *(1181–93) is a curious collection of anecdotes and stories. The letter* Valerius ad Ruffinum *was written and circulated separately in 1181, and then incorporated into the fourth Division of this work. It had been "eagerly seized, carefully copied, read with huge enjoyment," he says (see below, p. 444), and in this form it found its way into Jankyn's "book of wikked wyves" as "Valerie" (Wife of Bath's Prologue, 671). Despite Map's efforts to ensure recognition of his authorship, the work was most often attributed (as in Jankyn's book) to Valerius Maximus, Roman author of the popular* Factorum et dictorum memorabilium libri ix *("Nine Books of Memorable Deeds and Sayings": c. 31 A.D).*

The "Dissuasion from Marriage" is a literary form which reaches back to Juvenal's sixth Satire; *it provides the theme for Theophrastus'* Golden Book on Marriage *(see above, pp. 412–14). Chaucer's "Envoy à Bukton" makes use of this form, and it seems clear from lines 29–30 of that poem that he thought of the "matere" of his Wife of Bath's Prologue in a similar context, perhaps as an ironic "suasio."*

Trans. Frederick Tupper and Marbury Ogle, Master Walter Map's Book "De Nugis Curialium" (Courtiers' Trifles) *(New York: Macmillan, 1924), pp. 182–97. Reprinted by permission of Chatto & Windus Ltd.*

The Advice of Valerius to Ruffinus the Philosopher not to Marry

DIVISION IV, 2–5

2. I had a friend, a man of philosophic regime, whom, after long acquaintance and many visits, I found on a time greatly altered in clothes, carriage, and countenance, woefully sighing, pale of face and yet in far better apparel, speaking fewer but weightier words, arrogant with an unwonted dislike of other men. His former wit had vanished, and he was no longer merry as of old. He called himself a sick man, and he was indeed far from well. I beheld him seeking solitude and shunning my conversation as far as his regard for me permitted. I saw him possessed of Venus. For whatever was apparent in him smacked wholly of the lover and in no wise of the philosopher.[1] I felt a hope, however, that he would rise again after his fall. I was ready to pardon that of which I knew no part. I thought it a jest and it was deadly earnest. He strove for the treatment of a husband, not of a lover, and yearned not to become Mars but Vulcan.[2] And yet my sense left me and, because he seemed on the road to death, I was ready to go with him. I spoke to him and was rebuffed. I sent others to speak with him, and, as he would not listen to them, I said, "A most evil beast hath devoured my dearest friend";[3] and, in order to fulfil all the conditions of friendship, I wrote him a letter changing our names, calling me who am Walter, Valerius, and him who is John and red, Ruffinus. I headed the letter thus:

The Advice of Valerius to Ruffinus the Philosopher not to Marry.

3. I am forbidden to speak and yet I cannot be silent. . . .
Thou lovest parasites and players who whisper of sugared baits to come, and especially Circe, who doth cheat thee by pouring profusely sensual delights that are redolent of the aroma of sweetness long drawn out. For fear that thou be made swine or ass,[4] I cannot hold my peace.

Ministering Babel pledgeth thee in the honeyed poison;[5] it moveth itself aright, and awakeneth delight in thee and leadeth thy spirit's force whither it will.[6] Hence I am forbidden to speak.

I know that "at the last, it will bite as a serpent,"[7] and will make a wound which will defy every antidote (treacle).[8] Hence I cannot keep silent.

Thou hast had many advocates of thy pleasures, most practised in pleading against thy well-being. Shall I be the only one to hold the tongue—I, who alone proclaim the bitter truth which thou loathest? Hence I am forbidden to speak.

The foolish "voice of the goose among swans,"[9] which are trained only to give pleasure, hath been blamed, yet the voice of the goose taught the senators to save the city from burning, their treasures from theft, themselves from the enemy's weapons.[10] Perchance thou too wilt understand, with the senators, because thou art wise, that the swans chant death to you and the goose hisseth safety. Hence I cannot keep silent.

Thou are all aflame with thy desires, and, being ensnared by the beauty of a lovely person, thou knowest not, poor wretch, that what thou seekest is a chimera.[11] But thou art doomed to know that this tri-form monster, although it is beautified with the face of a noble lion, yet is blemished with the belly of a reeking kid, and is beweaponed with the virulent tail of a viper. Therefore I am forbidden to speak.

Ulysses was enticed by the song of the sirens, but because "he knew the voices of the sirens and the cups of Circe,"[12] he won for himself, by the fetters of virtue, the power of shunning the abyss. Moreover, I, trusting in the Lord, predict that thou wilt be the imitator of Ulysses, not of Empedocles, who, under the power of his philosophy, to say nothing of his melancholy, chose Etna as his tomb,[13] and that thou wilt hearken to the parable which thou hearest; but of this I am afraid. Hence I cannot keep silent.

Finally, stronger is that flame of thine by which a part of thee hath become the foe of thyself,[14] than that flame in thee by which thou art enkindled into love of me. Lest the greater draw the lesser to itself and I die, therefore I am forbidden to speak. . . .

The first wife of the first man [Adam] after the first creation of man, by the first sin, relieved her first hunger against God's direct command. Great hath been the spawn of Disobedience, which until the end of the world will never cease from assailing women and rendering them ever unwearied in carrying to the fell consequences their chief inherit-ance from their mother. O friend, a man's highest reproach is a diso-bedient wife.[15] Beware!

The truth of God, which cannot err, saith of the blessed David: "I have found a man after mine own heart."[16] Yet even he is a signal in-stance of descent, through the love of woman, from adultery to homi-cide,[17] that "offences may never come singly."[18] For every sin is rich in abundant company and surrendereth whatever home it entereth to the pollution of its fellow vices. O friend, Bathsheba spake not a word and maligned no man, yet she became the instigation of the overthrow of the perfect man and the dart of death to her innocent mate. Shall she be held guiltless who shall battle by her charm of speech as Samson's Delilah,[19] and by her grace of form as Bathsheba, although her beauty alone may have triumphed without her will? If thou art not more after God's heart than David, doubt not that thou too mayst fall.

That sun of men, Solomon,[20] treasure-house of the Lord's delights, chief dwelling-place of wisdom, was darkened by the inky blackness of shadows and lost the light of his soul, the fragrance of his fame, the glory of his home, by the witchery of women.[21] At the last, having bowed his knee to Baal,[22] he was degraded from a priest of the Lord to a limb of the devil, so that he seemed to be thrust over a yet greater precipice than Phoebus, who, even after Phaeton's fall, was changed from the Apollo of Jove into the shepherd of Admetus.[23] Friend, if thou art not wiser than Solomon—and no man is that—thou art not greater than he who can be bewitched by woman. "Open thine eyes and see."[24]

Even the very good woman, who is rarer than the phoenix,[25] cannot be loved without the loathsome bitterness of fear and worry and constant unhappiness. But bad women, of whom the swarm is so large that no spot is without their malice, punish bitterly the bestowal of love, and devote themselves utterly to dealing distress, "to the division of soul and body."[26] O friend, a trite moral is, "Look to whom thou givest." True morality is, "Look to whom thou givest thyself."[27]

Lucretia and Penelope, as well as the Sabine women, have borne aloft the banners of modesty and they have brought back trophies with but few in their following. Friend, there is now no Lucretia, no Penelope, no Sabine woman.[28] Fear all the sex. . . .

Jupiter, king of earth, who was also called king of heaven on account of his matchless might of body and his peerless excellence of mind, compelled himself to bellow for Europa. My friend, lo, him whom worth lifted above the heavens, a woman hath lowered to the level of brutes! A woman will have the power to compel thee to bellow unless thou art greater than Jupiter, to whose greatness no one else was equal. . . .[29]

Then there was Mars, who attained the name of "God of Battles" through the well-known number of victories, in which his ready valor stood him greatly in stead. Although he knew no fear for himself, he was bound with Venus by Vulcan in chains, invisible, to be sure, but tangible—this too amid the mocking applause and the derision of the heavenly court.[30] My friend, meditate at least upon the chains which thou dost not see and yet already in part feel, and snatch thyself away while they are still breakable, lest that lame and loathsome smith whom "no god ever honored at his board nor goddess with her bed"[31] shall chain thee in his fashion to his Venus and shall make thee like unto himself, lame and loathsome, or, what I fear more, shall render thee clubfooted; in such wise that thou canst not have the saving grace of a cloven hoof,[32] but, bound to Venus, thou wilt become the distress and laughing-stock of onlookers, while the blind applaud thee and those with sight threaten.

Pallas was condemned by a false judge of goddesses, since she promised to bestow not pleasure but profit.[33] Friend, dost thou, too, ever judge in this wise? . . .

. . . Thou indeed inclinest thine ear to me, the sender of this writing, as the asp to charmers;[34] but thou offerest thy mind as a boar to dogs. Thou art as soothed as the serpent, dipsas,[35] upon which the sun shone with equatorial rays. Thou are as thoughtful for thyself as was the betrayed Medea.[36] Thou pitiest thyself as the sea the shipwrecked. . . .

Cicero, after the divorce of Terentia, was unwilling to marry, professing himself unable to give his attention at once to a wife and to philosophy.[37] My friend, would that thy spirit would thus answer thee, or thy tongue me, and thou wouldst deign to imitate the master of eloquence at least in thy speech, in order to give me hope, even though it should prove vain! . . .

Pacuvius, in tears, said to his neighbor Arrius: "My friend, I have in my garden a barren tree on which my first wife hanged herself, and then my second, and just now my third." Arrius answered him: "I marvel that thou hast found cause for tears in such a run of good luck," and again, "Great heavens, what heavy costs to thee hang from that tree!' and thirdly, "My friend, give me of that tree some branches to plant."[38] And I say to thee, my friend, I fear that thou too wilt have to beg branches of that tree at a time when thou wilt not be able to find them.

Sulpicius felt where his shoe pinched him, seeing that he divorced a high-born and chaste wife. My friend, beware of a pinching shoe which cannot be pulled off.[39]

Cato of Utica said, "If the world could exist without women, our intercourse would not be without gods." My friend, Cato spoke only of what he had felt and known; nor doth any one curse the mockery of women unless tricked and tried by painful experiences. It is proper to trust such witnesses, because they speak with all truth: they know how enjoyment of love pleaseth and how it pricketh the beloved; they know that the flower of Venus is a rose, because under its crimson lurk many thorns. . . .

Livia slew her husband, whom she hated over-much; Lucilia hers, whom she over-much loved.[40] The one of her own will mixed aconite; the other by mistake mingled for her man a potion of madness, instead of a cup of love. My friend, they strive with opposite intent; neither, however, is cheated of the goal of woman's wiles, that is, her own natural evil. Women journey by widely different ways, but by whatever windings they may wander, and through however many trackless regions they may travel,[41] there is only one outlet, one goal of all their trails, one crown and common ground of all their differences—wickedness. Find a warning against them in the experience that a woman is bold for the gratification of all her love or hate and is an adept at hurting when she will, which is always. And frequently, when she is ready to assist, she hindereth; hence it cometh to pass that she doeth harm even against her own heart's wish. Thou art placed in a furnace: if thou art gold, thou wilt go forth gold.[42] . . .

Pray, what woman among thousands of thousands ever hath saddened with perpetual repulse the persistently solicitous suitor? What woman doth repeatedly reject the prayer of the petitioner? Her response hath a savor of favor, and however hard she seemeth, she will always have in some corner or other of her words some hidden kindling for thy craving. However much she may deny, she denieth not altogether.[43] . . .

My friend, are you amazed or are you, the rather, affronted, because in my parallels I point out heathen as worthy of your imitation, idolatries to a Christian, wolves to a lamb, evil men to a good? I wish you to be like unto the fruitful bee, which draweth honey from the nettle, "so that you may suck honey from the stone and oil from the hardest rock."[44] I know the superstition of the heathen; but every one of God's creatures furnisheth some honorable illustration, whence He himself is called lion, or serpent, or ram.[45] The unbelieving perform very many things perversely; nevertheless they do some things which, although barren in their case, would in ours bring forth fruit abundantly.[46] But if those who lived without hope, without faith, without charity, indeed without a preacher,[47] made coats of skins[48] (in human wise), and, if we should become asses or sows or brutes in some inhuman form, of what reward of faith, of charity, of hope should we be deemed worthy, although we might behold prophets, apostles, and chief of all Him, the Lord of the pure heart,[49] whom only pure eyes are permitted to perceive? Or if they have wearied themselves in the pursuit of their own designs with no perception of future bliss, but only with the hope of avoiding ignorant minds, what shall we have in return for our neglect of the sacred page, whose end is truth and whose illumination is "a lamp unto the feet" and "a light unto the path"[50] to eternal light? Would that thou mayst select this sacred page, would that thou mayst peruse this, would that "thou mayst bring this into thy chamber,"[51] that "the king may bring thee unto his"![52] Thou hast already ploughed closely this field of Holy Writ for the flowers of thy spring, in this thy summer "He expecteth thee to make grapes"; to the hurt of this do not marry another lest, in the time of harvest, "thou wilt make wild grapes."[53] I do not wish thee to be the bridegroom of Venus, but of Pallas. She will adorn thee with precious jewels; she will clothe thee in a marriage garment.[54] These nuptials will boast Apollo as the attendant; the Fescennine verses chanted there will be taught by the married Stilbon to the cedars of Lebanon.[55] Devoutly but fearfully have I conceived the hope of this solemn union, which I so greatly desire; for this reason have I planned this whole reading; to this end, the whole discourse, albeit slowly, will hasten. With the firmness of this dissuasion is armed the whole man of me, whose dart, hardened with many a point of steel, thou dost now feel.

The conclusion of the foregoing Epistle

4. Hard is the hand of the surgeon, but healing. "Hard is this speech also,"[56] but healthy; and may thou find it as useful as it is devoted. My friend, thou protestest that I inflict upon thee a narrow rule of living. So be it! For "narrow is the way which leadeth to life,"[57] nor is the path plain by which men proceed to a plenitude of joys. Nay, even to attain to moderate pleasures we must pass through rough places. Jason heard that he must voyage through a sea that up to this time had not been deflowered by ships or oars and must make his way by sulfur-breathing bulls and by the post of a poisonous serpent to the golden fleece. Employing a counsel that was sound but not sweet, he departed, and returned bringing the desired treasure.[58] Thus humility of mind accepteth the wormwood of surly truth; dutiful care doth fertilize it, and persistent service bringeth it to fruit. Thus Auster, the south wind, cup-bearer of the rains, bringeth up the seed, Aquilo (from the north), sweeper of the ways, strengtheneth it, Zephyr, the creator of flowers, advanceth it to a rich yield. Thus stern beginnings are rewarded with a sweet ending, thus a strait path leadeth to stately mansions;[59] thus a narrow road windeth to the land of the living.[60] But, to support belief in my words by the testimony of the ancients, read the *Aureolus* ("Little Golden Book") of Theophrastus and the story of Jason's Medea, and thou wilt find almost nothing impossible to a woman.

The End of the foregoing Epistle

5. My friend, may the omnipotent God grant thee power not to be deceived by the deceit of the omnipotent female, and may He illuminate thy heart, that thou wilt not, with eyes bespelled, continue on the way I fear. But, that I may not seem to thee the author of *Orestes*,[61] farewell!

We know that this discourse hath delighted many; it is eagerly seized, carefully copied, read with huge enjoyment. Yet there are some, but of the baser sort, who deny that it is mine. For they envy the epistle and rob it, by force, both of its honor and its author. My only fault is that I am alive. I have no intention, however, of correcting this fault by my death. In the title I have changed our names to the names of dead men, for I knew that this giveth pleasure. Otherwise men would have rejected it, as they have me. Wishing, therefore, to save this witless pamphlet from being thrown into the mud from the mantle, I shall bid it hide in my company. I know what will happen after I am gone. When I shall be decaying, then, for the first time, it will be salted; and every defect in it will be remedied by my decease, and in the most remote future its antiquity will cause the authorship to be credited to me, because, then as now, old copper will be preferred to new gold.

NOTES

1. The situation is similar to that described by Andreas Capellanus in his *De amore* about five years later; and both are like Juvenal's efforts to "save" his friend from marriage. Map's description makes use of characteristics conventional to the trope of the "lover." His "sickness" suggests Ereos, which Chaucer called the "loveris maladye" (Knight's Tale, 1373). The opposition of "love" and "philosophy" is a commonplace occasion of wit for medieval writers, including Chaucer. It appears in the selection from Proverbs above, p. 404, but probably derives here most immediately from Theophrastus (see above, pp. 412–14). The formula is reflected in the Wife of Bath's victory over Jankyn's "book."
2. That is, (cuckolded) husband, rather than lover. See Ovid, *Metamorphoses*, IV, 167 ff. for the best-known account of the story of Mars' seduction by Venus; also his *Ars amatoria*, II, 561–94. Medieval mythographers read the story as an allegory of *virtus corrupta libidine* (virtue [or manliness] corrupted by lust), a significance which Arcite ignores in his prayer to Mars (Knight's Tale, 2383–92). See Boccaccio's allusion to this story (above, p. 329), and below, p. 440.
3. Genesis xxxvii, 33.
4. The sorceress Circe transformed men into different kinds of beasts (see Ovid, *Metamorphoses*, XIV, 223 ff.) The mythographers identified Circe's wine with "sensual delights."
5. See Apocalypse xvi, 19.

6. See Ezechiel i, 12.
7. See Proverbs xxiii, 32.
8. Apparently an allusion to *De pomo*, a treatise on the immortality of the soul, once attributed to Aristotle, also referred to by Richard de Bury, *Philobiblon* XI. The image is of "the scorpion in treacle": i.e. something in itself poisonous that may be ministered as a medicine.
9. See Virgil, *Eclogues*, IX, 36.
10. See Virgil, *Aeneid*, VIII, 655–56.
11. See Horace, *Odes*, I, xxvii, 18–24.
12. Horace, *Epistles*, I, ii, 23.
13. A disciple of Pythagoras and Parmenides, Empedocles was said to have thrown himself into the volcano, to convince people that he was a god.
14. See Galatians v, 17.
15. The original sin is often identified as Disobedience (see above, p. 23). The basic premise of the Wife of Bath's philosophy is, ironically, Obedience (of husbands). See Wife of Bath's Prologue, 715–20.
16. Acts xiii, 22; see Psalm lxxxviii, 21, and 1 Kings xiii, 14.
17. See 2 Kings xi.
18. See Matthew xviii, 7.
19. See Judges xvi, 4–21; Wife of Bath's Prologue, 721–23.
20. Solomon's name is linked with the etymology *sol hominum*.
21. See 3 Kings xi. Compare Wife of Bath's Prologue, 35–43.
22. Compare Romans xi, 4.
23. Ovid, *Ars amatoria*, II, 239–40 (see above, p. 280).
24. See 4 Kings xix, 16.
25. Compare Theophrastus, p. 413 above.
26. Hebrews iv, 12 (paraphrased); comparison of woman's tongue to the "word of God," which is the subject of this verse, is a characteristic irony.
27. See Merchant's Tale, 1523–29.
28. *Lucretia*, chaste wife of Collatinus, ravished by Tarquin, killed herself. The episode is recounted by Livy, *Annales*, I, lviii ff. Important to a medieval understanding of her suicide are Augustine, *De civitate Dei* I, 19, and Jerome, *Adversus Jovinianum*, I, 45. See Chaucer's Legend of Good Women, V. *Penelope*, faithful wife of Ulysses, is cited by Jerome, *Adversus Jovinianum*, I, 46. For the *Sabine women* see Ovid, *Ars amatoria*, I, 101–32; Augustine, *De civitate Dei*, III, 13.
29. See Ovid, *Metamorphoses*, II, 843 ff. Jupiter disguised himself as a bull in order to seduce Europa. As a result of this escapade Jupiter became a model of the "bovine" lover made sottish by love. See *Ovide moralisée*, II, 4988–5021, and below, p. 440
30. Ovid, *Metamorphoses*, IV, 167 ff. See note 2, above.
31. Virgil, *Eclogues*, IV, 63.
32. See Leviticus xi, 3. The Douay gloss states: "The dividing of the hoof and chewing of the cud, signify discretion between good and evil, and meditating on the law of God; and where either of these is wanting a man is unclean."
33. The judge was Paris, who rejected the promise of Pallas (wisdom) and Juno (honorable estate) in favor of Venus' (fleshly pleasure), and thereby precipitated the Trojan War. See Ovid, *Heroides*, XVI, 51–88; *Ars amatoria*, I, 247–48.
34. See Psalm lvii, 5–6.
35. See Ovid, *Amores*, I, viii (above, pp. 407-10). In *The Bestiary*, "The *Dipsas* is a species of asp which is called a 'water-bucket' in Latin, because anybody whom it bites dies of thirst."
36. See Ovid, *Metamorphoses*, VII, 1 ff., and *Heroides*, XII, among many Classical accounts.
37. Derived from Jerome, *Adversus Jovinianum*, I, 48 (see above, p. 431).

38. Aulus Gellius couples Pacuvius and Attius (not Arrius) as tragic poets (*Noctes Atticae*, XIII, 2). The story of the tree appears in Cicero, *De oratore*, II, 69. In the *Gesta Romanorum* XXX it is related of one Arrius and Paletinus. The moral "application" in the *Gesta* reads: "My beloved, the tree is the cross of Christ. The man's three wives are pride, lusts of the heart, and lusts of the eyes [see 1 John ii, 15–6], which ought to be thus suspended and destroyed. He who solicited a part of the tree is any good Christian." The *Gesta* attributes the tale to "Valerius." See Wife of Bath's Prologue, 755–64.
39. See Jerome, *Adversus Jovinianum*, I, 48 (above, p. 432). See Wife of Bath's Prologue, 491–92; Merchant's Tale, 1553.
40. Livia poisoned her husband Drusus, the son of Tiberius, at the instigation of Sejanus, in 23 A.D. Lucilia was Lucretius' wife who, according to Jerome, brewed a fatal love-potion in the hope of reviving his affection.
41. Compare General Prologue, 467.
42. Compare Zacharias xiii, 9; Daniel xii, 10.
43. This corresponds to the stage of "daunger" in the ritual ascribed to "courtly love." See, for example, Franklin's Tale, 967 ff.; Miller's Tale, 3271 ff.
44. See Deuteronomy xxxii, 13.
45. See above, p. 88. Here the references are to Apocalypse v, 5; Psalm xxi, 7; Numbers v, 8; and Daniel viii, 3.
46. See, for example, Matthew iii, 10; vii, 17.
47. See Romans x, 14.
48. See Genesis iii, 21.
49. See Matthew v, 8.
50. See Psalm cxviii, 105.
51. See Genesis xxiv, 67. This, of course, in preference to Ruffinus' proposed wife.
52. See Canticles i, 3.
53. See Isaias v, 2.
54. A version of the "marriage" to Wisdom (Pallas Athene); see above, p. 404. See Isaias lxi, 10.
55. Map is referring to the *De nuptiis Philologiae et Mercurii* ("The Marriage of Mercury and Philology"), in which Martianus Capella had Mercury appear as "Stilbon." See Wife of Bath's Prologue, 699.
56. See John vi, 61.
57. Matthew vii, 14.
58. See Ovid, *Metamorphoses*, VII, 1 ff.
59. See John xiv, 2.
60. See Psalm xxvi, 13.
61. See Juvenal, *Satire* I, 6. Map may have thought of his letter as "Juvenalian" in the tradition of *Satire*, VI, a famous antifeminist poem.

Peter Abelard:
from *A Story of Misfortunes*

In the Foreword to his Historia calamitatum (1135) Peter Abelard (1079–
1142) at the age of fifty-six proposed his life as an exemplum "so that, in
comparing your sorrows with mine, you may discover that yours are in
truth nought, or at the most but of small account, and so shall you come
to bear them more easily." Of his misfortunes those attending his affair
with Héloise are only a small part, but they have been linked to the name
of Abelard more firmly than any of the others, or than any of his con-
siderable philosophical and theological works.

By his own account, Abelard deliberately seduced Héloise in the home of
her uncle Fulbert, a canon of the Cathedral of Paris. Upon discovering her
pregnancy, he secretly removed her to his birthplace, near Nantes, where
she bore a son whom she named Astrolabe. Then, in an effort to placate her
uncle, he offered to marry Héloise. Chapter VII of the Historia records the
arguments against marriage which Abelard attributes to her. Fulbert agreed
to the marriage since it provided him with the opportunity to carry out his
vengeance (its form was not an unusual penalty for fornication in the
twelfth century): "they cut off those parts of my body with which I had
done that which was the cause of their sorrow."

The arguments of "Helowys, / That was abbesse nat fer fro Parys" made
their way into Jankyn's antimatrimonial anthology (Wife of Bath's Pro-
logue, 677–78), possibly by way of the Roman de la rose (see below, p.
458). The points are not original, but this episode in Abelard's history
effectively dramatized the theme central to authorities on the subject—the
conflict between clerks and wives, books and women, philosophy and mar-
riage. Additionally poignant is the fact that this theme is treated in the
words of a "wise woman."

Trans. Henry Adams Bellows, The Story of My Misfortunes, New York: Mac-
millan, rept. 1972, pp. 23–29. Reprinted by permission of Macmillan Publishing
Co., Inc.

447

The Arguments of Héloise against Marriage

FROM CHAPTER VII

Forthwith I repaired to my own country, and brought back thence my mistress, that I might make her my wife. She, however, most violently disapproved of this, and for two chief reasons: the danger thereof, and the disgrace which it would bring upon me. She swore that her uncle would never be appeased by such satisfaction as this, as, indeed, afterwards proved only too true. She asked how she could ever glory in me if she should make me thus inglorious, and should shame herself along with me. What penalties, she said, would the world rightly demand of her if she should rob it of so shining a light! What curses would follow such a loss to the Church, what tears among the philosophers would result from such a marriage! How unfitting, how lamentable it would be for me, whom nature had made for the whole world, to devote myself to one woman solely, and to subject myself to such humiliation! She vehemently rejected this marriage, which she felt would be in every way ignominious and burdensome to me.

Besides dwelling thus on the disgrace to me, she reminded me of the hardships of married life, to the avoidance of which the Apostle exhorts us, saying: "Art thou loosed from a wife? seek not a wife. But and if thou marry, thou hast not sinned; and if a virgin marry, she hath not sinned. Nevertheless such shall have trouble in the flesh: but I spare you."[1] And again: "But I would have you to be free from cares."[2] But if I would heed neither the counsel of the Apostle nor the exhortations of the saints regarding this heavy yoke of matrimony, she bade me at least consider the advice of the philosophers, and weigh carefully what had been written on this subject either by them or concerning their lives. Even the saints themselves have often and earnestly spoken on this subject for the purpose of warning us. Thus St. Jerome, in his first book against Jovinianus, makes Theophrastus set forth in great detail the intolerable annoyances and the endless disturbances of married life, demonstrating with the most convincing arguments that no wise man should ever have a wife, and concluding his reasons for this philosophical exhortation with these words: "Who among Christians would not be overwhelmed by such arguments as these advanced by Theophrastus?"[3]

Again, in the same work, St. Jerome tells how Cicero, asked by Hircius after his divorce of Terentia whether he would marry the sister of Hircius, replied that he would do no such thing, saying that he could not devote himself to a wife and to philosophy at the same time.[4] Cicero does not, indeed, precisely speak of "devoting himself," but he does add that he did not wish to undertake anything which might rival his study of philosophy in its demands upon him.

Then, turning from the consideration of such hindrances to the study of philosophy, Héloise made me observe what were the conditions of honorable wedlock. What possible concord could there be between scholars and domestics, between authors and cradles, between books or tablets and distaffs, between the stylus or the pen and the spindle? What man, intent on his religious or philosophical meditations, can possibly endure the whining of children, the lullabies of the nurse seeking to quiet them, or the noisy confusion of family life? Who can endure the continual untidiness of children? The rich, you may reply, can do this, because they have palaces or houses containing many rooms, and because their wealth takes no thought of expense and protects them from daily worries. But to this the answer is that the condition of philosophers is by no means that of the wealthy, nor can those whose minds are occupied with riches and worldly cares find time for religious or philosophical study. For this reason the renowned philosophers of old utterly despised the world, fleeing from its perils rather than reluctantly giving them up, and denied themselves all its delights in order that they might repose in the embraces of philosophy alone. One of them, and the greatest of all, Seneca, in his advice to Lucilius, says: "Philosophy is not a thing to be studied only in hours of leisure; we must give up everything else to devote ourselves to it, for no amount of time is really sufficient thereto."[5]

It matters little, she pointed out, whether one abandons the study of philosophy completely or merely interrupts it, for it can never remain at the point where it was thus interrupted. All other occupations must be resisted; it is vain to seek to adjust life to include them, and they must simply be eliminated. This view is maintained, for example, in the love of God by those among us who are truly called monastics, and in the love of wisdom by all those who have stood out among men as sincere philosophers. For in every race, gentiles or Jews or Christians, there have always been a few who excelled their fellows in faith or in the purity of their lives, and who were set apart from the multitude by their continence or by their abstinence from worldly pleasures.

Among the Jews of old there were the Nazarites, who consecrated themselves to the Lord, some of them the sons of the prophet Elias and others the followers of Eliseus, the monks of whom, on the author-

ity of St. Jerome, we read in the Old Testament.[6] More recently there
were the three philosophical sects which Josephus defines in his *Book
of Antiquities,* calling them the Pharisees, the Sadducees, and the Es-
senes.[7] In our times, furthermore, there are the monks who imitate
either the communal life of the Apostles or the earlier and solitary life
of John.[8] Among the gentiles there are, as has been said, the philoso-
phers. Did they not apply the name of wisdom or philosophy as much
to the religion of life as to the pursuit of learning, as we find from the
origin of the word itself, and likewise from the testimony of the saints?

There is a passage on this subject in the eighth book of St. Augus-
tine's *City of God,* where he distinguishes between the various schools
of philosophy. "The Italian school," he says, "had as its founder Pytha-
goras of Samos, who, it is said, originated the very word 'philosophy.'
Before his time those who were regarded as conspicuous for the praise-
worthiness of their lives were called wise men, but he, on being asked
of his profession, replied that he was a philosopher, that is to say a stu-
dent or a lover of wisdom, because it seemed to him unduly boastful to
call himself a wise man."[9] In this passage, therefore, when the phrase
"conspicuous for the praiseworthiness of their lives" is used, it is evi-
dent that the wise, in other words the philosophers, were so called less
because of their erudition than by reason of their virtuous lives. In what
sobriety and continence these men lived it is not for me to prove by
illustrations, lest I should seem to instruct Minerva herself.

Now, she added, if laymen and gentiles, bound by no profession of
religion, lived after this fashion, what ought you, a cleric and a canon,
to do in order not to prefer base voluptuousness to your sacred duties,
to prevent this Charybdis from sucking you down headlong, and to save
yourself from being plunged shamelessly and irrevocably into such filth
as this? If you care nothing for your privileges as a cleric, at least uphold
your dignity as a philosopher. If you scorn the reverence due to God, let
regard for your reputation temper your shamelessness. Remember that
Socrates was chained to a wife, and by what a filthy accident he him-
self paid for this blot on philosophy, in order that others might be
made more cautious by his example. Jerome thus mentioned this affair,
writing about Socrates in his first book against Jovinianus: "Once when
he was withstanding a storm of reproaches which Xantippe was hurling
at him from an upper story, he was suddenly drenched with foul slops;
wiping his head, he said only, 'I knew there would be a shower after all
that thunder.' "[10]

Her final argument was that it would be dangerous for me to take
her back to Paris, and that it would be far sweeter for her to be called
my mistress than to be known as my wife; nay, too, that this would be

more honorable for me as well. In such case, she said, love alone would hold me to her, and the strength of the marriage chain would not constrain us. Even if we should by chance be parted from time to time, the joy of our meetings would be all the sweeter by reason of its rarity. But when she found that she could not convince me or dissuade me from my folly by these and like arguments, and because she could not bear to offend me, with grievous sighs and tears she made an end of her resistance, saying: "Then there is no more left but this, that in our doom the sorrow yet to come shall be no less than the love we two have already known." Nor in this, as now the whole world knows, did she lack the spirit of prophecy.

NOTES

1. 1 Corinthians vii, 27–28.
2. 1 Corinthians vii, 32.
3. *Adversus Jovinianum*, I, 47. See above, pp. 412–14.
4. *Adversus Jovinianum*, I, 48. See above, p. 431.
5. Seneca, *Epistle* LXXIII.
6. Jerome, *Epistles* IV and XIII.
7. *The Jewish Antiquities*, XVIII, i, 2–5.
8. That is, John the Baptist. See Matthew iii.
9. *De civitate Dei*, VIII, ii.
10. *Adversus Jovinianum*, I, 48. See above, p. 431.

Jean de Meun:
from the *Romance of the Rose*

Jean de Meun (c. 1240–c. 1305) studied at the University of Paris at a time of great intellectual activity. A clerk with encyclopedic interests, he was a defender of William of Saint-Amour in his attacks upon the mendicant orders. He translated Boethius' De consolatione Philosophiae *as* Li Livres de confort de Philosophie; *Vegetius'* De re militari *as* Le Livre de Vegèce de l'art de chevalerie; *Giraldus Cambrensis'* De mirabilibus Hiberniae *as the* Livre de merveilles d'Hirlande; *the* De spirituali amicitia *of Aelred of Rievaulx as* De spirituelle amitié; *and the* Epistolae *of Abelard and Héloise. He is best known, however, for his long concluding segment of the Ro-mance of the Rose.*

The Roman de la rose, *begun by Guillaume de Lorris (c. 1235) and fin-ished by Jean de Meun (c. 1275), was perhaps the most famous and influen-tial poem in the Middle Ages. In the* Legend of Good Women, *Chaucer had the god of Love accuse him of having written heresy against his law:*

> "Thow hast translated the Romauns of the Rose,
> That is an heresye ageyns my lawe,
> And makest wise folk fro me withdrawe;
> And thinkest in thy wit, that is ful col,
> That he nys but a verray propre fol
> That loveth paramours, to harde and hote."

$$(G, 255–60)$$

Whether or not the extant Romaunt of the Rose *is actually Chaucer's, this poem exerted an indelible influence upon his writing throughout his career.*

The account of le Jaloux *(the "Jealous Husband") in the* Roman *appears in an involved context.* Lamant *(the "Lover") who seeks to pluck the Rose has listened at length to* Raison *("Lady Reason"), who has recommended*

Trans. C. R. Dahlberg, The Romance of the Rose *(Princeton: Princeton University Press, 1971), pp. 155–69. Copyright © 1971 by Princeton University Press. Re-printed by permission of Princeton University Press.*

that he prefer herself to the Rose (4229–7185). Lamant then turns to Ami (the "Friend"), whose more congenial advice on how to gain the Rose contradicts that of Raison (7231–9999). The present passage is part of Ami's cynical recommendation to flatter, bribe, and even permit himself to be beaten, in order to achieve his objective. Le Jaloux is presented as an object-lesson in bad behavior.

The passage is surrounded by an account of the Golden Age, a time of Ami's version of "innocence." Jean de Meun's main literary models for this account are Juvenal, Ovid and Boethius—all of whom Ami is made to distort so as to equate Edenic "innocence" with Epicurean "liberty." The present passage begins with a description of "free love" in this "original" state, and presents le Jaloux as an example of the way "law" (here, the sacrament of marriage) contravenes the life of "love." Le Jaloux is Ami's "proof" that whoever seeks woman's love should avoid exercising "seignourie," but rather should grovel and serve in order to gain his end. Ami is presented as seriously recommending the cynical advice that Ovid ironically provided for "lovers" (e.g., The Art of Love, II, 197–232).

Jean de Meun used the picture of le Jaloux as an occasion to introduce commonplaces of antimatrimonial and antifeminist literature into his encyclopedic "romance." It is interesting that he did not give Raison these bitter observations. Jean's irony, like Chaucer's, whose Merchant is a latterday Jaloux, is subtle in that the subject is transferred from "dissuasion" to "complaint." The speech thus becomes an antitype to the cynical attitude of la Vieille, based on "experience" (the traditional enemy of "innocence"). Chaucer's Wife of Bath, who has learned the standard antimatrimonial topics from clerk Jankyn, combines both voices.

Le Jaloux's "authors" are an important collection of the central texts in the tradition; they may, indeed, have suggested Jankyn's "book of wikked wyves." Juvenal, Ovid, Theophrastus, "Valerius," Héloise are called upon in his vicious tirade. One can easily imagine his own wife coming away from the experience with the kind of ammunition which the Wife of Bath puts to her own use.

The Jealous Husband is often associated with the January–May type of marriage, a staple of medieval fabliaux. This association appears, for example, in the Miller's Tale as well as the Merchant's Tale, and in the Wife's first three marriages. In the Miller's Tale, John's failure to attend to the wisdom of "Catoun" that "man sholde wedde his simylitude" makes him "jalous" (lines 3224–32, 3851), and one source of humor in the tale is his placid failure to observe the furious suspicions of the stereotype. Thus the principles of the tradition are given further comic twist. In the Romance of the Rose Ami adapts clerical propaganda to a system of "courtly" values by putting them in the mouth of a villain; in the Miller's own remedy against such "jalousye" (lines 3152–66) the whole matter becomes thoroughly countrified.

[The Jealous Husband]

[Ami advises]

When the sky was calm, the weather sweet and pleasant, the wind soft and delightful as in an eternal springtime, and every morning the birds strove in their warbling to salute the dawn of the day, which makes all their hearts stir, then Zephirus and his wife Flora, the goddess and lady of flowers, spread out for men the counterpanes of little flowers.[1] (These two make flowers spring up. Flowers know no other master, for he and she go together throughout the whole world sowing flowers; they shape them and color them with those colors that the flowers use to bring honor, in gay and beautiful chaplets, to young girls and men who, with the love of pure lovers, value each other because of their great love.) The little flowers that they spread out reflected back such splendor among the grass, the meadows, and the woods that you would have thought that the earth was grown so haughty on account of its flowers that it wanted to take up war with heaven over the question of which had the better field of stars. Upon such couches as I describe, those who were pleased by Love's games would embrace and kiss each other without rapine or covetousness. The groves of green trees stretched out their pavilions and curtains over them with their branches and protected them from the sun. There these simple, secure people led their carols, their games and their idle, pleasant activities, free of all cares except to lead a life of gaiety in lawful companionship. No king or prince had yet committed any crime by robbing and seizing from another. All were accustomed to being equal, and no one wanted any possessions of his own. They knew well the saying, neither lying nor foolish, that love and lordship [*amour e seignourie*] never kept each other company nor dwelt together. The one that dominates separates them.[2]

It is the same in marriages, where we see that the husband thinks himself wise and scolds his wife, beats her, and makes her live a life of strife. He tells her that she is stupid and foolish for staying out dancing and keeping company so often with handsome young men.[3] They undergo so much suffering when the husband wants to have control over the body and possessions of his wife that good love cannot endure.[4]

"You are too giddy," he says, "and your behavior is too silly. As soon as I go to my work, you go off dancing and live a life so riotous that it

454

seems ribald, and you sing like a siren. And when I go off to Rome or Friesland with our merchandise, then immediately you become very coquettish—for word of your conduct goes around everywhere, and I know through one who tells me of it—and when anyone speaks about the reason that you conduct yourself so demurely in all the places where you go, you reply, 'Alas! It is on account of my love for my husband.' For me, sorrowful wretch that I am? Who knows whether I forge or weave, whether I am dead or alive? I should have a sheep's bladder shoved in my face. Certainly I am not worth a button if I don't scold you. You have created a great reputation for me when you boast of such a thing. Everyone knows very well that you lie. For me, sorrowful wretch! For me! I formed evil gauntlets with my own hands and deceived myself cruelly when I ever accepted your faith, the day of our marriage. For me you lead this life of riot! For me you lead this life of luxury! Who do you think you go around fooling? I never have the possibility of seeing these quaint little games, when these libertines, who go around spying out whores, greedy for pleasure and hot with desire, gaze and look upon you from top to bottom when they accompany you through the streets. For whom are you peeling these chestnuts? Who can trick me more than you? The instant I approach near you, you make a rain-cape out of me. I see that, in this coat and that wimple, you seem simpler than a turtle-dove or dove. It doesn't matter to you if it is short or long when I am all alone near you. No matter how good-tempered I am, I would not hold back, if someone gave me four bezants or if I did not refuse them out of shame, from beating you in order to subdue your great pride. Understand that it does not please me for you to wear any quaint adornment at a carol or dance, except in my presence.

"Furthermore—I can hide it no longer—do you have any lands to divide up between you and this young bachelor, Robichonnet of the green hat, who comes so quickly when you call? You cannot leave him alone; you are always joking together. I don't know what you want of each other that you can always talk with one another. Your silly conduct makes me mad with anger. By that God that doesn't lie, if you ever speak to him, your face will grow pale, in fact blacker than mulberry; God help me, before I get you away from this life of dissipation I will give you some blows in that face that is so pleasing to the libertines, and you will then stay meek and quiet. You will be held in good iron rings; you will never go out without me, and you will serve me in the house. The devils make you very secret with those rascals, full of lies, toward whom you should be distant. Didn't I take you to serve me?[5] Do you think that you deserve my love in order to consort with these dirty rascals just because they have such gay hearts and find you so gay in turn? You are a wicked harlot, and I can have no confidence, in you. The devils made me marry.

"Ah! If I had believed Theophrastus,[6] I would never have married a wife. He considers no man wise who takes a wife in marriage, whether she is beautiful or ugly, poor or rich, for he says, and affirms it as true in his noble book, *Aureolus* (a good one to study in school), that married life is very disagreeable, full of toil and trouble, of quarrels and fights that result from the pride of foolish women, full, too, of their opposition and the reproaches that they make and utter with their mouths, full of the demands and the complaints that they find on many occasions. One has great trouble keeping them in line and restraining their silly desires. He who wants to take a poor wife must undertake to feed her, clothe her, and put shoes on her feet. And if he thinks that he can improve his situation by taking a very rich wife, he will find her so proud and haughty, so overweening and arrogant, that he will again have great torment to endure her. And if, in addition, she is beautiful, everyone will run after her, pursue her and do her honor; they will come to blows, will work, struggle, battle, and exert themselves to serve her; and they all will surround her, beg her, try to get her favor, covet her, and carry on until in the end they will have her, for a tower besieged on all sides can hardly escape being taken.

"If, on the other hand, she is ugly, she wants to please everybody; and how could anyone guard something that everyone makes war against or who wants all those who see her? If he takes up war against the whole world, he cannot live on earth. No one would keep them from being captured, provided that they had been well-solicited. He who understood how to take a prize well would capture even Penelope, and there was no better woman in Greece.

[*Ami here recounts the story of Lucrece, so as to be able to conclude that no Lucrece or Penelope could defend herself from a knowledgeable suitor—lines 8608–60.*][7]

"Again, those who marry have a very dangerous custom, one so ill-arranged that it occurs to me as a very great wonder. I don't know where this folly comes from, except from raging lunacy. I see that a man who buys a horse is never so foolish as to put up any money if he does not see the horse unclothed, no matter how well it may have been covered. He looks the horse over everywhere and tries it out. But he takes a wife without trying her out, and she is never unclothed, not on account of gain or loss, solace or discomfort, but for no other reason than that she may not be displeasing before she is married. Then, when she sees things accomplished, she shows her malice for the first time; then appears every vice that she has; and then, when it will do him no good to repent, she makes the fool aware of her ways.[8] I know quite certainly that, no matter how prudently his wife acts, there is no man, unless he is a fool, who does not repent when he feels himself married.

"By Saint Denis! Worthy women, as Valerius bears witness, are fewer than phoenixes.[9] No man can love one but what she will pierce his heart with great fears and care and other bitter misfortunes. Fewer than phoenixes? By my head, a more honest comparison would say fewer than white crows,[10] however beautiful their bodies may be. Nevertheless, whatever I say, and in order that those who are alive may not say that I attack all women with too great impunity, a worthy woman, if one wants to recognize her, either in the world or in the cloister, and if he wants to put in some toil in seeking her, is a rare bird on earth, so easily recognized that it is like the black swan.[11] Even Juvenal confirms this idea when he reiterates it in a positive statement: 'If you find a chaste wife, go kneel down in the temple, bow down to worship Jupiter, and put forth your effort to sacrifice a gilded cow to Juno, the honored lady, for nothing more wonderful ever happened to any creature.'[12]

"And if a man wants to love the wicked women—of whom, according to Valerius, who is not ashamed to tell the truth, there are swarms, here and overseas, greater than those of the bees that gather in their hives—if he wants to love them, what end does he expect to come to? He brings harm to himself by clinging to such a branch; he who clings to it, I well recall, will lose both soul and body.[13]

"Valerius, who sorrowed because his companion Rufinus wanted to marry, made a stern speech to him: 'My friend,' he said, 'may omnipotent God keep you from ever being put into the snare of an all-powerful woman who smashes all things through cunning.'[14]

"Juvenal himself writes to Posthumus on his marriage: 'Do you want to take a wife, Posthumus? Can't you find ropes, cords, or halters for sale? Can't you jump out of one of the high windows that we can see? Or can't you let yourself fall from the bridge? What Fury leads you to this torment and pain?'[15]

"King Phoroneus himself, who, as we have learned, gave the Greek people their laws, spoke from his death-bed and said to his brother Leonce: 'Brother, I reveal to you that I would have died happy if I had never married a wife.' And Leonce straightway asked him the cause of that statement. 'All husbands,' said Phoroneus, 'test it and find it by experiment; and when you have taken a wife, you will know it well in every detail.'[16]

"Pierre Abelard, in turn, admits that Sister Héloise, abbess of the Paraclete and his former sweetheart, did not want to agree for anything that he take her as his wife. Instead, the young lady of good understanding, well educated, loving and well loved in return, brought up arguments to convince him not to marry; and she proved to him with texts and reasons that the conditions of marriage are very hard, no matter how wise the wife may be. For she had seen, studied, and known the books, and she knew the feminine ways, for she had them all in herself. She asked him to love her but not to claim any right of her except those of grace and freedom, without lordship or mastery, so that he might study, entirely his own man, quite free, without tying himself down, and that she might also devote herself to study, for she was not empty of knowledge. She told him also that in any case their joys were more pleasing and their comfort grew greater when they saw each other more rarely.[17] But, as he has written for us, he loved her so much that he afterward married her in spite of her admonition, and unhappiness resulted. After she had taken the habit of a nun at Argenteuil—by agreement of both of them together, as it seems to me— Pierre's testicles were removed, in his bed in Paris, at night; on this account he endured great suffering and torment.[18] After this misfortune, he was a monk of Saint Denis in France, then abbot of another abbey; then, it says in his *Life*, he founded a widely known abbey that he named the Abbey of the Paraclete, where Héloise, who was a professed nun before, was abbess.[19] She herself, without shame, in a letter to her lover, whom she loved so much that she called him father and lord, tells a wondrous thing that many consider demented. It is written in the letters, if you search the chapters well, that she sent to him by express, even after she was abbess: 'If the emperor of Rome, to whom all men should be subject, deigned to wish to take me as his wife and make me mistress of the world, I would still rather,' she said, 'and I call God to witness, be called your whore than be crowned empress.'[20] But, by my soul, I do not believe that any such woman ever existed afterward; and I think that her learning put her in such a position that she knew better how to overcome and subdue her nature, with its feminine ways. If Pierre had believed her, he would never have married her.

"Marriage is an evil bond, so help me Saint Julian, who harbors wandering pilgrims,[21] and Saint Leonard, who unshackles prisoners who are truly repentent, when he sees them lamenting.[22] It would have been better for me to go hang, the day I had to take a wife, when I became acquainted with so quaint a woman. With such a coquette I am dead. For Saint Mary's son, what is that quaintness worth to me, that costly, expensive dress that makes you turn your nose up, that is so long and trails behind you, that irks and vexes me so much, that makes you act so overbearing that I become mad with rage? What profit does it give me? No matter how much it profits others, it does me only harm; for when I want to divert msyelf with you, I find it so encumbering, so annoying and troublesome that I can come to no result. You make me so many turns and parries with your arms, legs, and hips, and you go twisting so much that I cannot hold you properly. I don't know how all this comes about, but I see very well that my love-making and my comforts are not pleasing to you. Even at night, when I lie down, before I receive you in my bed, as any worthy man does his wife, you have to undress yourself. On your head, your body, or your haunches you have only a head-covering of white cloth, with perhaps lace ornaments of blue or green, covered up underneath the head-covering. The dresses and the fur linings are then put on the pole to hang all night in the air. What can all that be worth to me then, except to sell or pawn? You will see me burn up and die with evil rage if I do not sell and pledge everything; for, since they give me such trouble by day and no diversion by night, what other profit can I expect of them except by selling or pawning them? And if you were to admit the truth, you are worth no more because of them, neither in intelligence, nor in loyalty, nor even, by God, in beauty.

"And even if any man, to confound me, wanted to oppose me by replying that the bounties of good things go well with many different kind of people and that beautiful apparel creates beauty in ladies and girls, then, no matter who said so in fact, I would reply that he lied. For the beauties of fair things, violets or roses, silk cloths or *fleurs de lys*, as I find it written in a book,[23] are in themselves and not in ladies. All women should know that no woman will ever, as long as she lives, have anything except her natural beauty. And I say the same about goodness as I have told you about beauty. Thus, to begin my speech, I say that if one wanted to cover a dung-heap with silken cloths or little flowers, well-arranged and beautifully colored, it would certainly still be a dung-heap, whose custom it is to stink just as it did before. Someone might want to say, 'If the dung-heap is ugly within it appears more lovely without; and in just the same way the ladies apparel themselves in order to appear more beautiful or to hide their ugliness.' If someone were to say thus, I do not know, by my faith, how to reply, except to say that such deception comes from the maddened vision of eyes that see them in all their fine apparel.[24] As a result, their hearts are led astray because of the pleasing impression of their imaginations, and they do not know how to recognize a lie or the truth, or how, for lack of clear vision, to explicate the sophism. But if they had the eyes of a lynx, they would never, for any sable mantles, surcoats, or skirts, any head ornaments, kerchiefs, undergarments, or pelisses, for any jewels or objects of value, for any covert, smirking coquetries, if one considered them well, for any gleaming exteriors, which make them look artificial, and never for any chaplets of fresh flowers, would they seem to them to be beautiful. However well Nature had formed Alcibiades, whose body was always beautiful in color and molding, anyone who could see within him would want to consider him very ugly. So Boethius tells us, a man wise and full of worth, and he draws upon the testimony of Aristotle, who observes that the lynx has a gaze so strong, piercing, and clear that he sees all that one shows him, quite open both without and within.[25]

"Thus I say that in no epoch were Beauty and Chastity ever at peace. Always there was such great strife that I have never heard it said or recounted in fable or song that anything could reconcile them. So mortal is the war between them that the one will never let the other hold a full foot of ground, provided that she might come out ahead. But things are very badly divided, since, with what Chastity received as her share, she knows so little of combat and parry when she attacks or defends herself that she has to surrender her arms; she has not the power to defend herself against Beauty, who is very cruel. Even Ugliness, Chastity's chambermaid, who owes her honor and service, does not love or value her enough not to chase her from her mansion; she runs after her, on her neck the club that is so huge and weighs so much that it vexes her exceedingly as long as her mistress remains active for the total of a single hour. Chastity is in a very bad situation, since she is attacked from two directions and has no help from anywhere. She has to flee the field, for she sees that she is alone in the combat. Even if she had sworn it by her throat, she would have her fill of struggle, and when everyone does battle against her, so that she cannot win, she would not dare to resist. Now cursed be Ugliness when she runs thus after Chastity, whom she should have defended and protected. If she could even have hidden her between her flesh and her shirt, she should have put her there. Beauty, also, is certainly very much to blame. She should have loved Chastity and, if it had pleased her, striven for peace between them. She should have at least done all she could to put herself in Chastity's good graces, since, if she had been worthy, courteous, and wise, she should have indeed done homage to her, not brought shame and disgrace; for even the letter bears witness, in the sixth book of Virgil, by the authority of the Sibyl, that no man who lives a chaste life can come to damnation.[26]

"There I swear by God, the celestial king, that a woman who wants to be beautiful, or who exerts herself to appear beautiful, examines herself and takes great trouble to deck herself out and look attractive, because she wants to wage war on Chastity, who certainly has many enemies.[27] In cloisters and abbeys all the women are sworn against her. They will never be so walled in that they do not hate Chastity so strongly that they all aspire to shame her. They all do homage to Venus, with no consideration for worth or harm; they primp and paint in order to fool those who look at them, and they go searching along through the streets in order to see, to be seen,[28] and to arouse desire in people, so that they will want to lie with them. Therefore they wear their finery to carols and churches, for not one of them would ever do so if she did not think that she would be seen and that she would thus more quickly give pleasure to those whom she could deceive. Certainly, if the truth be told, women give great shame to God. Misguided fools, they do not consider themselves rewarded with the beauty that God gives them.[29] Each one has on her head a crown of flowers, of gold, or of silk. She preens herself and primps as she goes through the town showing herself off, and thus the unhappy wretch abases herself in a very wicked way when, to increase and perfect her beauty, she wants to draw on to her head an object lower and more base than she. Thus she goes around despising God because she considers him inadequate, and in her foolish heart she thinks to herself that God did her a great outrage in that, when he proportioned the beauty in her, he acquitted himself very negligently. Therefore she searches for beauty in creations that God made with much worse appearance, things like metals or flowers or other strange things.

"As for men, it is the same, without fail. If, to be more beautiful, we make chaplets and adornments for the beauties that God has put in us, we misbehave toward him when we do not consider ourselves rewarded by the beauty that he has given us above all creatures that are born. But I have no interest in such tricks. I want only enough clothing to protect myself from cold and heat. This homespun of mine, lined with lamb, protects my body and head against wind, rain, and storm just as well—may God protect me as truly—as would fine sky-blue cloth lined with squirrel. It seems to me that I lose my money when I buy you a dress of blue, of camelot, of brown or scarlet material and line it with squirrel or costly gray fur. To do so makes you run wild, simpering and posturing as you go through dust and mud, while you value neither God nor me. Even at night when you lie all naked beside me in my bed, you can't be held, for when I want to embrace you to kiss you and comfort you, and when I am thoroughly warmed up, you sulk like a devil and do not want to turn your face toward me for anything that I may do. You pretend to be so sick, you sigh and complain so much and make so much resistance that I become so fearful that I don't dare attack you again, when I wake up after I have slept, so great is my fear of failing. It strikes me as a very great wonder how those ribalds attain anything when, by day, they hold you with your clothes on, if you twist about in the same way when you play with them and if you give them as much trouble as you do to me, both day and night. But I believe that you have no desire, that instead you go along singing and dancing through the gardens and meadows with these unlawful rogues.[30] They drag this married woman through the green grass with the dew on it and there they go along despising me and saying to each other, 'It's in spite of that dirty, jealous villain!' Now may the flesh and bones that have brought me such shame be given over to wolves and mad dogs! It is through you, lady slut, and through your wild ways, that I am given over to shame, you riotous, filthy, vile, stinking bitch. May your body never see the end of this year when you give it over to such curs! Through you and your lechery I am placed in the confraternity of Saint Ernoul, the patron of cuckolds,[31] from whom no man with a wife, to my knowledge, can be safe, no matter how much he may go about to guard her and spy on her, even though he may have a thousand eyes. All women get themselves attacked, and there is no guard worth anything. If it happens that they omit the deed, they never are without the wish, by which, if they can, they will jump to the deed, for they always carry their desire with them. But Juvenal gives one great comfort for this situation when he says, of the need that is called a woman's carnal need to be made happy, that it is the least of the sins by which the heart of a woman is stained, for their nature commands each of them to give their attention to doing worse.[32] Do we not see how the mothers-in-law cook up poisons for their sons-in-law, how they work charms and sorceries and so many other diabolical things that, no matter how stout his powers of thought, no man could combat them?[33]

"All you women are, will be, and have been whores, in fact or in desire, for, whoever could eliminate the deed, no man can constrain desire. All women have the advantage of being mistresses of their desires. For no amount of beating or upbraiding can one change your hearts, but the man who could change them would have lordship over your bodies.

"Now let us leave what cannot be. But O! fair sweet God, fair celestial king, what can I do with the rascals who thus shame me and oppose me? If I happen to threaten them, how seriously will they take my threat? If I go to fighting with them, they can kill me or beat me straightway, so cruel and unprincipled, so eager to do all sorts of wickedness, so young and handsome, so wild and headstrong are they. They will think me not worth a straw, for youth so inflames them, filling their hearts with fire and flame and inciting them, by necessity, to foolish, light, and giddy deeds, that each one thinks of himself Roland, indeed Hercules or Samson.

[*Lines 9184–312, concerning the fates of Hercules and Samson, and a tirade against expensive dress, are omitted.*][34]

"But now tell me without making up any lies. Where, for the sake of love, did you get that other rich new dress in which you fixed yourself up here the other day when you went to the carols, for I know very well that I am right to think that I never gave it to you. You swore to me by Saint Denis, Saint Philibert, and Saint Peter that it came to you through your mother, who sent you the cloth for it because, as you gave me to understand, her love for me is so great that she wants to spend her money in order to make me keep mine. May she be grilled alive, that dirty old whore, that priest's concubine, that mackerel, that pimping whore, and may you, for your merits, fry along with her, if the case is not exactly as you say. I would certainly ask her, but I would exert myself in vain; the whole thing would not be worth a ball to me: like mother, like daughter. I know that you have talked together, and it is obvious that you both have hearts touched by the same wand. I know which foot you jump with, and that dirty painted old whore agrees with your attitude; she used to act in the same way. She has followed so many roads that she has been bitten by many curs. But now, I know, her looks are so bad that she can make nothing by herself, and so now she sells you. Three or four times a week she comes in here and leads you out on the pretext of new pilgrimages according to her old customs—for I know the whole plan—and then she doesn't stop parading you, as one does with a horse for sale, while she grabs and teaches you to grab. Do you think that I don't know you well? Somebody hold me so that I don't break your bones with this pestle or this spit until you are like a pâté of baby chicks."

Then the jealous husband, sweating with anger, may seize her straightway by the hair and pull and tug her, break and tear her hair and grow mad with rage over her. A lion's rage at a bear would be nothing in comparison. In anger and rage, he drags her through the whole house and vilifies her foully. His intent is so evil that he doesn't want to hear excuses on any oath. Instead he hits her, beats her, thumps her, and knocks her about while she gives out howls and cries and sends her voice flying on the winds past windows and roofs. She reproaches him in every way she knows how, just as it comes into her mouth, in front of the neighbors who come there. The neighbors think them both crazy; with great difficulty they take her away from him while he is out of breath.

When the lady feels this torment and takes account of this riot and this diverting viol on which our jongleur plays to her, do you think that she will ever love him more? She would want him to be at Meaux, indeed in Romagna. I will say more; I don't think that she might ever want to love him. She might pretend, but if he could fly up to the clouds or raise his view so high that from there, without failing, he could see all the deeds of men, and if he reflected upon all at leisure, he still would have to choose into which peril he fell, and he has not seen all the frauds that a woman knows how to meditate in order to protect and defend herself. Afterward, if he sleeps in her company, he puts his life in very great peril. Indeed, sleeping and waking, he must fear most strongly that, in order to avenge herself, she may have him poisoned or hacked into pieces, or make him languish in a life of desperate ruses. Or he must fear that, if she cannot play any other way, she may take it into her head to flee. A woman values neither honor nor shame when anything rises up in her head; this is the truth without doubt. A woman has no reason whatever.[35] Valerius even claims that, toward whatever she hates and whatever she loves, a woman is bold, cunning, and studious of bringing injury to others[36]

My friend, consider this mad jealous boor—may his flesh be fed to the wolves—so filled with his jealousy, as I have described him for you here in this story. He makes himself lord over his wife, who, in turn, should not be his lady but his equal and his companion, as the law joins them together; and, for his part, he should be her companion without making himself her lord or master. Do you think that, when he arranges such torments for her and does not consider her his equal[37] but rather makes her live in such distress, he will not be displeasing to her and that the love between them will not fail? Yes indeed, without fail, whatever she says, he will not be loved by his wife if he wants to be called "lord," for love must die when lovers want lordship. Love cannot endure or live if it is not free and active in the heart.[38]

NOTES

1. See Ovid, *Metamorphoses*, I, 107–8; Legend of Good Women, F, 171–74; General Prologue, 5–7.
2. See Ovid, *Metamorphoses*, II, 846–47; the tale of Europa. Ovid says that Jove himself discovered the truth of this principle; therefore to seduce Europa he laid aside his *majestas* and took the form of a bull. In the tradition of Ovidian commentary represented by the *Ovide moralisée* he is seen as an emblem for lovers made sottish (or "bovine") by love (*Ov. mor.*, II, 5994–97). The *Ovide moralisée* sets as an antitype to the "fine amour" (II, 5003) of Jupiter, the love of Christ, who laid aside his divine majesty, to incarnate himself in order to secure the love of human nature (II, 5103–38). In becoming Ami's "seignourie," Ovid's *majestas* has degenerated into the authority of husbands over their wives. See Franklin's Tale, 761–66, and for yet another sense of the Ovidian principle, Knight's Tale, 1623–26.
3. See Theophrastus, above, p. 412; Wife of Bath's Prologue, 242–45, 303–6, 318–22, 544 ff.
4. Compare 1 Corinthians vii, 4: "The wife hath not power of her own body, but the husband. And in like manner the husband hath not power of his own body, but the wife." Saint Paul's idea of "good love" in marriage is obviously not that envisioned by Ami. See Jerome. *Adversus Jovinianum*, I, 7 (above, pp. 417–18); Wife of Bath's Prologue, 154–60, 312–19; Wife of Bath's Tale, 1061.
5. He recalls the wife's marital troth to "love, honor, and obey" (see above, p. 375).
6. The following passage amounts to a close paraphrase of the *Golden Book* of Theophrastus (above, pp. 412–14). Le Jaloux also regrets that he did not follow the advice of Walter Map's Valerius (see above, pp. 438–44); that is, he should have believed in "books." It seems clear from the extant commentaries on the *Valerius ad Ruffinum* that Theophrastus *was* "studied in school." Compare Merchant's Tale, 1310, and, in light of the following paraphrase, Wife of Bath's Prologue, 248–56, 265–70.
7. See Map, above, p. 440. For his account of Lucrece, Jean de Meun turned to Livy, *Annales*, I, lviii. For Penelope's ultimate concession see Ovid, *Ars amatoria*, I, 477.
8. See Theophrastus, above, p. 412; Wife of Bath's Prologue, 285–92.
9. See Map, above, p. 440.
10. Juvenal, *Satire* VII, 202.
11. Juvenal, *Satire*, VI, 165.
12. Juvenal, *Satire* VI, 47–49.
13. Map, above, p. 442. The image of bees is drawn from Ovid, *Ars amatoria*, I, 95–96.
14. Map, above, p. 444. See Miller's Tale, 3230.
15. Juvenal, *Satire* VI, 28–32.
16. Map, *Valerius ad Ruffinum*.
17. *Historia calamitatum*, VII (above, pp. 448–51).
18. *Historia calamitatum*, VII.
19. *Historia calamitatum*, VIII.
20. *Letter* II.
21. Saint Julian the Hospitaler. His story is told in the *Legenda aurea* (January 27). Compare General Prologue, 340.
22. According to the legend, this saint (sixth century?) received from the King of France the right to free all prisoners whom he visited—a privilege which he

exercised widely, both before and after his death. See *Acta sanctorum*, III, 6 November, and *Legenda aurea*, same date.

23. See Boethius, *De consolatione Philosophiae*, II, prose v. Like Chaucer, Jean de Meun translated Boethius.
24. See Boethius, III, prose viii.
25. See Boethius, III, prose vii.
26. Virgil, *Aeneid*, VI, 563.
27. Compare the advice of la Vieille, below, pp. 469–72.
28. The source is Ovid, *Ars amatoria*, I, 99: "They come to see, they come that they may be seen: to chastity that place [the theater] is fatal." See Wife of Bath's Prologue, 551–53.
29. With the following passage compare Boethius, *De consolatione Philosophiae*, II, prose v.
30. See Wife of Bath's Prologue, 563 ff.
31. Saint Ernoul is dignified with this patronage in other medieval texts as well.
32. Juvenal, *Satire* VI, 133–35.
33. Mothers-in-law are an insistent target in antifeminist literature. See Juvenal, *Satire* VI, 231–41; Wife of Bath's Prologue, 576.
34. This passage made the stories of Hercules and Dejanera, and Samson and Delilah, popularly available in the antifeminist context. Hercules and Samson were the standard clerical examples of strong men overcome by women: see Ovid, *Metamorphoses*, XV, 134–220; Map, above, p. 440; Wife of Bath's Prologue, 721–26.
35. Compare Proverbs ix, 13: "A foolish woman and clamorous, and full of allurements, and knowing nothing at all [*nihil omnino sciens*]." See Wife of Bath's Prologue, 440–42.
36. Map, above, p. 442.
37. See Parson's Tale, 926–28. "Equality," however, is a misnomer for Ami's own alternative to marital "seignourie."
38. See Franklin's Tale, 761–70.

Jean de Meun:
from the *Romance of the Rose*

The following selection is a small part of a very long lecture by la Vieille (the "Old Woman") to Bel Acueil ("Fair Welcoming") in the Roman de la rose. *Bel Acueil is one of numerous personified aspects of the Rose—that part of her nature which engages in social conversation, cast here as a young man presumably because French* acueil *is masculine in gender. La Vieille is presented as a governess or duenna, the position which medieval widows and older women were expected to occupy (see Physician's Tale, 72–82). She has been persuaded by Lamant and his friends to act as an intercessor for him, and her long speech (lines 12740–14546) is rendered on this occasion.*

Jean de Meun cast la Vieille in the tradition of the Latin vetula *(an old woman, wise in years); in fact, her performance contains significant echoes of Ovid's old procuress, Dipsas (see above, pp. 408–10). Her "advice" is based on her wide—and unhappy—experience with men. Thus, she says:*

"I was young and beautiful, foolish and wild, and had never been to a school of love where they read in the theory, but I know everything by practice. Experiments, which I have followed my whole life, have made me wise in love. Now that I know everything about love, right up to the struggle, it would not be right if I were to fail to teach you the delights that I know and have often tested. . . . I have so much knowledge upon which I can lecture from a chair that I could never finish. . . . And since I had good sense and manners, not without great harm to me, I have deceived many a worthy man when he fell captive in my nets. But I was deceived by many before I noticed. Then it was too late, and I was miserably unhappy. I was already past my youth. My door, which formerly was often open, both night and day, stayed constantly near its sill." (12801–35)

Trans. C. R. Dahlberg, The Romance of the Rose *(Princeton: Princeton University Press, 1971), pp. 229–36. Copyright © 1971 by Princeton University Press. Reprinted by permission of Princeton University Press.*

The *"education"* she proposes will, in effect, train Bel Acueil to accomplish her revenge upon the men who deceived her in her youth.

For his *la Vieille*, Jean de Meun formulated an ironic Ovidian context. If *la Vieille* is like *Dipsas*, Bel Acueil is being trained to make the Rose a courtesan. Her instructions, furthermore, are replete with rules drawn directly from Ovid's two *"handbooks"* on love—the Art of Love and the Remedies for Love. With characteristic humor, Ovid had pretentiously claimed that Venus had *"set him over tender Love as a master in the art"* (Ars amatoria, I, 7), and that he spoke from experience: *"The more violently Love has pierced and branded me, the better shall I avenge the wound that he has made"* (Ars amatoria, I, 23–24). Books I and II of the Ars provide practical advice in the art of seduction—the rules followed by the men who deceived *la Vieille*. Book III, which offers the same sort of advice for women, becomes a model for *la Vieille's* precepts. In turning Ovid's playful observations into earnest regulations, Jean de Meun made the Old Woman, broadly speaking, an Ovidian joke.

Chaucer's many echoes establish his Wife of Bath as a literary figure in the tradition of *la Vieille*. Though he dropped the explicit motive of cynical vengeance against men, he maintained the voice of experiential *"wisdom"* which preaches (as in lines 12739 and 14547 of the *Roman*) a doctrine of love to *"wise wyves."* The motif appears most explicitly in the *Wife of Bath's Prologue*, 165, and *Friar's Prologue*, 1271–77. *General Prologue*, 475–76, make it clear, too, that Chaucer recognized the Ovidian derivation of Alice's literary ancestor.

[Advice of la Vieille]

FROM *LINES* 13265–724

"Briefly, all men betray and deceive women; all are sensualists, taking their pleasure anywhere. Therefore we should deceive them in return, not fix our hearts on one. Any woman who does so is a fool; she should have several friends and, if possible, act so as to delight them to the point where they are driven to distraction. If she has no graces, let her learn them. Let her be haughtier toward those who, because of her hauteur, will take more trouble to serve her in order to deserve her love, but let her scheme to take from those who make light of her love. She should know games and songs and flee from quarrels and disputes. If she is not beautiful, she should pretty herself; the ugliest should wear the most coquettish adornments. . . .

"There is also a proper way to cry.[1] But every woman is adept enough to cry well on any occasion, for, even though the tears are not caused by grief or shame or hurt, they are always ready. All women cry; they are used to crying in whatever way they want. But no man should be disturbed when he sees such tears flowing as fast as rain, for these tears, these sorrows and lamentations flow only to trick him. A woman's weeping is nothing but a ruse; she will overlook no source of grief. But she must be careful not to reveal, in word or deed, what she is really thinking of.

"It is also proper to behave suitably at the table. . . . Let her guard against getting her fingers wet up to the joint in the sauce, against smearing her lips with soup, garlic, or fat meat, against piling up too large morsels and stuffing her mouth. When she has to moisten a piece in any sauce, either *sauce verte, cameline,* or *jauce,* she should hold the bit with her fingertips and bring it carefully up to her mouth, so that no drop of soup, sauce, or pepper falls on her breast. She must drink so neatly that she doesn't spill anything on herself, for anyone who happened to see her spill would think her either very clumsy or very greedy. Again, she must take care not to touch her drinking cup while she has food in her mouth. She should wipe her mouth so clean that grease will not stick to the cup, and should be particularly careful about her upper lip, for, where there is grease on it, untidy drops of it will show in her wine. She should drink only a little at a time, however great her appetite, and never empty a cup, large or small, in one breath, but rather drink little and often, so that she doesn't go around causing others to say that she gorges or drinks too much while her mouth is full. She should avoid swallowing the rim of her cup, as do many greedy nurses who are so foolish that they pour wine down their hollow throats as if they were casks, who pour it down in such huge gulps that they become completely fuddled and dazed. Now a lady must be careful not to get drunk, for a drunk, man or woman, cannot keep anything secret; and when a woman gets drunk, she has no defenses at all in her, but blurts out whatever she thinks and abandons herself to anyone when she gives herself over to such bad conduct. . . .[2]

"Further, a lady must be careful not to be too reluctant to play, for she might wait around so long that no one would want to offer her his hand. She should seek the diversion of love as long as youth deflects her in that direction, for, when old age assails a woman, she loses both the joy and the assault of Love.[3] A wise woman [*fame sage*][4] will gather the fruit of love in the flower of her age. The unhappy woman loses her time who passes it without enjoying love. And if she disbelieves this advice of mine, which I give her for the profit of all, be sure that she will be sorry when age withers her. But I know that women will believe me, particularly those who are sensible, and will stick to our rules and will say many paternosters for my soul, when I am dead, who now teach and comfort them. I know that this lesson will be read in many schools.

"O fair sweet son, if you live—for I see well that you are writing down in the book of your heart the whole of my teaching,[5] and that, when you depart from me, you will study more, if it please God, and will become a master like me—if you live I confer on you the licence to teach, in spite of all chancellors, in chambers or in cellars, in meadow, garden or thicket, under a tent or behind the tapestries, and to inform the students in wardrobes, attics, pantries, and stables, if you find no more pleasant places. And may my lesson be well taught when you have learned it well!

"A woman should be careful not to stay shut up too much, for while she remains in the house, she is less seen by everybody, her beauty is less well-known, less desired and in demand less. She should go often to the principal church and go visiting, to weddings, on trips, at games, feasts, and round dances,[6] for in such places the God and Goddess of Love keep their schools and sing mass to their disciples.

"But of course, if she is to be admired above others, she has to be well-dressed. When she is well turned out and goes through the streets, she should carry herself well, neither too stiffly nor too loosely, not too upright nor too bent over, but easily and graciously in any crowd. She should move her shoulders and sides so elegantly that no one might find anyone with more beautiful movements. And she should walk daintily in her pretty little shoes, so well made that they fit her feet without any wrinkles whatever. . . . She should be careful to let all the passersby see the fine shape of her exposed foot. And if she is the sort to wear a coat, she should wear it so that it will not too much hinder the view of her lovely body which it covers. . . .[7]

"A woman must always take care to imitate the she-wolf when she wants to steal ewes, for, in order not to fail completely, the wolf must attack a thousand to capture one; she doesn't know which she will take before she has taken it. So a woman ought to spread her nets everywhere to catch all men; since she cannot know which of them she may have the grace to catch, at least she ought to hook on to all of them in order to be sure of having one for herself. If she does so, it should never happen that she will have no catch at all from among the thousands of fools who will rub up against her flanks. Indeed, she may catch several, for art is a great aid to nature.[8]

"And if she does hook several of those who want to put her on the spit, let her be careful, however events run, not to make appointments at the same hour with two of them. If several were to appear together they would think themselves deceived and they might even leave her. An event like this could set her back a long way, for at the least she would lose what each had brought her. She should never leave them anything on which they might grow fat, but plunge them into poverty so great that they may die miserable and in debt; in this way she will be rich, for what remains theirs is lost to her.

"She should not love a poor man, for a poor man is good for nothing; even if he were Ovid or Homer, he wouldn't be worth two drinking mugs.[9] Nor should she love a foreign traveler, for his heart is as flighty as his body, which lodges in many places; no, I advise her not to love a foreigner.[10] However, if during his stay he offers her money or jewels she should take them all and put them in her coffer; then he may do as he pleases in haste or at his leisure. . . .

"And if any man, either an honest man or a swindler, should make promises, hoping to beg for her love and bind her to him by vows, she may exchange vows, but she must be careful not to put herself at his mercy unless she gets hold of the money also. If he makes any promise in writing, she must see if there is any deception or if his good intentions are those of a true heart. She may then soon write a reply, but not without some delay. Delay excites lovers, as long as it is not too great.

"Now when she hears a lover's request, she should be reluctant to grant all her love, nor should she refuse everything, but try to keep him in a state of balance between fear and hope.[11] When he makes his demands more pressing and she does not yield him her love, which has bound him so strongly, she must arrange things, through her strength and her craft, so that hope constantly grows little by little as fear diminishes until peace and concord bring the two together.[12] In giving in to him, she, who knows so many wily ruses, should swear by God and by the saints that she has never wished to give herself to anyone, no matter how well he may have pleaded; then she should say, 'My lord, this is my all; by the faith which I owe to St. Peter of Rome, I give myself to you out of pure love, not because of your gifts. The man isn't born for whom I would do this for any gift, no matter how greatly he desired it. I have refused many a worthy man, for many have gazed adoringly at me. I think you must have cast a spell over me; you have sung me a wicked song.' Then she should embrace him closely and kiss him so that he will be even better deluded.

"But if she wants my advice, she should think only of what she can get. She is a fool who does not pluck her lover down to the last feather, for the better she can pluck the more she will have, and she will be more highly valued when she sells herself more dearly. Men scorn what they can get for nothing; they don't value it at a single husk. If they lose it, they care little, certainly not as much as does one who has bought it at a high price.[13]

"Here then are the proper ways to pluck men: get your servants, the chambermaid, the nurse, your sister, even your mother, if she is not too particular, to help in the task and do all they can to get the lover to give them coats, jackets, gloves, or mittens; like kites, they will plunder whatever they can seize from him, so that he may in no way escape from their hands before he has spent his last penny. Let him give them money and jewels as though he were playing with buttons instead of money. The prey is captured much sooner when it is taken by several hands."

NOTES

1. Ovid *Ars amatoria,* III, 291–2: "How far does art not go? they learn to weep becomingly, and can wail when and how they choose."
2. See Ovid, *Ars amatoria,* III, 755–68 (above, p. 284). Compare General Prologue, 127–36 (description of the Prioress); the Prioress observes as well other recommendations of Ovid and la Vieille, some of which appear in this selection—to smile, to weep, to be amiable, to wear proper jewelry, to dress so as to show off good points, to go where one can be seen, to act haughtily enough to ensure men's respect. The combination of women and wine is also

treated by Juvenal, *Satire* VI, 300–305, and in the Wife of Bath's Prologue, 464–68.

3. For this argument see Horace, *Odes*, I, xxv; Ovid *Ars amatoria*, III, 59–98 (see above, p. 282). La Vieille's bitterness against "hungry lovers" made these lines inappropriate for Chaucer's Wife; but see Wife of Bath's Prologue, 331–36, a reference which indicates that Chaucer was perfectly aware of Jean de Meun's literary source.

4. The *fame sage* is a counterpart to the "wise man" whom antimatrimonial literature seeks to persuade "not to marry." Compare Wife of Bath's Prologue, 229–32, etc.

5. The following comparison between the "instruction" of la Vieille and the education of a clerk in the medieval University is a development of the antifeminist opposition between "women" and "books" (see above, pp. 401–2). Chaucer presents his Wife of Bath as a "teacher" and "preacher" of a similar "doctrine." The Wife's reference to her "dames loore" (Wife of Bath's Prologue, 583) may suggest not only the deceptions supposedly taught by mothers-in-law, and the authority of such a "school" as that proposed by la Vieille, but also (in parody) the law of "Mother Church."

6. See Ovid, *Ars amatoria*, III, 387–98 and 417–32. Compare the latter with Wife of Bath's Prologue, 587–99. For the more general principle, see Wife of Bath's Prologue, 555–59.

7. Ovid, *Ars amatoria*, III, 297–306. See General Prologue, 156–57.

8. Ovid, *Ars amatoria*, III, 419–26.

9. Ovid, *Ars amatoria*, II, 279–80; compare the advice of Dipsas, above, p. 409.

10. Ovid, *Heroides*, XVII (Helen to Paris), 191.

11. Ovid, *Ars amatoria*, III, 461–62.

12. Ovid, *Ars amatoria*, III, 469–78.

13. Compare the advice of Dipsas, above, p. 409.

nine

END OF
THE WORLD AND
LAST JUDGMENT

Just as the pilgrimage of Chaucer's Canterbury company will end at Becket's shrine, so the pilgrimage of the life of man is destined to come to an end, and the time and space (see General Prologue, 35) brought into being at the Creation will be abolished. The consummation of the Providential design unfolding in history was to be the Second Coming of Christ and the Last Judgment of the living and the dead. This awesome event, the subject of sermons during the season of Advent, served to cast the temporal endeavors of men in the light of eternity, and to emphasize their pettiness even when they were not overtly sinful. And though preachers spoke of God's desire for the salvation of mankind, their sermons describing the eternally damned made it clear that many would fail.

Chaucer's Parson's Tale brings just this perspective to the Canterbury Tales. As a treatise on penitence it covers the entire range of erring humanity's sinful ways, and urges the pilgrims to take "the righte wey of Jerusalem celestial" (line 80). This perspective is introduced at almost the last moment, as the Host's words in the Parson's Prologue stress:

"Telleth," quod he, "youre meditacioun.
But hasteth yow, the sonne wole adoun;
Beth fructuous, and that in litel space,
And to do wel God sende yow his grace!" (69–72)

In the course of the Parson's Tale we hear again themes, topics, issues, even actual phrases, which we have heard in the mouths of others in earlier tales, but they are now placed in the coherent framework of Christian eschatology—that is, given final authority—and are thus implicitly judged.

The texts in this section illustrate the kind of authority which lay behind such judgment.

Jacobus de Voragine: from *The Golden Legend*

The season of Advent begins on the Sunday nearest November 30 (Saint Andrew's Day). It is a period in which the faithful prepare to celebrate the Nativity. In the calendar of the Christian year it occurs at the end of the "period of pilgrimage" which "is that of our present life" (see above, p. 14). Contemplation of the Last Judgment, which will occur at Christ's Second Coming, is, as Chaucer's Parson points out, a powerful incentive to contrition (Parson's Tale, 158–230).

Trans. Granger Ryan and Helmut Ripperger, The Golden Legend (New York: Longmans, Green, 1941), pp. 2–6. Reprinted by permission of Granger Ryan.

Figure 16. Deathbed Scene. Bibliothèque Nationale MS lat. 9471, fol. 159 (Rohan Book of Hours).

The Spiritual Advent and the Return of the Lord

Advent is celebrated for four weeks, to signify that this coming of the Lord is fourfold; namely, that He came to us in the flesh, that He came with mercy into our hearts, that He came to us in death, and that He will come to us again at the Last Judgement. The last week is seldom finished, to denote that the glory of the elect, as they will receive it at the last advent of the Lord, will have no end. But while the coming is in reality fourfold, the Church is especially concerned with two of its forms, namely with the coming in the flesh and with the coming at the Last Judgement. Thus the Advent fast is both a joyous fast, and a fast of penance. It is a joyous fast because it recalls the advent of the Lord in the flesh; and it is a fast of penance in anticipation of the advent of the Last Judgement.

With regard to the advent in the flesh, three things should be considered: its timeliness, its necessity, and its usefulness. Its timeliness is due first to the fact that man, condemned by his nature to an imperfect knowledge of God, had fallen into the worst errors of idolatry, and was forced to cry out, 'Enlighten my eyes.'[1] Secondly, the Lord came in the 'fulness of time,' as Saint Paul says in the Epistle to the Galatians.[2] Thirdly, He came at a time when the whole world was ailing, as Saint Augustine says: 'The great physician came at a moment when the entire world lay like a great invalid.' That is why the Church, in the seven antiphons which are sung before the Feast of the Nativity, recalls the variety of our ills and the timeliness of the divine remedy. Before the coming of God in the flesh, we were ignorant, subject to eternal punishment, slaves of the Devil, shackled with sinful habits, lost in darkness, exiled from our true country. Hence the ancient antiphons announce Jesus in turn as our Teacher, our Redeemer, our Liberator, our Guide, our Enlightener, and our Saviour. . . .

As regards the second advent, at the time of the Last Judgement, we must consider in turn the circumstances which will precede it, and those that will accompany it.

The circumstances which will precede the Last Judgement are of three kinds: fearful signs, the imposture of the Antichrist, and a great fire. The signs which are to come before the Last Judgement are five; for Saint Luke says: 'There shall be signs in the sun, and in the moon, and in the stars; and upon the earth distress of nations, by reason of the confusion of the roaring of the sea and of the waves.'[3] All these things are explained in the Book of the Apocalypse.

Saint Jerome, on the other hand, has discovered, in the Annals of the Hebrews, fifteen signs which are to come before the Last Judgement:

On the first day, the sea will rise forty cubits higher than the mountains, and will rear up as a solid wall.

On the second day, it will sink so far that it will be barely visible.

On the third day, the monsters of the deep will appear on the surface of the sea, and their roaring will rise to the heavens. No one but God will understand it.

On the fourth day, the sea and all the waters will take fire.

On the fifth day, the trees and the plants will exude a bloody dew. And all of the birds of the air will come together, each of its kind, and they will neither eat nor drink, for fear of the strict Judge.

On the sixth day, all cities will collapse and all that is built, and fiery bolts of lightning will appear from sundown to sunrise.

On the seventh day, the stones will rub one against the other, and will break into four pieces.

On the eighth day, an earthquake will shake the whole earth, laying low man and beast.

On the ninth day, the earth will be levelled, mountains and hills being reduced to dust.

On the tenth day, men will come out of the caverns into which they will have fled, and will wander around like madmen, unable to converse with each other.

On the eleventh day, the skeletons of the dead will come forth from the tombs. And all the tombs will open from sunrise to sunset so that all the dead may come forth.

On the twelfth day, the stars will fall.

On the thirteenth day, all living beings will die, to rise again with the dead.

On the fourteenth day, the heavens and the earth will be consumed by fire.

On the fifteenth day, there will be a new heaven and a new earth, and all will rise again.

In the second place, the Last Judgement will be preceded by the imposture of the Antichrist, who will seek to deceive mankind in four ways: by a false explanation of the Scriptures, whereby he will try to prove that he is the Messiah promised by the Law; by working miracles; by the giving of gifts; by inflicting torments.[4]

In the third place, the Last Judgement will be preceded by a mighty fire, lighted by God to renew the world, to make the damned suffer, and to throw light upon the troop of the elect.

With regard to the circumstances which will accompany the Last Judgement, we must first mention the separation of the good from the wicked, for we know that the Judge will come down to the Valley of Josaphat, and will place the good at His right, and the wicked at His left.[5] This does not mean, as Saint Jerome very rightly says, that all men will succeed in finding room in that narrow valley (for that would be absurd), but simply that it will be the centre of the Judgement; although if God so chooses, nothing will prevent Him from making room in a small space for an infinite number of people.

Next comes the question of the number of categories into which men will be divided at the Last Judgement. Saint Gregory states that there will be four, two of the damned and two of the elect. For among the damned some will be judged, and others will already be condemned, namely those of whom it is said, 'He that does not believe, is already judged!'[6] On the side of the elect, some will be judged, and others, the perfect, will judge the rest, insofar as they will be seated beside the Judge. . . .

The Judge will be inexorably severe. He will not be influenced by fear, since He is all-powerful, nor by bribes, since He is Abundance itself, nor by hate, since He is Benevolence itself, nor by love, since He is Justice itself, nor by error, since He is Wisdom itself. Against His wisdom neither the pleading of advocates nor the sophisms of philosophers nor the discourses of orators nor the tricks of hypocrites will prevail.

The accuser will be as implacable as the Judge will be severe. Or rather the sinner will have against him three accusers: the Devil, sin itself, and the whole world. For, as Chrysostom says, 'On that day the heavens and the earth, the waters, the sun and the moon, the day and the night, in a word the whole world will stand against us before God, to bear witness to our sins.'

And in like manner, three witnesses will testify against us, all three infallible. In the first place, God Himself, Who tells us by the voice of Jeremiah, 'I am the judge and the witness.'[7] Secondly, our conscience. Thirdly, the Angel designated to watch over us, for we read in the Book of Job, 'The heavens (that is, the angels) shall reveal his iniquity.'[8]

Lastly, the sentence will be irrevocable, and for three reasons: the excellence of the Judge, the evidence of wrong, and the impossibility of putting off the punishment. In the sentence pronounced against us at the Last Judgement, these three conditions will be fulfilled, and there will be neither king nor emperor nor pope, to whom we may appeal from that judgement.

NOTES

1. Psalm xvii, 29.
2. Galatians iv, 4.
3. Luke xxi, 25. See Isaias xii, 19; Ezekiel xxxii, 7; Joel ii, 10, and iii, 7; Matthew xxiv, 29; Mark xii, 24.
4. See above, p. 245.
5. Joel iii, 2; Matthew xxv, 31–33.
6. John iii, 18.
7. Jeremias xxix, 23.
8. Job xx, 27.

Pope Innocent III:
from *On the Misery of the Human Condition*

De miseriis humane conditionis *was a work of such authority that over five hundred manuscripts survive in the libraries of all European countries. In his Legend of Good Women (G, Prologue, 414–15), Chaucer says that he had translated "the Wreched Engendrynge of Mankynde,/ As man may in Pope Innocent yfynde." Though this text has disappeared, Chaucer shows a translator's familiarity in his casual adaptations of Innocent's work, notably in the Man of Law's Tale. Here a striking revision of the* De miseria *in the Prologue depends for its effect on a popular knowledge of the original, and Chaucer's linking the treatise with his lawyer is interesting in view of Innocent's great reputation as a canonist and his low view of legalists.*

Pope Innocent III, born Giovanni Lotario dei Segni in 1160 or 1161, studied at the Universities of Paris, Rome, and Bologna, where he prepared for Church office. He served as a cardinal (1190–91) under his uncle, Pope Clement III. Elected Pope in 1198, he concerned himself with organizing the power of the Church and with ecclesiastical reforms such as those adopted in his Fourth Lateran Council (1215).

The De miseria *(1195) is a summation and distillation of the traditional* de contemptu mundi *theme, which insisted that a "contempt for the world" confirmed the humility with which God was to be loved. It is addressed to Pope Celestine III, a man who had deposed Innocent as cardinal in 1191.*

In the following passages, Pope Innocent conveniently collects many of the chief Scriptural authorities which shaped the medieval vision of Christ's Second Coming and the pains of Hell.

Trans. Margaret Mary Dietz, On the Misery of the Human Condition, ed. Donald R. Howard (New York: Bobbs-Merrill, 1969: Library of Liberal Arts), pp. 84–85, 74–75, 78. Copyright © 1969 by The Bobbs-Merrill Company. Reprinted by permission of the publisher.

"How the Lord Shall Come
to Judgment"

"Immediately after the tribulation of those days, the sun shall be darkened and the moon shall not give her light, and the stars shall fall from heaven, and the powers of heaven shall be moved; and then shall appear the sign of the Son of Man in heaven. And then shall all the tribes of the earth mourn over themselves."[1] "And the kings and princes and tribunes, the rich and the strong and every bondman and freeman shall hide themselves in the dens and the rocks of mountains, and they shall say to the mountains and the rocks, 'Fall upon us and hide us from the face of him who sits upon the throne and from the wrath of the Lamb, for the great day of their wrath is come, and who shall be able to stand?' "[2] "And he shall send his angels with a trumpet and a great voice and they shall gather his elect from the four winds of heaven, from the farthest parts of the heavens to the utmost bounds of them."[3]

Then "the Lord himself shall come down from heaven with commandment and with the voice of an archangel and with the trumpet."[4] And "all who are in the graves shall hear the voice of the Son of God and they that have done good things shall come forth unto the resurrection of life, but they that have done evil unto the resurrection of judgment."[5] "Death and hell shall give up the dead that were in them,"[6] and "every eye shall see him, and they also that pierced him,"[7] "the Son of Man coming in the clouds with great power and majesty."[8]

The Lord, however, will come to judgment not only with the angels but with the senators of his people: "He is honorable in the gates when he sits among the senators of the land."[9] For they will seat themselves "on twelve seats judging the twelve tribes of Israel."[10] "I beheld," he said, "till thrones were placed, and the Ancient of Days sat. His garment was white as snow, and the hair of his head like clean wool; his throne like flames of fire, the wheels of it like a burning fire. A swift stream of fire issued forth before him, thousands of thousands ministered to him and ten thousand times a hundred thousand stood before him."[11] "God shall come manifestly, our God shall come and shall not keep silence; a fire shall burn before him and a mighty tempest shall be round about him."[12] "Clouds and darkness are round about him, justice and judgment are the establishment of his throne."[13] "He shall call heaven from above and the earth to judge his people."[14] Then "All nations shall be gathered together before him, and he shall separate them

one from another, as the shepherd separates the sheep from the goats. And he shall set the sheep on his right hand, but the goats on his left."[15]

NOTES

1. Matthew xxiv, 29–30.
2. Apocalypse vi, 15–17.
3. Matthew xxiv, 31.
4. 1 Thessalonians iv, 15.
5. John v, 28–29.
6. Apocalypse xx, 13.
7. Apocalypse i, 7.
8. Luke xxi, 27.
9. Proverbs xxxi, 23.
10. Matthew xix, 28.
11. Daniel vii, 9–10.
12. Psalm xlix, 3.
13. Psalm xcvi, 2.
14. Psalm xlix, 4.
15. Matthew xxv, 32–33.

Figure 17. Christ in Judgment. British Library MS Add. 35313, fol. 134 (Book of Hours). Compare figure 9.

"On the Various Punishments of Hell"

III, 8

There are various punishments in hell for various kinds of sin. The first punishment is fire, the second cold. Of these the Lord says, "There will be weeping and gnashing of teeth,"[1] weeping because of the smoke, gnashing of teeth because of the cold. The third punishment will be stench. Of these three it is said, "Fire and brimstone and storms of winds shall be the portion of their cup."[2] The fourth is the never-failing worm, of which it is said, "Their worm shall not die and their fire shall not be quenched."[3] The fifth is the scourges of the lashers, of which it is said, "Judgments are prepared for the scorners and striking hammers for the bodies of fools."[4] The sixth is palpable darkness without and within, of which it is said, "A land of misery and darkness where the shadow of death is";[5] and elsewhere, "I go to a land that is dark and covered with the mist of death";[6] and again, "They shall never see light";[7] and in another place, "The wicked shall be silent in darkness."[8] The seventh punishment is the confusion of sinners; "For then," we read, "the books will be opened,"[9] that is, the consciences of men will be manifest to all. The eighth is the horrible sight of the demons, who will be glimpsed in the movement of blazing sparks arising from the fire. The ninth punishment is the chain of fire with which each of the limbs of the wicked is bound.

Now the first punishment of hell is for those of unbridled appetites; the second for those of malicious will; the third for the lecherous; the fourth for the envious and those who hate; the fifth is for those who in this world did not deserve to be beaten with scourges, because "the sinner hath provoked the Lord, according to the multitude of his wrath he will not seek him";[10] the sixth is for those walking in darkness who disdainfully refused to come to the true light, namely, Christ;[11] the seventh is for those who confess their sins and despise repentance; the eighth is for those who freely see the evils in this world and do them; and the ninth is for those who have wallowed in every vice, who travel the road of their own desires and follow only their own appetites.[12]

NOTES

1. Matthew xiii, 50.
2. Psalm x, 7.
3. Isaias lxvi, 24.
4. Proverbs xix, 29.
5. Job x, 22.
6. Job x, 21.
7. Psalm xlviii, 20.
8. 1 Kings ii, 9.
9. Apocalypse xx, 12.
10. Psalm ix, 4.
11. John viii, 12.
12. Ecclesiasticus xviii, 30.

"On the Despair of the Damned"

"They are laid in hell like sheep; death will feed on them."[1] This text is based on the similarity of the damned souls to beasts of burden, who do not tear up the grass by the roots but only chew the top, so that the grass grows again for pasture. Thus the wicked, as if eaten by death, spring to life again to die once more, and so are eternally dying.

> The liver of Tityus, unconsumed and ever growing,
> Wastes not—whence it can be devoured many times.[2]

Then death will never die, and those who are dead to life will live for death alone. They will seek death and never find it, having had life and lost it. Hear what John says in the Apocalypse: "In those days men will seek death and they will not find it, and they will desire to die and death will flee from them."[3] O death, how sweet you would be to these souls who when alive thought you so bitter; they will long for you and you alone—they who had despised you so in life.

NOTES

1. Psalm xlviii, 15.
2. Ovid, *Ex Ponto*, I, ii, 41–42.
3. Apocalypse ix, 6. See Parson's Tale, 216; Pardoner's Tale, 727–38.

Saint Augustine:
from *The City of God*

In The City of God *Augustine traced the history of the two "cities" from the Creation to the end of the world. In XIV, 28 he succinctly described the nature of these two "cities":*

> . . . Two cities have been formed by two loves: the earthly by the love of self, even to the contempt of God; the heavenly by the love of God, even to the contempt of self. The former, in a word, glories in itself, the latter in the Lord. For the one seeks glory from men; but the greatest glory of the other is God, the witness of conscience. The one lifts up its head in its own glory; the other says to its God, 'Thou art my glory, and the lifter up of mine head' [Psalm iii, 4].

The end of the earthly city is perdition; that of the heavenly city, "Jerusalem celestial" (Parson's Tale, 80), is the eternal felicity described in this, the concluding chapter of his work.

Trans. Marcus Dods, The City of God (*Edinburgh: T. & T. Clark, 1872: rept. New York: Hafner, 1948), Vol. II, pp. 540–45. Copyright 1948 by Hafner Publishing Company. Reprinted by permission of Macmillan Publishing Co., Inc.*

"Of the Eternal Felicity of the City of God, and of the Perpetual Sabbath"

How great shall be that felicity, which shall be tainted with no evil, which shall lack no good, and which shall afford leisure for the praises of God, who shall be all in all! For I know not what other employment there can be where no lassitude shall slacken activity, nor any want stimulate to labour. I am admonished also by the sacred song, in which I read or hear the words, "Blessed are they that dwell in Thy house, O Lord; they will be still praising Thee."[1] All the members and organs of the incorruptible body, which now we see to be suited to various necessary uses, shall contribute to the praises of God; for in that life necessity shall have no place, but full, certain, secure, everlasting felicity. For all those parts of the bodily harmony, which are distributed through the whole body, within and without, and of which I have just been saying that they at present elude our observation, shall then be discerned; and, along with the other great and marvellous discoveries which shall then kindle rational minds in praise of the great Artificer, there shall be the enjoyment of a beauty which appeals to the reason. What power of movement such bodies shall possess, I have not the audacity rashly to define, as I have not the ability to conceive. Nevertheless I will say that in any case, both in motion and at rest, they shall be, as in their appearance, seemly; for into that state nothing which is unseemly shall be admitted. One thing is certain, the body shall forthwith be wherever the spirit wills, and the spirit shall will nothing which is unbecoming either to the spirit or to the body. True honour shall be there, for it shall be denied to none who is worthy, nor yielded to any unworthy; neither shall any unworthy person so much as sue for it, for none but the worthy shall be there. True peace shall be there, where no one shall suffer opposition either from himself or any other. God Himself, who is the Author of virtue, shall there be its reward; for, as there is nothing greater or better, He has promised Himself. What else was meant by His word through the prophet, "I will be your God, and ye shall be my people,"[2] than, I shall be their satisfaction, I shall be all that men honourably desire,—life, and health, and nourishment, and plenty, and glory, and honour, and peace, and all good things? This, too, is the right interpretation of the saying of the apostle, "That God may be all in all."[3] He shall be the end of our desires who shall be seen without end, loved without cloy, praised without weariness. This out-going of affection, this employment, shall certainly be, like eternal life itself, common to all.

But who can conceive, not to say describe, what degrees of honour and glory shall be awarded to the various degrees of merit? Yet it cannot be doubted that there shall be degrees. And in that blessed city there shall be this great blessing, that no inferior shall envy any superior, as now the archangels are not envied by the angels, because no one will wish to be what he has not received, though bound in strictest concord with him who has received; as in the body the finger does not seek to be the eye, though both members are harmoniously included in the complete structure of the body. And thus, along with his gift, greater or less, each shall receive this further gift of contentment to desire no more than he has.

Neither are we to suppose that because sin shall have no power to delight them, free will must be withdrawn. It will, on the contrary, be all the more truly free, because set free from delight in sinning to take unfailing delight in not sinning. For the first freedom of will which man received when he was created upright consisted in an ability not to sin, but also in an ability to sin; whereas this last freedom of will shall be superior, inasmuch as it shall not be able to sin. This, indeed, shall not be a natural ability, but the gift of God. For it is one thing to be God, another thing to be a partaker of God. God by nature cannot sin, but the partaker of God receives this inability from God. And in this divine gift there was to be observed this gradation, that man should first receive a free will by which he was able not to sin, and at last a free will by which he was not able to sin,—the former being adapted to the acquiring of merit, the latter to the enjoying of the reward. But the nature thus constituted, having sinned when it had the ability to do so, it is by a more abundant grace that it is delivered so as to reach that freedom in which it cannot sin. For as the first immortality which Adam lost by sinning consisted in his being able not to die, while the last shall consist in his not being able to die; so the first free will consisted in his being able not to sin, the last in his not being able to sin. And thus piety and justice shall be as indefeasible as happiness. For certainly by sinning we lost both piety and happiness; but when we lost happiness, we did not lose the love of it. Are we to say that God Himself is not free because He cannot sin? In that city, then, there shall be free will, one in all the citizens, and indivisible in each, delivered from all ill, filled with all good, enjoying indefeasibly the delights of eternal joys, oblivious of sins, oblivious of sufferings, and yet not so oblivious of its deliverance as to be ungrateful to its Deliverer.

The soul, then, shall have an intellectual remembrance of its past ills; but, so far as regards sensible experience, they shall be quite forgotten. For a skilful physician knows, indeed, professionally almost all diseases; but experimentally he is ignorant of a great number which he himself has never suffered from. As, therefore, there are two ways of knowing evil things,—one by mental insight, the other by sensible experience, for it is one thing to understand all vices by the wisdom of a cultivated mind, another to understand them by the foolishness of an abandoned life,—so also there are two ways of forgetting evils. For a well-instructed and learned man forgets them one way, and he who has experimentally suffered from them forgets them another,—the former by neglecting what he has learned, the latter by escaping what he has suffered. And in this latter way the saints shall forget their past ills, for they shall have so thoroughly escaped them all, that they shall be quite blotted out of their experience. But their intellectual knowledge, which shall be great, shall keep them acquainted not only with their own past woes, but with the eternal sufferings of the lost. For if they were not to know that they had been miserable, how could they, as the Psalmist says, for ever sing the mercies of God?[4] Certainly that city shall have no greater joy than the celebration of the grace of Christ, who redeemed us by His blood. There shall be accomplished the words of the psalm, "Be still, and know that I am God."[5] There shall be the great Sabbath which has no evening, which God celebrated among His first works, as it is written, "And God rested on the seventh day from all His works which He had made. And God blessed the seventh day, and sanctified it; because that in it He had rested from all His work which God began to make."[6] For we shall ourselves be the seventh day, when we shall be filled and replenished with God's blessing and sanctification. There shall we be still, and know that He is God; that He is that which we ourselves aspired to be when we fell away from Him, and listened to the voice of the seducer, "Ye shall be as gods,"[7] and so abandoned God, who would have made us as gods, not by deserting Him, but by participating in Him. For without Him what have we accomplished, save to perish in His anger? But when we are restored by Him, and perfected with greater grace, we shall have eternal leisure to see that He is God, for we shall be full of Him when He shall be all in all. For even our good works, when they are understood to be rather His than ours, are imputed to us that we may enjoy this Sabbath rest. For if we attribute them to ourselves, they shall be servile; for it is said of the Sabbath, "Ye shall do no servile work in it."[8] Wherefore also it is said by Ezekiel the prophet, "And I gave them my Sabbaths to be a sign between me and them, that they might know that I am the Lord who sanctify them."⁹ This knowledge shall be perfected when we shall be perfectly at rest, and shall perfectly know that He is God.

This Sabbath shall appear still more clearly if we count the ages as days, in accordance with the periods of time defined in Scripture, for that period will be found to be the seventh. The first age, as the first day, extends from Adam to the deluge; the second from the deluge to Abraham, equalling the first, not in length of time, but in the number of generations, there being ten in each. From Abraham to the advent of Christ there are, as the evangelist Matthew calculates, three periods, in each of which are fourteen generations,—one period from Abraham to David, a second from David to the captivity, a third from the captivity to the birth of Christ in the flesh. There are thus five ages in all. The sixth is now passing, and cannot be measured by any number of generations, as it has been said, "It is not for you to know the times, which the Father hath put in His own power."¹⁰ After this period God shall rest as on the seventh day, when He shall give us (who shall be the seventh day) rest in Himself. But there is not now space to treat of these ages; suffice it to say that the seventh shall be our Sabbath, which shall be brought to a close, not by an evening, but by the Lord's day, as an eighth and eternal day, consecrated by the resurrection of Christ, and prefiguring the eternal repose not only of the spirit, but also of the body. There we shall rest and see, see and love, love and praise. This is what shall be in the end without end. For what other end do we propose to ourselves than to attain to the kingdom of which there is no end? . . .

NOTES

1. Psalm lxxxiii, 5.
2. Leviticus xxvi, 12.
3. 1 Corinthians xv, 28.
4. Psalm lxxxviii, 2.
5. Psalm xlv, 11.
6. Genesis ii, 2, 3.
7. Genesis iii, 5.
8. Deuteronomy v, 14.
9. Ezekiel xx, 12.
10. Acts i, 7.

Geoffrey Chaucer:
from *The Parson's Tale*

This final text is also the final passage in Chaucer's Canterbury Tales, if we discount his Retraction. Since this passage does not occur in his primary source, the Summa poenitentiae *("Summa on Penitence") of Raymund de Pennaforte, it is fair to conclude that Chaucer wished his own creation to reflect the design of the Creator. As salvation is the true end of Christian life, it was fitting to end his pilgrimage with a vision of the blessed, just as Saint Augustine and Dante had ended their great works. The journey which began in a London inn has been directed toward the cathedral of England's "hooly blisful martir," Saint Thomas Becket (General Prologue, 17). The Parson's Tale can be regarded as a "preparation" for the arrival at the shrine.*

[The Vision of the Blessed]

Men should understand what the fruit of penance is; and, according to the word of Jesus Christ, it is the endless bliss of heaven, where joy is not opposed by any grievance or woe; where all the evils of this present life have been left behind; where there is sure security from the pains of hell; where lives the blissful company who eternally rejoice, each in the others' joy; where the body of man, which was formerly foul and dark, is more bright than the sun; where the body, which formerly was sick, frail, and feeble, and mortal, is immortal, and so strong and so healthy that nothing can impair it; where there is neither hunger, nor thirst, nor cold, but where every soul is replenished with the vision of God in perfect understanding. Men may purchase this blessed kingdom by being poor in spirit,[1] and its glory by humility, its fullness of joy by hunger and thirst, and its rest by labor, and this life by death and the mortification of sin.

NOTE

1. *Poverte espiritueel*: the reference is clearly to Matthew v, 3.

Figure 18. Fortune's Wheel. British Library MS Harley 4373, fol. 14 (Valerius Maximus, *Factorum et dictorum memorabilium liber*). The four positions on Fortune's Wheel symbolize the feelings of those whom Fortune favors or deprives. From the top clockwise are represented: (1) *Regno* ("I rule"), a king who commands the gifts of Fortune; (2) *Regnavi* ("I have ruled"), an outcast courtier; (3) *Sum sine regno* ("I am without rule"), a beggar; and (4) *Regnabo* ("I will rule"), a favor-seeking courtier. (See figure 1.) In terms of figures 16 and 17, such "feelings" are ultimately illusory.

Chaucer Index

General Index

Italicized numbers refer to texts printed in this volume.